BBC

Bitesize

Bitesize
Pearson Edexcel GCSE (9–1)

COMBINED SCIENCE

REVISION WORKBOOK

Foundation

Series Consultant:
Harry Smith

Authors:
Sam Holyman
Alasdair Shaw
Janette Gledhill

Published by BBC Active, an imprint of Educational Publishers LLP, part of the Pearson
Education Group, 80 Strand, London, WC2R 0RL.

www.pearsonschools.co.uk/BBCBitesize

© Educational Publishers LLP 2020
BBC logo © BBC 1996. BBC and BBC Active are trademarks of the British Broadcasting Corporation.

Typeset by Newgen KnowledgeWorks Pvt. Ltd., Chennai, India
Produced and illustrated by Newgen Publishing UK
Cover design by Andrew Magee & Pearson Education Limited 2020
Cover illustration by Darren Lingard / Oxford Designers & Illustrators

The rights of Sam Holyman, Alasdair Shaw and Janette Gledhill to be identified as authors of this work have been asserted by them in
accordance with the Copyright, Designs and Patents Act 1988.

First published 2020

23 22 21 20
10 9 8 7 6 5 4 3 2 1

British Library Cataloguing in Publication Data
A catalogue record for this book is available from the British Library

ISBN 978 1 406 68573 2

Printed and bound in Slovakia by Neografia.

The Publisher's policy is to use paper manufactured from sustainable forests.

Acknowledgements
Content written by Karen Bailey, Mike Smith, Pauline Anning, Aidan Gill and Amani Leslie is included.

Text Credits:
P 31: Trinh P, Jung TH, Keene D, et al. Temporal and spatial associations between influenza and asthma hospitalisations in New York City from 2002
to 2012: a longitudinal ecological study, © BMJ Publishing Group Ltd. Used with Permission; **P 33:** Eldholm V, Rieux A, Monteserin J, et al. Impact of
HIV co-infection on the evolution and transmission of multidrug-resistant tuberculosis. Elife. 2016; **P 42:** Global Information System on Alcohol and
Health (GISAH), Age standardised death rates Liver cirrhosis 15+ years per 100,000 population. © World Health Organisation. Used with Permission;
P 42: Prescott, Eva, Hippe, Merete, Schnohr, Peter, Hein, Hans Ole, Vestbo, Jørgen, Smoking and risk of myocardial infarction in women and men:
longitudinal population study, © British Medical Journal 1998 Apr 4; 316(7137): 1043–1047. 10.1136/bmj.316.7137.1043; **P 43:** Data from Long-Term
Safety and Effectiveness of Mechanical Versus Biologic Aortic Valve Prostheses in Older Patients Results From the Society of Thoracic Surgeons Adult
Cardiac Surgery National Database by J. Matthew Brennan, September 15, © 2019, American Heart Association, Inc; **P 43:** Chung J, Shum-Tim D.
The Current Indications and Options for Aortic Valve Surgery. J Surgery. 2014;2(1): 6. Attribution 4.0 International (CC BY 4.0); **P 53:** Jakob Suckale,
Michele Solimena – Solimena Lab and Review Suckale Solimena 2008 Frontiers in Bioscience, original data: Daly et al. 1998. CC-BY 3.0; **P 64:** Global
average temperature 1850–2011,© 2014, Crown copyright. Contains public sector information licensed under the Open Government Licence v3.0;
P 65: Competition and parasitism in the native White Clawed Crayfish Austropotamobius pallipes and the invasive Signal Crayfish Pacifastacus
leniusculus in the UK by Jenny C. Dunn, © 2008, Springer Science+Business Media; **P 68:** Data from Hope Farm: Farming for food, profit and
wildlife, © 2012, Royal Society for the Protection of Birds **P 67:** The German Water Sector, Policies and Experiences, Umweltbundesamt (DE) – EEA
data service. Federal Ministry for the Environment, Nature Conservation and Nuclear Safety. Used with permission; **P 87:** Properties of materials,
© BBC; **P 159:** General rules, techniques and advice for all drivers and riders (103 to 158), © Crown Copyright. Contains public sector
information licensed under the Open Government Licence v3.0; **P 213:** National Diabetes Audit Executive Summary 2009–2010, The NHS Information Centre,
National Diabetes Audit Executive Summary, Copyright © 2011. Contains public sector information licensed under the Open Government Licence
v3.0; **P 213:** Adult obesity and type 2 diabetes, Public Health England, © Crown copyright 2014. Contains public sector information licensed under
the Open Government Licence v3.0. **P 224:** Digest of UK Energy Statistics: Chapter 5 Electricity, UK National Statistics, July 2019, © 2019,
Crown Copyright. Contains public sector information licensed under the Open Government Licence v3.0
BBC: pp1–209 © 2020.

Photo Credits:
(Key: T-top; B-bottom; C-centre; L-left; R-right)
123RF: Jarun Ontakrai 1, Pchweat 157, **Alamy Stock Photo:** Nigel Cattlin 36c, Nigel Cattlin 47, David Paterson/Picade LLC 165br, Photo Researchers/
Science History Images 210, **Getty Images:** Ed Reschke 5, De Agostini Picture Library 6, BSIP 15, **Science Photo Library:** Gary Carlson 14,
Edelmann 16, **Shutterstock:** Jeerawut Thiratrak 36r, Tyler Olsen 36l, Homydesign 152, Steve Meese 165t, Francois BOIZOT 165bl, IndustryAndTravel
166, Medwether 172, Bixstock 185, Olinchuk 188, Ruslan Ivantsov 163, 197, Brent Hofacker 205, Sathienpong Prempetch 207.

All other images © Pearson Education

Notes from the publisher
1. While the publishers have made every attempt to ensure that advice on the qualification and its assessment is accurate, the official specification and
associated assessment guidance materials are the only authoritative source of information and should always be referred to for definitive guidance.
Pearson examiners have not contributed to any sections in this resource relevant to examination papers for which they have responsibility.
2. Pearson has robust editorial processes, including answer and fact checks, to ensure the accuracy of the content in this publication, and every
effort is made to ensure this publication is free of errors. We are, however, only human, and occasionally errors do occur. Pearson is not liable for
any misunderstandings that arise as a result of errors in this publication, but it is our priority to ensure that the content is accurate. If you spot an
error, please do contact us at resourcescorrections@pearson.com so we can make sure it is corrected.

Websites
Pearson Education Limited is not responsible for the content of third-party websites.

Contents

Grades have been assigned to most questions in this workbook. These are intended to show you the level of challenge of those questions, and to help you track your progress. In your exam, your grade will be based on your overall mark, and not on your responses to individual questions.

☑ Tick off each topic as you go.

② Each bite-sized chunk has a **timer** to indicate how long it will take. Use them to plan your revision sessions.

▣ Scan the **QR codes** to visit the BBC Bitesize website. It will link straight through to revision resources on that subject. You can also access these by visiting www.pearsonschools.co.uk/BBCBitesizeLinks.

Levels of organisation

② Quick quiz

Draw **one** line from each keyword to its definition.

Keyword	Definition
tissue	the smallest structural and functional unit of an organism
organ system	a group of organs working together
cell	a group of similar cells working together

⑤ Organisation of the human body — Grade 3

1. The human body has four main levels of organisation. Use words from the box to complete the order of the levels of organisation in the circulatory system, from least complex (red blood cell) to most complex. **[3 marks]**

| blood | circulatory system | red blood cell | heart |

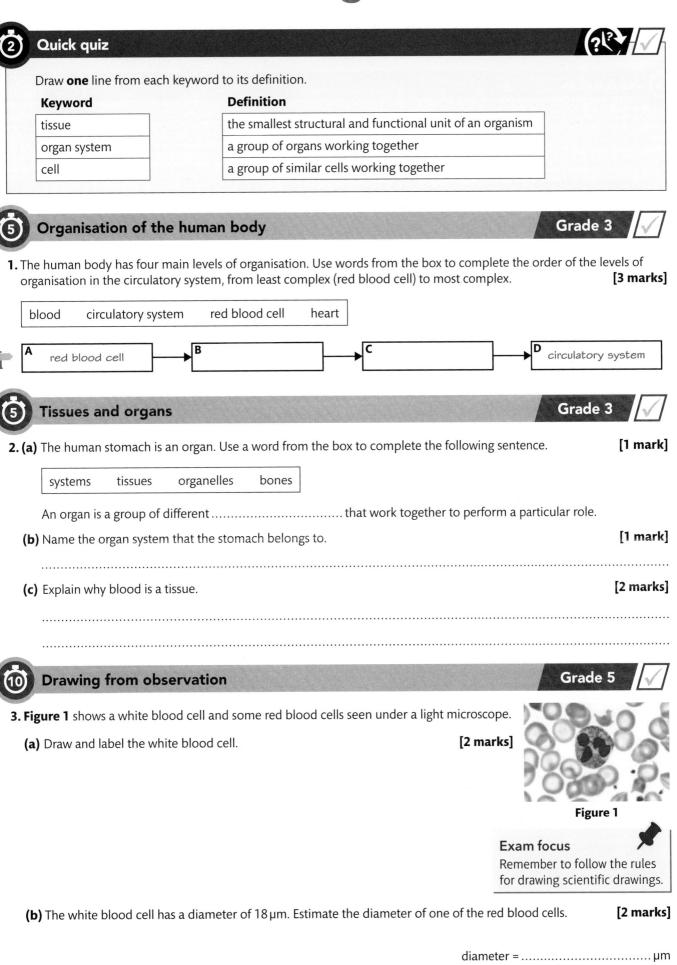

A red blood cell → B _____ → C _____ → D circulatory system

⑤ Tissues and organs — Grade 3

2. (a) The human stomach is an organ. Use a word from the box to complete the following sentence. **[1 mark]**

| systems | tissues | organelles | bones |

An organ is a group of different .... that work together to perform a particular role.

(b) Name the organ system that the stomach belongs to. **[1 mark]**

....

(c) Explain why blood is a tissue. **[2 marks]**

....

....

⑩ Drawing from observation — Grade 5

3. Figure 1 shows a white blood cell and some red blood cells seen under a light microscope.

(a) Draw and label the white blood cell. **[2 marks]**

Figure 1

Exam focus
Remember to follow the rules for drawing scientific drawings.

(b) The white blood cell has a diameter of 18 μm. Estimate the diameter of one of the red blood cells. **[2 marks]**

diameter = ... μm

 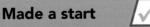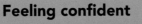

Eukaryotic and prokaryotic cells

2 Quick quiz

True or false?

Bacteria are eukaryotes.	**True / False**
Prokaryotic cells are usually bigger than eukaryotic cells.	**True / False**
Prokaryotic cells have cell walls.	**True / False**
Both prokaryotic and eukaryotic cells have ribosomes.	**True / False**
Eukaryotic cells have a nucleus.	**True / False**

15 Comparing prokaryotic and eukaryotic cells — Grade 5

1. Figure 1 shows a diagram of a prokaryotic cell.

(a) What is the structure labelled **A**? Tick **one** box. **[1 mark]**

cell membrane ☐

plasmid ☐

flagellum ☐

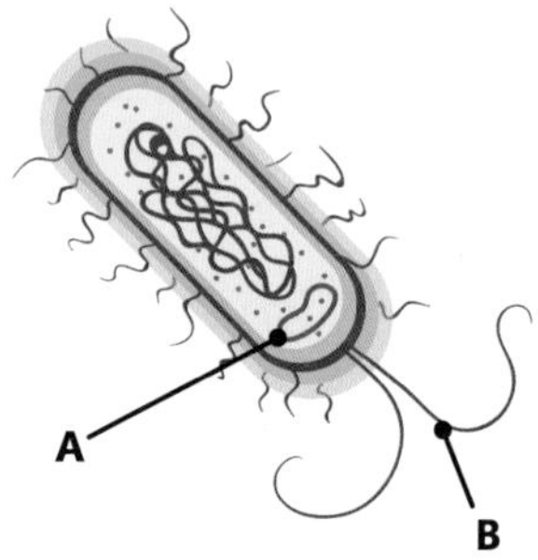

Figure 1

(b) Name structure **B**. .... **[1 mark]**

2. Give **one** similarity and **one** difference between prokaryotic cells and eukaryotic cells. **[2 marks]**

Similarity: ....

Difference: ....

3. Which part of a prokaryotic cell contains DNA? Tick **one** box. **[1 mark]**

cell wall ☐ flagella ☐ plasmid ☐

5 Cell size units — Grade 5

4. A scientist observed a kidney cell using an electron microscope. He calculated that the kidney cell was 16 μm wide.

(a) What does μm stand for? Tick **one** box. **[1 mark]**

centimetre ☐

millimetre ☐

micrometre ☐

nanometre ☐

Maths skills
You need to understand the scale and size of cells and use the correct prefixes: centi, milli, micro and nano.

(b) Give the width of the kidney cell in the following units.

(i) millimetres .... mm **[1 mark]**

(ii) nanometres .... nm **[1 mark]**

Maths skills
1 μm = 1000 nm (nanometres).
1 μm = 0.001 mm (millimetres).

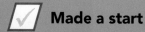

Animal and plant cells

② Quick quiz

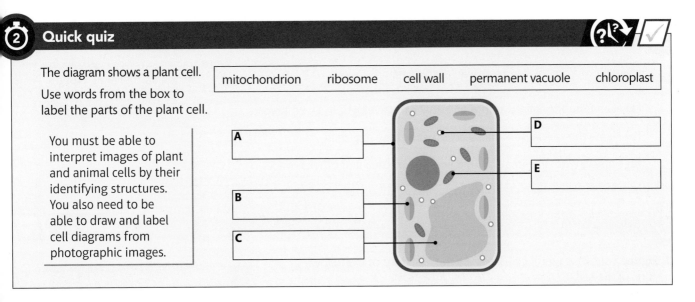

The diagram shows a plant cell.

Use words from the box to label the parts of the plant cell.

| mitochondrion | ribosome | cell wall | permanent vacuole | chloroplast |

You must be able to interpret images of plant and animal cells by their identifying structures. You also need to be able to draw and label cell diagrams from photographic images.

A

B

C

D

E

⑩ Sub-cellular structures of plant and animal cells — Grade 3

1. Animal and plant cells have many common sub-cellular structures. State the function of each of the following **five** sub-cellular structures. **[5 marks]**

Nucleus .....contains genetic material (DNA) that controls.............

Cell membrane .....controls which substances.............

Cytoplasm .....gel-like fluid where most.............

Ribosomes ....

Mitochondria ....

⑤ Plant cells — Grade 2

2. Some sub-cellular structures are only found in plant cells. Complete **Table 1** to show the name of the plant cell structure that matches each description. **[3 marks]**

Table 1

Cell structure	Description of the structure
	Made of cellulose which is strong and provides support for the cell.
	Contains dissolved minerals and sugars (cell sap). Gives the cell support.
	Carries out photosynthesis. Contains chlorophyll to trap light energy.

⑤ Comparing different plant and animal cells — Grade 5

3. Chloroplasts are structures that allow plant cells to carry out photosynthesis. Suggest why plant root cells do **not** have chloroplasts. **[2 marks]**

....

....

Exam focus

The command word 'suggest' means you need to apply your knowledge about plants to a new situation.

 Made a start   **Feeling confident**   **Exam ready**

3

Specialised animal cells

② Quick quiz

Use a word from the box to answer each question.

| bone | egg | ciliated epithelial | sperm |

(a) Name the specialised animal cells that can develop into an embryo. ....

(b) Name the specialised animal cells that fertilise egg cells. ....

(c) Name a type of animal cell that lines the trachea and other surfaces. ....

⑤ Sperm cells   Grade 4

1. Figure 1 shows a sperm cell. Describe the functions of the following parts of the cell.

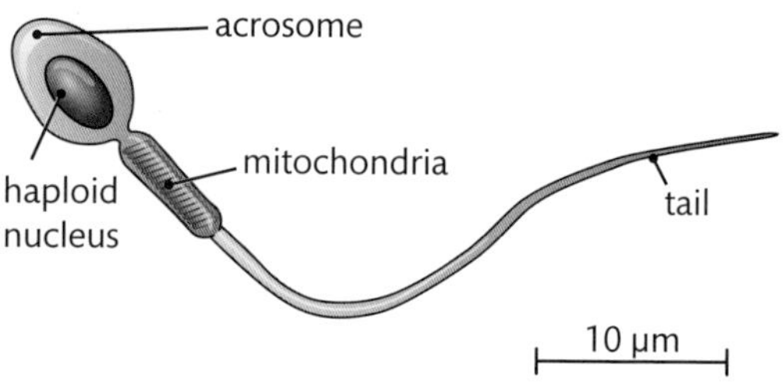

(a) haploid nucleus   **[1 mark]**

....

| Haploid means that it contains only one set of chromosomes. |

(b) acrosome   **[1 mark]**

....

| The acrosome contains substances that digest cell membranes. |

(c) mitochondria   **[1 mark]**

Release energy from .... so that the

....

Remember the function of mitochondria in respiration.

Figure 1 labels: acrosome, mitochondria, tail, haploid nucleus, 10 µm

Figure 1

⑤ Egg cells   Grade 4

2. (a) Describe the function of each of the following adaptations of egg cells.

(i) Nutrients in cytoplasm.   **[1 mark]**

....

(ii) Changes in cell membrane after fertilisation.   **[1 mark]**

....

(b) Sperm and egg cells have haploid nuclei with half the normal chromosome number. The full number of chromosomes is restored in a process in which the sperm and egg cell fuse. Name this process.   **[1 mark]**

....

⑤ Ciliated cells   Grade 5

3. Ciliated epithelial cells line airways in the lungs. Dirt and bacteria in the air stick to mucus on the surface of the airways. Explain how ciliated epithelial cells remove dirt and bacteria from the lungs.   **[3 marks]**

....

....

....

 Made a start   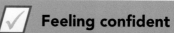 **Feeling confident**   **Exam ready**

Microscopy

② Quick quiz

Microscopes have developed over time. Complete each sentence by drawing a circle around the correct **bold** word in each statement about different kinds of microscopes.

Early microscopes were **light / electron** microscopes.

Improvements of early microscopes made it possible to see **cells / sub-cellular structures**.

Light microscopes have a **greater / lower** magnification than electron microscopes.

Electron microscopes let us see mitochondria in **less / more** detail than using light microscopes.

⑩ Calculating magnification   Grade 5

1. **Figure 1** shows cheek cells viewed with a light microscope.

   Suggest why the mitochondria are not clearly visible in the cells.   **[1 mark]**

   The mitochondria are too ....

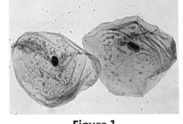

   The magnification of a light microscope is calculated by multiplying eyepiece lens magnification × objective lens magnification.

Figure 1

2. Animal cells are viewed through a microscope with an eyepiece lens of ×4 magnification. Calculate the total magnification with the following objective lenses:

   (a) ×40 objective lens (high power)   **[1 mark]**

   magnification = 4 (eyepiece lens) × 40 (objective lens) =

   magnification = ×.................................

   (b) ×10 objective lens (medium power)   **[1 mark]**

   magnification = ×.................................

   (c) ×4 objective lens (low power)   **[1 mark]**

   magnification = ×.................................

⑩ Magnification, resolution and cell size   Grades 3–5

3. **(a)** Give the meaning of the term 'magnification'. .... **[1 mark]**

   (b) Explain why electron microscopes are better than light microscopes for studying small cell structures.   **[2 marks]**

   ....

   ....

4. A scientist used an electron microscope to look at a mitochondrion in an animal cell.

   The size of the image was 30 mm. The magnification was ×10 000.

   (a) Calculate the real size of the sub-cellular structure using the equation:

   $$\text{size of real object} = \frac{\text{size of image}}{\text{magnification}}$$ **[2 marks]**

   real size = ... mm

   (b) A nucleus from the same cell measured 0.009 mm. Give the size of the nucleus in micrometres.   **[1 mark]**

   size = ... μm

Practical: Using microscopes

② Quick quiz

Use words from the box to label the diagram of a light microscope.

objective lens

eyepiece lens

course focus knob

stage clips

fine focus knob

lamp

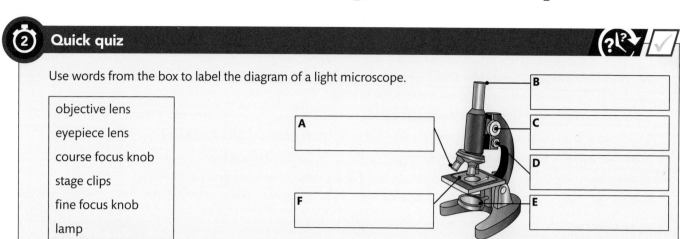

A

B

C

D

E

F

⑩ Magnification calculations　　　　Grade 5

1. Figure 1 shows a part of a kidney viewed with a light microscope.

The image of the kidney structure is 3 cm in diameter. The real size of this structure is 30 μm. Calculate the magnification of the image using the equation:

$$\text{magnification} = \frac{\text{size of image}}{\text{size of real object}}$$

[2 marks]

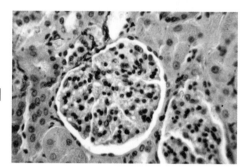

Figure 1

size of image = 3 cm = 3 × 10 000 μm

= .... μm

$$\text{magnification} = \frac{\text{..............}}{\text{..............}}$$

= ....

magnification = ×..............

Maths skills 🖩

Before using the equation, convert units so both are the same: 1 cm = 10 000 μm

⑩ Drawing and preparing slides　　　　Grade 3

2. (a) A student drew an epithelial cell as seen through a microscope (**Figure 2**).

Identify **three** improvements that would make this a better scientific drawing.　　**[3 marks]**

1 ....

2 ....

3 ....

(b) The student prepared the slide by using a mounted needle to lower a glass coverslip over the cells.

Explain why the coverslip must be carefully applied.　　**[1 mark]**

....

Figure 2

 Made a start　　 **Feeling confident**　　 **Exam ready**

Enzyme action

2 **Quick quiz**

The diagram shows the breakdown of a molecule by an enzyme to form two new molecules.

Use words from the box to label the diagram.

| active site |
| enzyme |
| products |
| substrate |

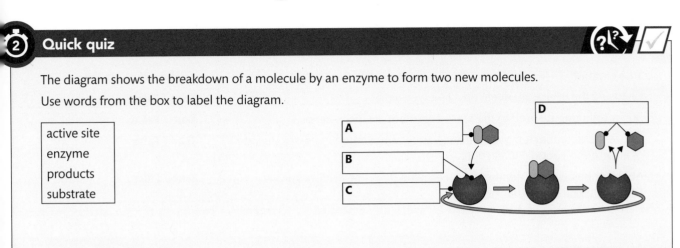

A

B

C

D

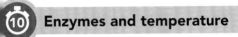

Enzymes and temperature **Grade 5**

1. **Figure 1** shows how the rate of breakdown of starch using human amylase depends on temperature.

(a) Use **Figure 1** to identify the optimum temperature for human amylase. **[1 mark]**

....

> The optimum temperature is when the rate of reaction is fastest.

(b) Describe the effect of temperature on rate of reaction between 0°C and 30°C. **[1 mark]**

As the temperature increases from 0°C to 30°C
....
the rate of reaction
....

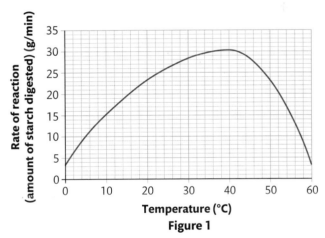

Figure 1

(c) Explain why the rate of reaction decreases at temperatures above 40°C. **[3 marks]**

The rate of reaction decreases because the enzyme is
....
This means that the shape of the active site .... making it more
difficult for the starch substrate to .... into the active site and so be broken down.

Enzymes and substrates **Grades 3–5**

2. **Figure 2** shows an enzyme and some possible substrates.

(a) Each enzyme is specific to only one substrate. Identify which substrate is specific to the enzyme. Give the letter of the substrate. **[1 mark]**

Substrate ....

(b) Explain why this substrate is specific to the enzyme. **[2 marks]**

....
....

Figure 2

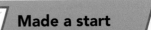 **Made a start** **Feeling confident** 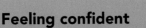 **Exam ready**

7

Practical: Enzymes

True or false?

Changing the pH has no effect on a lipase enzyme.	**True / False**
Buffer solutions are used to maintain a constant pH in a reaction.	**True / False**
Above the optimum temperature, increasing temperature increases the rate of an enzyme-controlled reaction.	**True / False**
Above or below the optimum pH, an enzyme does not work as quickly because its active site changes shape.	**True / False**

 Investigating enzyme action ⑩ Grade 5

1. Students investigated the effect of pH on digestion of starch by the enzyme amylase. **Figure 1** shows the results from a test at pH 6. Starch solution of a known pH was mixed with amylase. One drop of this mixture was taken immediately and then every 30 seconds. Each drop was added to iodine solution on a spotting tile.

(a) The top left spot on the tile in **Figure 1** was from the mixture at 0 seconds. Calculate the time taken for the starch to be completely digested. **[2 marks]**

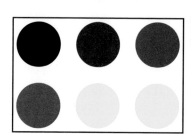

Figure 1

time = ... seconds

> Use your knowledge of your practical work to answer this question. Remember that the reaction is complete when the colour change is complete.

(b) The experiment was repeated at pH 7. The starch was fully digested after 90 seconds. Calculate the rate of reaction at pH 7 using the equation:

$$\text{rate of reaction} = \frac{1}{\text{time}}$$

Give your answer to 2 significant figures. **[2 marks]**

Maths skills

For two significant figures round to the first two non-zero digits.

rate = ... s^{-1}

(c) Explain why the starch/enzyme mixture was kept in a 30 °C water bath during the tests. **[2 marks]**

 To keep temperature .... because temperature also affects ....

....

 Amylase digestion ⑤ Grade 2

2. Figure 2 shows the rate of digestion of starch by amylase enzyme at different pHs.

(a) The optimum pH for amylase was 5.5. State what is meant by 'optimum pH'. **[1 mark]**

....

(b) Explain how iodine solution is used to test if starch has been digested. **[2 marks]**

....

....

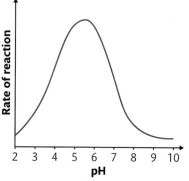

Figure 2

 Made a start **Feeling confident** ✓ **Exam ready**

Digestion and enzymes

② Quick quiz

Match each enzyme to its substrate and then to the products formed by digestion.

Enzyme	Substrate	Products
lipase	protein	amino acids
carbohydrase (e.g. amylase)	fat	glucose
protease	carbohydrates (e.g. starch)	fatty acids and glycerol

⑩ Enzymes in digestion   Grade 4

1. (a) Explain the role of enzymes in digestion of food.   **[2 marks]**

☞ Food molecules are too large to be ....

Digestive enzymes ....

(b) Protease enzymes in the intestines digest proteins in food. Name the products of this digestion.   **[1 mark]**

....

(c) Explain why enzymes are described as biological catalysts.   **[2 marks]**

☞ Enzymes are biological because ....

Enzymes are catalysts because ....

⑩ Substrate concentration   Grades 3–5

2. Figure 1 shows the products of digestion of a mixture of foods from a meal.

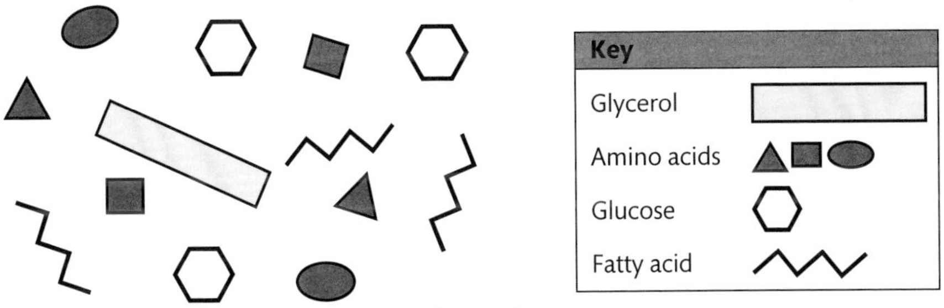

Key	
Glycerol	▭
Amino acids	▲ ■ ⬤
Glucose	⬡
Fatty acid	∿

Figure 1

(a) Fats were present in the mixture of foods. Name the enzyme that digests fats.   **[1 mark]**

....

(b) Name the products that result from the digestion of fats.   **[1 mark]**

....

(c) Larger molecules can be made from these products. Draw a carbohydrate that could be made from some of the products in **Figure 1**.   **[2 marks]**

....

....

Diffusion

② Quick quiz

Use words from the box to complete the diagram showing diffusion of particles across a cell membrane.

high concentration
low concentration
net movement

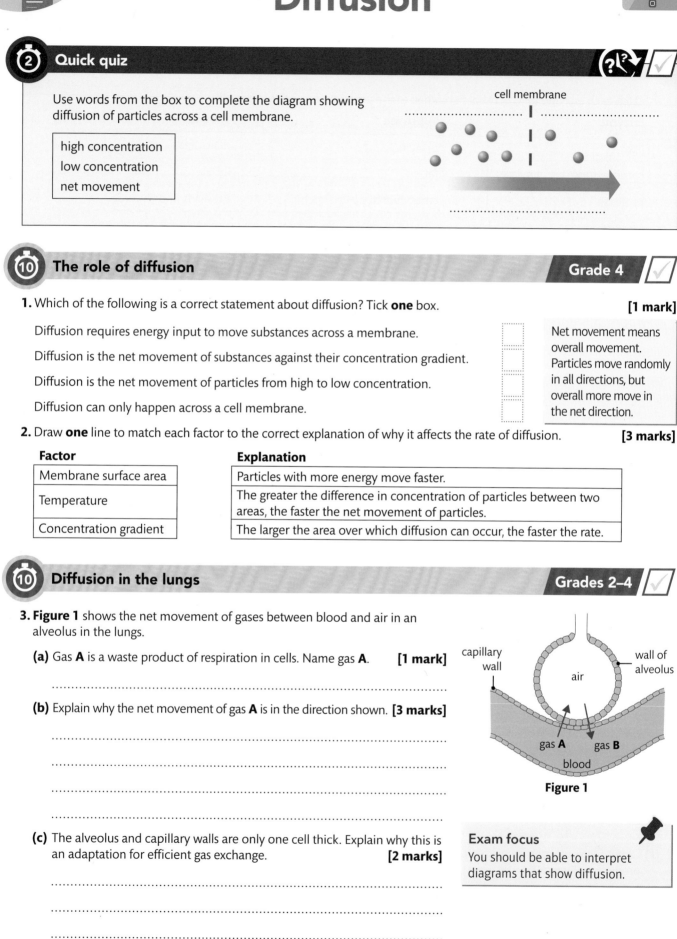

cell membrane

⑩ The role of diffusion

Grade 4

1. Which of the following is a correct statement about diffusion? Tick **one** box. **[1 mark]**

Diffusion requires energy input to move substances across a membrane.

Diffusion is the net movement of substances against their concentration gradient.

Diffusion is the net movement of particles from high to low concentration.

Diffusion can only happen across a cell membrane.

> Net movement means overall movement. Particles move randomly in all directions, but overall more move in the net direction.

2. Draw **one** line to match each factor to the correct explanation of why it affects the rate of diffusion. **[3 marks]**

Factor	Explanation
Membrane surface area	Particles with more energy move faster.
Temperature	The greater the difference in concentration of particles between two areas, the faster the net movement of particles.
Concentration gradient	The larger the area over which diffusion can occur, the faster the rate.

⑩ Diffusion in the lungs

Grades 2–4

3. Figure 1 shows the net movement of gases between blood and air in an alveolus in the lungs.

(a) Gas **A** is a waste product of respiration in cells. Name gas **A**. **[1 mark]**

....

(b) Explain why the net movement of gas **A** is in the direction shown. **[3 marks]**

....

....

....

....

Figure 1

(c) The alveolus and capillary walls are only one cell thick. Explain why this is an adaptation for efficient gas exchange. **[2 marks]**

....

....

....

....

> **Exam focus** 📌
> You should be able to interpret diagrams that show diffusion.

 Made a start   **Feeling confident**   **Exam ready**

Osmosis

② Quick quiz

Complete the table using the words 'high' or 'low'. One box has been completed for you.

	Concentration of salt molecules is	Concentration of water molecules is
Salt solution		low
Pure water		

⑤ Movement of water
Grade 5

1. A plant cell was placed in distilled water. The cell swelled and increased in size.

(a) Explain why the size of the cell increased when it was placed in distilled water. **[2 marks]**

> Water moves into the cell by the process of ....
>
> causing the cell to increase in size. This is because the solute concentration
>
> inside the cell is ....

> Distilled water contains no solutes. Any substance dissolved in water is a solute.

> Osmosis is the net movement of water from a low solute concentration to a high solute concentration.

(b) The cell is then placed in a concentrated sugar solution. Describe what happens to the cell. **[2 marks]**

> The cell .... as water moves ....
>
> ....

⑮ Investigating osmosis
Grades 2–5

2. Students investigated osmosis by filling some Visking tubing with sugar solution and leaving the tubing in a beaker of distilled water (**Figure 1**).

(a) Visking tubing is a partially permeable membrane. Which statement describes a partially permeable membrane? Tick **one** box. **[1 mark]**

an impermeable barrier ☐

a membrane that only allows certain molecules to pass through ☐

a membrane that does not allow water to pass through ☐

a membrane that holds the cell together ☐

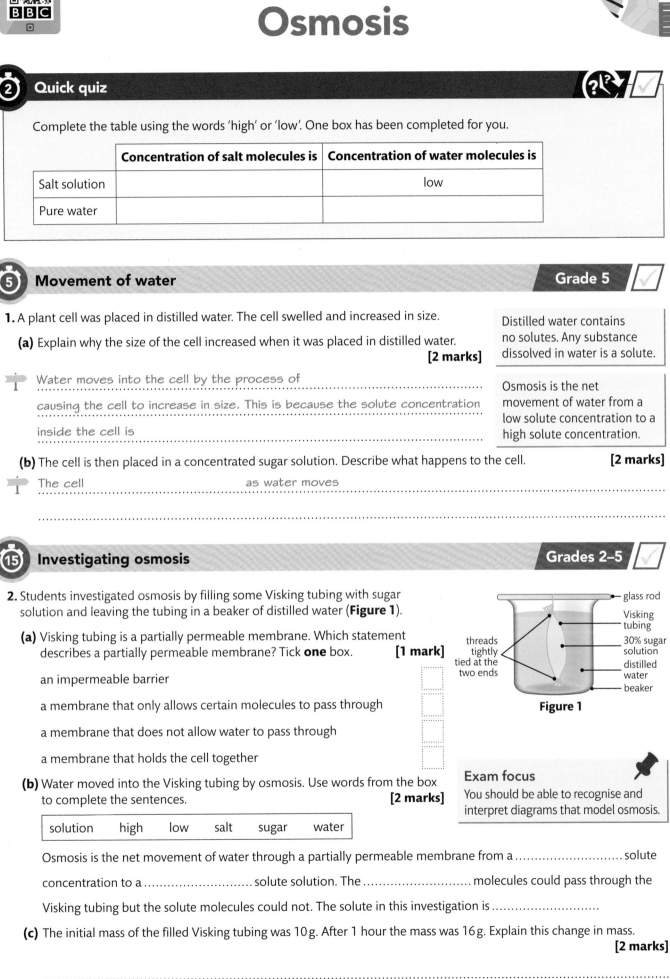

Figure 1 labels: glass rod, Visking tubing, 30% sugar solution, distilled water, beaker, threads tightly tied at the two ends

Figure 1

> **Exam focus** 📌
> You should be able to recognise and interpret diagrams that model osmosis.

(b) Water moved into the Visking tubing by osmosis. Use words from the box to complete the sentences. **[2 marks]**

solution	high	low	salt	sugar	water

Osmosis is the net movement of water through a partially permeable membrane from a .... solute

concentration to a .... solute solution. The .... molecules could pass through the

Visking tubing but the solute molecules could not. The solute in this investigation is ....

(c) The initial mass of the filled Visking tubing was 10 g. After 1 hour the mass was 16 g. Explain this change in mass. **[2 marks]**

....

....

 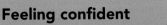

Practical: Osmosis

② Quick quiz

Complete the diagram of a model of osmosis by drawing an arrow to show the direction of movement of water molecules.

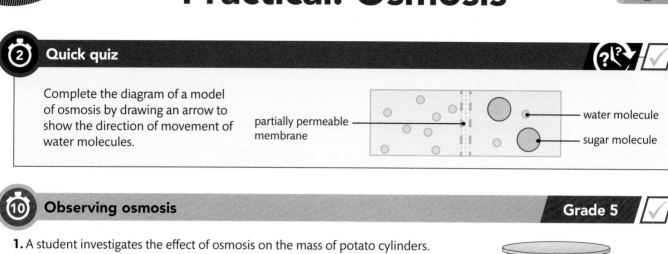

partially permeable membrane

water molecule

sugar molecule

⑩ Observing osmosis

Grade 5

1. A student investigates the effect of osmosis on the mass of potato cylinders. She places potato cylinders in beakers containing different concentrations of sugar solution. She records the mass of the cylinders at the start and end of the experiment. **Figure 1** shows the set-up of one beaker.

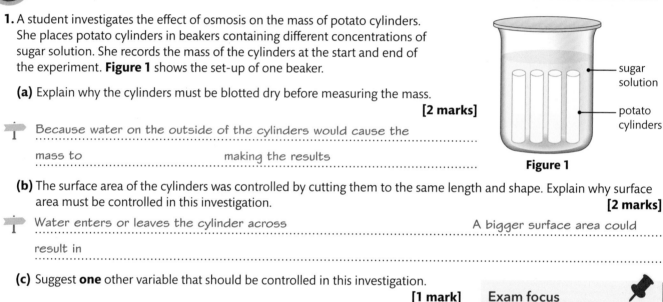

sugar solution

potato cylinders

Figure 1

(a) Explain why the cylinders must be blotted dry before measuring the mass. **[2 marks]**

Because water on the outside of the cylinders would cause the

mass to .... making the results ....

(b) The surface area of the cylinders was controlled by cutting them to the same length and shape. Explain why surface area must be controlled in this investigation. **[2 marks]**

Water enters or leaves the cylinder across .... A bigger surface area could

result in ....

(c) Suggest **one** other variable that should be controlled in this investigation. **[1 mark]**

....

This is a required practical so think back to how you carried out the experiment.

Exam focus 📌

Control variables are those that are kept constant, so that they do not affect the results.

⑩ Observing osmosis

Grades 3–5

2. (a) A potato cylinder had a mass of 1.13 g. The cylinders were placed in a beaker of distilled water for 30 minutes before being dried and reweighed. At the end of the experiment the mass of the cylinder was 1.25 g.

(i) Calculate the change in the mass of the potato cylinder. **[1 mark]**

.... g

(ii) Use your answer to calculate the percentage change in mass. **[1 mark]**

......................................%

Maths skills 🖩

$$\text{percentage change} = \frac{\text{change in mass}}{\text{initial mass}} \times 100\%$$

Always calculate change in mass first.

(b) Water moved into potato cells, changing the mass. State how water moves across cell membranes. **[1 mark]**

....

(c) A potato cylinder was placed in a concentrated solution. Explain what happens to the mass of this cylinder. **[2 marks]**

....

....

 Made a start 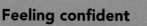 **Feeling confident** **Exam ready**

Active transport

② Quick quiz

Place a tick (✓) in one box in each row to show which method of transport is being described in each case.

Statement	Diffusion	Osmosis	Active transport
Movement of substances against a concentration gradient			
Movement of water across a partially permeable membrane			
Requires energy to take place			
Can describe the movement of gases			
Net movement of dissolved solute molecules down their concentration gradient			

⑩ Active transport in root hair cells | **Grades 3–5**

1. Figure 1 shows a root hair cell from a plant.

(a) Plants absorb water and mineral ions from the soil through the many root hair cells that cover the roots. Explain how these cells increase absorption. **[1 mark]**

> Think about the shape of the cell.

....

(b) Explain why some mineral ions must be absorbed into root hair cells by active transport. **[2 marks]**

Figure 1

 The concentration of mineral ions is higher in the ....

Therefore, the mineral ions need to be moved against ....

⑩ Transport in the small intestine | **Grade 5**

2. Digested food is absorbed into the blood in the small intestine. The small intestine is lined with cells like those shown in **Figure 2**.

(a) Glucose is moved from the gut into these cells by active transport. Suggest why glucose is transported by active transport rather than by diffusion. **[2 marks]**

....

....

(b) Mitochondria are sub-cellular structures. Explain why mitochondria are important for cells that carry out active transport. **[2 marks]**

....

Figure 2

....

Mitosis and the cell cycle

2 Quick quiz

Number the boxes 1-5 to show the order of the stages of mitosis. One has been done for you.

Metaphase - The chromosomes lie in the centre of the cell.	
Cytokinesis - The cell surface membranes of the new cells form.	
Anaphase - The two copies of each chromosome are pulled apart to opposite ends of the cell.	
Prophase - The chromosomes become visible as the DNA coils up tightly.	1
Telophase - Two new nuclei form.	

10 Process and use of mitosis — Grades 4–5

1. Mitosis is part of the cell cycle. During mitosis: **[1 mark]**

the cell gets bigger ☐

cell division takes place ☐

the number of chromosomes in the cell increases ☐

ribosomes become visible ☐

Mitosis produces two identical cells from a single cell.

5 Mitosis and the cell cycle — Grade 5

2. Figure 1 shows cells at different stages of the cell cycle.

(a) Identify the stage of mitosis that is shown by cell **B**. **[1 mark]**

....

(b) Cell **A** is **not** undergoing mitosis. Name the stage of the cell cycle shown by cell **A**. **[1 mark]**

....

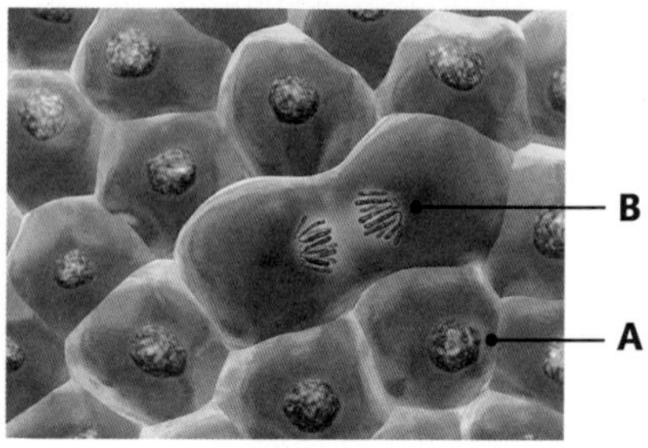

Figure 1

5 Cell division by mitosis — Grade 4

3. Figure 2 shows the chromosomes in the nucleus of a diploid cell that has four chromosomes. The cell undergoes a single division by mitosis.

(a) State how many daughter cells would be produced from this division. **[1 mark]**

....

(b) Describe how the chromosomes in the daughter cells would compare to the parent cell in **Figure 2**. **[2 marks]**

....

....

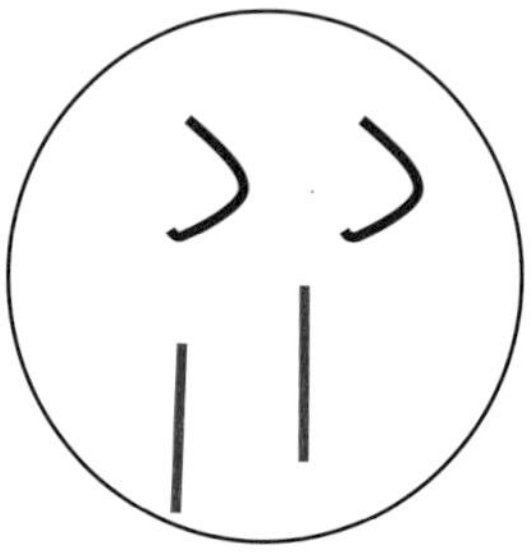
Figure 2

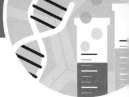

Importance of mitosis

2 Quick quiz

True or false?

A baby grows because its cells divide by mitosis to make more cells. **True / False**

Gametes (sex cells) are produced by mitosis. **True / False**

Mitosis is the type of cell division that occurs to replace damaged cells. **True / False**

Mitosis produces cells that are genetically different from the parent cell. **True / False**

10 Reproduction and cell division — Grades 3–5

1. Figure 1 shows a daffodil bulb in spring and in autumn. During the summer, daughter bulbs develop from the parent bulb. If the daughter bulbs are planted next year, they will produce new daffodil plants.

(a) Name the type of reproduction shown in **Figure 1**. **[1 mark]**

Remember how many parents are needed for asexual and sexual reproduction.

....

(b) Name the type of cell division that produced the daughter bulbs from the parent bulb. **[1 mark]**

Remember the functions of mitosis and meiosis.

....

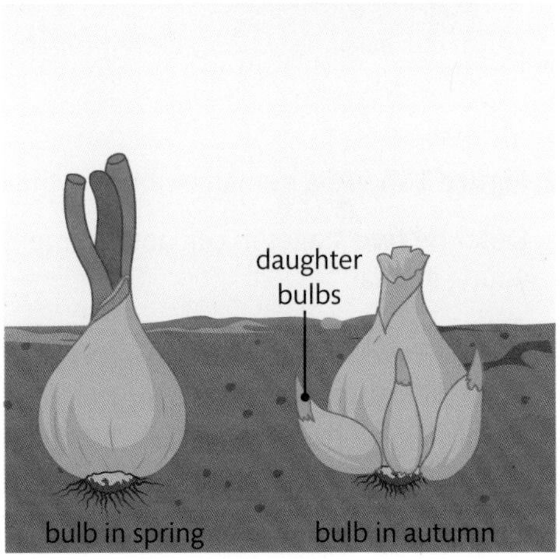

Figure 1

(c) Daffodil flowers can be yellow or white. The flowers produced by the parent bulb in **Figure 1** were white. State and explain the colour of the flowers in the daughter bulbs. **[2 marks]**

Colour The flowers of the daughter bulbs would be white.

Explanation Because offspring produced by asexual reproduction are genetically

....

5 Cancer — Grades 3–4

2. Figure 2 shows a cancer tumour growing on a person's skin.

(a) State the type of cell division that produces a tumour. **[1 mark]**

....

(b) A tumour is produced because **[1 mark]**

the division of cells is uncontrolled ☐

the cells produced are discoloured ☐

the cells produced are larger than usual ☐

the division of cells is inhibited. ☐

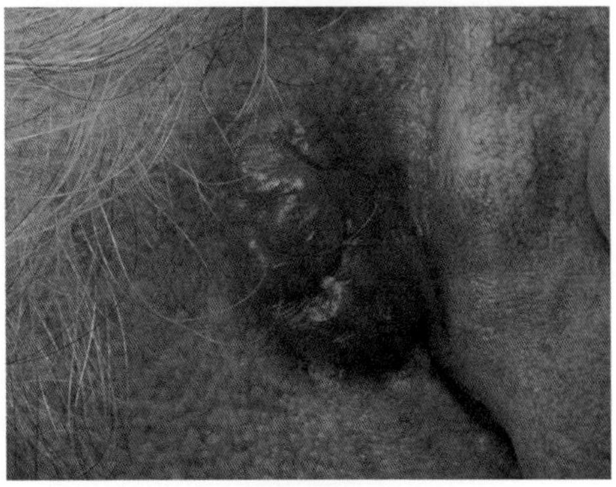

Figure 2

Cell differentiation and growth

2 Quick quiz

True or false?

Most types of animal cell can differentiate at any time in the animal's life. **True / False**

Many types of plant cell can differentiate at any time during the plant's life. **True / False**

10 Differentiation in animal growth — Grade 4

1. State what is meant by the term 'differentiation'. **[1 mark]**

A specialised cell has a particular shape and structure to carry out a certain function.

Differentiation is when an unspecialised cell develops to become ....

....

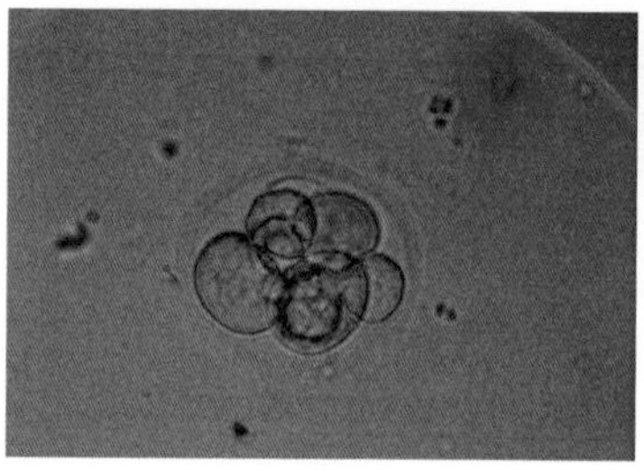

Figure 1

2. Figure 1 shows a human embryo at the eight-cell stage.

Describe **two** stages in cell development that take place to bring about growth in a young animal. **[2 marks]**

The first stage is cell .... which produces many new unspecialised cells.

The second stage is cell .... which produces ....

5 Growth in plants — Grade 4

3. Figure 2 shows the tip of a root of a garlic plant showing the position of the meristem.

(a) Growth of the root begins in the meristem. Describe what happens within the meristem. **[1 mark]**

....

(b) Use words from the box to complete the sentences to describe plant growth. **[2 marks]**

transpiration	elongation	compaction
duplication	differentiation	

The small, unspecialised cells produced by the meristem get bigger by the process of ....

Cells must also undergo .... to form specialised cells.

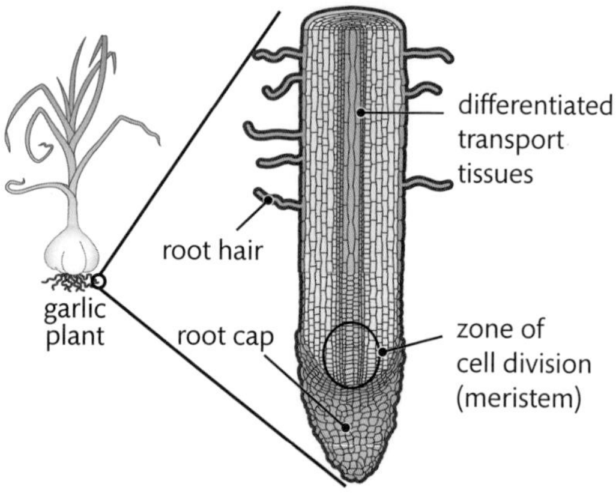

garlic plant
root hair
root cap
differentiated transport tissues
zone of cell division (meristem)

Figure 2

5 Growth in children — Grades 3–5

4. A child's growth is plotted on a percentile chart, which shows growth curves for boys or girls with different birth weights.

(a) State what the 50th percentile growth curve indicates. **[1 mark]**

....

(b) Explain why doctors use percentile charts to monitor the health of babies. **[1 mark]**

....

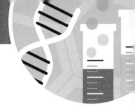

Stem cells

2 Quick quiz

Draw **one** line from each keyword to its definition.

Keyword	Definition
embryonic stem cell	plant cells that divide and differentiate into any type of plant cell
adult stem cell	unspecialised cell that can give rise to all of the different types of cells in a human body
meristem	unspecialised cell in tissue that can produce some types of differentiated cell

15 Embryonic and adult stem cells — Grades 4–5

1. Blood cells are not able to divide. Explain how new blood cells are produced in bone marrow tissue to replace old or damaged cells. **[2 marks]**

New blood cells are produced by division of ....

....

2. Type 1 diabetes is caused when pancreas cells do not produce the hormone insulin. Stem cell therapies are being developed to help people with type 1 diabetes.

(a) One therapy begins by taking adult cells from a person and reprogramming those cells to become embryonic stem cells. Explain why embryonic stem cells are used rather than adult stem cells. **[2 marks]**

....

....

(b) Describe how stem cell therapy may one day be used to cure type 1 diabetes. **[2 marks]**

Stem cells could be used to replace faulty cells in the pancreas with ....

The healthy cells would then ....

(c) Explain the advantage of using stem cells that are made from a patient's own cells. **[2 marks]**

Remember the response of the immune system to foreign cells in the body. Foreign cells have different alleles.

....

....

5 Plant stem cell uses — Grade 4

3. Most new banana plants are produced using stem cells from mature plants.

(a) Name the special tissue that contains plant stem cells. **[1 mark]**

....

(b) Describe **one** benefit of using stem cells to produce new banana plants. **[1 mark]**

....

(c) Explain why stem cells from a banana shoot can be used to produce a whole new banana plant. **[2 marks]**

....

....

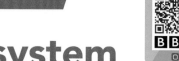

The human nervous system

2 Quick quiz

Number the steps 1–5 to give the correct order for the response of a reflex arc in the nervous system. One has been done for you.

Sensory receptor cells	1
Relay neurone in spinal cord	
Effector cells	
Motor neurone	
Sensory neurone	

10 Synapses — Grade 5

1. Figure 1 is a partly-labelled diagram of a synapse.

(a) State what is meant by the term 'synapse'. **[1 mark]**

A synapse is where ....

(b) Figure 1 shows events at a synapse. Describe what is happening at steps **2**, **3** and **4**. **[3 marks]**

Step 2 The impulse causes the axon terminal to release ....

....

Step 3 The neurotransmitter ....

Step 4 This causes a new electrical ....

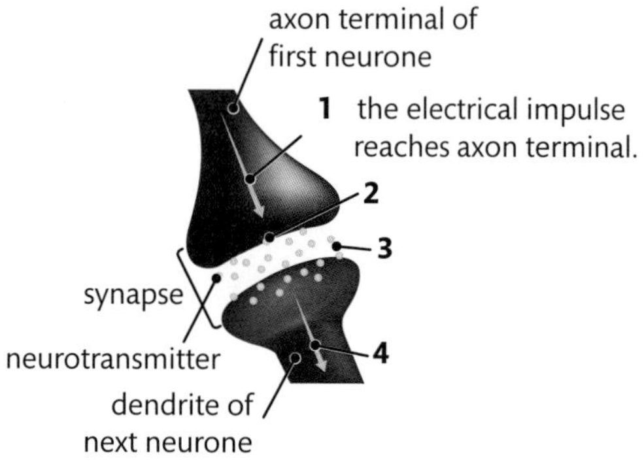

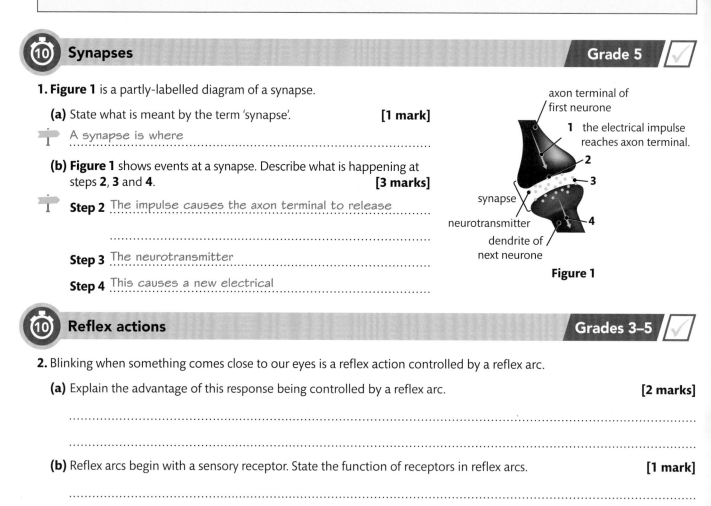

axon terminal of first neurone
1 the electrical impulse reaches axon terminal.
2
3
4
synapse
neurotransmitter
dendrite of next neurone

Figure 1

10 Reflex actions — Grades 3–5

2. Blinking when something comes close to our eyes is a reflex action controlled by a reflex arc.

(a) Explain the advantage of this response being controlled by a reflex arc. **[2 marks]**

....

....

(b) Reflex arcs begin with a sensory receptor. State the function of receptors in reflex arcs. **[1 mark]**

....

5 Features of the nervous system — Grade 4

3. Figure 2 shows a sensory neurone.

Sensory neurones carry impulses from sensory receptors to the central nervous system. Give **two** ways in which the sensory neurone is adapted to its function. **[2 marks]**

....

....

....

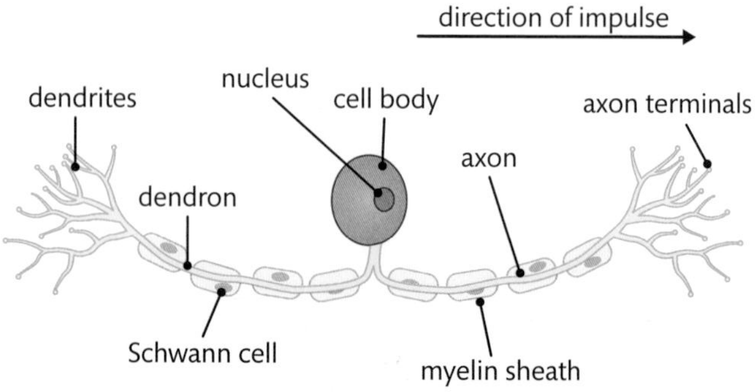

direction of impulse
dendrites
nucleus
cell body
axon terminals
axon
dendron
Schwann cell
myelin sheath

Figure 2

Meiosis

Quick quiz

True or false?

Meiosis happens in cells in reproductive organs.	**True / False**
Gametes are always produced by mitosis.	**True / False**
Fertilisation is when the male and female sex cells fuse together.	**True / False**

Process of meiosis   Grade 5

1. A body cell from a cat contains 38 chromosomes.

(a) State the number of chromosomes found in an egg cell from a female cat.   **[1 mark]**

....

(b) Explain why meiosis is needed to produce gametes for sexual reproduction.   **[3 marks]**

> Think about what happens to the chromosome number when gametes fuse in fertilisation.

Meiosis produces gametes that have .... the normal number of chromosomes. When two

gametes fuse during .... their chromosomes are combined in the fertilised cell.

This restores .... in the fertilised cell.

2. A sperm-forming cell divides by meiosis to form sperm.

(a) Describe what must happen in the sperm-forming cell before division can occur.   **[1 mark]**

> When a cell divides, its chromosomes are split between the daughter cells.

....

(b) State how many sperm cells are produced from each sperm-forming cell.   **[1 mark]**

....

Comparison of mitosis and meiosis   Grades 3–5

3. Reproduction in plants can involve cell division by meiosis or mitosis.

(a) Name the type of reproduction that involves cell division by meiosis.   **[1 mark]**

....

(b) Meiosis produces daughter cells which are all genetically different from each other. Explain the advantage of these genetic differences in reproduction.   **[2 marks]**

....

....

(c) There are several differences between mitosis and meiosis. Which is **not** a correct difference? Tick **one** box.   **[1 mark]**

Mitosis involves one division but meiosis involves two. ☐

Mitosis produces two daughter cells but meiosis produces four. ☐

Mitosis produces cells with one set of chromosomes while meiosis produces cells with two sets. ☐

Daughter cells in mitosis are genetically identical but daughter cells in meiosis are genetically different. ☐

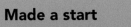

The structure of DNA

BBC

---

② **Quick quiz**

The stages of extracting DNA from a banana are given below out of order. Number the stages 1–4 to show the order they should occur.

Stage	Stage order
Pour ice-cold ethanol down the inside of the tube very carefully.	
Remove the banana skin and mash it up very thoroughly.	
Filter the mixture.	
Mix the banana mash with a mixture of salt, detergent and water and warm in a water bath for 20 minutes.	

---

⑩ **DNA structure** **Grades 2–5**

1. Figure 1 shows a small section of DNA.

(a) Which term scientifically describes the shape of a DNA molecule? Tick **one** box.   **[1 mark]**

spiral ☐   double coil ☐   double helix ☐   double twist ☐

(b) Use **Figure 1** to identify the number of DNA strands in a DNA molecule.   **[1 mark]**

....

(c) The strands of DNA are linked by complementary base pairs. State what 'complementary' means in this case.   **[1 mark]**

🚩 A particular base will only pair with
....

(d) The order of bases on DNA provides the genetic code of an organism. State how many different bases are found in this code.   **[1 mark]**

| Use the colours on the diagram to help you. |

....

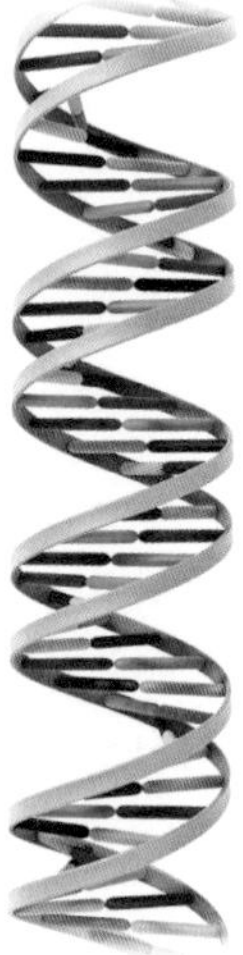

Figure 1

---

⑩ **DNA bases** **Grade 5**

2. Figure 2 shows a very short section of DNA.

(a) Name the units that are formed from one sugar, one phosphate group and one base.   **[1 mark]**

....

(b) Give a reason why DNA is described as a polymer.   **[1 mark]**

....

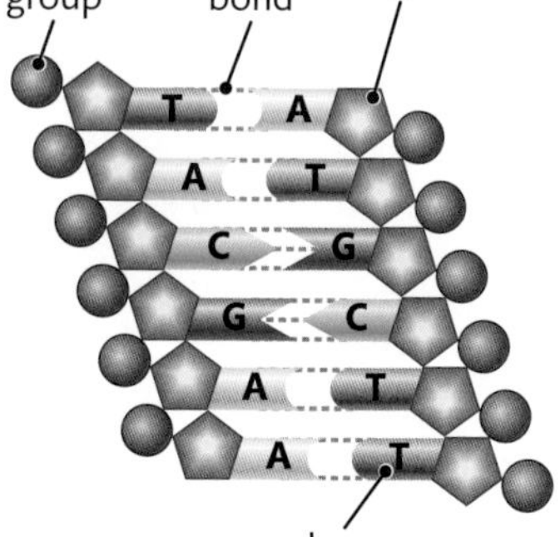

phosphate group   hydrogen bond   sugar

T — A
A — T
C — G
G — C
A — T
A — T

base

Figure 2

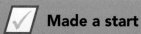

✓ **Made a start**   ✓ **Feeling confident**   ✓ **Exam ready**

DNA and the genome

(2) Quick quiz

Use words from the box to complete the sentences.

| chromosomes | DNA | helix | nucleus | polymer | two |

The genetic material in a cell is composed of a chemical called ....

This chemical is a .... because it is made of repeating units.

The units are joined together to make .... strands, which twist round each other forming a double

.... The strands combine with other molecules to form structures called ....

(10) Genes and genome   Grades 2–3

1. The human genome consists of about 20 000 genes.

(a) Give the meaning of the term 'human genome'.   **[1 mark]**

> It means the whole .... of a human.

(b) State what is meant by the term 'gene'.   **[2 marks]**

> A gene is a short section of DNA that ....

....

Remember that each gene is the code for making a particular molecule.

(c) Genes are found on chromosomes. Describe where chromosomes are found within a eukaryotic cell.   **[1 mark]**

....

Remember that eukaryotic cells include animal and plant cells but not bacterial cells.

(10) The human genome   Grades 3–4

2. The aim of the Human Genome Project was to map and identify all the genes in the human genome.

(a) Use words from the box to complete the sentences.   **[2 marks]**

| chromosome | lipid | carbohydrate | nucleus | protein | nucleotide |

Mapping the genes included finding out which .... they were located on.

Identifying the genes involved working out their function and which particular .... they code for.

(b) One other potential benefit of the Human Genome Project is identifying people who have an increased risk of certain diseases. There are advantages if a person knows their risk of developing a particular disease. Suggest **one** advantage.   **[1 mark]**

....

Genetic inheritance

2 Quick quiz

The diagram shows a pair of chromosomes found in a body cell. Use the words in the box to label the diagram.

different genes
homozygous recessive allele pair
alleles of gene A
homozygous dominant allele pair
heterozygous allele pair

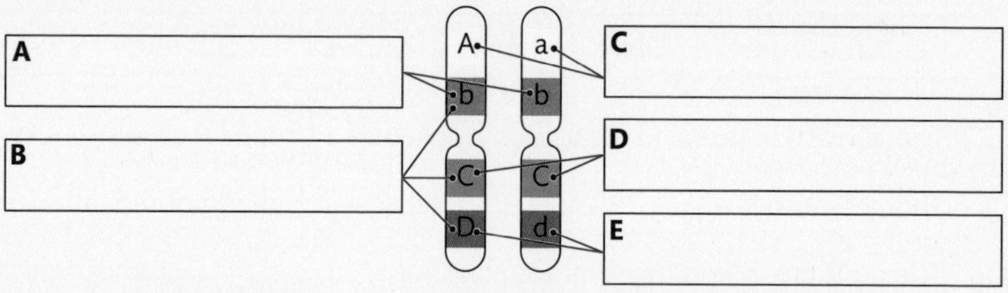

Remember that alleles are alternative forms of the same gene.

15 Genetic cross and Punnett squares

Grades 3–5

1. What do most phenotype features result from? Tick **one** box. **[1 mark]**

a single gene ☐ multiple interacting genes ☐

a recessive allele ☐ a dominant allele ☐

Phenotype is the observable characteristics of an organism, or its appearance.

2. (a) Cystic fibrosis is a disorder of cell membranes caused by a recessive allele. State what is meant by the term 'recessive'. **[1 mark]**

A recessive allele is only expressed if ....

(b) Complete the Punnett square to show the possible genotypes of offspring from parents who are both heterozygous for the gene related to cystic fibrosis. **[1 mark]**

Remember that gametes of the parents can only contain one allele but the cells of the offspring will have two.

	F	f
F	FF	
f		

(c) State the probability of a child of these parents developing cystic fibrosis. **[1 mark]**

Probability ....

Maths skills
Probability is a measure of how likely something is to happen. Probabilities can be written as fractions, decimals or percentages.

5 Inheritance

Grade 5

3. Being able to taste bitter PTC is caused by a dominant allele, **T**. A person who is homozygous recessive for the trait has the genotype **tt** and cannot taste PTC.

(a) The Punnett square shows the possible genotypes of offspring when one parent is heterozygous for the PTC gene and one parent cannot taste PTC. Complete the Punnett square to show the alleles of the heterozygous parent. **[2 marks]**

t	Tt	tt
t	Tt	tt

(b) State the percentage of the offspring that will not be able to taste PTC. **[1 mark]**

....

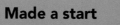

Made a start ☐ Feeling confident ☐ Exam ready ☐

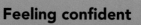

Genetic diagrams

② Quick quiz

Draw **one** line to link each term to its meaning.

inherited disorder	affects the phenotype even if only one copy of the allele is present in the genotype
recessive allele	a disorder caused by a faulty allele
dominant allele	affects the phenotype only when there are two copies in the genotype

⑩ Family pedigree   Grades 3–5

1. **Figure 1** shows a family pedigree identifying which family members have an inherited disorder caused by a dominant allele.

   (a) State how many women shown in **Figure 1** have the disorder.   **[1 mark]**

   ....

   | Use the key to help you. |

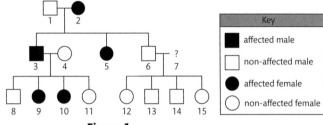

Figure 1

   (b) D represents the dominant allele for the disorder and **d** the recessive allele. State and explain the genotype of person 2.   **[2 marks]**

   > Remember that a person has two alleles of each gene but only passes on one allele to each child.

   The genotype must be **Dd** because ....

   ....

   (c) Person 6 does not have the disorder, but they are worried that they may be a carrier. Explain why they cannot be a carrier of the disorder.   **[3 marks]**

   Person 6 must have the genotype **dd**. They cannot be a carrier because this disorder is caused by a ....

   ....so if they were a carrier with one faulty allele they would ....

⑩ Genetic diagrams   Grade 5

2. Dwarf pea plants are caused by a recessive allele represented as **t**. The dominant allele **T** gives tall pea plants. **Figure 2** shows a cross between two heterozygous plants.

   (a) State the phenotype of both parent plants.   **[1 mark]**

   ....

   (b) Complete the genetic diagram in **Figure 2** to show the possible genotypes and phenotypes of the offspring.   **[2 marks]**

   (c) Give the percentage of seeds produced from this cross that will produce dwarf plants. Use your completed diagram to help you.   **[1 mark]**

genotypes of parents

possible gametes

possible offspring genotypes

possible offspring phenotypes

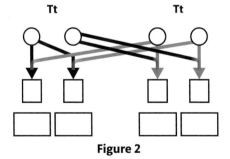

Figure 2

   ....

Sex determination

② Quick quiz

Complete the sentences by choosing words from the box below.

| DNA | fertilisation | pairs | parent | XX | XY | YY | genes | zygote |

The sex of an individual is determined at .... when the two gametes fuse to form a

.... One of the chromosome pairs in each cell carries ....

that determine the sex of the individual. In human females, the two sex chromosomes are

.... In human males, the two sex chromosomes are ....

⑩ Sex chromosomes   Grade 4

1. (a) Name the type of cell division which gives rise to the formation of sex cells.   **[1 mark]**

....

(b) State the proportion of human sperm cells that contain an X chromosome.   **[1 mark]**

....

> Remember that only one chromosome from each pair enters the gamete during cell division.

(c) The sex of a human baby is determined by the inheritance of sex chromosomes. Explain why it is the chromosomes from the father that determine whether the baby is a girl or a boy.   **[3 marks]**

The egg cell from the mother can contain only
....

Sperm cells may contain either
....

So, the sex chromosome that is present in the sperm that fertilises the egg determines
....

....

⑩ Sex determination   Grades 2–4

2. (a) Complete the Punnett square to show the inheritance of sex in humans. Use the symbols **X** and **Y** for the chromosomes. **[2 marks]**

(b) A couple are having a baby. Using your Punnett square, determine the chance of the baby being a girl.
Tick **one** box.   **[1 mark]**

		Sperm cells from father	
		X	Y
Egg cells from mother	X		

0% ☐   50% ☐   25% ☐   75% ☐

(c) A different couple already have two boys and a girl. The woman is expecting another child. State the probability that the baby will be a girl.   **[1 mark]**

....

(d) Genetic tests show that an embryo has the genotype **XX**. Explain what this shows.   **[1 mark]**

....

 Made a start   **Feeling confident**   ✓ **Exam ready**

Variation and mutation

② Quick quiz

Each statement below describes an example of variation. Circle the correct word after each statement to show if the statement describes genetic or environmental variation.

Seeds from tall plants usually produce plants that grow to be tall. **Environmental / Genetic**

Seeds from tall plants may not grow tall because they cannot get enough water. **Environmental / Genetic**

Plants that usually have green leaves may develop pale leaves if grown in the dark. **Environmental / Genetic**

Green-leaved plants may occasionally produce seeds that grow into plants with unusually pale leaves. **Environmental / Genetic**

⑩ Variation and mutations   Grades 2–5

1. (a) Give the meaning of the term 'variation'. **[1 mark]**

Variation is the .... in characteristics that are seen between individuals.

(b) Give the meaning of the term 'mutation'. **[1 mark]**

A mutation is a change in ....

(c) A baby may have many genetic mutations that its parents do not have. Describe the likely effect of these mutations on the baby. **[3 marks]**

They are likely to have no effect on the baby because most genetic mutations ....

....

Very rarely a mutation may ....

⑩ Cause of variation   Grade 4

2. (a) What are two causes of genetic variation? Tick **one** box. **[1 mark]**

sexual reproduction and mutations in DNA ☐

changes in an individual over their lifetime ☐

asexual reproduction and mutations in RNA ☐

mitosis and the cell cycle ☐

(b) Explain why children of the same parents may show a large variation in height even when they grow up in similar environments. **[2 marks]**

....

....

> Human height is determined by both inherited and environmental factors.

....

(c) Suggest **one** environmental factor that may cause variation in the height of children. **[1 mark]**

....

(d) Hair colour is also determined by genes. Parents who have a genotype for dark hair may very rarely have a child who has pale hair. Explain how this could happen. **[1 mark]**

....

Evolution by natural selection

2 Quick quiz

Use words from the box to complete the sentences on Darwin's theory of natural selection.

adapted	characteristics	evolution	alleles	natural	simple	offspring

Darwin's theory of .... describes how organisms may change over time through .... selection. It explains how changes in the environment can lead to changes in .... of species as only the best .... individuals survive and breed, passing on their characteristics to their .... in their ....

15 Evolution of resistance — Grade 5

1. Figure 1 shows how an antibiotic resistant population of bacteria develops. Each shape represents a bacterium. Explain how this provides evidence in support of Darwin's theory of evolution. **[6 marks]**

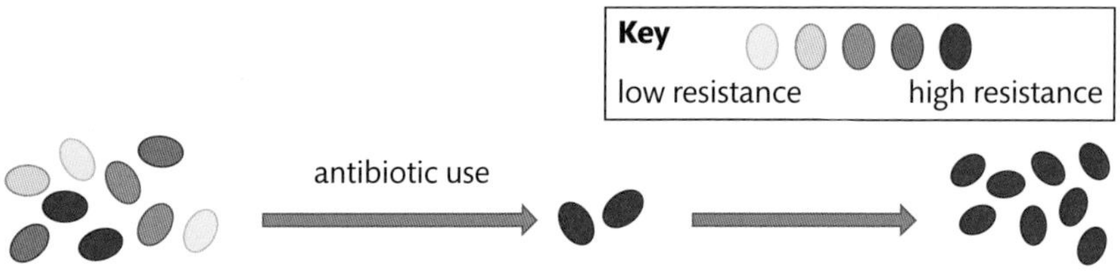

Figure 1

The population of bacteria has existing genetic ....

Some bacteria are more ....

This is caused by ....

People misuse antibiotics by ....

Those bacteria that are not resistant die. The resistant bacteria ....

This is an example of ....

The population of bacteria changes due to natural selection. This is evidence of ....

Remember that the mutations for resistance arise randomly and are already present in the population; the antibiotic does not cause the mutations.

Exam focus
Some marks in a 6-mark question are for a sensible ordering of your answer. Always use information from any diagram provided.

5 New species — Grades 2–4

2. Polar bears and brown bears are thought to have evolved from a common ancestor that was similar to the brown bear. Polar bears have thick white fur and wide feet. They live in Arctic areas that are covered in ice and snow for most of the year. Brown bears have brown fur and smaller feet. They are found in warmer areas with no snow for most of the year.

(a) State what is meant by the term 'evolution'. **[2 marks]**

....

....

(b) Explain how **one** adaptation shown by polar bears allows them to survive in Arctic areas. **[2 marks]**

....

....

Evidence for human evolution

② Quick quiz

True or false?

The Leakey family found fossils of human-like species that lived in Africa 1.6 million years ago. **True / False**

'Lucy' is a fossil of a human-like species from 6.2 million years ago. **True / False**

'Ardi' belongs to the human-like species *Ardipithecus ramidus* and lived 4.4 million years ago. **True / False**

⑩ Fossil evidence — Grade 5

1. Figure 1 shows the upper leg bone of two living species (human and chimp) and of the fossil skeleton known as 'Lucy'. The position of each bone shows its alignment in the whole skeleton.

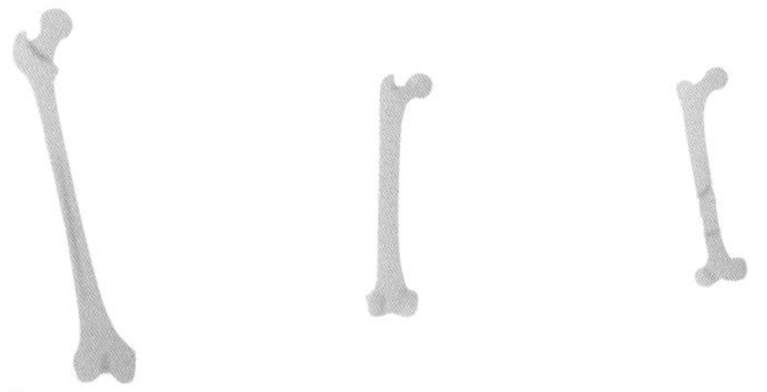

(a) Use evidence from **Figure 1** to suggest how Lucy's height compares with that of a modern human and chimp. **[2 marks]**

Lucy's leg bone is nearer in length to a

than   This suggests she was a

similar height to a modern

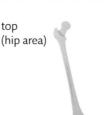

top (hip area)

knee

modern human knees close together for upright walking

modern chimpanzee knees apart – four-legged 'knuckle' walking

'Lucy'

Figure 1

(b) **Figure 1** shows that the position of Lucy's leg bone and knee is closer to that of a modern human. Comment on what this tells us about how Lucy walked. **[2 marks]**

This shows that her knees would have been

and suggests that she would have walked

⑩ Stone tools — Grades 3–5

2. Figure 2 shows two stone hand axes and their dates.

Explain how the differences between these axes provides evidence for human evolution. **[3 marks]**

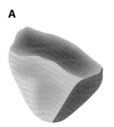 

A   B

1.9 million years old

1.5 million years old

Figure 2

Exam focus
When a question asks you to use evidence given, make sure you refer to the evidence in your answer.

Classification

② Quick quiz

Draw **one** line to link each kingdom with a feature shared by organisms in that kingdom.

Kingdom	Feature
prokaryotes	usually multi-celled organisms that are able to photosynthesise
protists	usually multi-celled organisms that digest food outside their bodies
fungi	single cells with genetic material free in cytoplasm
plants	multi-celled organisms that digest food inside their bodies
animals	usually single cells with nucleus and other sub-cellular structures

⑩ Classification systems   Grade 4 ✓

1. (a) In the 18th century, Carl Linnaeus developed a classification system for organisms based on observable characteristics. Use words from the box to complete the sentences about this classification system. **[2 marks]**

> The smallest group contains individuals with the most similar characteristics.

genus	phylum	order	species	domain	class

All living things were placed into one of five large groups called kingdoms. The second largest group

is called a .... The smallest group in Linnaeus' system is the ....

(b) In the 20th century, a new classification for organisms was developed based on genetics. Explain why Linnaeus did not use this evidence. **[1 mark]**

🚏 Knowledge about genetic material and how to analyse it was
....

⑩ Domains versus kingdoms   Grade 5 ✓

2. The older classification system grouped living things into five kingdoms. A more recent system groups them into three domains: bacteria, archaea and eukaryota.

(a) Organisms in the eukaryota have cells with DNA inside a nucleus. Name **two** kingdoms from the old classification system that are now placed in the eukaryota. **[2 marks]**

1 ....   **2** ....

(b) The relationships between the three domains are shown in **Figure 1**. The closer together the domains the more similar they are.

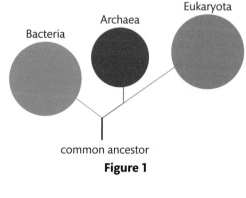

Figure 1

(i) Describe how organisms were placed into three domains. **[1 mark]**

....

(ii) Suggest why archaea are placed between bacteria and eukaryota in the domain system. **[2 marks]**

....

....

....

....

 Made a start   Feeling confident   Exam ready

Selective breeding

② Quick quiz

Suggest **one** feature of each organism that has been selectively bred.

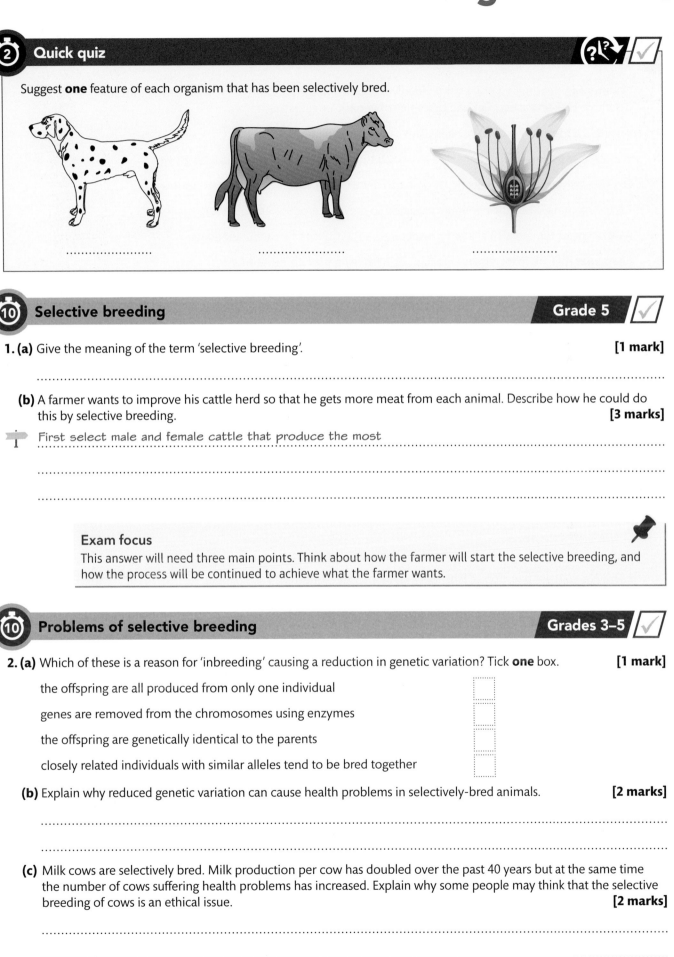

....

⑩ Selective breeding

Grade 5

1. (a) Give the meaning of the term 'selective breeding'. **[1 mark]**

....

(b) A farmer wants to improve his cattle herd so that he gets more meat from each animal. Describe how he could do this by selective breeding. **[3 marks]**

First select male and female cattle that produce the most
....

....

....

> **Exam focus**
> This answer will need three main points. Think about how the farmer will start the selective breeding, and how the process will be continued to achieve what the farmer wants.

⑩ Problems of selective breeding

Grades 3–5

2. (a) Which of these is a reason for 'inbreeding' causing a reduction in genetic variation? Tick **one** box. **[1 mark]**

the offspring are all produced from only one individual

genes are removed from the chromosomes using enzymes

the offspring are genetically identical to the parents

closely related individuals with similar alleles tend to be bred together

(b) Explain why reduced genetic variation can cause health problems in selectively-bred animals. **[2 marks]**

....

....

(c) Milk cows are selectively bred. Milk production per cow has doubled over the past 40 years but at the same time the number of cows suffering health problems has increased. Explain why some people may think that the selective breeding of cows is an ethical issue. **[2 marks]**

....

....

✓ **Made a start** ✓ **Feeling confident** ✓ **Exam ready**

Genetic engineering

② Quick quiz

Genetic engineering is a process that involves modifying the genome of an organism to introduce desirable characteristics. Tick the examples of genetic engineering.

A gene is added to rice cells so that a plant can produce vitamin A.

A disease-resistant strain of banana is cloned so that lots of resistant plants can be grown.

Disease-resistant cotton plants that have had a gene from a bacterium inserted into them.

Bacteria that have had their genome modified so they will produce an antibiotic.

A new type of tomato with alleles for sweeter fruit is produced by careful breeding.

Plum trees that are made disease resistant by modifying their chromosomes.

⑩ Genetic engineering of cells   Grade 5

1. Bacteria have been genetically engineered to produce human insulin.

(a) Describe how bacteria can be genetically engineered to produce human insulin.   **[3 marks]**

The gene for human insulin is
....

The gene is then inserted into
....

The modified bacterium will then produce
....

(b) People with type 1 diabetes must use insulin every day to stay healthy. Most insulin used is now genetically engineered insulin. Previously, diabetics used insulin extracted from pigs. Suggest an advantage of using genetically engineered insulin.   **[1 mark]**

....

> This is a 'suggest' question so look for clues in the whole question. For example, you are told that the genetically engineered insulin is human insulin.

⑩ Genetic modification of crops   Grade 4

2. Maize (sweetcorn) has been genetically modified to contain a gene that codes for a poison that kills caterpillars which eat the plant. The gene comes from a bacterium.

(a) Explain why growing this type of genetically modified maize can increase the yield (amount of food harvested) from each plant.   **[2 marks]**

....

....

(b) Explain why some people are concerned that growing genetically modified maize might affect the environment.   **[2 marks]**

....

....

 Made a start   **Feeling confident**   ✓ **Exam ready**

Health issues

2 Quick quiz

These are some examples of communicable and non-communicable diseases. Draw a circle around the diseases that are **non-communicable**.

HIV	chalara ash dieback	cholera	lung cancer	cardiovascular disease	tuberculosis	malaria

5 Health and disease — Grades 2–3

1. The World Health Organization defines health as being more than just the absence of disease. State **two** factors that a doctor should consider when assessing if a patient is in good health or not. **[2 marks]**

Well-being can be influenced by physical, mental and social factors, as well as disease.

2. Explain why some diseases are described as communicable and others as non-communicable diseases. **[2 marks]**

Communicable diseases are caused by a pathogen and can be passed

Non-communicable diseases have other causes, such as genes or faults in the way cells work, and

15 Data interpretation — Grade 5

3. Regularly drinking large amounts of alcohol can lead to mental illness. UK figures for 2016 recorded 5507 alcohol-specific deaths. Of these, 441 were linked to mental illness. Calculate the percentage of alcohol-specific deaths that were linked to mental illness. **[2 marks]**

4. Flu is a communicable disease of the nose, throat and lungs. **Figure 1** shows the number of people in hospital for either flu infection or asthma attack between 2002 and 2012. Describe the relationship shown between flu infection and asthma attacks in **Figure 1**. **[2 marks]**

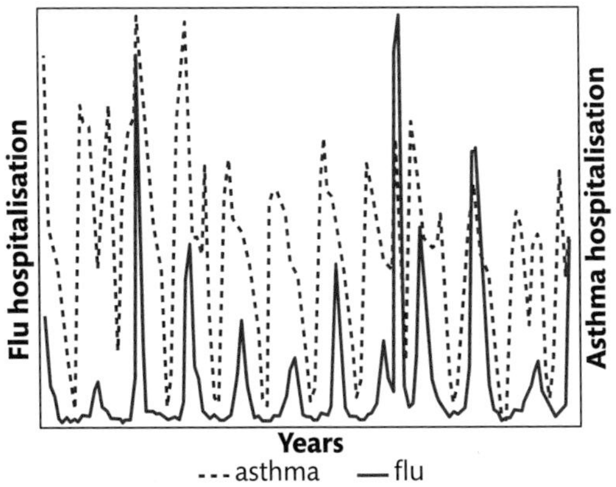

Figure 1

Communicable diseases

② Quick quiz

Draw **one** line to link each infection with the type of pathogen that causes it.

Infection	Pathogen that causes it
chalara ash dieback	virus
chlamydia	fungus
HIV	protist
malaria	bacterium

⑩ Preventing the spread of disease **Grades 3–5**

1. State what is meant by the term 'pathogen'. **[1 mark]**

....

2. Communicable diseases can be spread in different ways. Complete **Table 1** by ticking the boxes to show how the disease is spread. **[2 marks]**

Table 1

	Water	Airborne	Animal vector
Tuberculosis		✓	
Chalara ash dieback			
Malaria			

3. Cholera is a common infectious bacterial disease that can be spread through contaminated water. What are **two** ways that the spread of cholera can be stopped? **[2 marks]**

ensuring good ventilation ☐   killing mosquitoes ☐

sterilising drinking water ☐   careful treatment and disposal of sewage ☐   Tick **two** boxes.

⑩ Understanding data **Grade 5**

4. People who have been treated for tuberculosis may develop the disease again. **Table 2** shows the results of a study into the relationship between smoking and developing tuberculosis a second time.

Table 2

Number of cigarettes smoked each day	Total number in group	Number with a second tuberculosis infection	Percentage of group (%)
0	4280	55	1.3
1–10	250	3	1.2
>10	602	19	

(a) Complete **Table 2** by calculating the percentage of people who smoked more than 10 cigarettes a day who developed tuberculosis again. **[1 mark]**

(b) Describe the effect of smoking on the risk of developing tuberculosis for a second time. **[3 marks]**

....

....

....

 Made a start   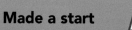 **Feeling confident**   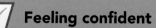 **Exam ready**

Viral diseases

② Quick quiz

True or false?

Some viral infections can make a person more likely to catch other infections.	**True / False**
Cholera is caused by a virus.	**True / False**
Some viral pathogens are spread in droplets through air when someone sneezes.	**True / False**
Diseases caused by viruses can be cured using antibiotics.	**True / False**

⑩ HIV   Grades 3–5

1. Human immunodeficiency virus (HIV) is a human viral pathogen.

(a) Describe **one** way in which HIV can be spread.   **[1 mark]**

HIV is spread through exchange of body fluids, for example,
....

....

(b) Describe **one** way in which the risk of spreading HIV can be reduced during sexual activity.   **[1 mark]**

The risk of spreading HIV during sexual activity can be reduced by
....

....

(c) Name the type of cell that HIV infects.   **[1 mark]**

White ....

(d) HIV destroys the cells that it infects. Explain why this leads to the onset of acquired immune deficiency syndrome (AIDS).   **[3 marks]**

White blood cells are part of the
....

With fewer white blood cells, the body is not able to
....

So AIDS develops, in which a person
....

⑩ TB and HIV   Grades 4–5

2. Figure 1 shows the proportion of people with HIV and the proportion of people with tuberculosis (TB), in 50 different countries.

(a) Describe the trend shown in the scatter diagram.   **[1 mark]**

....

....

(b) Which of these statements explains the relationship shown in the scatter diagram?   **[1 mark]**

People with TB are less likely to get HIV. ☐

HIV damages the immune system so people with HIV are more likely to be infected with TB. ☐

HIV is caused by a virus, but TB is a bacterial infection. ☐

TB infection can develop into HIV. ☐

Proportion of people with TB

Proportion of people with HIV

Figure 1

Bacterial diseases

② Quick quiz

Draw a circle round the infections caused by bacteria.

chlamydia   cholera   malaria   chalara ash dieback   tuberculosis   HIV

⑩ Chlamydia infections   Grade 5

1. Chlamydia is a sexually transmitted disease (STD).

   Figure 1 shows how the number of chlamydia infections per 100 000 males in different age groups has changed between 2009 and 2017 in England.

   Free screening tests for chlamydia infection are offered in England for people under the age of 25. Use **Figure 1** to suggest why they are offered to this age group and not older age groups. **[2 marks]**

   > Look at the difference in infection rates between age groups. Testing everyone would be too expensive.

Chlamydia (males)

Rate per 100000 population

— 15–19
— 20–24
— 25–34
— 35–44
— 45–64

Year

Figure 1

....

....

⑩ Cholera and tuberculosis   Grades 2–5

2. Cholera bacteria can cause a severe illness in humans.

   (a) Describe **one** symptom of cholera infection. **[1 mark]**

   ....

   (b) In areas where there is poor sanitation and poor hygiene (where drinking and cooking water contains human waste) cholera outbreaks happen. Explain why. **[2 marks]**

   ....

   ....

   (c) Explain how a person could reduce their risk of infection by cholera when there is an outbreak. **[2 marks]**

   ....

   ....

3. **(a)** Tuberculosis is a bacterial disease. Identify **one** symptom of tuberculosis. **[1 mark]**

   skin rashes and vomiting ☐   lung damage ☐

   destruction of white blood cells ☐   diarrhoea ☐

   (b) Describe **two** ways that the spread of tuberculosis can be reduced. **[2 marks]**

   1 ....

   2 ....

 Made a start   **Feeling confident**   ✓ **Exam ready**

Fungal diseases

(2) Quick quiz

Circle the classification domain that fungi belong to.

archaea   bacteria   eukaryota

---

(15) Impact of chalara ash dieback   Grades 3–5

1. Chalara ash dieback is a fungal infection of ash trees. **Figure 1** shows how infection spreads.

(a) Describe the symptoms of chalara ash dieback.   **[2 marks]**

Chalara ash dieback causes damaged areas of bark called

lesions and ....

(b) The fungus blocks the xylem tubes in the leaves and stems. Explain how this could cause the symptoms you described in part **(a)**.   **[2 marks]**

Stopping water and nutrients reaching the leaf and stem cells

....

....

> Use clues from the diagram. Remember that the spread of chalara ash dieback is airborne.

healthy ash tree   infected ash tree

summer

spring   autumn

winter

spores released from fruiting bodies on infected leaf stalks   dying leaves fall to the ground

Figure 1

(c) Explain how chalara ash dieback fungus on leaf stalks can infect healthy trees more than 10 miles away.   **[2 marks]**

....

....

---

(5) Controlling chalara ash dieback   Grade 4

2. (a) The advice to tree owners is to cut down ash trees infected with chalara ash dieback, and burn or bury infected wood and leaves. Explain how this advice can help reduce the spread of ash dieback.   **[1 mark]**

....

(b) Ash trees are abundant in some woodlands. Explain why removing infected trees can affect biodiversity in these woodlands.   **[3 marks]**

....

....

....

> Use your knowledge of the interdependence of organisms to answer this question.

 Made a start   **Feeling confident**   **Exam ready**

Protist diseases

② Quick quiz

True or false?

Malaria is a disease caused by a protist pathogen.	**True / False**
Protists are a type of bacteria.	**True / False**
Mosquitoes are pathogens that cause malaria.	**True / False**
An animal vector is an animal that carries pathogens from infected people to others.	**True / False**

⑩ Malaria　　　　　　　　　　　　　　　　　　Grade 5

1. **(a)** Give **two** health problems caused by a malaria infection.　　　**[2 marks]**

　1　recurrent bouts of fever ....

　　　..

　2　..

> The protist first infects the liver then reproduces in red blood cells, bursting out at intervals.

(b) Mosquitoes spread malaria. They lay their eggs in water. The larval stage develops in water until it turns into an adult. During the day, female mosquitoes rest in shady areas. At night, they feed on blood from animals, including humans. Using this information, explain **two** ways to reduce the spread of malaria.　　　**[4 marks]**

　1　Spray water with insecticide to kill young/larval mosquitoes so ....

　　　..

　2　..

　　　..

⑩ Data interpretation　　　　　　　　　　　　　　Grade 2

2. **Figure 1** shows how malaria is spread.

person
with malaria　　　　　　　　→　　　　　　A　　　　　　　→　　　　　　B

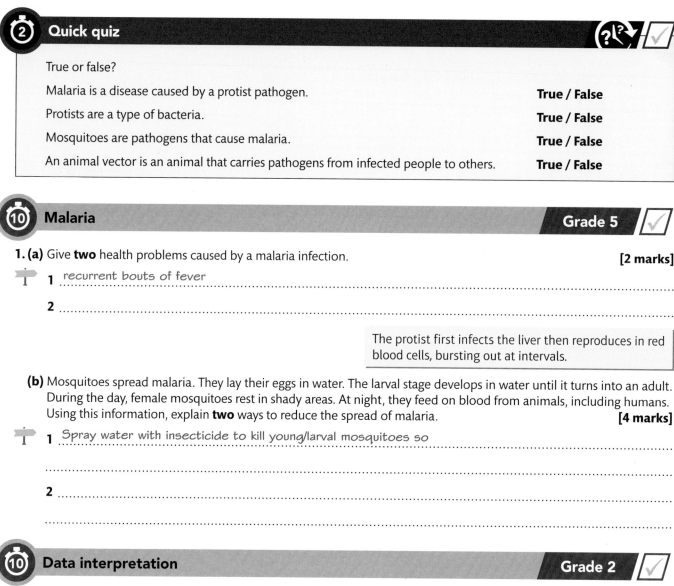

Figure 1

Draw **one** line to link each box (**A** and **B**) with its correct label.　　　**[2 marks]**

Box	Label
A	The mosquito bites another person, passing on malaria when the pathogens grow under their skin.
	The mosquito bites another person, passing on malaria when the pathogens enter the human bloodstream.
B	Mosquito bites a person with malaria, taking in the protist inside skin cells.
	Mosquito bites a person with malaria, taking in the protist in blood that it feeds on.

 Made a start　　　 **Feeling confident**　　　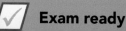 **Exam ready**

Human defence systems

② **Quick quiz**

True or false?

The human body produces antibiotics to fight off disease.	**True / False**
Lymphocytes are white blood cells that produce antibodies to destroy pathogens.	**True / False**
Antigens on the pathogen trigger the immune response.	**True / False**

⑩ **Defence against infection**   **Grades 4–5**

1. **(a)** The human body has physical barriers that help to prevent pathogens entering.

For each physical feature give **one** reason why it defends the body.

(i) Thick skin makes it difficult .... [1 mark]

(ii) Sticky mucus in the nose traps .... [1 mark]

(iii) Cells lining the trachea and bronchi have cilia (tiny hairs) on their surface that ....

.... [1 mark]

(b) Chemical defences can also provide protection from pathogens by destroying them before they cause an infection. Describe how **one** chemical defence helps to prevent infection.   **[2 marks]**

....

....

⑮ **Specific defence against disease**   **Grades 3–5**

2. **(a)** Describe the function of the immune system.   **[2 marks]**

....

....

(b) White blood cells play an important role in the immune system. Describe **three** ways in which white blood cells protect against disease.   **[3 marks]**

1 ....

2 ....

3 ....

3. **Figure 1** shows how the concentration of antibodies in the blood changes after a bacterial infection.

Use words from the box to complete these sentences to explain the changes shown in **Figure 1**.   **[2 marks]**

| antibodies | antigens | pathogens | lymphocytes |

Molecules known as .... on the bacteria trigger an

immune response. White blood cells called .... begin

to produce .... that target the molecule and destroy

the bacteria. When the .... have been destroyed the

antibody production decreases.

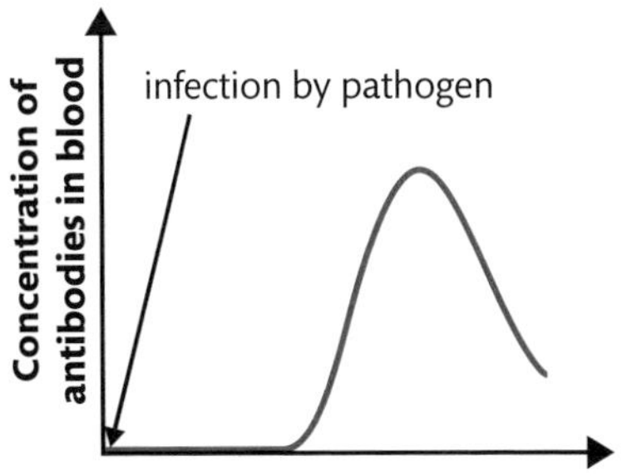

Concentration of antibodies in blood

infection by pathogen

Time

Figure 1

Immunisation

⏱ ② Quick quiz

Use the words in the box to complete the sentences.

| specific | antigens | illness | communicable |

Vaccines used in immunisation contain the .... of a pathogen.

Immunisation has been used to prevent the spread of .... diseases such as polio.

A vaccine is .... to the pathogen that causes a particular disease.

Immunisation is used to prevent .... in an individual.

⏱ ⑩ The body's response to immunisation   Grades 4–5

1. The majority of children in the UK are immunised against polio, a disease caused by the polio virus.

   (a) Polio vaccine contains a weakened or inactive form of the polio virus. Explain why a weakened form of the virus is used.
   [2 marks]

   ....

   ....

   > Explain why the virus used is inactive. Use the term 'antigen' in your answer.

   (b) Immunisation using the polio vaccine triggers an immune response in which antibodies and memory lymphocytes are produced. Explain how this immune response protects the child from polio infection.   **[3 marks]**

   The memory lymphocytes ....

   This means that if the child is infected later with the polio virus ....

   ....

   This will destroy the virus before symptoms can occur and prevent ....

   ....

⏱ ⑩ Widespread immunisation   Grade 5

2. Smallpox was an infectious viral disease with serious symptoms, including death. In 1966, 10–15 million people in more than 50 countries had smallpox, and 1.5–2 million people died of the disease.

   (a) Compulsory immunisation against smallpox began in 1853 in the UK. Suggest **two** reasons why smallpox immunisation was made compulsory.   **[2 marks]**

   Reason 1 ....

   Reason 2 ....

   (b) Explain why a person who had been immunised against smallpox did not become infected with the disease during a later smallpox epidemic.   **[2 marks]**

   ....

   ....

   (c) Worldwide smallpox immunisation was carried out from 1965. The last case of smallpox in the UK occurred in 1971. Give a reason why children in the UK are no longer immunised against smallpox.   **[1 mark]**

   ....

 Made a start   Feeling confident   ✓ Exam ready

Antibiotics

② Quick quiz

Draw **one** line to link each word with its definition.

antibiotic	stimulates the immune system to attack a pathogen
antibody	medicine used to cure bacterial disease
painkiller	produced by immune system in response to infection
antigen	medicine used to reduce symptoms of disease

⑩ Choosing the right medicine   Grades 3–4

1. Flu is a viral disease that causes a high temperature, muscle aches, a runny nose and sore throat.
   Explain why someone who has flu is not given antibiotics such as penicillin to treat their infection. **[2 marks]**

   Antibiotics only kill ....

   so they will have no effect ....

   > Think about what antibiotics can or cannot kill.

2. Antibiotics are used to treat pneumonia infections. Explain why antibiotics will kill the pneumonia bacteria but do not
   harm the cells of the patient. **[2 marks]**

   Antibiotics only inhibit cell processes in .... such as ....

   They do not affect ....

⑩ Drawbacks of antibiotic use   Grade 5

3. **Figure 1** shows the number of deaths in the US between 1990 and 1996, per 100 000 people per year, from
   infectious diseases.

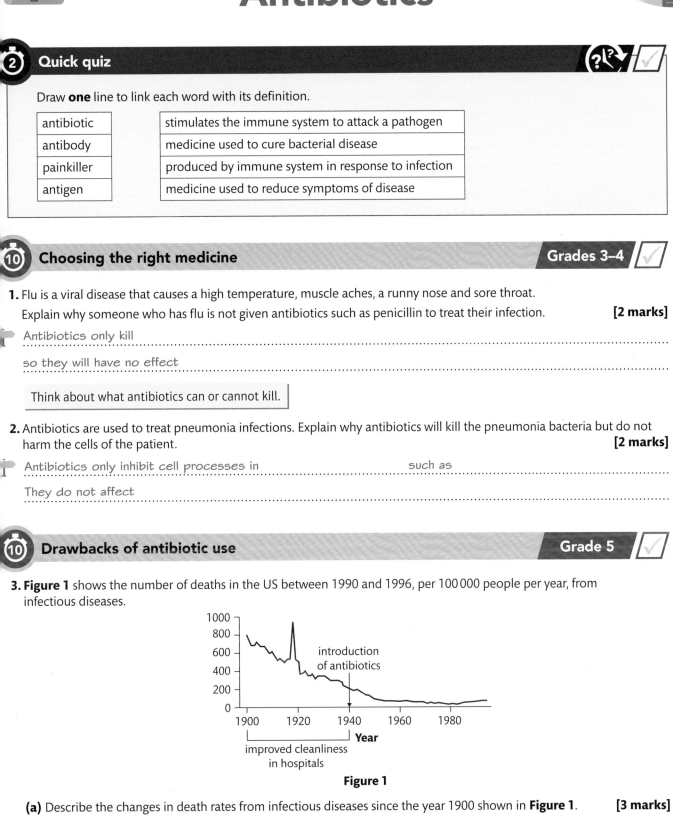

Figure 1

   (a) Describe the changes in death rates from infectious diseases since the year 1900 shown in **Figure 1**. **[3 marks]**

   ....

   ....

   ....

   (b) Suggest why doctors are very concerned that many strains of bacteria are becoming resistant to antibiotics. **[2 marks]**

   ....

   ....

Development of drugs

② Quick quiz

New drugs are tested for toxicity, efficacy and dose. Draw **one** line to link each term with its definition.

placebo	unintended harm caused by a drug
side effect	how much drug to use at a time
dose	appears exactly like the drug but without any active ingredients

⑩ Discovery and development   Grade 3

1. (a) Use words from the box to complete the following sentences.   **[2 marks]**

development   placebo   discovery   distraction   prescription

The first stage of the process in producing a new medicine is ...discovery...............

The source of many old medicines was from plants. When they have a possible new medicine, the next process

is a stage of .... when the structure of the molecule may be studied and modifications made.

(b) The use of computers is now an important part of drug discovery. Computers can be used to find a match between the structure of potential drug molecules and molecules that are linked to disease.

Suggest why computers are used for this task.   **[1 mark]**

Computers will be able to compare molecules more
....

⑩ Drug trials   Grades 3–5

2. One important stage in drug development is pre-clinical testing.

(a) Describe **two** stages of pre-clinical testing.   **[2 marks]**

1 ....

2 ....

(b) Give **one** reason why pre-clinical testing is done before the drug is tested on people.   **[1 mark]**

....

(c) The clinical stage of drug trialling involves testing first on healthy volunteers and then on patients who have the target disease. Explain why each phase is carried out.   **[2 marks]**

Tests on small numbers of healthy volunteers ....

....

Tests on patients who have the target disease ....

....

(d) It usually takes many years to develop a new drug and do safety tests. Suggest why a faster process with less testing is occasionally allowed for drugs for life-threatening diseases.   **[1 mark]**

....

Non-communicable diseases

⏱ 2 Quick quiz

True or false?

All cancers are inherited.	**True / False**
Cancer is caused by controlled cell division.	**True / False**
Liver cancer may be caused by drinking large amounts of alcohol.	**True / False**
Cardiovascular diseases are non-communicable.	**True / False**

⏱ 10 Risk factors   Grade 5

1. (a) Which of the following is **not** a risk factor for liver disease? Tick **one** box.   **[1 mark]**

drug abuse ☐

air pollution ☐

diabetes ☐

genetic factors ☐

(b) Obesity has been identified as one factor that can cause cardiovascular disease. Give **two** other factors that may also contribute to the risk of developing cardiovascular disease.   **[2 marks]**

1 ....smoking...

2 ....

⏱ 5 Nutritional diseases   Grade 3

2. Malnutrition can result from a diet which does not have the correct balance of nutrients.

(a) Suggest why a person who is a healthy weight may still suffer from malnutrition.   **[1 mark]**

....

(b) Anaemia is a condition in which the ability of blood to carry oxygen is reduced. Anaemia can be caused when the diet does not contain enough: **[1 mark]**

iron ☐

nitrate ☐

potassium ☐

calcium ☐

⏱ 5 HPV and cancer   Grade 4

3. Human papilloma virus (HPV) is a trigger for several cancers, including cervical cancer in women.

(a) Vaccination against HPV has been offered to 11 to 13-year-old girls since 2008. Predict the effect of vaccination on the numbers of women developing cervical cancer since 2008.   **[1 mark]**

....

(b) Explain your prediction.   **[1 mark]**

....

 Made a start   Feeling confident   Exam ready

Effects of lifestyle

 Quick quiz

Draw **one** line to link each aspect of lifestyle with the disease for which it is a risk factor.

Aspect of lifestyle	Disease
smoking tobacco	type 2 diabetes
obesity	liver disease
drinking large amounts of alcohol	skin cancer
high dose of UV radiation from sunshine	lung cancer

 Smoking and cardiovascular disease | **Grade 5**

1. **Table 1** shows the results of a study into the relationship between smoking and cardiovascular disease.

Table 1

	People who have never smoked	People who smoke		
Mass of tobacco smoked (g/day)	0	1–14	15–24	>24
Comparative risk of heart attack	1.0	1.60	1.75	2.09

(a) Compare the risk of heart attack for someone who smokes 1–14 g tobacco per day with the risk for someone who has never smoked. **[1 mark]**

People who smoke 1–14 g/day have a risk of heart attack that is 1.6 times

....

(b) Use the information in **Table 1** to describe the relationship between risk of having a heart attack and the amount of tobacco smoked per day. **[1 mark]**

As the mass of tobacco smoked per day .... *the risk of having a heart attack*

....

 Alcohol and liver disease | **Grade 4**

2. **Figure 1** shows how the amount of alcohol consumed per person per year, and number of deaths from liver disease in the UK, changed between 1970 and 2009.

(a) Describe the change in alcohol consumption between 1970 and 2009. **[1 mark]**

....

....

(b) Deaths from liver disease increased between 1970 and 2009. Suggest **one** reason for the relationship between the changes in alcohol consumption and deaths shown in **Figure 1**. **[2 marks]**

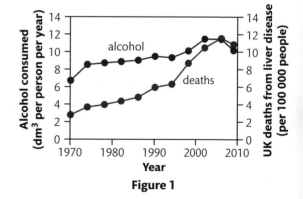

Figure 1

....

....

 Made a start **Feeling confident** ✓ **Exam ready**

Cardiovascular disease

② Quick quiz

Use words from the box to complete the sentences about cardiovascular disease.

| blood flow   arteries   oxygen   blood vessels |

Cardiovascular disease (CVD) is a general term for conditions affecting the heart or ....

CVD can be caused when blood vessels called ....that take oxygen to the heart muscle

become narrowed. Fat deposited in the walls of these blood vessels reduces ....

to the muscle cells beyond the blockage. The cells receive less ....which they need for respiration, and so may die.

⑩ Surgical treatment of heart disease   Grade 5

1. Faulty heart valves can be replaced during surgery with either a mechanical or a biological valve.

(a) Explain why a heart with faulty valves is less efficient at pumping blood.   **[2 marks]**

Heart valves prevent blood from moving
....

So, with faulty valves the amount of blood
....

Figure 1 compares the performance of mechanical and biological replacement valves. The graph on the left shows the risk of death after surgery. The graph on the right shows the risk that the new valve will need to be replaced again.

(b) Comment on the success of each type of valve over 15 years as shown in **Figure 1**.
[3 marks]

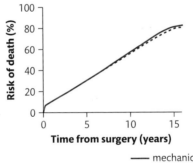
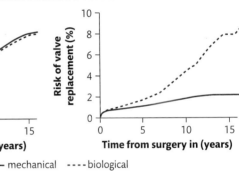

—— mechanical   - - - - biological

Figure 1

Write two sentences comparing the mechanical and biological valves – one sentence for each graph. Then make a comment about which type of valve is best based on what you have written.

....

....

....

⑩ Medication and lifestyle changes   Grade 4

2. Doctors will advise lifestyle changes for patients with cardiovascular disease (CVD).

(a) Explain why doctors may recommend more frequent gentle exercise to reduce CVD.   **[2 marks]**

....

....

(b) Give **one** dietary change a doctor may advise to reduce the risk of CVD.   **[1 mark]**

....

Photosynthesis

② Quick quiz

Which is the correct word equation for photosynthesis? Tick **one** box.

water + carbon dioxide → glucose + oxygen ☐

oxygen + water → glucose + carbon dioxide ☐

carbon dioxide + glucose → oxygen + water ☐

glucose + oxygen → carbon dioxide + water ☐

⑩ Photosynthesis reaction   Grades 3–5

1. (a) Describe the importance of photosynthesis in food chains.   **[2 marks]**

Plants are producers that use photosynthesis to make ....

This is the source of .... in the food chain.

(b) Explain why photosynthesis is an example of an endothermic reaction.   **[2 marks]**

More energy is transferred from the environment to .... than is transferred

from the reaction to ....

(c) Explain why light is needed for photosynthesis.   **[2 marks]**

Light provides the .... for the reaction. Energy is needed to allow carbon dioxide and

....

⑩ The site of photosynthesis   Grades 3–4

2. Figure 1 shows the structure of a leaf in cross-section.

(a) Name the sub-cellular structures in plant cells where photosynthesis occurs.
   [1 mark]

....

(b) Name the pigment in plant cells that captures energy from light.   **[1 mark]**

....

(c) Use **Figure 1** to explain why most photosynthesis takes place in palisade tissue.   **[2 marks]**

....

....

....

(d) Gases diffuse into and out of the air space in the leaf. Name the gas that is needed for photosynthesis.   **[1 mark]**

....

(e) Glucose is produced in photosynthesis. Give **one** way that the glucose is used by the plant.   **[1 mark]**

....

cuticle
(waxy coating)

upper epidermis

chloroplast

palisade tissue

spongy tissue

lower epidermis containing stomata

guard cell

Figure 1

 Made a start   Feeling confident   ✓ Exam ready

BBC

Rate of photosynthesis

---

② **Quick quiz**

Circle the **three** factors that can affect the rate of photosynthesis.

| light intensity | temperature | biomass | oxygen concentration | carbon dioxide concentration |

---

⑮ **Carbon dioxide and temperature** **Grade 5**

1. Figure 1 shows how increasing the concentration of carbon dioxide affects the rate of photosynthesis.

(a) Explain why the graph at point **X** shows that carbon dioxide concentration is a limiting factor. **[1 mark]**

Because on this part of the graph, as carbon dioxide concentration increases ....

....

(b) Explain why carbon dioxide concentration can limit the rate of photosynthesis. **[1 mark]**

> Think of the word equation for photosynthesis and the role of carbon dioxide.

....

(c) Explain why an increase in CO_2 does not lead to an increase in rate of photosynthesis at point **Y**. **[2 marks]**

At point **Y** some other factor ....

....

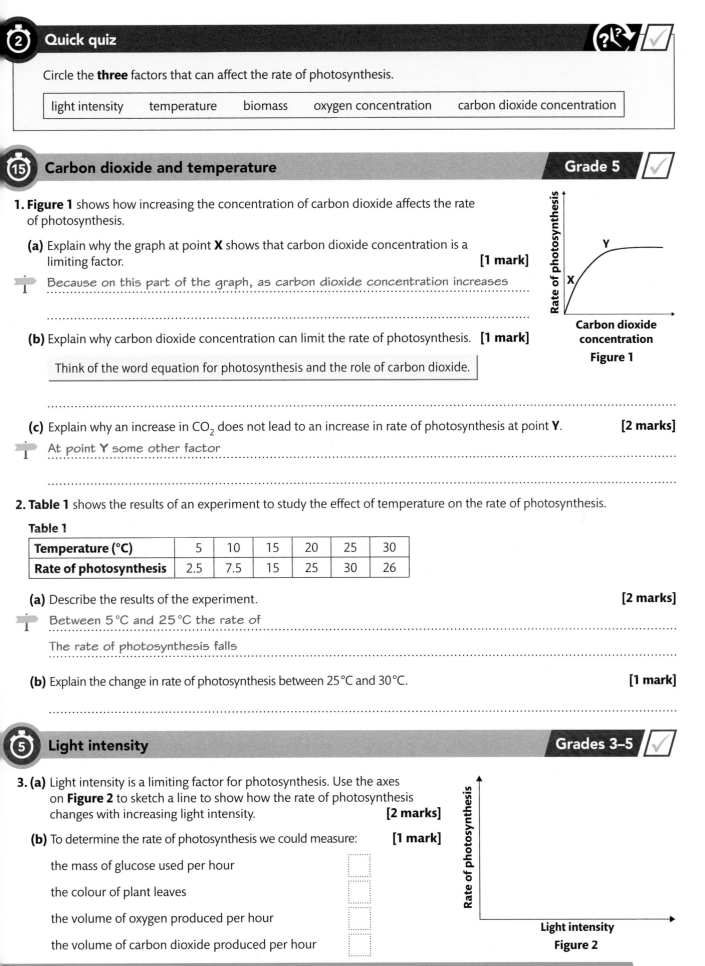

Figure 1

Rate of photosynthesis (y-axis) vs Carbon dioxide concentration (x-axis), with points X and Y marked.

2. Table 1 shows the results of an experiment to study the effect of temperature on the rate of photosynthesis.

Table 1

Temperature (°C)	5	10	15	20	25	30
Rate of photosynthesis	2.5	7.5	15	25	30	26

(a) Describe the results of the experiment. **[2 marks]**

Between 5 °C and 25 °C the rate of ....

The rate of photosynthesis falls ....

(b) Explain the change in rate of photosynthesis between 25 °C and 30 °C. **[1 mark]**

....

---

⑤ **Light intensity** **Grades 3–5**

3. (a) Light intensity is a limiting factor for photosynthesis. Use the axes on **Figure 2** to sketch a line to show how the rate of photosynthesis changes with increasing light intensity. **[2 marks]**

(b) To determine the rate of photosynthesis we could measure: **[1 mark]**

the mass of glucose used per hour ☐

the colour of plant leaves ☐

the volume of oxygen produced per hour ☐

the volume of carbon dioxide produced per hour ☐

Rate of photosynthesis (y-axis) vs Light intensity (x-axis)

Figure 2

 Made a start **Feeling confident** **Exam ready** **45**

Practical: Photosynthesis

(2) Quick quiz

Use words from the box to complete the sentences.

| carbon dioxide | limiting factor | increase | light intensity | oxygen |

During the morning, the rate of photosynthesis in a garden plant will .... because

.... is increasing. The rate then levels off because of another ....

such as temperature or .... concentration.

(10) Investigating photosynthesis   Grade 5

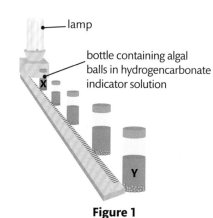

Figure 1

1. The effect of light intensity on the rate of photosynthesis was investigated in balls containing algae.

   Figure 1 shows the equipment used. Hydrogencarbonate indicator solution is yellow when carbon dioxide concentration is high. It becomes orange then red as the carbon dioxide concentration becomes lower. All bottles were yellow at the start of the investigation.

   (a) The dependent variable in this investigation is the colour of the indicator solution. Name the independent variable in this investigation.   **[1 mark]**

   > Think about the algae and about factors that affect the rate of photosynthesis.

   > The independent variable is the condition you change. The dependent variable is what you measure.

   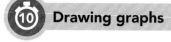 Light   (distance from the lamp)

   (b) Suggest **two** variables that should be controlled in this investigation.   **[2 marks]**

   1 ....   2 ....

   (c) After 1 hour the indicator in bottle **Y** was orange. Predict the colour of the indicator in bottle **X**.   **[1 mark]**

   ....

   > Photosynthesis uses carbon dioxide. Higher light intensity would mean more photosynthesis.

(10) Drawing graphs   Grade 5

2. **Table 1** shows results from an investigation that measured the number of bubbles of oxygen released from pondweed at different distances from a lamp.

   Draw a graph of the results to show number of bubbles against distance from the lamp.   **[2 marks]**

Table 1

Distance from lamp (cm)	10	15	20	25	40
Number of bubbles produced in 1 min	22	9	5	4	2

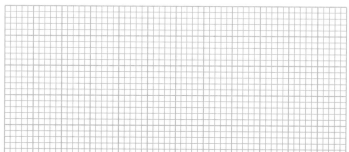

Made a start   Feeling confident   Exam ready

Specialised plant cells

Quick quiz

Draw **one** line to link each type of cell to its function and structural adaptation.

Type of cell	Function	Structural adaptation
xylem	absorbs water and minerals from soil	dead and lignified
phloem	transports water and minerals	large surface area
root hair	transports sucrose (sugar)	holes in end wall, lots of mitochondria

Adaptations of root hair cells — Grades 3–4

1. **Figure 1** shows a germinating seed, showing a young root with many root hairs. Each hair is a single cell.

   (a) Explain how the structure of root hair cells is related to their function. **[2 marks]**

   Root hair cells have a large .... which increases the ....

   rate at which ....

   (b) Root hair cells absorb mineral ions from soil using active transport. Explain why root hair cells contain many mitochondria. **[2 marks]**

   > Mitochondria are the site of respiration in a cell. Think how this relates to active transport.

   ....

   ....

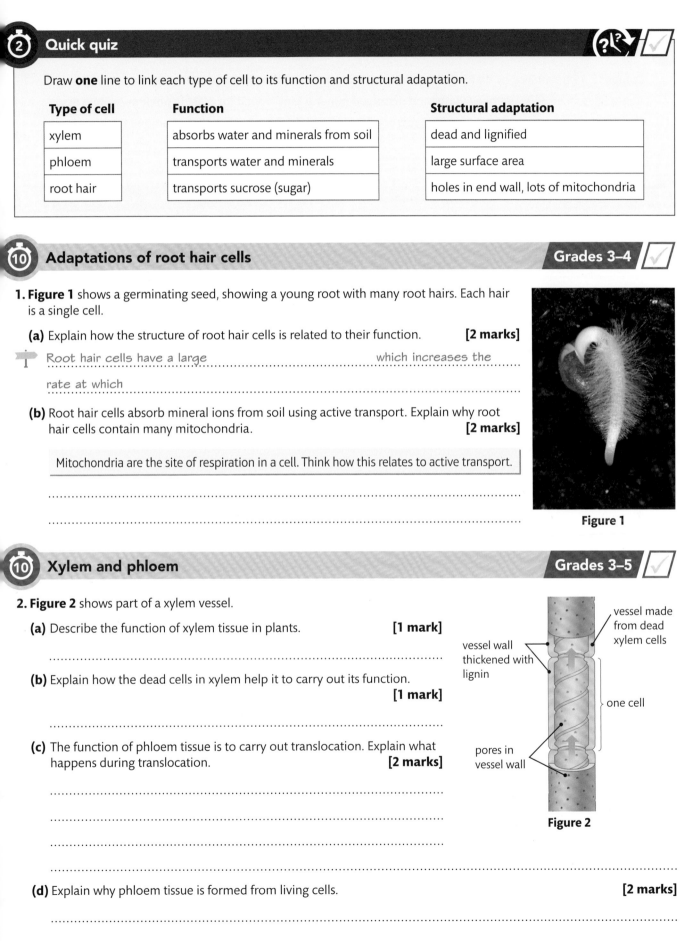

Figure 1

Xylem and phloem — Grades 3–5

2. **Figure 2** shows part of a xylem vessel.

   (a) Describe the function of xylem tissue in plants. **[1 mark]**

   ....

   (b) Explain how the dead cells in xylem help it to carry out its function. **[1 mark]**

   ....

   (c) The function of phloem tissue is to carry out translocation. Explain what happens during translocation. **[2 marks]**

   ....

   ....

   ....

   ....

   (d) Explain why phloem tissue is formed from living cells. **[2 marks]**

   ....

   ....

Figure 2 labels: vessel made from dead xylem cells; vessel wall thickened with lignin; one cell; pores in vessel wall

Made a start   Feeling confident   Exam ready

Transpiration

② Quick quiz

Complete each sentence by drawing a circle around the correct words in **bold** in each sentence.

Transpiration transports **sucrose / water and dissolved mineral ions** around the plant in **phloem / xylem** tissue.

Translocation is the transport of dissolved **sucrose / water and dissolved mineral ions** around the plant in **phloem / xylem** tissue.

⑩ Transport of water and mineral ions   Grades 2–5

1. (a) Use words from the box to complete the sentences.   **[3 marks]**

| active transport | leaves | osmosis | roots | translocation | transpiration |

Water enters a plant through its .....roots...

Water moves into plant cells from the soil by the process of ....

Water and mineral ions move through the plant by the process of ....

(b) Explain how water is returned to the environment from cells in the leaves.   **[2 marks]**

Water .... from the surface of cells inside the leaf and then diffuses

....

2. (a) Name the type of plant cell that absorbs mineral ions from the soil.   **[1 mark]**

....

(b) Mineral ions are absorbed from the soil by active transport. Explain why minerals cannot move into the plant from the soil by diffusion.   **[2 marks]**

....

....

> The concentration of minerals is higher inside plant cells than in the soil. Think about the concentration gradient.

⑩ Stomata   Grade 5

3. Stomata are small pores on a plant leaf. **Figure 1** shows a single stoma surrounded by two guard cells.

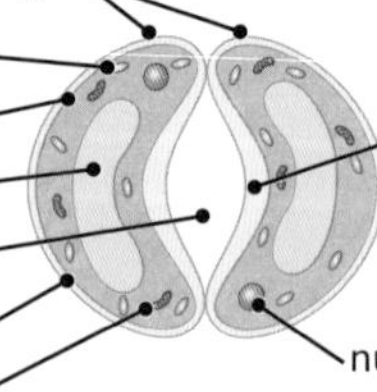

(a) Describe the function of stomata.   **[1 mark]**

....

(b) Describe how the guard cells act to open and close the stomata.   **[2 marks]**

....

....

guard cells swollen with water and rigid
chloroplast
cell membrane
vacuole
stoma
thin cell wall
mitochondrion
thick cell wall
nucleus
stoma open
Figure 1

(c) Gas exchange between leaf cells and the atmosphere can take place when stomata are open.

Stomata open during daylight hours. Explain why stomata open during daylight hours.   **[2 marks]**

....

....

(d) Stomata close at night. Suggest **one** advantage to the plant of stomata closing at night.   **[1 mark]**

....

| Made a start | Feeling confident | Exam ready |

Water uptake in plants

② Quick quiz

True or false?

The transport of water through a plant is called translation.	**True / False**
Sugars made in leaf cells by photosynthesis are transported to other parts of the plant in phloem.	**True / False**
Water is lost from plant leaves to the environment through stomata.	**True / False**

⑩ Environmental effects   Grade 4

1. Water uptake by plants depends upon the rate at which water is lost from the plant's leaves.

(a) Explain why the rate of water loss from a plant is faster on a sunny day than on a cloudy day.   **[2 marks]**

> Think about the effect of light intensity on stomata and how their response affects rate of water loss.

Stomata are opened more as .... so more water molecules

can evaporate from the leaf when it is ....

(b) Explain how temperature affects the rate of water uptake on a warm day compared with a cold day.   **[2 marks]**

On a warm day more water is lost by ....

So, on a warm day more water is ....

⑩ Rate of water uptake   Grades 3–5

2. Figure 1 shows apparatus used for measuring the rate of water uptake by a plant.

(a) Transpiration is the flow of water through a plant and evaporation from the leaves. Explain why the rate of water uptake by a plant depends on transpiration.   **[2 marks]**

....

....

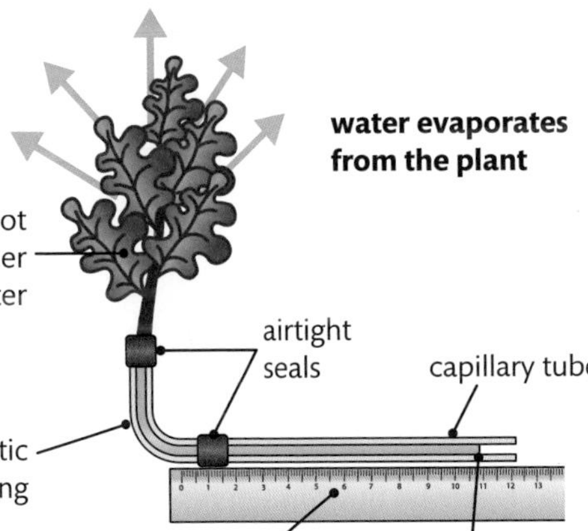

The results for the distance travelled by the air bubble in the tube in 5 minutes are shown in **Table 1**.

water evaporates from the plant

leafy shoot cut under water

airtight seals

capillary tube

plastic tubing

graduated scale

movement of meniscus is measured over time

Figure 1

Table 1

Test	1	2	3	Mean
Distance in 5 min (mm): 25 °C	39.5	36.8	40.4	38.9
Distance in 5 min (mm): 15 °C	28.5	26.4	29.1	

(b) Complete **Table 1** by calculating the mean distance travelled over 5 minutes at 15 °C.   **[1 mark]**

(c) The results show water uptake over 5 minutes. Calculate the **mean rate of water uptake per minute** at 25 °C.   **[1 mark]**

(d) The same plant was used in each experiment so that the surface area of the leaves was the same. Explain why leaf surface area must be controlled in the experiment.   **[2 marks]**

....

....

 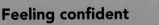

Human endocrine system

2 Quick quiz

Use the words in the box to label the diagram to show the positions of the endocrine glands.

pituitary gland
thyroid gland
adrenal glands
pancreas

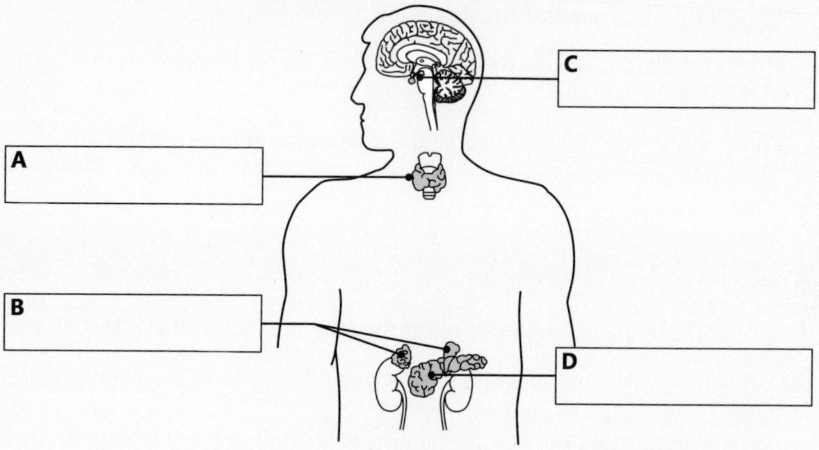

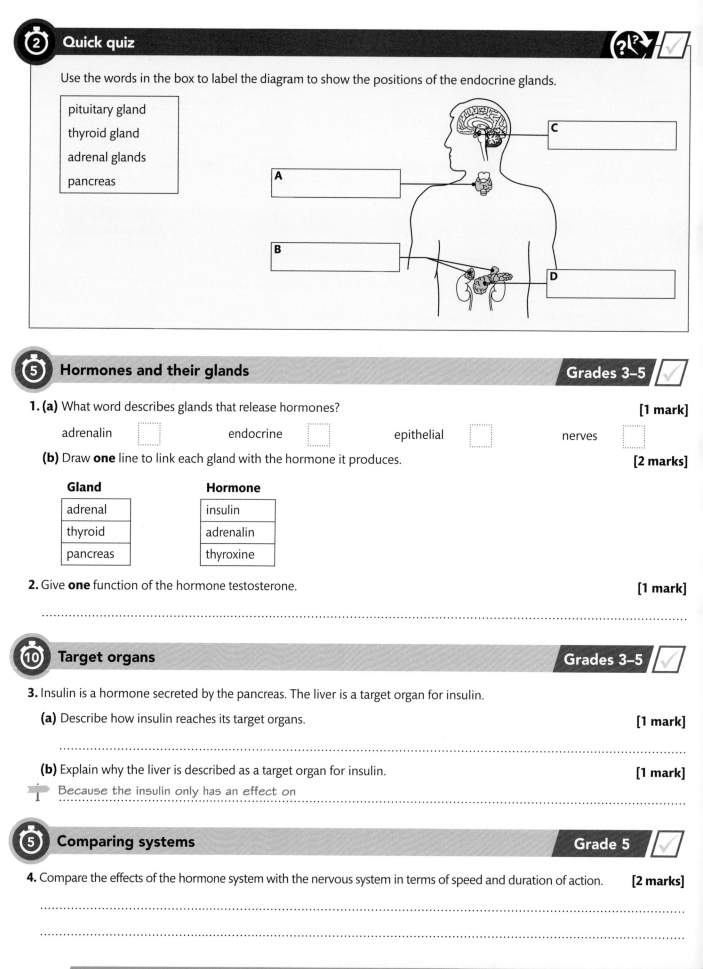

5 Hormones and their glands — Grades 3–5

1. (a) What word describes glands that release hormones? **[1 mark]**

adrenalin ☐ endocrine ☐ epithelial ☐ nerves ☐

(b) Draw **one** line to link each gland with the hormone it produces. **[2 marks]**

Gland	Hormone
adrenal	insulin
thyroid	adrenalin
pancreas	thyroxine

2. Give **one** function of the hormone testosterone. **[1 mark]**

....

10 Target organs — Grades 3–5

3. Insulin is a hormone secreted by the pancreas. The liver is a target organ for insulin.

(a) Describe how insulin reaches its target organs. **[1 mark]**

....

(b) Explain why the liver is described as a target organ for insulin. **[1 mark]**

Because the insulin only has an effect on ....

5 Comparing systems — Grade 5

4. Compare the effects of the hormone system with the nervous system in terms of speed and duration of action. **[2 marks]**

....

....

Hormones in reproduction

2 Quick quiz

Draw **one** line to link each word with its definition.

puberty	features that develop in response to increasing sex hormone concentrations
oestrogen	female hormone that causes development of breasts and start of menstrual cycle
secondary sexual characteristics	time when the body starts developing in ways that will allow reproduction

5 Hormones and the menstrual cycle — Grade 3

1. Describe the role of the following hormones in the control of the female menstrual cycle.

(a) Oestrogen **[2 marks]**

It causes the lining of the uterus to start to ....

and causes the release of another hormone that triggers ....

(b) Progesterone **[1 mark]**

It maintains the ....

5 Details of the menstrual cycle — Grade 5

2. (a) State the meaning of the term 'ovulation'. **[1 mark]**

....

(b) Name the endocrine gland that produces oestrogen and progesterone. **[1 mark]**

....

10 Interpreting data — Grades 4–5

3. Figure 1 shows how concentrations of two hormones change during the menstrual cycle. Use **Figure 1** to help you answer the following questions.

(a) Describe the changes in oestrogen and progesterone levels in the blood. **[2 marks]**

....

....

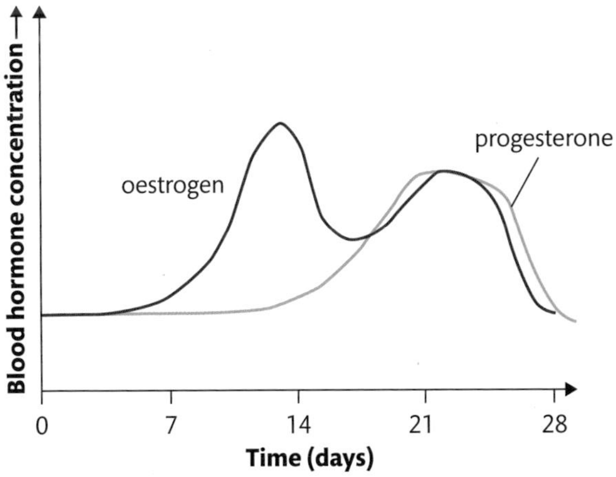

Figure 1

After day 28 the cycle begins again. Menstruation occurs between days 0 and 5.

(b) Describe what happens during menstruation. **[1 mark]**

....

(c) Explain why menstruation takes place at this time. **[2 marks]**

....

....

Contraception

2 Quick quiz

What is contraception used for? Tick **one** box.

prevent brain damage ☐

prevent pregnancy ☐

prevent lung cancer ☐

prevent obesity ☐

10 Evaluating contraceptives

Grades 3–5

1. The cards below show facts about the use of hormone implants and male condoms as contraceptives.

Hormone implant or patch

- >99% effective
- minor surgery to insert implant; lasts for up to 3 years
- hormones can cause side effects, e.g. irregular menstrual periods, depression, nervousness
- can be removed at any time

Male condom

- perfect use is 98% effective; typical use 82% effective
- protects against transmission of sexually transmitted disease
- needs to be put on when penis is erect

(a) An implant, or patch, contains progesterone. Explain how an implant works as a contraceptive. **[2 marks]**

Progesterone stops any ....

So there are no eggs available that can be ....

(b) The hormone implant or patch is >99% effective; this means that fewer than 1 woman in 100 will get pregnant during a year. Calculate the number of women in 100 who may get pregnant with typical use of a male condom. **[1 mark]**

100 − 82 = ...

(c) Using the information provided, state which type of contraceptive is more effective. **[1 mark]**

....

(d) Use the cards to identify **two** advantages of using a male condom rather than a hormone implant as a contraceptive. **[2 marks]**

The male condom does not cause any ....

Condoms also protect against ....

5 How contraception works

Grade 4

2. Draw **one** line to link each type of contraception to how it works. **[3 marks]**

condom	stops ovulation
IUD	provides a physical barrier so sperm don't reach the egg
spermicide	prevents fertilised egg from implanting in the uterus
contraceptive pill	kills sperm

Control of blood glucose

2 Quick quiz

Use words from the box to complete the sentences.

blood glucose	cells	constant	external	internal

Homeostasis is the control of the .... environment of the body in response to internal and .... change. Homeostasis makes sure that conditions, such as temperature, water levels and .... concentration are kept relatively .... so that processes inside .... continue to work well.

15 Interpreting graphs of blood glucose and insulin — Grade 5

1. **Figure 1** shows how blood glucose and insulin concentrations change over 24 hours. The graphs show the range of values for people who do not have diabetes. Use **Figure 1** to answer the questions.

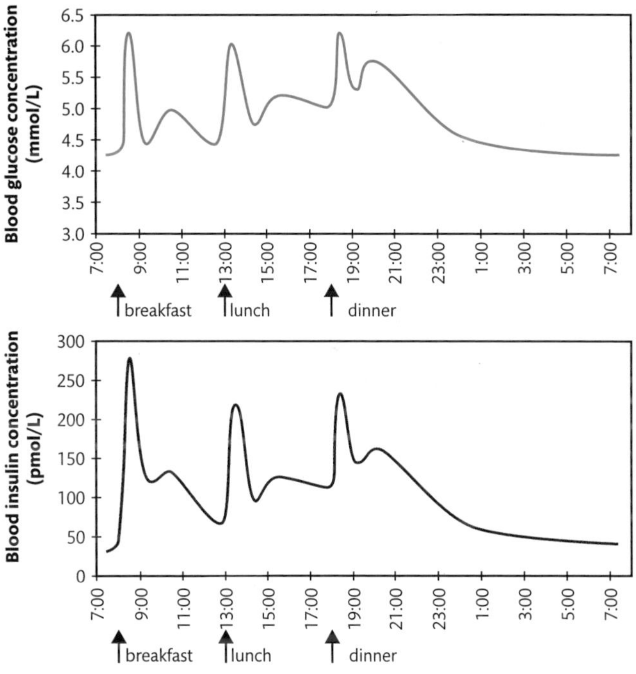

Figure 1

(a) Describe the effect of food on blood glucose concentration. **[1 mark]**

After each meal the blood glucose concentration ....

....

(b) Describe how insulin concentration changes in response to blood glucose changes after meals. **[1 mark]**

An .... in blood glucose ....

concentration is followed by ....

....

(c) Describe the effect of the hormone insulin on blood glucose concentrations. **[1 mark]**

Insulin causes blood glucose levels to ....

Look at the relationship between the blood glucose level and insulin level

5 Insulin — Grades 3–4

2. Insulin reduces the blood glucose level when it becomes too high.

(a) Use words from the box to complete the sentences. **[2 marks]**

glycogen	pancreas	glucose	blood	liver	hydrogen

Insulin causes glucose to move out of the .... and into cells. The excess glucose is converted into .... and stored in muscles and the liver.

(b) The organ that produces insulin and monitors blood glucose levels is the: **[1 mark]**

liver ☐ kidney ☐ stomach ☐ pancreas ☐

Diabetes

② Quick quiz

True or false?

Blood glucose concentration is controlled by the hormone insulin.	**True / False**
The organ that monitors blood glucose concentration is the pancreas.	**True / False**
Type 2 diabetes occurs when a person does not produce their own insulin.	**True / False**

 Obesity and diabetes   **Grade 3**

1. Figure 1 shows how mean body mass and percentage of people with type 2 diabetes changed between 1990 and 2000.

(a) Use **Figure 1** to identify any correlation between mean body mass and the risk of developing type 2 diabetes. **[3 marks]**

Between 1990 and 2000, mean body mass

....

....

Over the same time, the percentage of people with

type 2 diabetes

....

This means that

....

....

Figure 1

(b) One measure of obesity is body mass index (BMI). This uses measurements of both height and body mass of the individual. Explain why BMI is a better indication of obesity than body mass alone.

> Think about how height can affect body mass.

[1 mark]

....

 Causes and effects of diabetes   **Grades 3–4**

2. (a) State the causes of type 1 and type 2 diabetes. **[2 marks]**

Type 1 ....

Type 2 ....

(b) Describe how insulin injections are used to control type 1 diabetes. **[2 marks]**

....

....

(c) Type 2 diabetes is not usually controlled using insulin injections. Explain how type 2 diabetes is controlled. **[4 marks]**

> This is an 'explain' question, so you should say how each method works or why it is used.

....

....

....

....

 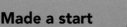

Transport in animals

② Quick quiz

Complete each sentence by drawing a circle around the correct word in **bold** in each sentence.

The waste product from amino acid breakdown that is removed from the blood by the kidneys is **urea / urine**.

Plants and animals must transport **oxygen / carbon dioxide** into all their cells for respiration. If too much water is absorbed from food and drink, the excess must be transported **into / out of** the body to protect cells from swelling.

Gases are exchanged between the human body and the environment through the **lungs / small intestine**.

⑩ Surface area and volume   Grade 5

1. Table 1 shows calculations of surface area and volume for three cubes.

Table 1

Length (cm)	Surface area of cube (cm^2)	Volume of cube (cm^3)	Surface area : volume ratio
l	$6 \times l^2$	l^3	surface area : volume
1	$6 \times 1^2 = 6$	$(1 \times 1 \times 1 =) 1$	6 : 1
2	24	8	3 : 1 (24 : 8)
4	96		

(a) Complete the bottom row of **Table 1** by calculating the values. **[2 marks]**

volume = 4^3 =

surface area : volume ratio =

Maths skills

The surface area of the cube is calculated by working out the area of one side of the cube, then multiplying by six because there are six sides to a cube.

(b) Describe the relationship between surface area : volume ratio and length shown in **Table 1**. **[1 mark]**

As length increases, surface area : volume ratio ....

(c) Describe how increasing surface area : volume ratio affects the rate of exchange by diffusion. **[1 mark]**

Increasing surface area : volume ratio would .... the rate of diffusion.

⑩ Adaptations for exchange   Grade 5

2. The small intestine is part of the digestive system. **Figure 1** shows how the small intestine is lined with folds called villi.

(a) Describe the function of the small intestine. **[1 mark]**

....

(b) Explain the importance of villi in the small intestine. **[2 marks]**

....

....

(c) Describe how digested food is transported to cells in the body. **[1 mark]**

....

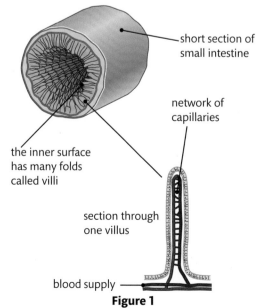

short section of small intestine

network of capillaries

the inner surface has many folds called villi

section through one villus

blood supply

Figure 1

Alveoli

2 Quick quiz

Use words from the box to complete the sentences.

air	alveoli	carbon dioxide	capillaries	kidneys	lungs	oxygen

The human organs in which gas is exchanged with the air are called the ....

Air passes into the body through the nose and mouth and reaches tiny sacs in these organs called .... The gas .... which is needed for cellular respiration, passes into the blood from these tiny sacs. The gas .... which is a waste product of respiration, passes from the blood into the .... in the tiny sacs.

10 Structure of alveolus — Grades 3–5

1. Figure 1 shows gas exchange in one alveolus.

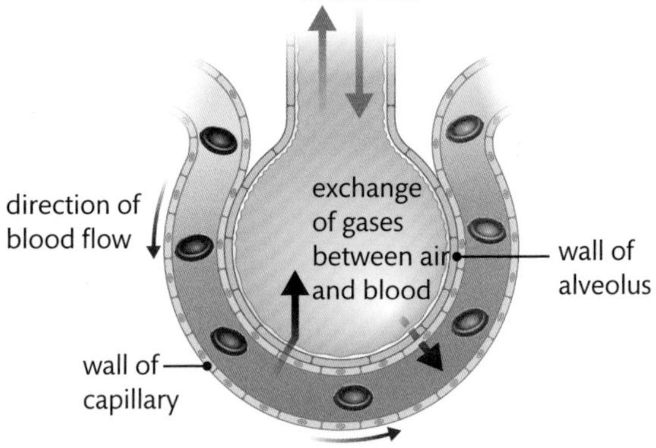

in and out
direction of blood flow
exchange of gases between air and blood
wall of alveolus
wall of capillary

Figure 1

(a) Which method of transport is used to exchange gases between air and blood? Tick **one** box. **[1 mark]**

active transport ☐ osmosis ☐
diffusion ☐ phagocytosis ☐

(b) Explain why the concentration of carbon dioxide is higher in the blood coming to the alveolus than in the air in the alveolus. **[2 marks]**

The carbon dioxide is coming from body cells. Think about what process produces carbon dioxide.

Carbon dioxide concentration is higher in the blood because the blood is ....

....

(c) The lungs contain millions of alveoli. Explain why this is important. **[1 mark]**

Think about the effect of surface area on exchange of substances across a surface.

....

5 Adaptations for exchange — Grade 4

2. The alveoli of the lungs have adaptations to increase gas exchange between air in the lungs and blood in capillaries. Draw **one** line to link each adaptation with the explanation of how it increases gas exchange by diffusion. One has been done for you. **[3 marks]**

adaptation	explanation
membranes of the alveolus and capillary are very thin	good blood flow increases the concentration gradient between air and blood
alveoli are ventilated by breathing	reduces distance for diffusion
alveoli are surrounded by many capillaries	gives a large surface area over which diffusion can take place
there are many alveoli in each lung	refreshes the air and so maintains a high concentration gradient for diffusion

Made a start ☐ Feeling confident ☐ Exam ready ☐

The blood

② Quick quiz

Draw **one** line to link each part of the blood to its function.

red blood cell	destroys pathogens
white blood cell	carries dissolved substances
plasma	causes blood to clot where blood vessels are damaged
platelet	carries oxygen

⑩ Erythrocyte structure   Grades 3–5

1. Figure 1 shows an erythrocyte (red blood cell).

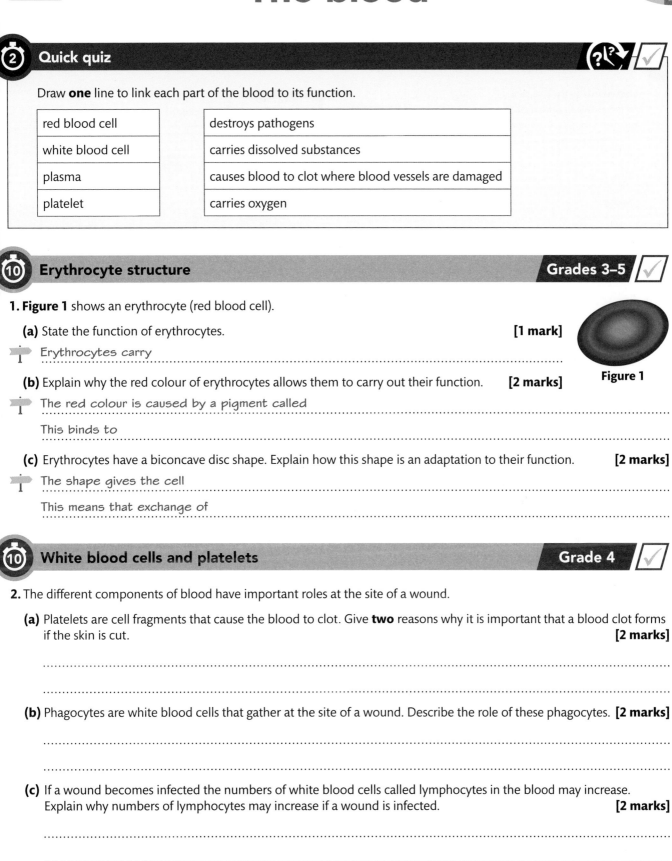

(a) State the function of erythrocytes.   **[1 mark]**

Erythrocytes carry ....

Figure 1

(b) Explain why the red colour of erythrocytes allows them to carry out their function.   **[2 marks]**

The red colour is caused by a pigment called ....

This binds to ....

(c) Erythrocytes have a biconcave disc shape. Explain how this shape is an adaptation to their function.   **[2 marks]**

The shape gives the cell ....

This means that exchange of ....

⑩ White blood cells and platelets   Grade 4

2. The different components of blood have important roles at the site of a wound.

(a) Platelets are cell fragments that cause the blood to clot. Give **two** reasons why it is important that a blood clot forms if the skin is cut.   **[2 marks]**

....

....

(b) Phagocytes are white blood cells that gather at the site of a wound. Describe the role of these phagocytes.   **[2 marks]**

....

....

(c) If a wound becomes infected the numbers of white blood cells called lymphocytes in the blood may increase. Explain why numbers of lymphocytes may increase if a wound is infected.   **[2 marks]**

....

....

 Made a start   **Feeling confident**   ✓ **Exam ready**

Blood vessels

② Quick quiz

Use words from the box to label the diagram of the human circulatory system.

artery

capillary

heart

vein

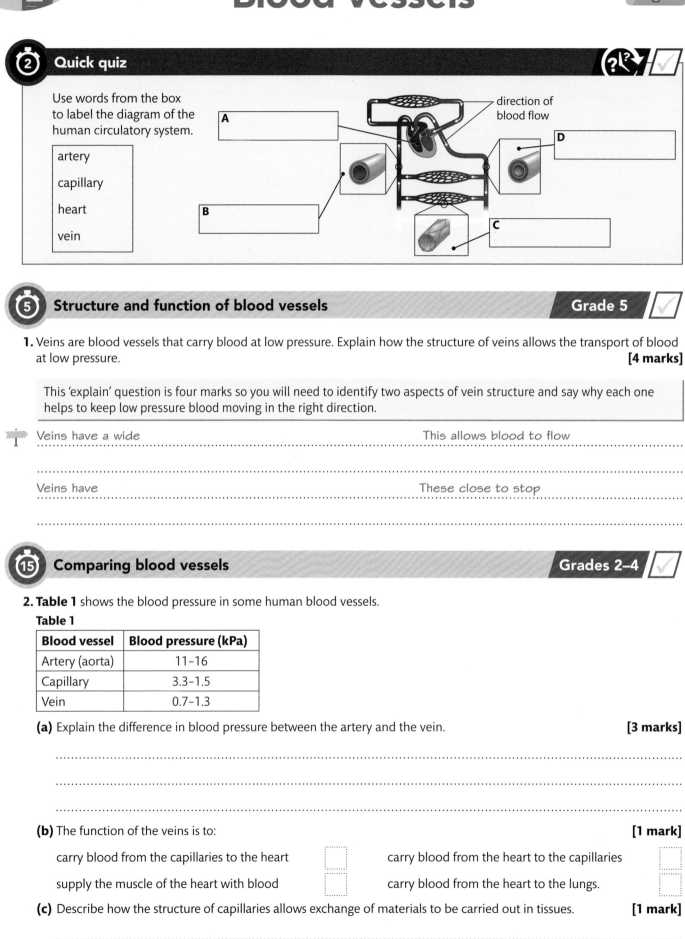

direction of blood flow

A

B

C

D

⑤ Structure and function of blood vessels **Grade 5**

1. Veins are blood vessels that carry blood at low pressure. Explain how the structure of veins allows the transport of blood at low pressure. **[4 marks]**

This 'explain' question is four marks so you will need to identify two aspects of vein structure and say why each one helps to keep low pressure blood moving in the right direction.

Veins have a wide .... This allows blood to flow ....

....

Veins have .... These close to stop ....

....

⑮ Comparing blood vessels **Grades 2–4**

2. Table 1 shows the blood pressure in some human blood vessels.

Table 1

Blood vessel	Blood pressure (kPa)
Artery (aorta)	11–16
Capillary	3.3–1.5
Vein	0.7–1.3

(a) Explain the difference in blood pressure between the artery and the vein. **[3 marks]**

....

....

....

(b) The function of the veins is to: **[1 mark]**

carry blood from the capillaries to the heart ☐   carry blood from the heart to the capillaries ☐

supply the muscle of the heart with blood ☐   carry blood from the heart to the lungs. ☐

(c) Describe how the structure of capillaries allows exchange of materials to be carried out in tissues. **[1 mark]**

....

 Made a start   **Feeling confident**   ☑ **Exam ready**

The heart

② Quick quiz

Label the parts of the heart.

> Labelling of the heart is as viewed from the front, so left is on the right and vice versa.

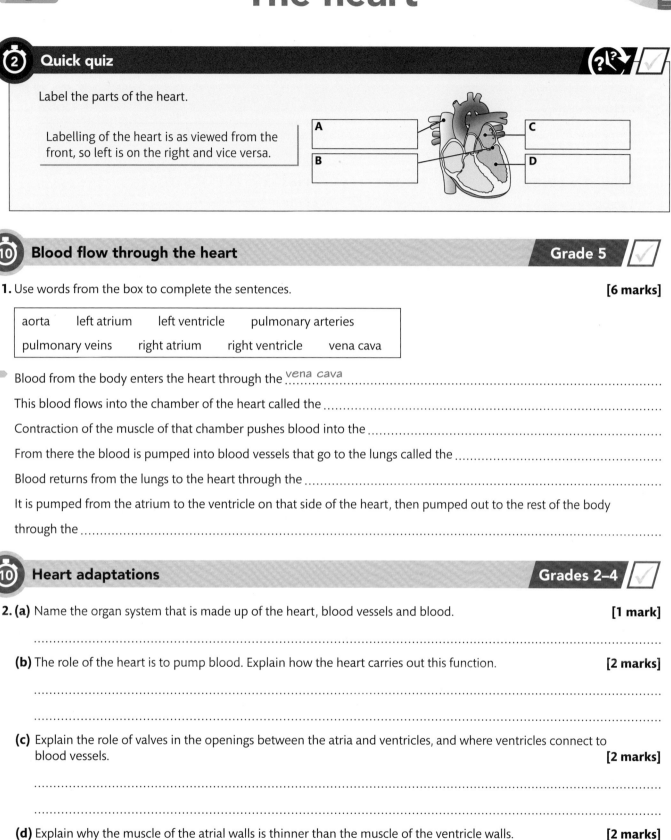

A

B

C

D

⑩ Blood flow through the heart　　　　Grade 5

1. Use words from the box to complete the sentences.　　　　**[6 marks]**

aorta	left atrium	left ventricle	pulmonary arteries
pulmonary veins	right atrium	right ventricle	vena cava

Blood from the body enters the heart through the ......vena cava..

This blood flows into the chamber of the heart called the ....

Contraction of the muscle of that chamber pushes blood into the ....

From there the blood is pumped into blood vessels that go to the lungs called the ....

Blood returns from the lungs to the heart through the ....

It is pumped from the atrium to the ventricle on that side of the heart, then pumped out to the rest of the body

through the ....

⑩ Heart adaptations　　　　Grades 2–4

2. (a) Name the organ system that is made up of the heart, blood vessels and blood.　　　　**[1 mark]**

....

(b) The role of the heart is to pump blood. Explain how the heart carries out this function.　　　　**[2 marks]**

....

....

(c) Explain the role of valves in the openings between the atria and ventricles, and where ventricles connect to blood vessels.　　　　**[2 marks]**

....

....

(d) Explain why the muscle of the atrial walls is thinner than the muscle of the ventricle walls.　　　　**[2 marks]**

....

....

(e) Explain why the muscle of the left ventricle wall is thicker than the muscle of the right ventricle wall.　　　　**[2 marks]**

....

....

 Made a start　　 **Feeling confident**　　 **Exam ready**　　**59**

Aerobic and anaerobic respiration

② Quick quiz

Draw lines to link each type of respiration in muscle cells to its correct reactant and product.
Products and reactants may be used more than once.

Type of respiration	Reactant	Product
aerobic	oxygen	carbon dioxide
anaerobic (in muscle cells)	glucose	lactic acid
		water

⑩ Cellular respiration   Grades 3–5 ☑

1. (a) Name the sub-cellular structures in which respiration occurs. **[1 mark]**

....

(b) Write a word equation to describe the process of aerobic respiration. **[2 marks]**

glucose + ...

(c) Explain why respiration is described as an exothermic reaction. **[1 mark]**

....

> You will also have studied exothermic reactions in chemistry. The same ideas about transfer of heat energy are important here.

⑤ Anaerobic respiration   Grades 4–5 ☑

2. (a) Anaerobic respiration can take place in muscle cells. Complete the word equation for anaerobic respiration in muscle cells. **[1 mark]**

glucose → ....

(b) Explain why muscle cells can respire anaerobically only for a limited time. **[1 mark]**

....

(c) The process of anaerobic respiration in yeast is different from animals and is called fermentation. Name the **two** products of anaerobic respiration in yeast. **[2 marks]**

1 ....   2 ....

⑤ Comparing respiration   Grade 5 ☑

3. (a) Explain why muscle cells must sometimes use anaerobic respiration to release energy. **[2 marks]**

....

....

(b) Give **one** advantage of aerobic respiration compared with anaerobic respiration. **[1 mark]**

....

(c) Name the substance that builds up in muscles during anaerobic respiration. **[1 mark]**

....

 Made a start   Feeling confident   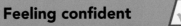 Exam ready

Practical: Rate of respiration

Quick quiz

True or false?

Aerobic respiration can only occur when there is enough oxygen available. **True / False**

A product of anaerobic respiration in muscle cells is carbon dioxide. **True / False**

Aerobic respiration releases more energy from each glucose molecule than anaerobic respiration. **True / False**

Respirometer investigation   Grade 5

1. **Figure 1** shows a simple respirometer for measuring the rate of respiration in living organisms.

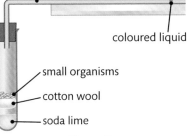

capillary tube   scale

coloured liquid

small organisms

cotton wool

soda lime

Figure 1

(a) When organisms are respiring the coloured liquid moves to the left. Explain why the coloured liquid moves in this way.   **[2 marks]**

It moves because the organisms are using up ....

in the process of ....

(b) State the function of the soda lime in the respirometer.   **[1 mark]**

Soda lime absorbs ....

produced during respiration.

(c) Describe a suitable control for this investigation.   **[2 marks]**

....

A control is an experiment that tells us if the changes we see are due to the independent variable (in this case, the organisms) or caused by something else. Everything else in the control set-up should be the same.

Effect of temperature on respiration rate   Grade 3

2. **Table 1** shows results from an investigation on the effect of temperature on the respiration of mealworms.

Table 1

Temperature (°C)	Distance coloured liquid moves in 5 min (mm)
10	8
15	14
20	13
25	22
30	34

(a) One result was anomalous. Identify the anomalous result. .... **[1 mark]**

(b) Explain how this investigation could be improved to account for any anomalous results.   **[2 marks]**

....

....

(c) Ignoring any anomalous results, use **Table 1** to describe the effect of temperature on the rate of respiration in mealworms.   **[2 marks]**

....

 Made a start   **Feeling confident**   ✓ **Exam ready**   61

Response to exercise

2 Quick quiz

The table shows data for a person at rest and during exercise. For each row, tick (✓) the correct box to identify if the data are for a person at rest or who is exercising.

	Heart	Muscles	Rest	Exercise
Blood flow (cm^3/min)	300	1500		
Blood flow (cm^3/min)	890	2500		

10 The body's response to exercise — Grades 4–5

1. (a) Describe how oxygen is transported to the muscles. **[1 mark]**

....

(b) Explain why each of the following changes during exercise.

(i) breathing rate **[2 marks]**

Breathing rate increases so more oxygen is ....

and more carbon dioxide from ....

(ii) heart rate **[2 marks]**

Heart rate .... so that ....

....

(c) Describe how heart rate could be measured. **[2 marks]**

Count the number of ....

10 Cardiac output — Grades 3–5

2. At rest, an athlete's heart was beating at 55 beats per minute and the volume of blood pumped out of their heart in each pulse was 0.081 litres.

Cardiac output is calculated using the equation: cardiac output = stroke volume × heart rate

(a) Calculate the athlete's resting cardiac output in litres/min to 2 decimal places. **[2 marks]**

....

(b) An unfit person had the same cardiac output in litres/min as the athlete but their heart rate was 69 beats per minute. Calculate the stroke volume of the unfit person in litres to 3 decimal places. **[2 marks]**

....

5 Heart rate and stroke volume — Grade 4

3. Give a definition of stroke volume. **[1 mark]**

....

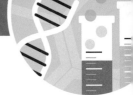

Communities

② Quick quiz

Complete each sentence by drawing a circle around the correct words in **bold** in each sentence.

A population is all the organisms of **the same / different** species living in **the same area / different areas**.

A community is all the populations of **the same / different** species living in **the same area / different areas**.

⑩ Interdependence   Grade 4

1. State the term that describes all the organisms within a community and the environment that affects that community.

[1 mark]

....

2. Blackberry plants form large bushes in hedges. Blackbirds nest in the hedges in the summer. During the autumn they eat blackberry fruits. Seeds from the fruits may be dropped far from the hedge, in the blackbirds' faeces.

(a) Describe how blackberry plants and blackbirds are interdependent.   **[2 marks]**

> Interdependence means how different organisms need each other for survival.
> Look for factors given in the text that indicate what each species is
> getting from the other.

Blackbirds depend on blackberry plants for ....

Blackberry plants depend on blackbirds for ....

(b) Explain what would happen to the population of blackbirds if blackberry bushes were cut down.   **[2 marks]**

If the number of blackberry plants in the area decreased, the number of blackbirds might ....

....

....

⑩ Interdependence in a food web   Grade 4

3. Figure 1 shows the feeding relationships between some organisms that live in a woodland. The arrows show different food chains within the woodland. Use **Figure 1** to answer the questions.

(a) Name the **two** species eaten by foxes.   **[1 mark]**

....

(b) Figure 1 shows competition between roe deer and rabbits. State what they are competing for.   **[1 mark]**

....

(c) Explain how the number of rabbits in the wood might change if roe deer numbers increase.   **[2 marks]**

....

....

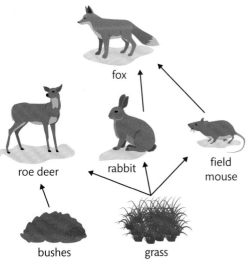

Figure 1

Abiotic factors

2 Quick quiz

These are some of the factors that affect organisms in an ecosystem. Circle the abiotic factors.

light intensity	temperature	predation	water availability	competition for food
soil nutrient concentration	pollutants	carbon dioxide concentration in air		

5 Temperature — Grade 5

1. Figure 1 shows the change in UK mean air temperature since 1860.

(a) Describe the trend after 1980 shown in **Figure 1**. **[1 mark]**

....

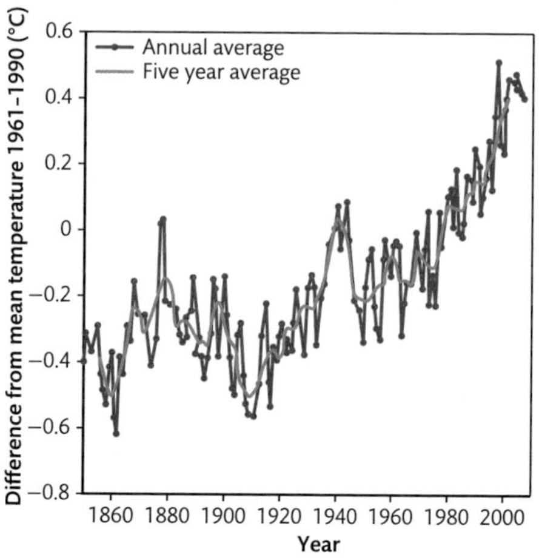

Figure 1

Scientists studying the effect of temperature on insects found that a few days of high temperatures can reduce the number of healthy sperm in male insects.

(b) Suggest how the changing climate in the UK could affect insect populations. **[2 marks]**

As the temperature ....

this could cause more male insects to ....

....

which could cause the size of insect populations to ....

5 Pollution — Grades 3–5

2. Plastic is becoming a major pollution problem. For example, plastic waste caught on coral reefs increases the risk of coral becoming diseased.

(a) Give the meaning of the term 'pollution'. **[1 mark]**

....

(b) Coral reef ecosystems are highly biodiverse. Explain how plastic pollution may affect coral reef communities. **[2 marks]**

....

....

5 Identifying abiotic factors — Grade 5

3. Chalara ash dieback is a disease that causes ash trees to lose their leaves. This changes abiotic conditions of the woodland floor. Suggest why plants on the woodland floor under diseased trees may show increased growth. **[3 marks]**

....

....

....

Made a start Feeling confident Exam ready

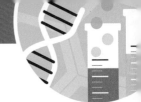

Biotic factors

② Quick quiz

Complete each sentence by drawing a circle around the correct word in **bold** in each sentence.

Scabies is caused by mites that lay their eggs in the skin of animals. The mites and their young feed on the skin and cause an intense itch in the animal's skin. This is an example of **parasitism / mutualism**.

Bees feed on nectar in flowers and collect pollen for feeding their young. Pollen on the bee's body is transferred to other flowers, which leads to fertilisation of the plant. This is an example of **parasitism / mutualism**.

⑩ Impact of non-indigenous species   Grade 4

1. Signal crayfish were introduced to the UK in the 1970s. Since then, their numbers have increased rapidly across the country. Signal crayfish are voracious predators, eating a wide range of small aquatic animals, and are having a significant impact on native white-clawed crayfish. **Figure 1** compares the size distribution of white-clawed crayfish in populations where signal crayfish are present or absent.

   (a) Use **Figure 1** to describe the differences in size of white-clawed crayfish when signal crayfish are present or absent. **[2 marks]**

   Most white-clawed crayfish are larger when the signal

   crayfish are .... The most frequent size class

   with signal crayfish is 20–29 mm but ....

   ....

   (b) Use the information in the question to suggest **two** possible ways that signal crayfish could affect white-clawed crayfish. **[2 marks]**

   1 ....

   2 ....

   > Think about how animals in the same habitat may affect each other.

Figure 1: Population chart — Frequency (y-axis 0–40) against Size class (mm) (x-axis: 10–19, 20–29, 30–39, 40–49). Keys: % with signal crayfish; ■ no signal crayfish.

Figure 1

⑩ New pathogens   Grade 5

2. Grey squirrels were introduced to the UK in the 1870s. Since then, they have spread across most of England, Wales and parts of Scotland. Where the number of grey squirrels has increased, the number of native red squirrels has fallen.

   (a) Grey squirrels eat more than red squirrels. Suggest how this could affect red squirrel populations. **[2 marks]**

   ....

   ....

   (b) Squirrel pox virus can kill squirrels. Grey squirrels can carry squirrel pox virus without suffering from the disease. Suggest what effect this may have on red squirrel populations. **[2 marks]**

   ....

   ....

   (c) Pine martens are predators of squirrels. Research shows that red squirrel numbers are higher than grey squirrels in areas with more pine martens. Suggest why. **[2 marks]**

   ....

   ....

Practical: Population studies

2 Quick quiz

Use words from the box to write the correct term beside each definition.

| abundance | community | quadrat | belt transect | quorum | distribution |

A line along which measurements are taken to identify the effect of an abiotic factor. ....

How the individuals of a species are spread throughout an area. ....

How many organisms there are in a given area. ....

A square frame used to sample organisms in the environment. ....

10 Calculating population size   **Grade 5**

1. Students estimated the population size of buttercups in a field by taking six quadrat samples. The field was 25 m by 34 m.

(a) Explain why the quadrats should be placed randomly. **[1 mark]**

➡ The buttercups may not be spread
....

(b) Explain how random sampling may help to avoid bias in the results. **[1 mark]**

➡ Random sampling may help to avoid bias in the results from choosing
....

....

Table 1 shows the results of the sampling.

Table 1

Quadrat	A	B	C	D	E	F
Number of buttercup plants in quadrat	3	2	0	0	2	1

Maths skills

To calculate the mean, find the total number of plants and divide that by the number of quadrats sampled.

(c) Calculate the mean number of buttercup plants per quadrat to 1 decimal place. **[1 mark]**

mean = ...

(d) Each quadrat had an area of 100 cm². Use your answer to part **(c)** to calculate the population size of buttercups in the field. **[3 marks]**

➡ total area of field = ... m²

total area of quadrat = 100 cm² = $\dfrac{100}{100 \times 100}$ .... m²

population size = ...

10 Using a transect   **Grades 3–5**

2. Students wanted to study the effect of a tree on daisies. They measured the abundance of daisy plants in quadrats placed along a transect from the tree to the open field.

(a) Name **one** abiotic factor that could affect the distribution of daisies. **[1 mark]**

....

(b) Explain why quadrats were placed along a transect rather than being placed randomly. **[1 mark]**

....

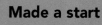 **Made a start**   **Feeling confident**   **Exam ready**

Biodiversity

② Quick quiz

Use words from the box to complete the sentences.

| ecosystem | food | habitats | less | live | more | species |

Biodiversity is all the different .... on Earth or within an ....

A higher biodiversity means that each species may depend on more than one other species for

resources such as .... or shelter. This makes it .... likely that the

community will be harmed if there is a change in the environment.

⑩ Eutrophication   Grade 4

1. **Figure 1** shows the oxygen concentration of water in the River Rhine in Germany between 1955 and 1997, and the number of invertebrate species sampled in the river in a selection of years.

   (a) The oxygen concentration decreased between 1955 and 1971. This was due to eutrophication of the water. State what is meant by the term 'eutrophication'. **[2 marks]**

   > Remember that eutrophication may be linked to algal growth followed by die-off.

....

....

....

Figure 1

   (b) Describe the relationship between changes in species number and changes in oxygen concentration shown in **Figure 1**. **[2 marks]**

   As oxygen concentration decreases, ...

   When oxygen concentration increases, ...

⑩ Fish farming   Grades 2–5

2. Some people think that eating farmed fish can protect biodiversity and is better for the environment.

   (a) Give the meaning of the term 'fish farming'. **[1 mark]**

   ....

   (b) Suggest how eating farmed fish could protect biodiversity in seas or lakes. **[1 mark]**

   ....

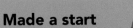 Made a start   Feeling confident   ✓ Exam ready

Maintaining biodiversity

② Quick quiz

True or false?

Deforestation increases biodiversity.	**True / False**
All human activities have a negative impact on biodiversity.	**True / False**
Conservation is the protection of species or habitats to maintain biodiversity.	**True / False**
Breeding programmes in zoos and conservation areas can help protect endangered species from becoming extinct.	**True / False**

⑩ Conservation of birds   Grade 5

1. At a farm, studies are being carried out to find ways of farming that also improve biodiversity. **Table 1** shows the number of skylarks, a bird species that feeds on insects in summer and seeds in winter.

Table 1

Year	2000	2001	2002	2003	2004	2005	2006	2007	2008	2009	2010	2011
Skylarks	10	18	24	27	27	34	32	30	23	44	41	42

(a) In the UK, since the 1970s, skylark numbers have fallen by over 75%. Compare the trends in skylark populations in the UK nationally with those on the farm. **[2 marks]**

 The national trend for skylarks is

....

The trend on the farm for skylarks is

....

(b) One reason for the national decrease is that farmers have changed to planting crops in autumn rather than in spring. This reduces the food available for birds over the winter but produces a greater yield of grain. Suggest why many farmers choose to change to autumn-sown crops. **[1 mark]**

More yield means

....

(c) Efforts to conserve skylark populations include planting field edges with wildflowers that attract insects in summer, along with planting seed-bearing species that are left in the field over winter. Explain how these actions may bring an increase in skylark numbers. **[2 marks]**

> Look back at the information on skylark feeding in the first part of the question.

....

....

⑩ Reforestation   Grade 5

2. In 2018, the UK government announced a plan to create a new forest of around 50 million new trees. Suggest how the new forest should be planted to maximise the biodiversity of organisms living in it. You should consider habitats and diversity of plants and animals in your answer. **[6 marks]**

....

....

....

....

....

....

Carbon cycle

 Quick quiz

The following processes are involved in the carbon cycle. Identify whether each process causes an increase or a decrease in carbon dioxide in the atmosphere by circling the correct word.

Respiration **Increase / Decrease**

Photosynthesis **Increase / Decrease**

Decay by microorganisms **Increase / Decrease**

 Carbon cycling **Grades 3–4**

1. Many substances cycle through the abiotic and biotic components of an ecosystem. One example is carbon.

(a) Name the process that converts carbon in fossil fuels into carbon dioxide in the air.
[1 mark]

> This happens, for example, in coal fires and in car engines.

....

(b) Name the process that converts carbon dioxide in the air to carbon compounds in plants. **[1 mark]**

> The carbon compound made in plants is glucose.

....

(c) State how carbon found in compounds within plants can be transferred to carbon compounds in animals. **[1 mark]**

> Think about food chains.

....

(d) Carbon compounds are transferred to the environment in animal faeces and urine. Explain how these carbon compounds are converted to carbon dioxide in air. **[2 marks]**

They are broken down by .... that release

....
carbon dioxide in the process of ....

 Carbon and decay **Grades 2–5**

2. A student decided to investigate the production of carbon dioxide during decomposition of leaves in a sealed bag. A carbon dioxide sensor and datalogger was used to record the results. The results are shown in **Figure 1**.

(a) What causes the leaves to decompose? Tick **one** box. **[1 mark]**

lack of light in the bag ☐

carbon dioxide concentrations ☐

microorganisms such as bacteria and fungi ☐

lack of oxygen in the bag ☐

% CO₂ / Time

Figure 1

(b) Explain why the concentration of carbon dioxide increases during the experiment. **[1 mark]**

....

(c) Explain why decomposition is an important process in ecosystems. **[1 mark]**

....

Water cycle

② Quick quiz

Use words from the box to complete the sentences.

| cytoplasm | plasma | phloem | reactions | vacuole | xylem |

Water is essential to living organisms. It is a major component of cell .... where many cell

.... take place. Plant cells depend on water to fill their central .... to help support the plant.

Water is essential in transport systems. For example, blood carries many substances around the body dissolved in the .... In plants, mineral ions dissolved in water are transported in the

.... and dissolved sucrose is transported around the plant in the ....

⑩ The water cycle
Grade 4

1. (a) Explain the importance of the water cycle to living organisms. **[2 marks]**

The water cycle provides fresh water
....

The water also dissolves
....

(b) Figure 1 shows the water cycle. Identify each lettered process in the cycle and describe what happens in each process. **[3 marks]**

A Evaporation is when
....

B Condensation
....

C Precipitation
....

> Remember the processes in which water changes from one state to another.

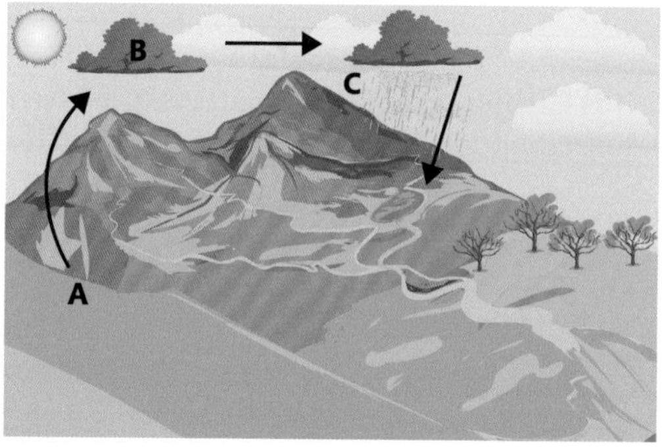

Figure 1

⑩ Desalination
Grade 5

2. Figure 2 is a diagram of an emergency solar still which might be found in a lifeboat. The still can be used to produce potable water from sea water.

(a) State what is meant by the term 'potable water'. **[1 mark]**

....

(b) Describe how potable water is produced from sea water in the solar still. **[2 marks]**

....

....

(c) Give a reason why this process is an example of desalination. **[1 mark]**

....

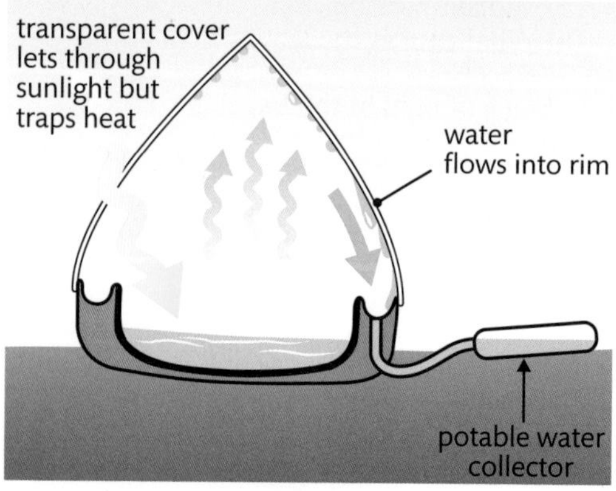

transparent cover lets through sunlight but traps heat

water flows into rim

potable water collector

Figure 2

 Made a start   Feeling confident   ☑ Exam ready

Nitrogen cycle

② Quick quiz

True or false?

Nitrogen is found in proteins and DNA in the biotic components of an ecosystem.	**True / False**
Plants absorb nitrogen from the air through their leaves.	**True / False**
Animals can absorb nitrogen directly from the environment.	**True / False**
Nitrogen cycles from the biotic components to the abiotic components of an ecosystem by decay.	**True / False**

> Remember that biotic means living things and abiotic means non-living.

⑩ The nitrogen cycle — Grade 4

1. Figure 1 shows the effect of mass of nitrogen in fertiliser on the yield (mass of harvested food) of a crop.

(a) Describe the relationship between mass of nitrogen and yield shown in **Figure 1**. **[1 mark]**

As the mass of nitrogen is increased, the yield
....

(b) The growing crop takes nitrogen from the soil. Name the form of nitrogen that is absorbed by plant roots. **[1 mark]**

....

> Plants take up nitrogen as a mineral ion in which nitrogen is combined with oxygen. Names of compounds that include oxygen often end in '-ate'

(c) Explain why plants need nitrogen to grow. **[2 marks]**

Nitrogen is needed so the plant can make .... which is an

important substance for ....

Yield (tonne/ha)

3.0
2.5
2.0
1.5
1.0
0.5
0

0   45   90

**Mass of nitrogen added
to soil in fertiliser (kg)**

Figure 1

⑩ Different farming practices — Grade 5

2. Farmers use a variety of ways to increase the amount of nitrogen available to plants in the soil of their fields.

(a) Explain how each of the following practices can increase soil fertility.

(i) Plough the old crop stalks into the ground and allow the dead plant material to rot. **[2 marks]**

....
....

(ii) Add artificial fertiliser powder to the soil. **[1 mark]**

....

(b) Denitrifying bacteria convert nitrate into nitrogen gas. This action of denitrifying bacteria will: **[1 mark]**

increase the amount of soil nitrogen available to plants ☐

increase the organic material in the soil ☐

improve the soil moisture content ☐

reduce the amount of soil nitrogen available to plants. ☐

 Made a start   **Feeling confident**   **Exam ready**

Atoms, elements and compounds

2 Quick quiz

Draw **one** line to match each word to its definition.

atom	consists of two or more different elements chemically joined
element	the smallest part of an element that can exist
compound	made of only one type of atom

5 Chemical equations — Grade 3

1. When calcium reacts with oxygen a compound is formed. Complete the word equation for the reaction. **[1 mark]**

Exam focus
Look at every part of a question carefully. Often the words and diagrams will have all the information you need to answer the question. The examiner is testing to see if you can understand what is happening during the reaction.

calcium + ... → ....

2. When copper carbonate is heated, it decomposes to form a metal oxide and carbon dioxide gas. Write the word equation for the reaction. **[1 mark]**

.... → .... + ...

10 Elements and compounds — Grades 2–3

3. Use the periodic table (on page 252) to complete **Table 1**. **[4 marks]**

Table 1

Element name	Element symbol
	Na
Bromine	
	Pb
Iron	

4. The chemical formula for carbon dioxide is CO_2. How many atoms are in a molecule of carbon dioxide? **[1 mark]**

1 ☐ 2 ☐ 3 ☐ 4 ☐

5 Reactions and compounds — Grade 4

5. What compound is made when barium and chlorine react? Tick **one** box. **[1 mark]**

chlorine baride ☐
chlorine barate ☐
barium chlorate ☐
barium chloride ☐

6. (a) Determine the number of atoms present in Fe_2O_3. .... **[1 mark]**

(b) Determine the number of different elements present in Fe_2O_3. .... **[1 mark]**

7. When zinc carbonate is heated, it decomposes to form zinc oxide and carbon dioxide. Write the word equation for the reaction. **[1 mark]**

....

The model of the atom

 Quick quiz

Number the boxes from 1–4 to show the order in which these events occurred.

Chadwick shows that neutrons exist.	
Electrons are discovered.	
Alpha particle scattering experiments, carried out by Rutherford, Geiger and Marsden, led to the nuclear model of the atom.	
The plum pudding model of the atom was developed.	

 Atomic models **Grade 4**

1. **Figure 1** shows two models for the structure of an atom.

   Table 1 shows different features. Complete **Table 1** by placing a tick (✓) in the box if the model has the feature.
   [4 marks]

Plum pudding model

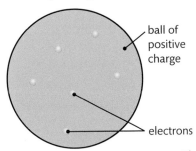
ball of positive charge

electrons

Nuclear model

electrons

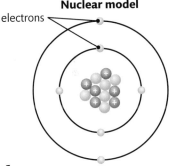

Figure 1

Table 1

Feature	Plum pudding model	Nuclear model
Protons in a nucleus		✓
Contains electrons		
Contains positive charges		
Electrons at fixed distances		

Some rows will have two ticks in them.

 Evidence for the nuclear model **Grade 4**

2. The plum pudding model was tested. Positively charged alpha particles were aimed at a thin sheet of gold foil.
   Draw **one** line from each observation to the correct conclusion. **[3 marks]**

Observation

Most alpha particles passed straight through.
Some alpha particles were deflected.
A very small number of alpha particles were deflected backwards.

Conclusion

The nucleus has most of the atom's mass.
Most of the atom is empty space.
The nucleus is negatively charged.
The nucleus is positively charged.

Not every conclusion is supported by an observation so there will only be three lines to draw.

 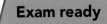

Subatomic particles

② Quick quiz

(a) Name the parts of the atom shown by labels **A**, **B** and **C**.

A ....

B ....

C ....

(b) Give the name of the part of the atom where **B** and **C** are found.

....

⑩ Subatomic particles   Grade 4

1. Complete **Table 1** to show the names of the three subatomic particles and their position in an atom.   **[3 marks]**

Table 1

Name of subatomic particle	Position in the atom
proton	nucleus
neutron	
	shell

2. Name the subatomic particle that gives an element its atomic number.   **[1 mark]**

....

3. Give a reason why atoms have no overall electrical charge.   **[1 mark]**

....

⑩ Atomic structure   Grade 5

4. A carbon atom contains 6 protons and 6 neutrons. Deduce the atomic number of carbon.   **[1 mark]**

....

5. A sodium atom contains 11 protons. Work out the number of electrons in a sodium atom.   **[1 mark]**

....

6. The radius of an atom is about 0.1 nm.

What is the radius of an atom in m? Tick **one** box.   **[1 mark]**

0.000 1 m   ☐

0.000 000 1 m   ☐

0.000 000 000 1 m   ☐

0.000 000 000 000 1 m   ☐

 Made a start   **Feeling confident**   ☑ **Exam ready**

Size and mass of atoms

2 Quick quiz

Complete the table to show the names of the three subatomic particles and their relative charges.

Name of subatomic particle	Relative charge
proton	
	0

10 Atomic number and mass number

Grade 3

1. State what is meant by the term 'mass number'. **[1 mark]**

Mass number is the total number of protons and ....

2. An atom of gold has the symbol: $^{197}_{79}Au$

(a) Identify the atomic number of this atom. **[1 mark]**

....

(b) Identify the mass number of this atom. **[1 mark]**

....

3. The mass number of an aluminium atom is 27. Its proton number is 13. Calculate the number of neutrons in this atom. **[1 mark]**

number of neutrons = mass number – atomic number

Number of neutrons = ...

5 Ions and subatomic particles

Grade 5

4. An atom of iron has an atomic number of 26. The ion Fe^{3+} forms when iron reacts with oxygen. Calculate the number of electrons in an Fe^{3+} ion. **[2 marks]**

Ions have the same mass number and atomic number as the atom they came from, but a different number of electrons (fewer for a positively charged ion, more for a negatively charged ion).

Number of electrons = ...

10 Particle numbers

Grade 5

5. The atomic number of beryllium is 4. The mass number of a beryllium atom is 9. Calculate the number of protons and neutrons in an atom of beryllium. **[2 marks]**

Protons .... Neutrons ....

6. State where in the atom most of the mass is found. **[1 mark]**

....

Made a start | Feeling confident | Exam ready

Isotopes and relative atomic mass

② Quick quiz

True or false?

Isotopes have the same mass number but a different atomic number.	**True / False**
Isotopes have the same chemical properties.	**True / False**
Isotopes have the same number of protons and neutrons, but a different number of electrons.	**True / False**
Isotopes can have different percentage abundances.	**True / False**

⑩ Isotopes   Grade 5

1. An isotope of oxygen, oxygen-16, is represented as: $^{16}_{8}O$

(a) Deduce the number of each subatomic particle present in an atom of oxygen-16.   **[3 marks]**

> For all atoms other than hydrogen-1, $^{1}_{1}H$, mass number is greater than atomic number. Check your periodic table to find the atomic number for atoms of an element.

protons ....   neutrons ....   electrons ....

(b) Oxygen-16 and oxygen-18 are isotopes of the same element. Describe what isotopes of an element are.   **[2 marks]**

Isotopes are atoms of an element that have the same number of .... but different numbers of ....

....

2. One of the isotopes of helium is $^{3}_{2}He$.

(a) Deduce the number of each type of subatomic particle found in an atom of this isotope of helium.   **[3 marks]**

....

(b) Give a reason why the relative atomic mass of helium is given as 4 rather than 3.   **[1 mark]**

....

3. Table 1 shows some information about isotopes. Which two are isotopes of the same element? Tick **two** boxes.   **[1 mark]**

Table 1

	Number of protons	Number of electrons	Number of neutrons
☐	21	21	24
☐	10	10	10
☐	24	24	28
☐	10	10	12

Developing the periodic table

2 Quick quiz

Fill in the gaps using words from the box.

periods	different	similar	elements	groups	Mendeleev	atomic mass	atomic number

.... arranged elements in order of their increasing relative .... He put elements with .... properties into .... He changed the order of some .... to fit the trend better.

10 Mendeleev's periodic table — Grades 4–5

1. Mendeleev was a Russian chemist who developed an early periodic table.
Describe how Mendeleev first ordered the elements in his periodic table. **[1 mark]**

....

2. (a) Explain how Mendeleev was able to predict the existence of elements that had not been discovered at that time. **[2 marks]**

....

....

(b) Give a reason why Mendeleev changed the order of some elements in his periodic table. **[1 mark]**

....

5 Early periodic tables — Grade 3

3. Figure 1 shows the first version of the periodic table written by Mendeleev in the late 1800s.

(a) Explain why there were question marks in Mendeleev's periodic table. **[1 mark]**

....

....

....

(b) Give a difference between Mendeleev's periodic table and the modern periodic table. **[1 mark]**

....

....

Row	Group 1	2	3	4	5	6	7	8
1	H	-	-	-	-	-	-	-
2	Li	Be	B	C	N	O	F	-
3	Na	Mg	Al	Si	P	S	Cl	-
4	K	Ca	?	Ti	V	Cr	Mn	Fe, Co, Ni, Cu
5	(Cu)	Zn	?	?	As	So	Br	-
6	Rb	Sr	Yt	Zr	Nb	Mo	?	Ru, Rh, Pd, Ag

Figure 1

(c) Give the symbol of the element that is below aluminium in Mendeleev's periodic table. **[1 mark]**

....

The periodic table

② **Quick quiz**

1. Match each element to its group number.

potassium		Group 0
nitrogen		Group 1
argon		Group 5

2. True or false?

A column in the periodic table is a group.	**True / False**
A row in the periodic table is a period.	**True / False**
Elements in the same groups have similar reactions.	**True / False**
Elements in the same group have the same number of electron shells.	**True / False**

⑩ **Periodic table positions** **Grade 4**

1. Fluorine is a non-metal element and found on the right of the periodic table.

(a) Give the group number that fluorine belongs to. **[1 mark]**

> In the periodic table, the columns are the groups. The rows are the periods.

....

(b) Give the symbol of an atom of fluorine. **[1 mark]**

....

2. Carbon is a non-metal element.

(a) Give the group number of carbon. .... **[1 mark]**

(b) State the period that carbon can be found in. .... **[1 mark]**

(c) Give the atomic number of carbon. .... **[1 mark]**

(d) Give the number of electrons in the outer shell of carbon. .... **[1 mark]**

> Remember, the period number tells you the number of electron shells and the group number tells you the number of electrons in the outer shell.

3. Element X has an atomic number of 17.

(a) Deduce the name of element X. .... **[1 mark]**

(b) Determine the group number of element X. .... **[1 mark]**

> **Exam focus** 📌
> Use your periodic table to help you answer these types of question.

⑩ **Predicting reactions** **Grade 4**

4. Rubidium is an element in Group 1. It forms an oxide that dissolves in water to give an alkaline solution. Francium is also in Group 1. Predict whether francium oxide will form an acidic or alkaline solution. Give a reason for your answer. **[2 marks]**

 It will form an alkaline solution because elements in the same group have ....

....

 Made a start **Feeling confident** 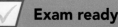 **Exam ready**

Electronic configuration

② Quick quiz

(a) Complete the table to show the maximum number of electrons in the first three shells.

Shell	Maximum number of electrons
1	
2	
3	

(b) Determine the group of an element with electronic configuration 2.8.6.

....

(c) Deduce which period this element is found in.

....

⑤ Electronic structure   Grade 4

1. (a) The electronic configuration of potassium is 2.8.8.1.
Complete **Figure 1** to show this configuration.   **[2 marks]**

> number of protons = number of electrons

(b) Give the number of protons in the potassium atom.   **[1 mark]**

....

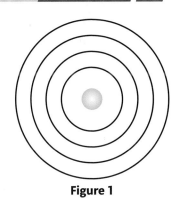

Figure 1

⑮ Using electronic configuration   Grade 5

2. Magnesium atoms have 12 electrons. The electronic structure for magnesium can be represented by **Figure 2**.

Give the electronic structure of magnesium. .... **[1 mark]**

3. (a) Give the electronic configuration of the following elements.

(i) oxygen .... **[1 mark]**

(ii) hydrogen .... **[1 mark]**

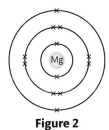

Figure 2

(b) Describe the relationship between electronic configuration and group number in the periodic table.   **[1 mark]**

....

4. Calcium atoms have 20 electrons. Complete **Figure 3** to show the electronic configuration of a calcium atom.   **[2 marks]**

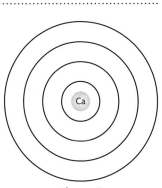

Figure 3

 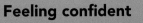

Metals and non-metals

BBC

② Quick quiz

Complete the labels on the diagram to show where metals and non-metals are found in the periodic table.

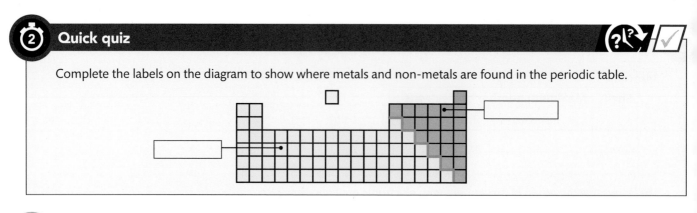

⑤ Properties of metals and non-metals   Grade 3

1. Metals and non-metals have different properties. Complete **Table 1** by placing a tick (✓) in each row to show whether each property is typical of metals or of non-metals.   **[2 marks]**

Table 1

Property	Poor conductor of electricity	Good conductor of heat	Brittle	Dull	Malleable
Metals					✓
Non-metals					

⑩ Elements, ions and electrons   Grade 5

2. Metals and non-metals form ions when they react together. Describe the difference between the ions formed by metals and the ions formed by non-metals.   **[2 marks]**

> Decide whether negatively charged ions or positively charged ions are formed in each case.

Metals lose electrons to form ....

Non-metals gain electrons to form ....

3. Metals are elements that have fewer than four electrons in their outer shell. This is true for most of the elements in the first three rows of the periodic table.

(a) An element has the electronic configuration 2.8.3. Determine whether this element is a metal or a non-metal. Give a reason for your answer.   **[1 mark]**

....

(b) Helium has the electronic configuration 2. Explain why this is unusual.   **[2 marks]**

> Is helium a metal or a non-metal? What information about electronic configurations are you given in the question?

....

....

⑤ Electron configurations   Grade 2

4. Draw **one** line to match each element with the correct electron configuration.   **[3 marks]**

Li
Ca
Na
F

2.7
2.1
2.8.8.2
2.8.1

> Use the periodic table to help you.

 Made a start   **Feeling confident**   **Exam ready**

Chemical bonds

True or false?

Ionic bonding happens between a metal and a non-metal element.	**True / False**
Two types of metal are needed to make a metallic bond.	**True / False**
Covalent bonding uses transfer of electrons.	**True / False**
Metallic bonding and ionic bonding both have delocalised electrons.	**True / False**
Covalent bonds form in non-metals only.	**True / False**

10 Types of bonding — Grade 4

1. Hydrogen chloride (HCl) is an example of a compound that contains covalent bonds.

(a) State what is meant by a 'covalent bond'. **[1 mark]**

A bond that is formed when two atoms share a pair of ....

(b) Hydrogen chloride is a compound of hydrogen and chlorine. Explain why the atoms must be held by covalent bonds. **[1 mark]**

Both hydrogen and chlorine are non-metals and so can only ....

2. Table 1 shows information about compounds and the elements that they are made from. Some elements react together to form compounds containing ionic bonds. Other elements form compounds that contain covalent bonds. Complete **Table 1** by placing a tick to show the type of bond in each compound. **[2 marks]**

Table 1		Type of bond	
Compound	**Made from**	**Ionic**	**Covalent**
water	hydrogen + oxygen		✓
carbon dioxide	carbon + oxygen		
sodium chloride	sodium + chlorine	✓	
iron sulfide	iron + sulfur		
methane	carbon + hydrogen		
magnesium oxide	magnesium + oxygen		

> Compounds made from a metal and a non-metal contain ionic bonds.

3. Complete the sentence about metallic bonding. Use words from the box. **[3 marks]**

attraction	electrons	an electrostatic	ions	a magnetic	repulsion

Metallic bonding is .... force of .... between ions and delocalised ....

10 Ionic and metallic bonding — Grade 5

4. Magnesium is a metal element. State and describe the type of bonding present in magnesium. **[3 marks]**

....

....

....

> You can include a labelled diagram to help you describe the bonding.

....

Ionic bonding

(2) Quick quiz

Give the symbol for the ion that each element forms. (For example, lithium forms Li⁺.)

magnesium ....   oxygen ....   sodium ....

aluminium ....   fluorine ....   calcium ....

(5) Losing and gaining electrons   Grades 4–5

1. Metals and non-metals form ions when they react together.

Which statement about the formation of ions is correct? Tick **one** box.   **[1 mark]**

Metals lose electrons to form negative ions. ☐

Metals gain electrons to form positive ions. ☐

Non-metals lose electrons to form positive ions. ☐

Non-metals gain electrons to form negative ions. ☐

2. Give the number of electrons an atom from a Group 2 element will lose when it reacts. Explain your answer.   **[3 marks]**

Atoms of Group 2 elements will lose two electrons, because all atoms of elements in Group 2 have

....

....

To be stable,

....

3. Lithium reacts with chlorine to form lithium chloride. Complete the dot and cross diagrams (**Figure 1**) to show outer shells of the ions formed in lithium chloride. Show the charge on each ion.   **[2 marks]**

Lithium is in Group 1 and chlorine is in Group 7.

$$\left[\enspace Li \enspace \right] \quad \left[\enspace Cl \enspace \right]$$

Figure 1

(10) Forming an ionic compound   Grade 5

4. Magnesium reacts with chlorine to form magnesium chloride.

(a) Write a word equation for this reaction.   **[1 mark]**

....

(b) The formula of magnesium chloride is $MgCl_2$. Give the formula of the positive ion in this compound.   **[2 marks]**

....

(c) Describe the bonding in magnesium chloride.   **[3 marks]**

....

....

....

Ionic compounds

2 Quick quiz

List four different ways of representing the structure of ionic compounds.

....

....

15 Representing ionic compounds

Grade 5

1. Calcium sulfide is an ionic compound of calcium and sulfur. It has a similar structure to sodium chloride. **Figure 1** is a two-dimensional diagram that represents the structure of calcium sulfide.

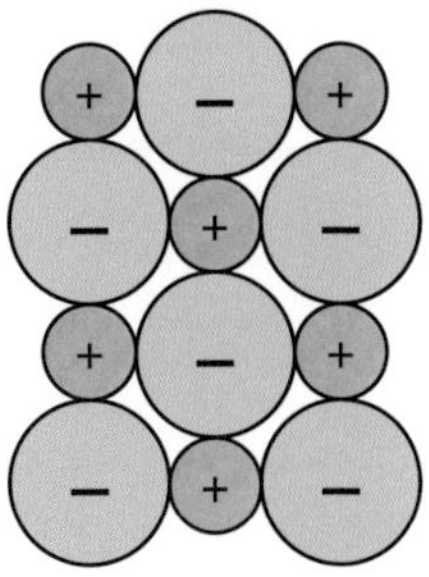

Figure 1

(a) What type of structure does calcium sulfide have? Tick **one** box. **[1 mark]**

giant ☐ molecular ☐

metallic ☐ simple ☐

(b) Name what the labelled circles represent. **[1 mark]**

....

(c) Describe ionic bonding. **[2 marks]**

It is strong electrostatic forces of attraction between ....

....

(d) Determine the empirical formula of calcium sulfide. **[2 marks]**

Use the periodic table to look up the symbols for calcium and sulfur.

....

....

5 Ionic lattice

Grades 4–5

2. The ionic lattice structure for magnesium oxide is shown in **Figure 2**.

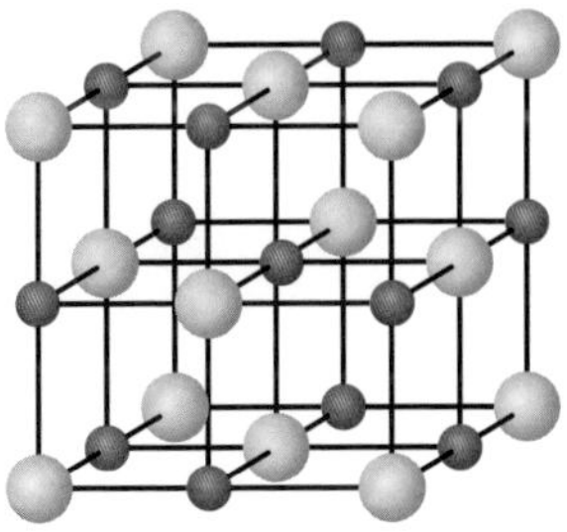

Figure 2

(a) Describe the structure of an ionic lattice. **[2 marks]**

....

....

....

(b) Deduce the formula for magnesium oxide. **[2 marks]**

....

....

Properties of ionic compounds

⏱ 2 Quick quiz

Tick the boxes of the substances that are ionic compounds.

sodium chloride ☐   aluminium ☐

water ☐   diamond ☐

magnesium oxide ☐   copper sulfate ☐

⏱ 5 Ionic compounds   Grade 3

1. Choose the correct answer. Tick **one** box for each part.

(a) Ionic compounds: **[1 mark]**

conduct electricity when solid ☐

conduct electricity when dissolved ☐

cannot conduct electricity when molten ☐

cannot conduct electricity when dissolved ☐

(b) Ionic compounds have a high melting point because: **[1 mark]**

they cannot conduct electricity ☐

there are strong forces of attraction between ions ☐

they can easily conduct electricity ☐

they have strong forces of attraction between molecules ☐

⏱ 5 Structure and bonding   Grade 4

2. Complete the sentence about ionic bonding. Use words from the box. **[3 marks]**

| atoms   electrons   electrostatic   ions   oppositely   same |

Ionic bonding is the ...electrostatic... force of attraction in all directions between .... charged ....

⏱ 10 Properties of ionic compounds   Grade 5

3. Explain why the ionic compound calcium chloride does **not** conduct electricity when solid. **[2 marks]**

The ions in a solid are in fixed positions. In order to conduct electricity,
....

....

4. Explain why an aqueous solution of sodium chloride can conduct electricity. **[2 marks]**

....

....

....

Covalent bonding

2 Quick quiz

Choose the correct answers.

(a) Chemical bonding involves:

- electrons ☐
- protons ☐
- neutrons ☐
- nuclei ☐

(b) Covalent bonds form in:

- metals ☐
- small molecules ☐
- polymers ☐
- giant covalent structures ☐

10 Sharing electrons — Grade 5

1. The structures of some covalent substances are shown in **Figure 1**. They are labelled **A**, **B**, **C** and **D**.

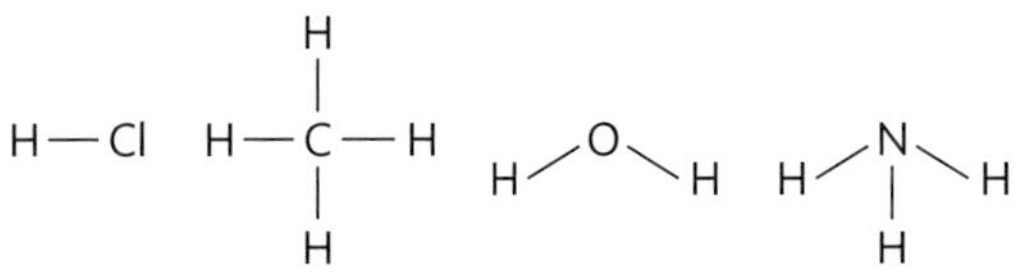

A **B** **C** **D**

Figure 1

Methane has the formula CH_4.

(a) Give the letter of the molecule which represents methane. **[1 mark]**

....

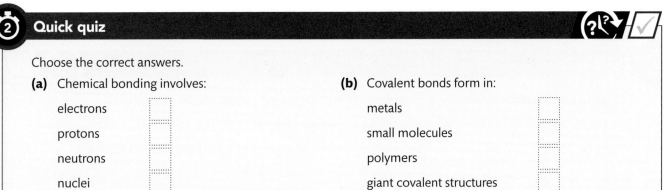

(b) Give the formula of molecule **D**. **[1 mark]**

....

(c) Give the name of molecule **C**. **[1 mark]**

....

5 Ball and stick and dot and cross — Grade 5

2. Covalent compounds can be represented by ball and stick diagrams and by dot and cross diagrams.

(a) Give **one** limitation of a ball and stick diagram. **[1 mark]**

....

(b) Give **one** limitation of a dot and cross diagram. **[1 mark]**

....

10 Dot and cross diagrams — Grade 5

3. Oxygen is a simple molecular, covalent substance. The electronic configuration of an atom of oxygen is 2.6. Draw the dot and cross diagram of an oxygen molecule, O_2. Show outer electrons only. **[2 marks]**

4. Carbon dioxide molecules contain double bonds. Draw the dot and cross diagram of a carbon dioxide molecule, CO_2. Show outer electrons only. **[2 marks]**

Exam focus
Use your periodic table to work out the number of outer shell electrons in each atom that form the molecule.

Properties of simple molecular substances

2 Quick quiz

Complete each sentence by drawing a circle around the correct word in **bold** in each sentence.

Substances that consist of simple molecules are usually **solids / liquids** or gases at room temperature.

Simple molecular substances consist of simple molecules that contain **ionic / covalent** bonds and have intermolecular forces between molecules.
They:
- have relatively **low / high** melting and boiling points
- are **good / poor** conductors of electricity
- are usually **soluble / insoluble** in water.

10 Intermolecular forces — Grade 4

1. Carbon dioxide exists as simple molecules. Explain why it is a gas at room temperature. **[2 marks]**

Carbon dioxide is a gas at room temperature because the forces of attraction between the molecules are ....

....

2. **Table 1** shows the molecular formula and boiling points of some hydrocarbons.

Table 1

Name	Molecular formula	Boiling point in °C
Ethene	C_2H_4	−104
Propene	C_3H_6	−48
Butene	C_4H_8	−6
Pentene	C_5H_{10}	30
Hexene	C_6H_{12}	63

(a) State which hydrocarbon in **Table 1** has the lowest boiling point. **[1 mark]**

For a negative value, the larger the number the lower the value.

....

(b) Describe how the size of a hydrocarbon molecule affects its boiling point. **[1 mark]**

As the size of the molecule increases ....

5 Conducting electricity — Grade 4

3. Explain why carbon dioxide does not conduct electricity. **[2 marks]**

....

....

Giant covalent structures

BBC

② Quick quiz

Label each diagram to show whether it is a giant covalent structure or a simple molecular structure.

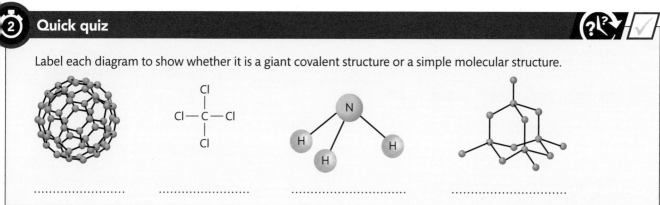

....

⑩ Giant covalent structures   Grade 4

1. Glass is mainly made of silicon dioxide. **Figure 1** shows a diagram of the structure of silicon dioxide. It is an example of a substance with a giant covalent structure.

(a) **Figure 1** shows part of the structure of silicon dioxide. How are the atoms arranged in silicon dioxide? Tick **one** box.   **[1 mark]**

In a giant structure with a regular pattern ☐

In a giant structure with a random pattern ☐

In a simple structure with a regular pattern ☐

In a simple structure with a random pattern ☐

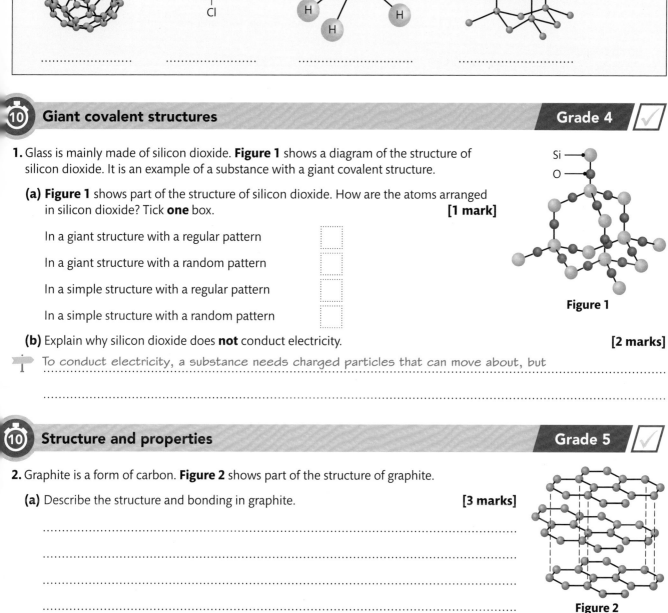

Figure 1

(b) Explain why silicon dioxide does **not** conduct electricity.   **[2 marks]**

To conduct electricity, a substance needs charged particles that can move about, but

....

....

⑩ Structure and properties   Grade 5

2. Graphite is a form of carbon. **Figure 2** shows part of the structure of graphite.

(a) Describe the structure and bonding in graphite.   **[3 marks]**

....

....

....

....

Figure 2

(b) Predict **two** physical properties that you would expect graphite to have.   **[2 marks]**

....

....

Diamond

2 Quick quiz

Use words from the box to complete the sentences.

covalent	four	hard	high	soft	three

Each atom in diamond is bonded to .... other atoms. All the atoms are joined by .... bonds. Diamond has a .... melting point. Diamond is suitable for cutting tools because it is ....

10 Structure and bonding in diamond — Grade 4

1. Diamond is a form of carbon. **Figure 1** shows part of the structure of diamond.

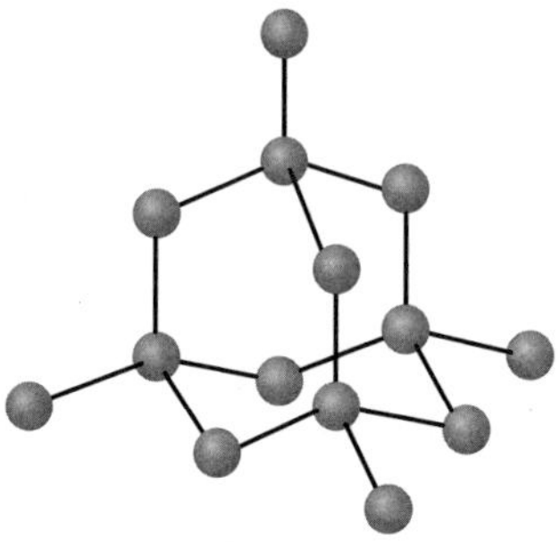

Figure 1

(a) How many bonds can a carbon atom form? Tick **one** box. **[1 mark]**

1 ☐ 2 ☐ 3 ☐ 4 ☐

(b) Name the type of bond present in diamond. **[1 mark]**

....

Types of bond include ionic bonds, covalent bonds and metallic bonds.

(c) Complete the sentence about diamond. Use words from the box. **[2 marks]**

giant	random	regular	small

The atoms in diamond have a ....giant.... structure with a .... arrangement.

2. Give **one** reason why diamond is unable to conduct electricity. **[1 mark]**

....

5 Properties of diamond — Grade 4

3. Which row in **Table 1** about the boiling point and bonding in diamond is correct? **[1 mark]**

Table 1

	Boiling point	Bonding
☐	Low	Strong
☐	Low	Weak
☐	High	Strong
☐	Low	Weak

Graphite

2 Quick quiz

Give **two** uses of graphite.

....

5 Graphite structure — Grade 4

1. Graphite has a giant structure.

(a) Name the type of bonding in graphite. .... **[1 mark]**

(b) Give the number of bonds each atom forms. .... **[1 mark]**

2. Describe the structure of graphite. **[3 marks]**

Graphite forms layers of ....

These are arranged ....

Between the layers there are ....

Exam focus
There are three marks so you need to make three points.

15 Properties of graphite — Grade 5

3. Diamond is hard and is used in cutting tools. Graphite is slippery and is used as a lubricant.

(a) Which type of bonding is found in **both** diamond and graphite? Tick **one** box. **[1 mark]**

covalent ☐

ionic ☐

metallic ☐

intermolecular forces ☐

(b) Give the difference in the number of bonds between the carbon atoms in graphite and in diamond. **[1 mark]**

....

(c) Explain why graphite is suitable for use as a lubricant. **[2 marks]**

A lubricant reduces friction when applied to the surface of moving parts.

....

....

(d) Suggest and explain which form of carbon, diamond or graphite, is suitable for use as electrodes. **[3 marks]**

....

....

....

....

Graphene and fullerenes

② Quick quiz

True or false?

Graphene is a single layer of graphite.	**True / False**
Each carbon atom in graphene forms four covalent bonds.	**True / False**
Fullerenes can form rings with different numbers of carbon atoms.	**True / False**
Graphene and fullerenes cannot conduct electricity.	**True / False**

⑩ Graphene and graphite   Grade 5

1. Figure 1 shows part of the structure of graphene.

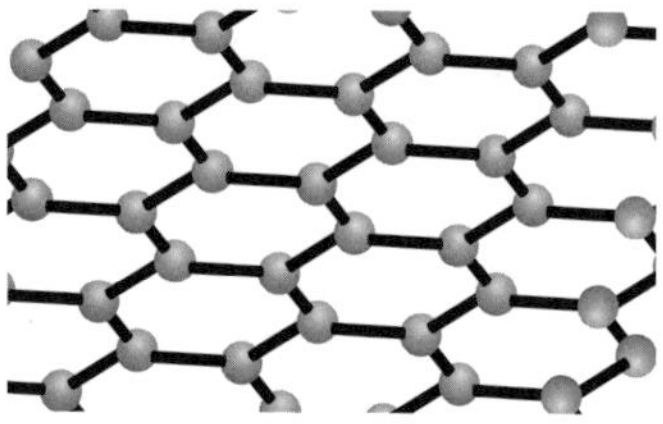

(a) Determine the number of covalent bonds formed by each carbon atom.

[1 mark]

....

(b) Give **two** ways in which the properties of graphene and graphite are similar.

[2 marks]

⊤ Both have high melting and boiling points so are solid at room temperature.

....

....

Figure 1

2. Explain, in terms of structure and bonding, why graphene is strong.   **[3 marks]**

....

....

....

> Remember to mention both the structure *and* the bonding in your answer.

⑩ Fullerenes   Grade 5

3. Figure 2 shows the structure of carbon nanotubes. They are cylindrical fullerenes. Which statement describes some of their properties?   **[1 mark]**

high tensile strength, very low length to diameter ratios ☐

high tensile strength, very high length to diameter ratios ☐

low tensile strength, very high length to diameter ratios ☐

low tensile strength, very low length to diameter ratios ☐

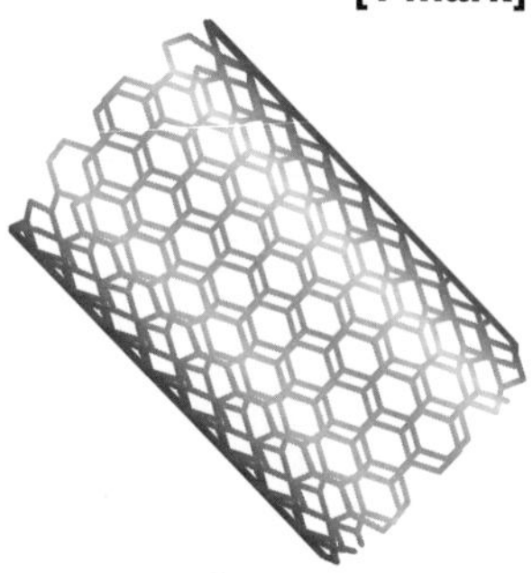

4. Figure 3 shows the structure of buckminsterfullerene. Buckminsterfullerene is a form of carbon with the molecular formula C_{60}.

(a) Describe the structure and bonding in buckminsterfullerene.   **[2 marks]**

....

....

Figure 2

(b) Suggest and explain whether buckminsterfullerene can conduct electricity.   **[3 marks]**

....

....

....

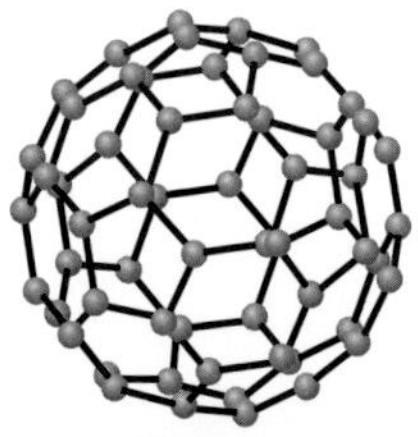

Figure 3

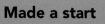 **Made a start**   **Feeling confident**   **Exam ready**

Polymers

② Quick quiz

Complete each sentence by drawing a circle around the correct word in **bold** in each sentence.

Poly(ethene) molecules are **large / small**. The atoms are held together by **covalent / ionic** bonds. The intermolecular forces between poly(ethene) molecules are **stronger / weaker** than the intermolecular forces between ethene molecules. Properties of poly(ethene) include:

- relatively **high / low** melting point
- **does / does not** conduct electricity.

⑤ Formation of polymers · Grade 5

1. (a) State what is meant by the term 'polymer'. **[1 mark]**

A polymer is a large molecule made from

....

(b) Name the type of bonds which hold together the atoms in a polymer. **[1 mark]**

> Consider whether the atoms are from metals or non-metals.

....

⑮ Polymer properties · Grade 5

2. Figure 1 shows the ball and stick diagram of part of poly(ethene). Poly(ethene) is a polymer with many uses.

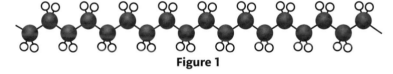

Figure 1

(a) Give the name of the element shown as the black balls. **[1 mark]**

....

(b) State the symbol of the element shown as the white balls. **[1 mark]**

....

(c) Describe the structure of poly(ethene). **[2 marks]**

....

....

3. Give a reason, in terms of its structure and bonding, why poly(ethene) does not conduct electricity. **[1 mark]**

> Think about the type of particles in the polymer.

....

....

Metals

② Quick quiz

The diagram shows part of the structure of a metal.

(a) Label the diagram to show a delocalised electron and a metal particle.

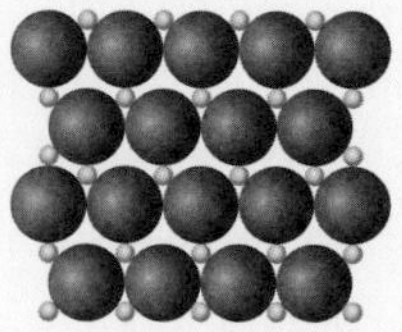

(b) True or false?

Metals are good conductors of electricity.	**True / False**
Metals have low boiling points.	**True / False**
Metals have low density.	**True / False**

⑤ Describing metallic bonding   Grade 4

1. (a) Name the main type of force of attraction between the particles in metals. Tick **one** box.   **[1 mark]**

magnetic ☐   gravitational ☐

electrostatic ☐   contact ☐

(b) Give the charge of a metal ion from Group 1.   **[2 marks]**

....

⑤ Properties of metals   Grade 4

2. Metals are malleable. Which of the following correctly explains the meaning of malleable? Tick **one** box.   **[1 mark]**

can be drawn into a wire ☐

conducts electricity ☐

is shiny when freshly cut ☐

can be hammered into shape without breaking ☐

3. Explain why metals have high boiling points.   **[1 mark]**

| Think about the strength of metallic bonding. |

....

⑤ Conducting electricity   Grade 4

4. Explain why metals are good conductors of electricity.   **[2 marks]**

....

....

 Made a start   **Feeling confident**   ☑ **Exam ready**

Relative formula mass

2 Quick quiz

True or false?

Relative formula mass is the mass of one atom of an element. **True / False**

Relative formula mass is found by adding the atomic numbers of the elements together. **True / False**

Relative formula masses have the unit grams. **True / False**

5 Simple calculations — Grade 5

1. (a) Give the relative atomic masses of the following elements. Use your periodic table to help you. **[3 marks]**

Use the periodic table to find out the relative atomic masses.

Carbon 12 ....

Sodium ....

Mercury ....

(b) Calculate the relative formula mass of the following molecules. (Relative atomic masses: O = 16, F = 19, Cl = 35.5) **[3 marks]**

You can find relative atomic masses and atomic numbers in the periodic table on page 252.

Oxygen (O_2) $2 \times 16 =$ ....

Fluorine (F_2) ....

Chlorine (Cl_2) ....

5 Complex calculations — Grade 5

2. Calculate the relative formula mass of the following compounds. (Relative atomic masses: H = 1, C = 12, N = 14, O = 16, Na = 23, S = 32, Cl = 35.5, Ca = 40, Cu = 63.5)

(a) $CuSO_4$ $Cu + S + (4 \times O) =$ .... **[1 mark]**

(b) Na_2CO_3 $2 \times$ .... **[1 mark]**

(c) NaCl .... **[1 mark]**

(d) NH_4OH .... **[1 mark]**

(e) $Ca(OH)_2$ $Ca + (2 \times O) + (2 \times H) =$ .... **[1 mark]**

If there are brackets within the formula, you need to multiply the contents of the brackets by the number that follows, e.g. $(OH)_2$ means 2 × OH (two 'units' of OH) = 2 × O and 2 × H.

15 Calculating relative formula mass — Grade 5

3. Calculate the relative formula mass of the following compounds. (Relative atomic masses: N = 14, O = 16, Na = 23, S = 32, K = 39, Mn = 55, Fe = 56, Cu = 63.5)

(a) $FeSO_4$ .... **[1 mark]**

(b) $KMnO_4$ .... **[1 mark]**

(c) $Cu(NO_3)_2$ .... **[1 mark]**

Empirical formulae

② Quick quiz

Draw lines to link each term with its definition and example.

Formula	Definition	Example
molecular formula	shows every atom and every bond	H–O–O–H
empirical formula	shows the number and type of atom	CH
displayed formula	smallest whole number ratio of atoms in a compound	C_6H_6

⑩ Empirical formulae　　　　Grade 5

1. Figure 1 shows the structure of ethane.

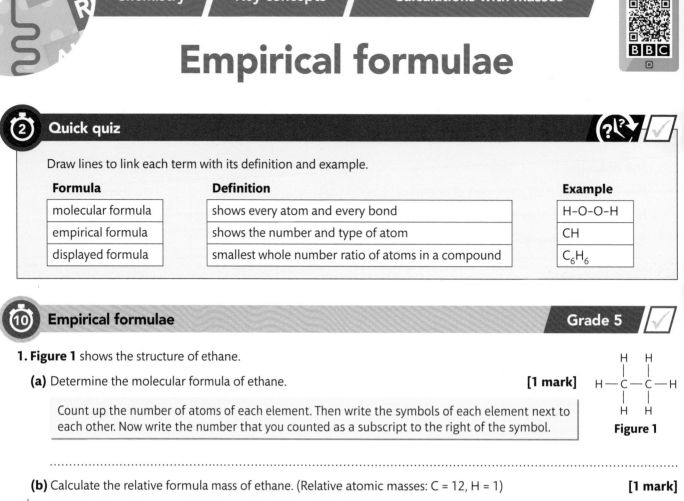

Figure 1

(a) Determine the molecular formula of ethane. **[1 mark]**

> Count up the number of atoms of each element. Then write the symbols of each element next to each other. Now write the number that you counted as a subscript to the right of the symbol.

....

(b) Calculate the relative formula mass of ethane. (Relative atomic masses: C = 12, H = 1) **[1 mark]**

Relative formula mass of C_2H_6 = (2 × 12) + (6 × 1) = ...

(c) Determine the empirical formula of ethane. **[1 mark]**

> This is the smallest whole number ratio of elements in the compound.

....

2. The empirical formula of a hydrocarbon is C_2H_5. Its relative formula mass is 58. Show that its molecular formula is C_4H_{10}. **[3 marks]**

Relative formula mass of C_2H_5 = (2 × 12) + (5 × 1) = ...

Then divide 58 by this value ....

This shows that you need .... empirical formulae to make the molecular formula. So, the

molecular formula must be ....

⑩ Experimental determination of empirical formulae　　　　Grade 5

3. A student carried out an experiment to determine the empirical formula of magnesium oxide.

magnesium + oxygen → magnesium oxide

The student obtained the following results:

mass of magnesium reacted = 2.4 g　　　mass of magnesium oxide formed = 4.0 g

Describe an experimental method which could be used to collect these results. **[6 marks]**

> You should list the measurements that you will take as well as the main stages in the method. You might want to include a labelled diagram of the equipment.

....

....

....

> Continue on your own paper if you need more space.

 Made a start **Feeling confident** **Exam ready**

Balancing equations

② Quick quiz

Tick each correctly balanced equation.

$Na + Cl_2 \rightarrow NaCl$ ☐

$N_2 + 2H_2 \rightarrow 2NH_3$ ☐

$2Ca + O_2 \rightarrow 2CaO$ ☐

$CH_4 + 2O_2 \rightarrow CO_2 + 2H_2O$ ☐

⑩ Balancing equations   Grade 5

1. Complete the following chemical equations by balancing them.

> Remember in a chemical reaction, no atoms are created or destroyed they are just rearranged. So there must be the same number and type of atom on each side of the equation.

(a) $BaO + ..2..HCl \rightarrow BaCl_2 + H_2O$ **[1 mark]**

(b) $......Na + ...Br_2 \rightarrow ......NaBr$ **[1 mark]**

(c) $......Mg + ...CuSO_4 \rightarrow ......MgSO_4 + ...Cu$ **[1 mark]**

(d) $......Li + ...H_2O \rightarrow ......LiOH + ...H_2$ **[1 mark]**

(e) $.....Al_2O_3 \rightarrow .....Al + ...O_2$ **[1 mark]**

> $2H_2 + O_2 \rightarrow 2H_2O$
> $2 \times 2 = 4H \quad\quad 2 \times 2 = 4H$
> $1 \times 2 = 2O \quad\quad 2 \times 1 = 2O$
> It can help to write the number of atoms of each element underneath the equation.

⑩ Balancing symbol equations   Grade 5

2. Potassium is a very reactive metal.

(a) Potassium can react with oxygen in the air to make potassium oxide. Write the word equation for this reaction. **[1 mark]**

....

(b) Potassium can react with water (H_2O) to make potassium hydroxide (KOH) and hydrogen (H_2). Write a balanced chemical equation for this reaction. **[2 marks]**

....

(c) Potassium can react with chlorine to make potassium chloride. Write a balanced chemical equation for this reaction. **[3 marks]**

.... $\rightarrow$ KCl ....

3. Carbon is a non-metal found in Group 4 of the periodic table.

(a) Carbon can undergo incomplete combustion to make carbon monoxide and carbon dioxide. Write a word equation for this reaction. **[1 mark]**

....

(b) Carbon can be used to remove oxygen from metal compounds. Write a balanced chemical equation for the reaction between copper oxide (CuO) and carbon to make copper and carbon dioxide (CO_2). **[2 marks]**

....

(c) Carbon can react with oxygen in the air to make carbon dioxide. Write a balanced chemical equation for this reaction. **[2 marks]**

....

Conservation of mass

② Quick quiz

Which of the following reactions give off a gas? Tick all the correct answers.

Heating copper carbonate

Reacting sodium hydroxide and sulfuric acid

Reacting hydrochloric acid and magnesium

Reacting magnesium and oxygen

⑩ Changes in mass   Grade 5

1. Silver oxide, Ag_2O, decomposes when heated. Two products form, silver and oxygen, O_2.

(a) Write a balanced chemical equation for the reaction.   **[2 marks]**

$2Ag_2O \rightarrow \qquad Ag + \qquad O_2$

(b) When 6.22 g of silver oxide decomposes, 5.79 g of silver is produced. Calculate the expected mass of oxygen produced in the reaction.   **[1 mark]**

$6.22g - 5.79g =$ ....

expected mass of oxygen = ... g

(c) The actual mass of silver metal collected and weighed was less than the expected mass. Describe **one** step in the experiment that could lead to this observation.   **[1 mark]**

....

⑮ Mass changes   Grade 5

2. Magnesium will react with the oxygen in the air when it is heated. A student weighed some magnesium in a crucible, covered it with a lid and then heated it. The mass appeared to increase.

The results of the experiment are:

crucible + lid = 30.10 g   magnesium + crucible + lid = 30.34 g   magnesium oxide + crucible + lid = 30.50 g

Use the results to calculate the mass of magnesium, magnesium oxide and oxygen in the experiment.   **[2 marks]**

3. A teacher weighs a strip of copper, then heats it in a boiling tube containing iodine vapour. A layer of yellow-brown copper iodide forms on the surface of the copper. The teacher weighs the strip again.

(a) Write a word equation for the reaction that takes place.   **[1 mark]**

....

(b) Suggest an explanation for why the mass of the strip increases. Explain your answer.   **[2 marks]**

....

....

      Made a start   **Feeling confident**   **Exam ready**

Calculating masses in reactions

② Quick quiz

192 g of magnesium reacts with oxygen to produce 320 g of magnesium oxide. How much oxygen has been used?

132 g ☐   512 g ☐   128 g ☐   1.67 g ☐

⑩ Conservation of mass in reactions | **Grade 5** ✓

1. Two students investigated the reaction between solid calcium carbonate and dilute hydrochloric acid. Before they carried out the experiment, each student made a prediction about the results. They completed the experiment and noted the mass of the beaker at the start and end of the experiment.

   Student 1 wrote: When the reaction is finished, the mass of the products will be less than the mass of the reactants.

   Student 2 wrote: When the reaction is finished, the mass of the products will be equal to the mass of the reactants.

   (a) Justify each student's prediction. **[3 marks]**

   Student 1 The reaction produces a gas. ....

   ....

   Student 2 ....

   ....

   (b) Write a balanced chemical equation to show the reaction between calcium carbonate and hydrochloric acid. Include state symbols. **[3 marks]**

   $CaCO_3(s)$ + ... → $CaCl_2(aq)$ + ... + ...

   (c) Name the measuring instrument that the students would have used to measure the dependent variable. **[1 mark]**

   ....

⑩ Law of conservation of mass | **Grade 5** ✓

2. Give the meaning of the 'law of conservation of mass'. **[1 mark]**

   ....

3. Give the meaning of the term 'closed system'. **[1 mark]**

   ....

4. When heated, 50 g of calcium carbonate decomposes to form carbon dioxide and 28 g of solid calcium oxide.

   (a) Calculate the mass of carbon dioxide formed. **[1 mark]**

   mass = ... g

   (b) Give your answer to part **(a)** as a percentage of the mass of calcium carbonate. Give your answer to 2 significant figures. **[2 marks]**

   percentage = ... %

 Made a start   Feeling confident   Exam ready   97

Concentrations of solutions

② Quick quiz

Draw **one** line to link each variable to its unit.

concentration	dm^3
mass	g/dm^3
volume	g

⑩ Concentration calculations — Grade 3

1. The volume of a solution is $250\,cm^3$. Calculate this volume in dm^3. **[1 mark]**

$$\text{volume in } dm^3 = \frac{\text{volume in } cm^3}{1000} = \frac{250}{1000} = \text{......................} \ dm^3$$

> Remember that $1000\,cm^3 = 1\,dm^3$.

2. $3.7\,g$ of salt is dissolved in water to make $100\,cm^3$ of solution.

(a) Give the volume of this solution in dm^3. **[1 mark]**

Volume = ... dm^3

(b) Calculate the concentration of this solution. **[3 marks]**

$$\text{concentration in } g/dm^3 = \frac{\text{mass in } g}{\text{volume in } dm^3} = \text{......................}$$

concentration of solution = ... g/dm^3

⑩ Concentration and mass calculations — Grade 4

3. A student dissolves $2\,g$ of sugar in $50\,cm^3$ of water. Calculate the concentration of the solution made. **[3 marks]**

concentration of solution = ... g/dm^3

4. Calculate the mass of salt needed to make $125\,cm^3$ of a $4\,g/dm^3$ salt solution. **[3 marks]**

mass of salt = ... g

 Made a start   **Feeling confident**   **Exam ready**

States of matter

② Quick quiz

Fill in the gaps in the table about the states of matter.

State	Particle arrangement	Particle movement	Forces of attraction
solid	close together regular lattice arrangement		
liquid	close together random arrangement	move around each other	weak
gas		move around freely in all directions	

⑩ Changes of state and state symbols   Grade 5

1. Heating affects the arrangement, movement and energy of the particles when a solid melts.

(a) State what happens to the energy of the particles.   **[1 mark]**

....

(b) Describe what happens to the arrangement of the particles.   **[2 marks]**

The particles move further apart
....

....

(c) Describe what happens to the movement of the particles.   **[1 mark]**

....

2. Figure 1 shows particles of the same substance in three different states of matter.

(a) Complete the sentences. Use words from the box.   **[3 marks]**

gas   liquid   solid   slowly   quickly   two   all

Particles can only vibrate in fixed positions in a ....

In a gas, particles move .... in .... directions.

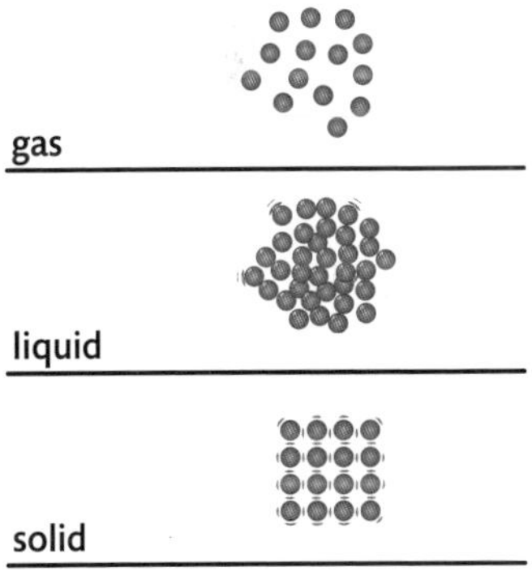

gas
_____

liquid
_____

solid
_____

cold

Figure 1

(b) Describe how the boiling points of different substances depend on the strength of the forces between their particles.
                    [2 marks]

As the strength of the forces increases, the boiling point
....

....

(c) Describe what happens to the movement and arrangement of the particles when the liquid is cooled until it changes into a solid.
                    [2 marks]

....

....

Pure substances

② Quick quiz

Circle the diagrams that represent pure substances.

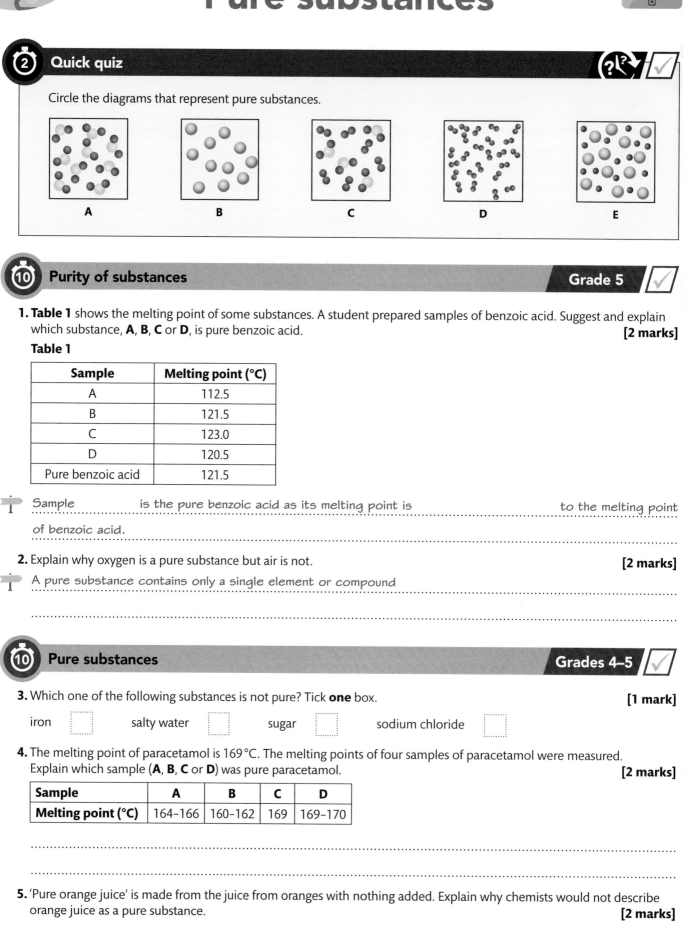

A   B   C   D   E

⑩ Purity of substances   Grade 5

1. Table 1 shows the melting point of some substances. A student prepared samples of benzoic acid. Suggest and explain which substance, **A**, **B**, **C** or **D**, is pure benzoic acid. **[2 marks]**

Table 1

Sample	Melting point (°C)
A	112.5
B	121.5
C	123.0
D	120.5
Pure benzoic acid	121.5

Sample .... is the pure benzoic acid as its melting point is .... to the melting point

of benzoic acid. ....

2. Explain why oxygen is a pure substance but air is not. **[2 marks]**

A pure substance contains only a single element or compound ....

....

⑩ Pure substances   Grades 4–5

3. Which one of the following substances is not pure? Tick **one** box. **[1 mark]**

iron ☐   salty water ☐   sugar ☐   sodium chloride ☐

4. The melting point of paracetamol is 169 °C. The melting points of four samples of paracetamol were measured. Explain which sample (**A**, **B**, **C** or **D**) was pure paracetamol. **[2 marks]**

Sample	A	B	C	D
Melting point (°C)	164–166	160–162	169	169–170

....

....

5. 'Pure orange juice' is made from the juice from oranges with nothing added. Explain why chemists would not describe orange juice as a pure substance. **[2 marks]**

....

....

 Made a start   **Feeling confident**   **Exam ready**

Mixtures

② Quick quiz

Draw lines to match the component in the mixture to the best technique used to separate it out.

coal from slurry
ethanol from a mixture of alcohols
water from coal slurry
salts from sea water
pure water from sea water
coloured substances from leaves, dissolved in ethanol

simple distillation
paper chromatography
filtration and drying
filtration
fractional distillation
crystallisation

⑩ Crystallisation · Grade 5

1. (a) State what is meant by the term 'mixture'. **[1 mark]**

A mixture consists of two or more ....

(b) Figure 1 shows common laboratory apparatus. A sample of pure dry crystals of copper sulfate can be made by reacting copper oxide and sulfuric acid. Describe the main steps in a laboratory method for a student to safely crystallise copper sulfate from its solution. **[6 marks]**

> The student has already made a solution of copper sulfate and has some unreacted copper oxide in the mixture.

To remove unreacted copper oxide the student should ....

....

> Then think about how to get the blue crystals of copper sulfate to form from the solution.

To get the copper sulfate solute from the solution the student should ....

....

> Finally, think about how you would dry the crystals.

The blue copper sulfate crystals can be removed and dried by ....

....

stirring rod · spatula · beaker · filter funnel and paper · evaporating basin

Bunsen burner · tripod, gauze and mat · conical flask

Figure 1

⑩ Separating mixtures · Grade 5

2. A student collects a bucket of sand and sea water from the beach.

(a) Explain how filtration can be used to separate the sand and other solids from the liquid. **[3 marks]**

....

....

(b) The liquid that the student separates is not pure. Give the experimental process that the student could use to make pure water. **[1 mark]**

....

 Made a start · Feeling confident · Exam ready

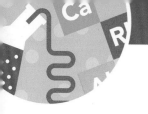

Chromatography

2 Quick quiz

True or false?

Under the same conditions, the R_f value of a substance is always the same. **True / False**

The paper used in chromatography is called the mobile phase. **True / False**

The smaller the R_f value, the more soluble the ink in the solvent. **True / False**

5 Chromatograms — Grade 5

1. **Figure 1** shows a chromatogram of different inks. The black ink is a mixture of blue, red and yellow substances. Complete **Figure 1** to show the chromatogram of this black ink. **[2 marks]**

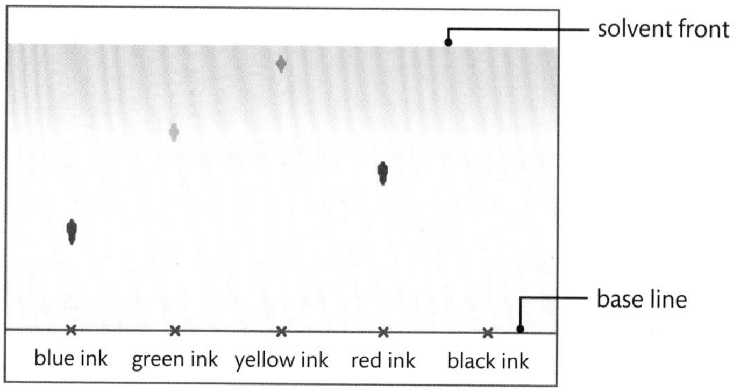
solvent front
base line
blue ink
green ink
yellow ink
red ink
black ink

Figure 1

5 Calculating R_f values — Grade 4

2. A student carried out chromatography on food colouring. The solvent front travelled 7.3 cm and the yellow food colouring travelled 3.7 cm. Calculate the R_f value for the food colouring. Use the formula below. Give your answer to 2 significant figures. **[3 marks]**

$$R_f = \frac{\text{distance moved by substance}}{\text{distance moved by solvent}}$$

$$R_f = \frac{3.7}{7.3}$$

=

R_f = ...

R_f values have no units. This is because both values used are distances and so their units will cancel out.

Maths skills

You need to know how to give answers to a stated number of significant figures (usually 1, 2 or 3 significant figures). To work out the number of significant figures, start at the first non-zero number, then count the number of figures you need to the right (including zeros). If the number after that is 5 or more, round up. If it is 4 or less, do not round up. For example, 2.13 rounds to 2.1 to 2 significant figures but 2.17 rounds to 2.2 to 2 significant figures.

10 Chromatography — Grade 5

3. Paper chromatography is an experimental technique that can be used to separate inks and dyes. Describe how paper chromatography works. **[4 marks]**

....

....

....

....

Remember that all types of chromatography rely upon two different phases.

Practical: Investigating inks

2 Quick quiz

Draw lines to match the terms with their definitions.

stationary phase	the level reached by the solvent
R_f value	the chromatography paper
mobile phase	the distance a substance travels relative to the solvent
solvent front	the liquid solvent

5 Preparing and analysing chromatograms — Grade 5

1. Give the steps a student would follow to prepare a chromatogram to separate the dyes in ink. Use the terms 'base line', 'mobile phase' and 'stationary phase'. **[4 marks]**

Step 1: Draw the base line using a ruler and ....

Step 2: Put small spots of ink ....

Step 3: ....

Step 4: ....

5 Using chromatograms — Grade 5

2. Figure 1 shows a chromatogram of ink samples from an original ink drawing and from a suspected forgery.

(a) Determine the number of coloured substances in the original green ink. **[1 mark]**

....

(b) Explain whether the suspected forgery was drawn with the same green ink. **[3 marks]**

The original green ink and the ink from the suspected forgery have a different ....

number of ....

One of the spots ....

So, the suspected forgery ....

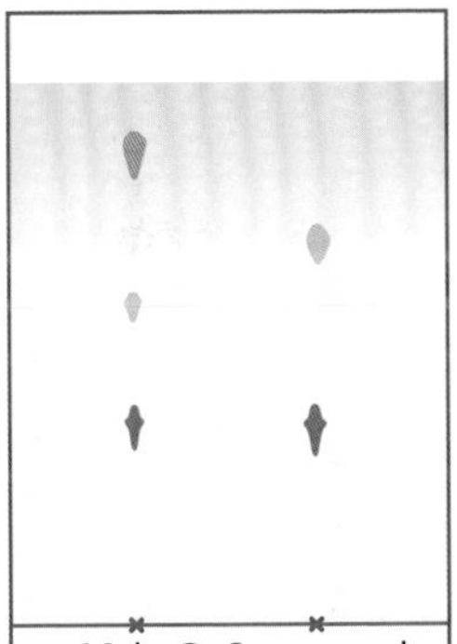

Figure 1

10 Analysis of chromatograms — Grade 5

3. A student carried out an investigation on a sample of red food colouring. They drew a base line on a piece of chromatography paper and placed a spot of the colouring on the line.

(a) State and explain what would be used to draw the base line. **[2 marks]**

....

....

(b) Describe the **two** measurements that the student would need to take to calculate the R_f values. **[2 marks]**

1 ....

2 ....

Potable water

② Quick quiz

(a) Give **two** sources of fresh water.

....

(b) Give **one** source of salty water.

....

⑩ Potable water   Grade 5

1. (a) State what is meant by the term 'potable'.   **[1 mark]**

....

(b) Describe how potable water is different from pure water.   **[1 mark]**

....

(c) Potable water can be produced from sea water by distillation.

Describe the **two** stages of the process of distillation in the production of potable water.   **[2 marks]**

1 The sea water is heated to ....

2 The water vapour is then ....

⑩ Making potable water   Grade 3

2. Figure 1 shows how fresh water can be treated to make it potable. Label steps **A, B** and **C** to complete the diagram. Use words from the box.   **[3 marks]**

sedimentation	chlorination	filtration

water in   pump   storage tank

| screening and coarse filtration | **A** | **B** | fine filtration | **C** | drinking water supply to homes |

Figure 1

3. Why is distillation a suitable method to make water suitable for use in analysis? Tick **one** box.   **[1 mark]**

The water must not contain dissolved salts. ☐

The water must be pure. ☐

The water must be potable. ☐

The water must be sterilised. ☐

 Made a start   Feeling confident   Exam ready

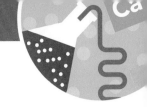

The pH scale and neutralisation

2 Quick quiz

Label the pH scale to show the acidic, alkaline and neutral sections.

0 1 2 3 4 5 6 7 8 9 10 11 12 13 14

10 pH and neutralisation — Grade 3

1. Describe what the pH scale represents. **[1 mark]**

It is a measure of the acidity

2. Table 1 shows the results of a student who measured the pH of different solutions.

Table 1

Solution	Baking soda	Vinegar	Shampoo	Battery acid	Tomato juice	Pure water
pH	8.3	2.6	7.5	1.0	4.5	7.0

(a) Identify the acidic solutions. **[3 marks]**

Battery acid,

(b) Identify the alkaline solutions. **[2 marks]**

5 Neutralisation — Grade 4

3. Aqueous solutions of acids and alkalis always contain certain ions.

(a) Complete **Table 2** to show the names and formulae of these ions. **[4 marks]**

Table 2

	Acidic solutions	**Alkaline solutions**
Name of ion	Hydrogen	
Formula of ion		OH^-

(b) Complete the equation to show how these ions react together during a neutralisation reaction. **[1 mark]**

.... + OH^- → ....

5 Estimating pH of solutions — Grade 3

4. Describe how to use universal indicator to measure the approximate pH of a solution. **[3 marks]**

Made a start | Feeling confident | Exam ready

Practical: pH change

② Quick quiz

True or false?

When acid is added to alkali the pH of the alkali solution falls.	**True / False**
Calcium oxide and hydrochloric acid react to produce calcium chloride and hydrogen.	**True / False**
A pH probe measures the pH more accurately than universal indicator paper.	**True / False**

⑤ Neutralisation   Grade 5

1. Complete the word equations for the following neutralisation reactions.

(a) calcium oxide + hydrochloric acid → .... + water .... **[1 mark]**

(b) calcium hydroxide + hydrochloric acid → .... + ... **[1 mark]**

> Remember that hydrochloric acid makes chlorides.

2. In a neutralisation reaction, acids and alkalis react with each other.

(a) Name the ion which is present in all acids. **[1 mark]**

....

(b) Name the ion which is present in all alkalis. **[1 mark]**

....

> Look at the formulae of these acids to help you: HCl, H_2SO_4, HNO_3.

⑮ Practical method   Grade 5

3. Which one of the following could be used to determine the pH of vinegar? Tick **one** box. **[1 mark]**

methyl orange ☐   pipette ☐   thermometer ☐   universal indicator solution ☐

4. In an experiment, a student put 25.0 cm³ hydrochloric acid solution into a beaker and measured the pH. The student then added 0.2 g of calcium hydroxide powder to the beaker, stirred the mixture and recorded the pH. She continued to add 0.2 g amounts of powder and measure the pH until a total of 2.4 g had been added.

(a) Name a suitable piece of apparatus used to measure out 25.0 cm³ of hydrochloric acid. **[1 mark]**

....

> **Exam focus**
> Make sure you are familiar with different measuring instruments which could be used to measure volumes. Pipettes and burettes are more accurate than measuring cylinders.

(b) Name the piece of apparatus used to measure out 0.2 g of calcium hydroxide powder. **[1 mark]**

....

(c) Write a word equation for this reaction. **[2 marks]**

....

(d) Predict what would happen to the pH of the solution in the beaker during the experiment. **[3 marks]**

....

....

....

 Made a start   **Feeling confident**   **Exam ready**

Salt production

② Quick quiz

Draw **one** line to match the name of the acid with the salt that it will make.

Acid	Salt
hydrochloric	sulfate
sulfuric	nitrate
nitric	chloride

⑩ Salt equations   Grade 5

1. Complete the word equations for the following neutralisation reactions.

(a) magnesium oxide + sulfuric acid → magnesium sulfate + ... **[1 mark]**

(b) magnesium hydroxide + sulfuric acid → .... + ... **[1 mark]**

(c) copper carbonate + nitric acid → .... + ... + carbon dioxide **[1 mark]**

> When metal carbonates react with acids, they make a salt, water and carbon dioxide gas.

(d) iron oxide + hydrochloric acid → .... **[1 mark]**

(e) zinc carbonate + hydrochloric acid → .... **[1 mark]**

2. When acids react with carbonates, carbon dioxide is formed. Describe the chemical test for carbon dioxide.   **[2 marks]**

....

....

⑮ Ions and neutralisation equations   Grades 4–5

3. Predict the name of the salt formed in the following reactions.

(a) sodium hydroxide + hydrochloric acid .... **[1 mark]**

(b) copper oxide + sulfuric acid .... **[1 mark]**

(c) zinc carbonate + nitric acid .... **[1 mark]**

4. Give the formulae of the ions in the following salts.

(a) magnesium chloride

positive ion: .... negative ion: ....   **[1 mark]**

(b) silver nitrate

positive ion: .... negative ion: ....   **[1 mark]**

5. Deduce the formula of the salt formed from the ions given below.
Name the salt.

(a) Ca^{2+} and Cl^- .... **[1 mark]**

(b) Pb^{2+} and Br^- .... **[1 mark]**

> Remember that the charges have to balance. So, you are going to need two chlorine ions for just one calcium ion.

Reactions of acids with metals

BBC

② **Quick quiz**

Name the gas produced when a metal reacts with an acid.

....

⑩ Redox reactions   Grade 5

1. When metals react with an acid, a salt and hydrogen are made.

   (a) Give the meaning of the term salt.   **[1 mark]**

   A salt is a compound made from
   ....

   (b) Complete the word equation for the reaction between magnesium and hydrochloric acid.   **[2 marks]**

   magnesium + hydrochloric acid → .... + ...

   (c) Name the acid that can be reacted with calcium to make calcium sulfate.   **[1 mark]** | Use the second part of the name of the salt to work out the name of the acid.
   ....

   (d) Give the formula of the gas made when zinc reacts with nitric acid.   **[1 mark]** | This should be a formula and not a name.
   ....

2. The balanced chemical equation for the reaction between magnesium and hydrochloric acid is:

   $$Mg(s) + 2HCl(aq) \rightarrow MgCl_2(aq) + H_2(g)$$

   (a) Name the salt which is produced in this reaction.   **[1 mark]** | The products are on the right hand side. The acid is hydrochloric so the salt will be a chloride.
   ....

   (b) Explain the observations you would see during this reaction.   **[2 marks]**

   Observation: Bubbles ....

   Reason: ....

⑩ Reactants and products   Grade 5

3. Nitric acid reacts with magnesium to form a salt and a gas.

   (a) Name the salt formed in this reaction.   **[1 mark]**

   ....

   (b) Which of these is the gas produced in this reaction? Tick **one** box.   **[1 mark]**

   carbon dioxide ☐   hydrogen ☐   oxygen ☐   nitrogen ☐

4. Zinc reacts with sulfuric acid (H_2SO_4) to form hydrogen gas and zinc sulfate ($ZnSO_4$).

   (a) Write the balanced chemical equation for this reaction.   **[2 marks]**

   ....

   (b) Describe the test to show that the gas produced is hydrogen.   **[2 marks]**

   ....

   ....

Soluble salts

② Quick quiz

True or false?

Soluble substances can dissolve in water.	**True / False**
Salts can be made by reacting an acid and a carbonate.	**True / False**
Copper reacts with dilute sulfuric acid.	**True / False**
Sodium hydroxide is a soluble base.	**True / False**

⑩ Choosing reactants   Grade 5

1. Soluble salts can be made by reacting an acid with an insoluble substance. Some insoluble substances cannot be used.

(a) Suggest and explain why potassium chloride should not be made by reacting the metal with hydrochloric acid.   **[1 mark]**

....

> Think about the reactivity series of metals.

(b) Suggest why silver cannot be used to make silver nitrate.   **[1 mark]**

....

2. A student makes magnesium sulfate solution using magnesium ribbon.

(a) Predict **two** observations that the student would see.   **[2 marks]**

The magnesium ribbon would become smaller or disappear, and
....

....

(b) Describe how the student could remove unreacted magnesium from the reaction mixture.   **[1 mark]**

....

⑩ Making soluble salts   Grade 4

3. Zinc chloride is a soluble salt. It can be made by reacting dilute hydrochloric acid with insoluble zinc hydroxide.

(a) Name **three** other solids that could be reacted with hydrochloric acid to make zinc chloride.   **[3 marks]**

1 ....

2 ....

3 ....

(b) Write a word equation for the reaction between hydrochloric acid and one of the substances you named in part **(a)**.
[1 mark]

....

Practical: Making salts

② Quick quiz

The diagram shows apparatus for making salts. Use the words in the box to label the equipment.

| tripod | filter funnel | beaker | evaporating dish | Bunsen burner |

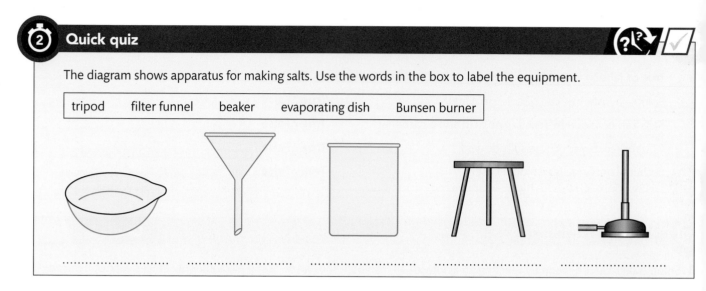

....

⑩ Making a salt   Grade 3

1. **Table 1** gives the steps for making a sample of pure, dry copper chloride crystals using dilute hydrochloric acid and insoluble copper carbonate.

   The statements are not in the correct order. Put the statements in order by writing a number in the second column of **Table 1**. The first step has been done for you.   **[5 marks]**

Table 1

Description of step	Step number
Add copper carbonate to the acid until no more reacts.	
Filter the mixture to remove the excess copper carbonate.	
Leave the filtrate to cool so that crystals form.	
Add dilute hydrochloric acid to a beaker.	1
Warm the acid gently in the beaker.	
Pat the crystals dry with filter paper.	
Heat the filtrate gently in an evaporating basin.	

⑩ Experimental methods   Grade 4

2. Devise a method to make pure, dry crystals of zinc nitrate from dilute nitric acid and solid zinc oxide. Use some of the apparatus from the box.   **[5 marks]**

| beaker | Bunsen burner | conical flask | evaporating basin |
| filter funnel | filter paper | gauze mat | stirring rod | tripod |

Warm some nitric acid gently in a beaker using a Bunsen burner. Add zinc oxide one spatula at a time
....

....

....

....

....

| You only need to describe essential steps in your answer. |

Titration

② Quick quiz

Methyl orange indicator is added to hydrochloric acid in a conical flask. What colour change happens when sodium hydroxide solution is added to the solution? Tick **one** box.

orange to yellow ☐   orange to red ☐   red to yellow ☐   yellow to red ☐

⑩ Titration method   Grade 5 ☑

1. A titration was used to prepare sodium chloride crystals from $25.0\,cm^3$ of sodium hydroxide solution. A few drops of phenolphthalein indicator and dilute hydrochloric acid were added until the indicator first changed colour permanently. The volume of acid added was recorded.

(a) Figure 1 shows the apparatus used to measure out $25.0\,cm^3$ of sodium hydroxide solution. Label the diagram.   **[3 marks]**

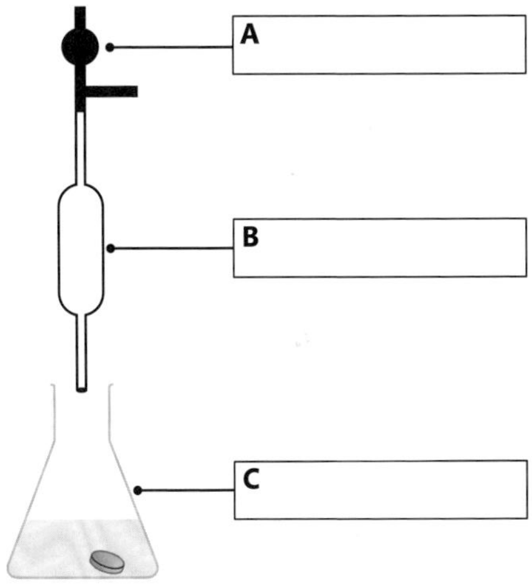

(b) Give a reason why the conical flask is placed on a white tile during the titration.   **[1 mark]**

....

(c) Name **one** other piece of measuring apparatus, not shown in **Figure 1**, which must be used in a titration.   **[1 mark]**

....

(d) State the colour change at the end point.   **[2 marks]**

From .... to ....

A ▢

B ▢

C ▢

Figure 1

Think about what type of substance is in the conical flask. Phenolphthalein is colourless in acidic solutions and pink in alkaline solutions.

⑩ Using a titration to prepare a salt   Grade 8 ☑

2. Potassium sulfate solution is formed by neutralising potassium hydroxide solution with dilute sulfuric acid. Pure crystals of potassium sulfate can be obtained from this solution. The volumes of potassium hydroxide solution and dilute sulfuric acid required to form the potassium sulfate solution must be found by titration.

Devise a method to prepare a solution of pure, dry potassium sulfate from potassium hydroxide solution and dilute sulfuric acid.

Use some of the apparatus from the box.

You need to complete a titration to find out the amount of acid needed. Then re-do the titration without an indicator, adding the volume of acid measured in the first titration. Then evaporate off the water to get a pure sample of the salt.

| pipette   burette   stand   boss and clamp   phenolphthalein indicator |
| white tile   crystallising dish   water bath |

[6 marks]

....

....

Remember that alkalis should be in the conical flask.

....

....

Sulfuric acid should be in the burette.

....

....

You can pat dry with absorbent paper, use a drying oven or leave the crystals out on a warm sunny window sill.

....

Solubility rules

② Quick quiz

The table below shows the solubility rules. Complete the table by putting a tick (✓) in the correct box to show if the substances are soluble.

Rule	Soluble (observation: dissolves in water)	Insoluble (observation: makes a precipitate)
All common sodium, potassium and ammonium salts		
Nitrates		
Common chlorides (except for silver chloride)		
Common sulfates (except for lead sulfate, barium sulfate and calcium sulfate)		
Common hydroxides (except for sodium, potassium and ammonium salts)		
Common carbonates (except for sodium, potassium and ammonium salts)		

⑮ Solubility rules   Grade 4

1. A student mixed an ammonium sulfate solution with a barium chloride solution. Two salts were formed, one was a precipitate and one was in the solution.

(a) Write the word equation for the reaction.   **[1 mark]**

.... + barium chloride → .... + barium sulfate

(b) Name the precipitate formed.   **[1 mark]**

....

> A precipitate is an insoluble solid formed in a reaction.

2. Write word equations for the precipitation reactions between the following solutions.

(a) potassium iodide and lead nitrate   **[2 marks]**

....

(b) sodium chloride and silver nitrate   **[2 marks]**

....

⑤ Precipitation reactions   Grade 5

3. Which of these salts is insoluble in water? Tick **one** box.   **[1 mark]**

calcium chloride ☐   lead chloride ☐   potassium sulfate ☐   sodium carbonate ☐

4. Solutions of potassium carbonate and zinc chloride are mixed. A precipitate of zinc carbonate and a solution of potassium chloride are formed. Describe how pure, dry zinc carbonate can be obtained from the mixture.   **[3 marks]**

....

....

....

 Made a start   **Feeling confident**   **Exam ready**

Electrolysis

2 Quick quiz

(a) Match each keyword to its description. Draw **one** line to link each term with its description.

electrode	using electricity to decompose a compound
electrolysis	a solid electrical conductor
electrolyte	a liquid or solution that can conduct electricity

(b) What are the charged particles in an electrolyte called? ....

5 The components of electrolysis — Grade 3

1. Give the names of these two electrodes:

(a) negative electrode .... **[1 mark]**

(b) positive electrode .... **[1 mark]**

2. What happens to the ions in an ionic compound when it is melted? **[1 mark]**

They become free to ....

Think about the movement of the particles in a liquid.

3. There must be an electricity supply, two electrodes and an electrolyte for electrolysis to work.

(a) Name **one** non-metal that can be used as an electrode. **[1 mark]**

....

(b) Give **two** ways that sodium chloride can become an electrolyte. **[2 marks]**

1 Dissolve it in water ....

2 ....

5 The process of electrolysis — Grade 4

4. Complete the sentences. Use words from the box. Words can be used more than once. **[4 marks]**

atoms	compounds	elements	ions	negative	positive

During electrolysis, ...positive...... ions move to the negative electrode.

Negative ions move to the .... electrode. .... are discharged at the electrodes, producing ....

10 An electrolysis experiment — Grade 4

5. Copper sulfate solution is an electrolyte. Describe a simple electrolysis experiment to show that copper ions are positively charged. **[4 marks]**

Your answer could include a diagram. Continue on your own paper if needed.

....

....

....

....

Electrolysis of molten ionic compounds

② Quick quiz

Complete the sentences by circling the correct words in **bold**.

Ionic compounds cannot conduct electricity when **solid / liquid / molten**.

When an ionic compound conducts electricity it is called **a metal / an ion / an electrolyte**.

In electrolysis, positive ions always travel to the **anode / cathode / electrolyte**.

In electrolysis, negative ions always travel to the **anode / cathode / electrolyte**.

⑩ Electrolysis of molten salts
Grade 5

1. Molten magnesium chloride can be electrolysed as shown in **Figure 1**.

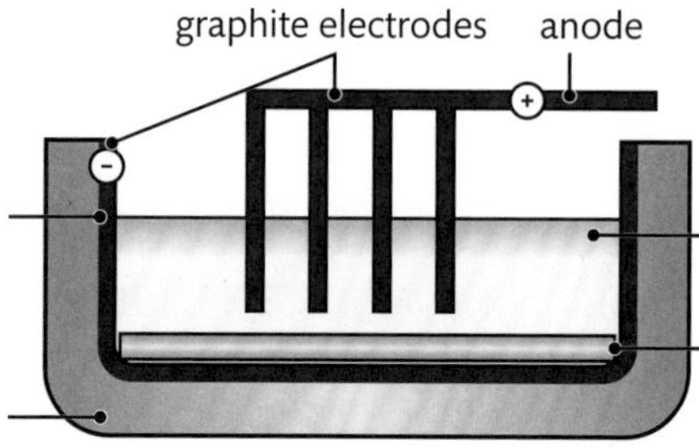

(a) Explain why magnesium metal forms at the negatively charged electrode (cathode). **[3 marks]**

> Magnesium ions have

....

....

....

....

....

Figure 1

graphite electrodes   anode
cathode
molten magnesium chloride
magnesium
steel case

Remember that the anode is the positive electrode. The cathode is the negative electrode.

(b) Name the product at the positively charged electrode. **[1 mark]**

....

⑩ Electrolysis and equations
Grade 4

2. Lead bromide can undergo electrolysis to form two elements.

(a) Name the electrode at which lead will form. **[1 mark]**

....

(b) Name the substance formed at the other electrode. **[1 mark]**

....

(c) Write a word equation for this reaction. **[2 marks]**

....

(d) Give **one** safety precaution used in this experiment. **[1 mark]**

....

 Made a start   **Feeling confident**   **Exam ready**

Electrolysis of aqueous solutions

② Quick quiz

(a) Name the positive electrode. ....

(b) Name the negative electrode. ....

(c) What is an electrolyte? ....

⑤ At the negative electrode   Grade 4

1. Table 1 shows a reactivity series of some metals, with hydrogen included.

Predict the products formed at the **negative electrode** during the electrolysis of the following aqueous solutions.

> Hydrogen is produced if the metal is more reactive than hydrogen.

(a) Sodium chloride .....hydrogen..................... **[1 mark]**

(b) Copper sulfate .... **[1 mark]**

(c) Magnesium bromide .... **[1 mark]**

(d) Silver nitrate .... **[1 mark]**

Table 1

potassium	Most reactive
sodium	
magnesium	
zinc	↓
hydrogen	
copper	
silver	Least reactive

⑤ At the positive electrode   Grade 4

2. Predict the products formed at the **positive electrode** during the electrolysis of the following aqueous solutions.

(a) Sodium chloride ...chlorine................... **[1 mark]**

(b) Copper sulfate .... **[1 mark]**

> Oxygen is produced unless the solution contains halide ions.

(c) Magnesium bromide .... **[1 mark]**

(d) Silver nitrate .... **[1 mark]**

⑤ Ions in solution   Grade 4

3. (a) A small proportion of water molecules, H_2O, break down to produce two types of ion.

Identify these two ions.   **[2 marks]**

Hydroxide ions ....

....

(b) Identify the ions that produce oxygen during the electrolysis of aqueous solutions.   **[1 mark]**

....

4. Predict the product formed at each electrode during the electrolysis of:

(a) sodium hydroxide solution .... **[1 mark]**

(b) potassium iodide solution .... **[1 mark]**

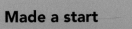 **Made a start**   **Feeling confident**   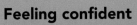 **Exam ready**   115

Practical: Electrolysis of copper sulfate

② Quick quiz

Label the diagram for the electrolysis of copper sulfate solution using the words in the box.

| anode |
| cathode |
| electrolyte |
| cell |

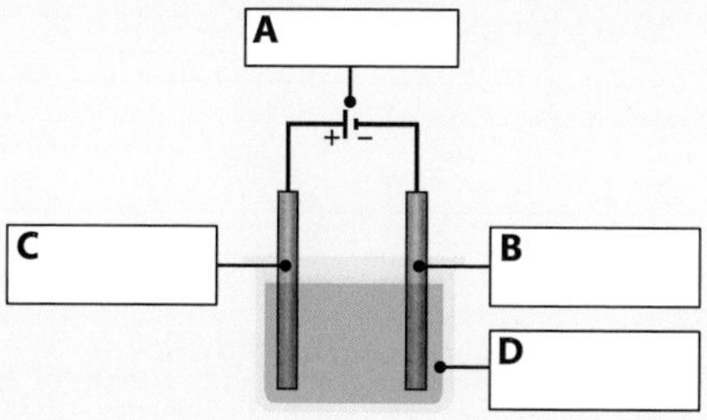

A

C

B

D

⑮ Electrolysis of copper sulfate — Grade 4

1. The diagram above shows how the electrolysis of copper sulfate solution can be carried out with inert electrodes.

(a) Name the substance made at the positive electrode. **[1 mark]**

....

(b) Give the symbol of the substance made at the negative electrode. **[1 mark]**

....

(c) Describe a method for the electrolysis of copper sulfate solution. **[4 marks]**

Inert electrodes are placed in the electrolyte, which is ....

....

....

....

(d) State what is meant by the term 'inert electrode'. **[1 mark]**

An electrode provides a surface for a reaction to happen on and does not have to react with the substances involved.

....

⑤ Purifying copper — Grade 5

2. Copper sulfate solution can undergo electrolysis with inert or copper electrodes. The products of these two electrolysis experiments will be different.

(a) Explain the difference between inert and copper electrodes. **[1 mark]**

....

(b) The electrolysis was carried out with inert electrodes. Name the substance produced at each inert electrode. **[2 marks]**

Cathode ....

Anode ....

 Made a start   Feeling confident   Exam ready

The reactivity series

② Quick quiz

Fill in the missing metals in each reactivity series using words from the box.

| copper   magnesium   sodium   iron |

potassium .... magnesium

calcium .... zinc

zinc .... copper

⑩ Ordering metals   Grades 4–5

1. A student investigated the reactions of three metals (**X**, **Y** and **Z**) with a dilute acid. **Table 1** shows the results.

(a) Identify the most reactive metal in **Table 1**. Give a reason for your answer. **[2 marks]**

➥ Metal Z because
....

....

Table 1

Metal	Reaction with a dilute acid
X	Slow bubbling
Y	No reaction
Z	Vigorous bubbling

(b) Deduce the order of decreasing reactivity of these metals. **[1 mark]**

....

(c) Identify the metal in **Table 1** that will most easily lose electrons to form positive ions. **[1 mark]**

> The reactivity of metals is related to how readily they lose electrons.

....

⑩ Metal reactions   Grade 5

2. A student investigates the reactions of three metals (**A**, **B** and **C**) with solutions of their salts. **Table 2** shows the results ('NC' means 'no visible change').

Table 2

Metal	A nitrate solution	B nitrate solution	C nitrate solution
A	NC	NC	NC
B	Black coating on metal	NC	Brown coating on metal
C	Brown coating on metal	NC	NC

(a) Determine the order of reactivity of the metals. **[1 mark]**

....

(b) Explain your answer to part **(a)**. **[3 marks]**

....

....

....

Extraction of metals and reduction

② Quick quiz

Place these metals in order of **decreasing** reactivity. Write **1** for the most reactive and **4** for the least reactive.

aluminium	copper	iron	gold

⑤ Ores
Grade 3

1. (a) State what is meant by the term 'ore'. **[2 marks]**

A naturally occurring rock that contains
....

(b) Some metals are found in the Earth as the metal itself. Name **one** of these metals. **[1 mark]**

| These metals are unreactive metals. |

....

⑤ The reactivity series
Grade 4

2. Table 1 shows a reactivity series with carbon included. Some metals can be extracted by heating their ores with carbon.

Table 1

Most reactive				Least reactive
potassium	magnesium	carbon	zinc	copper

(a) Identify **one** metal that can be extracted from its ore by heating with carbon. **[1 mark]**

....

(b) Give the symbol of **one** metal from the list above that cannot be extracted from its ore using carbon. **[1 mark]**

....

⑤ Extracting iron
Grades 4–5

3. Iron ore contains iron oxide. Iron is extracted by heating iron ore with carbon. Carbon dioxide is also produced in the reaction.

(a) Write a word equation for the reaction. **[1 mark]**

.... + carbon → iron + ...

(b) Give **one** reason why iron can be extracted from its ore by heating with carbon. **[1 mark]**

....

(c) Identify the substance that is oxidised and the substance that is reduced. Give reasons for your answers. **[2 marks]**

| Oxidation is gain of oxygen. |

Oxidised ....

Reduced ....

 Made a start   **Feeling confident**   ☑ **Exam ready**

Electrolysis to extract metals

 Quick quiz

Place these metals in order of decreasing reactivity. Write **1** for the most reactive and **4** for the least reactive.

iron	copper	potassium	zinc

 Electrolysis Grade 4

1. Some metals can be extracted by heating their ores with carbon. However, electrolysis must be used if the metal is more reactive than carbon. **Table 1** shows a reactivity series with carbon included.

Table 1

Most reactive				Least reactive
sodium	magnesium	carbon	iron	gold

Name **one** metal that must be extracted from its ore using electrolysis. **[1 mark]**

....

2. The ions in an electrolyte must be free to move for electrolysis to happen. Give the **two** ways an ionic compound can act as an electrolyte. **[2 marks]**

When the compound is dissolved in water and when it is
....

3. Aluminium is extracted by the electrolysis of a molten mixture of aluminium oxide and cryolite.

Table 2 shows the melting points of aluminium oxide and cryolite.

(a) Give **one** reason for using cryolite and not water as the solvent for this electrolysis. **[1 mark]**

Table 2

Compound	Melting point (°C)
Aluminium oxide	2072
Cryolite	1012

....

(b) Explain how using cryolite reduces the energy cost of extracting aluminium. **[2 marks]**

Cryolite melts at a lower temperature than aluminium oxide, so
....

....

 Extracting aluminium Grades 4–5

4. Aluminium is extracted by the electrolysis of a molten mixture of aluminium oxide and cryolite.
A lot of energy is needed to melt the compounds for electrolysis.

(a) Give **one** other reason why extracting aluminium using electrolysis is very expensive. **[1 mark]**

....

(b) Predict the product discharged at the anode during the extraction of aluminium. **[1 mark]**

....

(c) The anodes are made from carbon. Explain why the anodes must be replaced regularly. **[2 marks]**

....

....

 Made a start 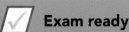 **Feeling confident** **Exam ready** **119**

Metal oxides

② Quick quiz

True or false?

Metal oxides have a high boiling point.	**True / False**
Metal oxides contain ionic bonding.	**True / False**
Metal oxides usually have a low melting point.	**True / False**

⑤ Naming oxides — Grade 3

1. Name the oxides produced in the following reactions:

(a) calcium reacting with oxygen _calcium oxide_ ....
[1 mark]

(b) iron wool burning in air ....
[1 mark]

(c) magnesium burning in air ....
[1 mark]

2. Name these compounds:

(a) PbO_2 _lead oxide_ .... **[1 mark]**

(b) ZnO .... **[1 mark]**

(c) Na_2O .... **[1 mark]**

(d) Al_2O_3 .... **[1 mark]**

⑤ Oxidation reactions — Grades 4–5

3. (a) Write a word equation for the reaction between aluminium and oxygen. **[1 mark]**

....

(b) Give a reason why this reaction is described as an 'oxidation reaction'. **[1 mark]**

In the reaction, aluminium gains
....

⑤ Identifying oxidation and reduction — Grade 5

4. When heated, copper oxide reacts with hydrogen: $CuO + H_2 \rightarrow Cu + H_2O$
Identify the substance that is reduced and the substance that is oxidised. Give reasons for your answer. **[2 marks]**

Copper oxide is reduced because it loses
....

Hydrogen is oxidised because it
....

⑤ Oxidation and reduction — Grade 5

5. Iron oxide can react with carbon in a chemical reaction. The word equation for this is:

iron oxide + carbon → iron + carbon dioxide

Explain which substance is oxidised and which substance is reduced. **[4 marks]**

....

....

....

....

 Made a start   **Feeling confident**   **Exam ready**

Recycling and life-cycle assessment

② Quick quiz

Give **three** factors that are considered in a life-cycle assessment (LCA) of a product.

....

⑩ Considerations for LCAs   Grade 5

1. Describe what is meant by a 'life-cycle assessment'.   **[2 marks]**

A life-cycle assessment assesses the impact of
....

....

2. Suggest **three** factors a company would consider for a life-cycle assessment when producing shopping bags.   **[3 marks]**

1 Energy used to extract
....

2 ....

3 ....

3. Shopping bags are often single use and made of plastic.

(a) Suggest an explanation for why re-using plastic bags could reduce the negative environmental impact of plastic bags.
[2 marks]

Using the plastic bag more times will reduce the amount of plastic bags needed to be made and
....

....

(b) Justify how recycling single use plastic bags may harm the environment more than re-using them.   **[3 marks]**

....

....

(c) Plastic bags that are thrown away can be burnt. Suggest and explain **one** way to make this process more environmentally friendly.   **[2 marks]**

....

....

⑩ Analysing LCA data   Grade 5

4. Table 1 compares the life-cycle assessments for the manufacture of two types of drinking cup.

Identify which cup is less damaging to the environment. Justify your answer using your knowledge and the data in **Table 1**. You should comment on the reuse, recycling and how it will be disposed of.   **[6 marks]**

Table 1

Type of cup	Plastic	Paper
Raw materials	Crude oil	Wood
Energy used (J)	12 000	21 000
Mass of CO_2 produced (g)	270	603

....

....

....

....

Continue on your own paper if you need more space.

....

✓ **Made a start**   ✓ **Feeling confident**   ✓ **Exam ready**   121

Reversible reactions

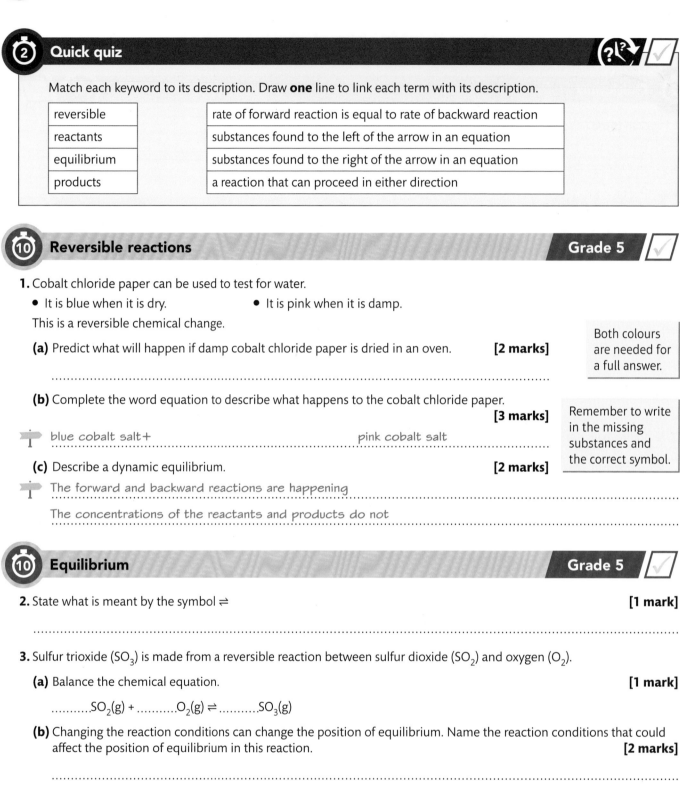

② Quick quiz

Match each keyword to its description. Draw **one** line to link each term with its description.

reversible	rate of forward reaction is equal to rate of backward reaction
reactants	substances found to the left of the arrow in an equation
equilibrium	substances found to the right of the arrow in an equation
products	a reaction that can proceed in either direction

⑩ Reversible reactions   Grade 5

1. Cobalt chloride paper can be used to test for water.

- It is blue when it is dry.
- It is pink when it is damp.

This is a reversible chemical change.

> Both colours are needed for a full answer.

(a) Predict what will happen if damp cobalt chloride paper is dried in an oven.   **[2 marks]**

....

(b) Complete the word equation to describe what happens to the cobalt chloride paper.

[3 marks]

> Remember to write in the missing substances and the correct symbol.

🚏 blue cobalt salt+ ....   pink cobalt salt ....

(c) Describe a dynamic equilibrium.   **[2 marks]**

🚏 The forward and backward reactions are happening ....

The concentrations of the reactants and products do not ....

⑩ Equilibrium   Grade 5

2. State what is meant by the symbol ⇌   **[1 mark]**

....

3. Sulfur trioxide (SO_3) is made from a reversible reaction between sulfur dioxide (SO_2) and oxygen (O_2).

(a) Balance the chemical equation.   **[1 mark]**

...........SO_2(g) + ...O_2(g) ⇌ ....SO_3(g)

(b) Changing the reaction conditions can change the position of equilibrium. Name the reaction conditions that could affect the position of equilibrium in this reaction.   **[2 marks]**

....

....

4. White anhydrous copper sulfate reacts with water in a reversible reaction. Blue hydrated copper sulfate forms.

(a) Write a word equation for this reaction.   **[2 marks]**

....

(b) Describe the observations that would be made if one drop of water was placed on the anhydrous copper sulfate.

[2 marks]

....

✓ **Made a start**   ✓ **Feeling confident**   ✓ **Exam ready**

Dynamic equilibrium and the Haber process

② Quick quiz

True or false?

The reaction goes to completion.	**True / False**
The rates of the forward and reverse reactions are equal.	**True / False**
The reaction mixture must be in a closed system.	**True / False**
There are always more product particles than reactant particles.	**True / False**

⑩ Dynamic equilibrium   Grades 3–4

1. The reaction between nitrogen and hydrogen in the Haber process is reversible and can reach a dynamic equilibrium.

(a) State what is meant by the term 'dynamic equilibrium'.   **[2 marks]**

➡ Dynamic equilibrium occurs in a closed system when the rate of the forward
....

....
The concentrations of the reactants and products
....

(b) Describe the **three** conditions for the Haber process.   **[3 marks]**

➡ Temperature of 450°C
....

....

(c) Give the name of the product from the Haber process.   **[1 mark]**

> You have been asked for a name – this is a word, not the formula of the product.

....

⑩ The Haber process   Grades 4–5

2. Figure 1 shows how nitrogen and hydrogen react in the Haber process to form ammonia.

(a) Name the **two** raw materials from which nitrogen and hydrogen are obtained.   **[2 marks]**

1 ....

2 ....

(b) Describe how the ammonia is removed from the reaction mixture.   **[3 marks]**

....

....

....

....

....

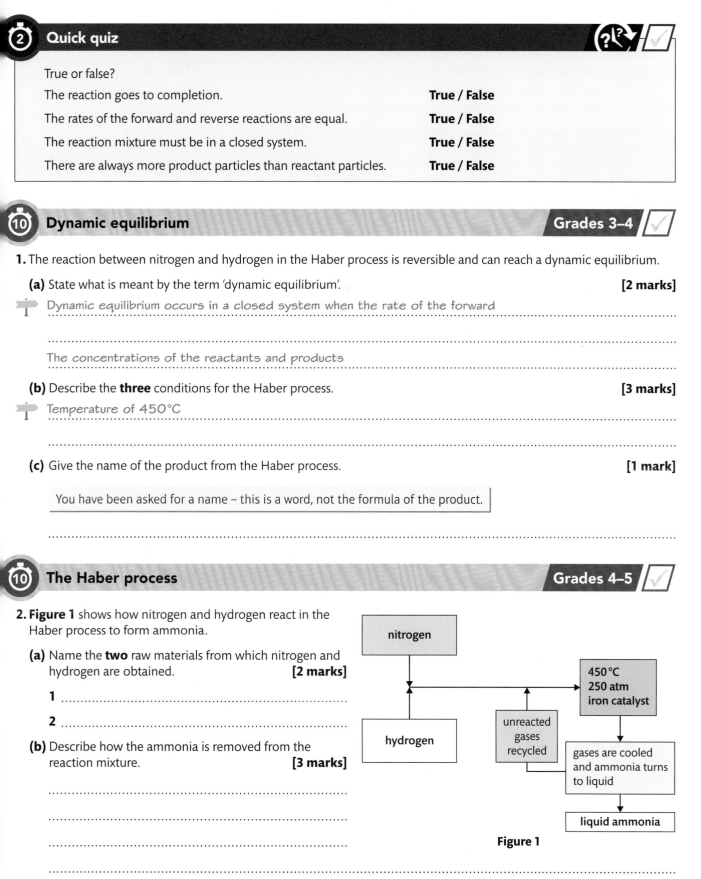

nitrogen

450°C
250 atm
iron catalyst

unreacted gases recycled

hydrogen

gases are cooled and ammonia turns to liquid

liquid ammonia

Figure 1

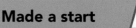 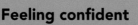

Group 1

② Quick quiz

True or false?

Group 1 elements float on the surface of the water.	**True / False**
Group 1 elements all produce an orange flame.	**True / False**
Group 1 elements fizz in water.	**True / False**
Group 1 elements all explode at the end of the reaction.	**True / False**
Universal indicator turns red when added to the solution after the reaction of Group 1 elements with water.	**True / False**

⑩ Reactions of Group 1 elements   Grades 3–4

1. When the Group 1 elements react with water, an alkaline solution and a gas are produced.

(a) Which **two** statements about the reactions of lithium, sodium and potassium with water are correct?   **[2 marks]**

They all sink in the water. ☐

They all produce an orange flame. ☐

They all fizz in the water. ☐

They all explode at the end of the reaction. ☐

The water turns universal indicator purple after all the reactions. ☐

(b) Write a word equation to show the reaction of potassium with water.   **[1 mark]**

potassium + water → potassium hydroxide + ...

2. Lithium reacts with oxygen to produce lithium oxide.

(a) Write a word equation for this reaction.   **[1 mark]**

....

(b) Give the colour of the flame that is seen during the reaction.   **[1 mark]**

....

> Group 1 metals burn with coloured flames, such as lilac, red or yellow–orange.

⑩ Pattern in reactivity of alkali metals   Grade 5

3. Alkali metals react with water and are found in Group 1 of the periodic table.

(a) State **two** properties of alkali metals.   **[2 marks]**

....

(b) Describe **two** observations that would be seen when a piece of sodium is dropped into a container of water.   **[2 marks]**

....

....

(c) Complete the chemical equation for the reaction of potassium with water by adding the state symbols.   **[1 mark]**

$2K$ .... + $2H_2O$ .... → $2KOH$ .... + H_2 ....

 Made a start   **Feeling confident**   **Exam ready**

Group 7

Circle the correct word of each pair in **bold**.

Group 7 elements have **low / high** melting and boiling points.

Group 7 elements are **metals / non-metals**.

The halogens are **good / poor** conductors of electricity.

Group 7 elements exist as **single atoms / molecules**.

⑩ **Properties of the halogens** Grade 4

1. Which row of **Table 1** shows the correct appearance and state of a halogen? **[1 mark]**

Table 1

	Halogen	Colour	State at room temperature
☐	Bromine	Red-brown	Gas
☐	Chlorine	Colourless	Gas
☐	Iodine	Grey	Solid
☐	Iodine	Brown	Liquid

Exam focus
The colour of substances are not usually something you can work out– spend time learning the colours of the halogens.

2. The halogens are elements that are found in Group 7 of the periodic table.

   (a) Give the number of electrons in the outer shell of the halogens. **[1 mark]**

   ....

   (b) Describe the chemical test for chlorine. **[3 marks]**

   The number of outer shell electrons are the same as the group number.

   ....

   ....

   (c) State and explain the trend in boiling point in the halogens. **[3 marks]**

   The boiling point increases as you go down the group
   ....

   ....

   ....

⑩ **Properties of Group 7** Grade 5

3. **(a)** Name a halogen that is a liquid at room temperature. **[1 mark]**

   ....

   (b) Give the formula of a halogen that is a solid at room temperature. **[1 mark]**

   ....

   (c) Name the halogen that makes damp blue litmus paper bleach. **[1 mark]**

   ....

   (d) Predict the state of astatine at room temperature (20 °C). **[1 mark]**

   ....

 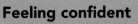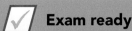

Group 7 reactivity

⑤ Quick quiz

Fill in the gaps using the correct words from the box.

seven	easier	electron configuration	fluorine	reactivity	one

The .... of a halogen depends on its .... All Group 7 elements

have .... outer electrons and gain .... more to make a full

outer shell. The .... it is for the atom to gain an electron, the more reactive it is. So, as

.... is the smallest atom it is the most attractive to electrons and so the most reactive halogen.

⑩ Displacement reactions　　　　　　　　　　　　　　　Grade 5

1. **Table 1** shows the results of an experiment. A student investigated the displacement reactions between halogens and aqueous solutions of their salts. The student placed a tick in **Table 1** if a reaction occurred, and a cross if no reaction took place.

Table 1

Halogen	Salt		
	Potassium chloride	**Potassium bromide**	**Potassium iodide**
chlorine	not done	✓	✓
bromine	✗	not done	✓
iodine	✗	✗	not done

(a) State what is meant by the term 'displacement reaction'.　　　　　　　　**[2 marks]**

➤　A more reactive element

....

....

(b) Deduce the most reactive halogen.　　　　　　　　　　　　　　　　　**[1 mark]**

> Look at **Table 1** and see which halogen has the most ticks.

....

(c) Give a reason why the student did not investigate the reaction between potassium chloride and chlorine.　**[1 mark]**

....

(d) Write a word equation for the reaction between potassium iodide and bromine.　**[2 marks]**

....

⑩ Properties of Group 7　　　　　　　　　　　　　　　　　　　Grade 4

2. Displacement reactions can happen when a more reactive halogen takes the place of a less reactive halogen in a compound. One displacement reaction is described by the following word equation:

sodium bromide + chlorine → sodium chloride + bromine

(a) Name the halogen that is a reactant.　　　　　　　　　　　　　　　　**[1 mark]**

....

(b) Give the formula of the halide ion that is the product.　　　　　　　　　**[1 mark]**

....

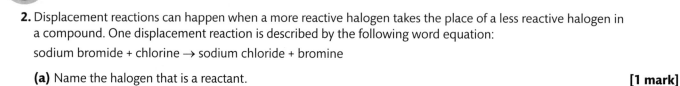

 Made a start　　 Feeling confident　　 Exam ready

Group 0

② Quick quiz

True or false?

The Group 0 gases are inert, or unreactive.	**True / False**
Helium is placed at the bottom of Group 0.	**True / False**
Neon exists as single atoms.	**True / False**
The size of the atoms increases down Group 0.	**True / False**
The noble gases all have 8 electrons in their outer shell.	**True / False**

⑤ Trends in properties of Group 0   Grade 5

1. Table 1 gives information about some of the noble gases.

Table 1

Noble gas	Relative atomic mass	Melting point in °C	Boiling point in °C
Helium	4	−272	−269
Neon	20	−248	−246
Argon	40	−189	
Krypton	84	−157	−153

Predict the melting and boiling point for argon. Write your answers in **Table 1**.   **[2 marks]**

⑩ Chemical properties of Group 0   Grade 5

2. The electronic configurations of neon and argon are 2.8 (neon) and 2.8.8 (argon).

(a) Describe what these two electronic configurations have in common.   **[2 marks]**

 They both have eight electrons in their outer shells, so they both have
....

....

(b) The electronic configuration of helium is 2. Give **one** way in which this differs from the electronic configurations of neon and argon.   **[1 mark]**

....

(c) Give **one** way in which the electronic configurations of helium, neon and argon are similar.   **[1 mark]**

....

⑩ Melting and boiling points   Grade 5

3. Table 2 gives the melting and boiling points of some of the noble gases.   **Table 2**

(a) Deduce approximate values for the melting and boiling points of neon.   **[2 marks]**

(b) State the trend in boiling point down the group.   **[1 mark]**

....

(c) Give **two** reasons why helium is used in balloons.   **[2 marks]**

Noble gas	Melting point (°C)	Boiling point (°C)
Helium	−272	−269
Neon		
Argon	−189	−186
Krypton	−157	−153

....

....

Calculating rate of reaction

② Quick quiz

Tick the boxes that show the correct units for rate of reaction.

mol/s ☐

mol^3/s^3 ☐

cm^3/s^3 ☐

cm^3/s ☐

⑤ Calculating rate   Grade 3

1. A student investigates the reaction between magnesium and dilute hydrochloric acid. 0.12 g of magnesium is put into a beaker of acid. It takes 50 s for the magnesium ribbon to completely disappear.

   Calculate the mean rate of this reaction. Give the units for rate in your answer.   **[2 marks]**

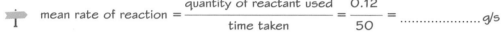

$$\text{mean rate of reaction} = \frac{\text{quantity of reactant used}}{\text{time taken}} = \frac{0.12}{50} = \text{.................... } g/s$$

⑩ Calculating rate   Grade 4

2. **Figure 1** shows the volume of gas released during a reaction.

   (a) Describe how you can tell that the reaction finished at 60 s.   **[1 mark]**

   Look at what the line on the graph does after 60 s.

   ....

   (b) Draw a tangent to the line at 10 s.   **[1 mark]**

   (c) The slope of the line changes as the reaction goes on.

   Explain what this means.   **[2 marks]**

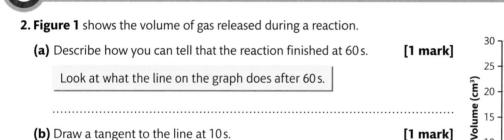

   The slope decreases, for example, from 10 s to the end of

   the reaction. This means that the rate

   ....

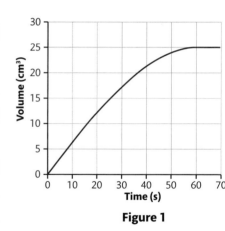

Figure 1

⑮ Interpreting rate graphs   Grades 4–5

3. **(a)** Calculate the mean rate of the reaction shown in **Figure 1**. Give the units for rate in your answer.   **[2 marks]**

   The total time of the reaction is from 0 s to when it ends at 60 s.

   (b) Draw a tangent to the line at 40 s on **Figure 1**.   **[1 mark]**

 Made a start   **Feeling confident**   **Exam ready**

Factors affecting rate of reaction

② Quick quiz

Write 'increase' or 'decrease' to complete these sentences.

An increase in the concentration of reactants will .... the rate of reaction.

Decreasing the pressure of reacting gases will .... the rate of reaction.

A catalyst will .... the rate of reaction.

Decreasing the surface area of reactants will .... the rate of reaction.

⑩ Factors affecting rate of reaction　　　　　　　　　　Grade 5

1. Give **two** reasons why the rate of reaction increases as the temperature increases.　　　**[2 marks]**

Particles collide more often and with more

....

....

2. Give a reason why a catalyst speeds up the rate of reaction.　　　**[1 mark]**

It reduces

....

⑩ Surface area and rate　　　　　　　　　　Grade 4

3. **Table 1** shows the results of an investigation into the reaction of marble chips and acid. The mass lost after 60 s is measured with different sized chips.

Table 1

Size of chips	Mass lost (g)
Small	2.1
Medium-sized	1.3
Large	0.5

(a) Explain what the results show about the rate of this reaction.　　　**[2 marks]**

....

....

(b) Identify the factor that changes as the size of the marble chips is changed.　　　**[1 mark]**

....

(c) Give **two** other ways to change the rate of this reaction.　　　**[2 marks]**

1 ....

2 ....

Practical: Monitoring rate of reaction – colour change

2 Quick quiz

List three ways which can be used to measure the rate of a reaction.

1 ....

2 ....

3 ....

5 Sodium thiosulfate and acid — Grade 5

1. Sodium thiosulfate solution reacts with dilute hydrochloric acid to make a pale yellow solid.

sodium thiosulfate + hydrochloric acid → sodium chloride + water + sulfur dioxide + sulfur

(a) Describe how the rate of reaction could be monitored. **[2 marks]**

....

> The products on the right of the arrow include a yellow precipitate of sulfur. How could this precipitate be used to monitor the reaction?

(b) Complete the symbol equation for the reaction. **[1 mark]**

$Na_2S_2O_3$ + ... HCl → ..... NaCl + H_2O + SO_2 .....

(c) State and explain one safety precaution you would take during this experiment. **[2 marks]**

....

....

> Look for a hazardous substance in the equation, then say what precaution you would take and why.

15 Changing the temperature — Grade 3

2. A student investigated the effect of changing the temperature on the rate of the reaction between sodium thiosulfate solution and hydrochloric acid. The time for a fixed amount of sulfur to be formed was measured. The experiment was repeated using hydrochloric acid at different temperatures.

(a) Use the words in the box to label the diagram **(Figure 2)**. **[3 marks]**

white tile	conical flask	thermometer

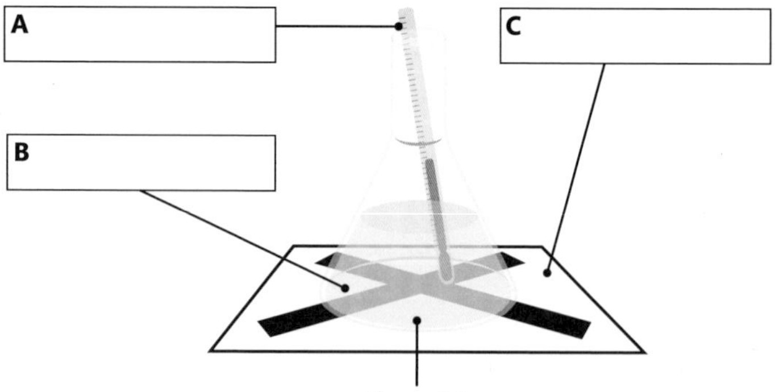

Figure 2

(b) Deduce the independent variable in this experiment. **[1 mark]**

....

(c) Name the piece of equipment used to measure the dependent variable. **[1 mark]**

....

(d) Give **one** variable which must be controlled to make the student's results valid. **[1 mark]**

....

Made a start | Feeling confident | Exam ready

Practical: Monitoring rate of reaction – gas production

② Quick quiz

Which of the following reactions can be monitored by collecting gas in a gas syringe?
Tick the correct answers.

magnesium + hydrochloric acid ☐   sodium hydroxide + hydrochloric acid ☐

calcium carbonate + hydrochloric acid ☐   copper sulfate + sodium hydroxide ☐

sodium thiosulfate + hydrochloric acid ☐   zinc + sulfuric acid ☐

⑩ Calcium carbonate and hydrochloric acid   Grade 4

1. A student measures the volume of carbon dioxide produced when calcium carbonate reacts with dilute hydrochloric acid. **Figure 1** shows the apparatus used.

   (a) Give the letter of the conical flask. .... [1 mark]

   (b) Give the letter of the delivery tube. .... [1 mark]

   (c) Name the equipment labelled as **A**. ....[1 mark]

   (d) Give a reason why the bung must be inserted immediately once the calcium carbonate is added to the acid.   [1 mark]

   ....

   ....

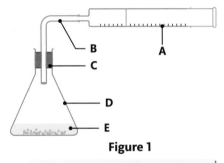

Figure 1

Think about what the student is recording in this experiment.

⑮ Measuring the rate of reaction   Grade 4

2. A student investigated the effect of concentration on the rate of reaction between excess dilute hydrochloric acid and magnesium ribbon. The volume of gas was collected every 30 seconds in a gas syringe.

   (a) Name the gas made in this reaction.   [1 mark]

   ....

   (b) Give **one** observation which would be seen in the conical flask.   [1 mark]

   ....

   (c) The surface area of the magnesium ribbon must be the same for every concentration that is investigated. Give **one** variable that must be controlled to make this a valid test.   [1 mark]

   ....

   Exam focus
   In a valid test only the independent variable is changed by the experimenter, in this case the concentration.

   (d) Describe how the student would know when the reaction was complete.   [1 mark]

   ....

Collision theory and activation energy

(5) Quick quiz

Draw a line to match an increase in each factor to the explanation of how it affects the rate of a reaction.

temperature	There are more particles present in the same volume and so a higher chance of collisions.
concentration	The volume in which the particles are located is reduced, therefore the particles are more likely to collide.
pressure	Particles have more energy and move faster, colliding more frequently.

(10) Activation energy
Grades 4–5

1. Figure 1 shows the results from an experiment in which an excess of calcium carbonate was added to dilute hydrochloric acid. A student investigated how the temperature of the acid affected the rate of reaction.

(a) A change in the reaction conditions causes a change in the rate of reaction. Complete **Table 1** by placing a tick in each correct box. **[3 marks]**

Table 1

Change in reaction condition	Reaction rate increased	Reaction rate decreased
Concentration decreased		
Surface area to volume ratio increased		
Temperature increased		

(b) Draw a second line on the graph to show the reaction at a higher temperature, but with all the other conditions unchanged. **[2 marks]**

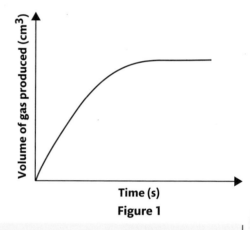
Figure 1

The reaction will be faster but the final volume of gas produced when the reaction ends will be the same because the same amounts of reactants are used.

(c) State and explain how reducing the temperature of the acid will affect the rate of reaction. **[4 marks]**

The rate of reaction will .... as the lower

temperature means that the particles have .... and they are

less likely to .... This means there are fewer successful collisions

in a given time and ....

(10) Factors affecting rate
Grade 5

2. Figure 1 shows how the rate of reaction between marble chips and acid changes over time.

(a) Describe how the rate of reaction changes in **Figure 1**. **[2 marks]**

....

....

(b) Explain why the rate of reaction changes during the investigation. **[3 marks]**

....

....

Made a start | Feeling confident | Exam ready

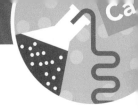

Reaction profiles

2 Quick quiz

The diagram shows a reaction profile for an exothermic reaction. Label it to show reactants, products, activation energy and the overall energy change.

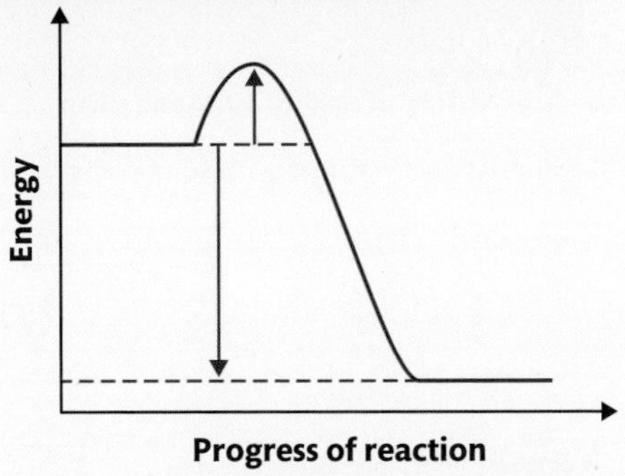

15 Reaction profiles — Grade 5

1. The reaction profile in **Figure 1** shows an exothermic reaction.

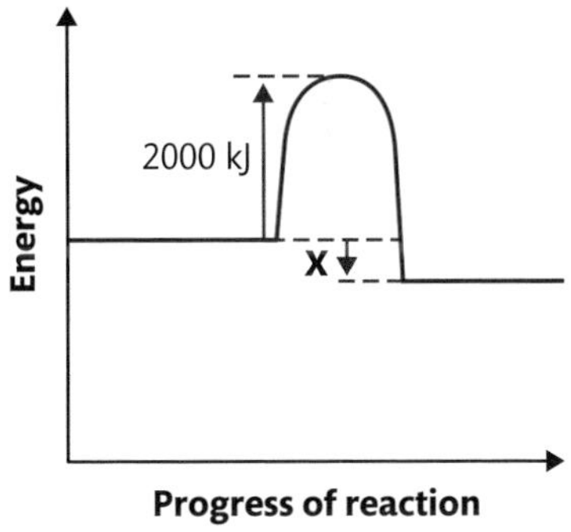

Figure 1

(a) State how you can tell from the diagram that the reaction is exothermic. **[1 mark]**

The products have less energy than ....

(b) Identify what is shown by **X**. **[1 mark]**

X is the overall ....

(c) State what is meant by the term 'activation energy'. **[1 mark]**

The minimum energy ....

5 Endothermic reaction profile — Grade 5

2. Draw a labelled reaction profile for an endothermic reaction. Use words from the box for your labels. **[3 marks]**

reactants	products	activation energy	overall energy change

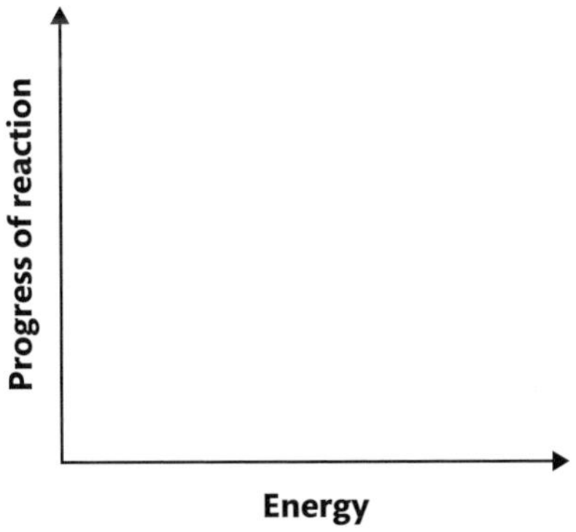

Exam focus

The number of marks indicates how much information is required. Marks will be awarded for drawing and correctly labelling the following:

- reactant(s) and product(s) labelled in their correct positions **[1]**
- correct placement of the energy of reactants compared with the energy of products **[1]**
- the activation energy **[1]**.

For an endothermic reaction the energy of the reactants will be lower than the energy of the products.

Catalysts

(2) Quick quiz

True or false?

A catalyst has no effect on a reaction. **True / False**

A catalyst permanently changes into a different substance in the reaction. **True / False**

The catalyst in the Haber process is iron. **True / False**

The mass of the catalyst present at the end of the experiment is less than at the start. **True / False**

(10) Properties of catalysts **Grade 5**

1. Catalysts are used to speed up many chemical reactions in industry.

(a) Explain how a catalyst increases the rate of reaction. **[4 marks]**

 Catalysts provide a different pathway for the reaction which has a lower activation energy. This means

there are more ....

(b) Name the catalyst used in the Haber process. .... **[1 mark]**

(5) Identifying catalysts **Grade 3**

2. A student adds manganese dioxide powder to hydrogen peroxide solution. The mixture starts to bubble rapidly. The word equation for the reaction is:

hydrogen peroxide → water + oxygen

(a) State what is meant by the term 'catalyst'. **[2 marks]**

 A substance that changes the rate of a chemical reaction but

....

....

(b) Give a reason why the word equation shows that manganese dioxide is a catalyst for this reaction. **[1 mark]**

> Think about the substances that the student mixes together.

....

(10) Reaction profiles and catalysts **Grade 5**

3. (a) Complete the reaction profile in **Figure 1** to show an exothermic reaction, using the labels in the box. **[3 marks]**

| reactants products activation energy overall energy change |

(b) Describe how the reaction profile would look different for the same reaction with a catalyst added. **[1 mark]**

....

(c) Explain why a catalyst makes the reaction happen more quickly. **[2 marks]**

....

....

Energy

Progress of reaction

Figure 1

Exothermic and endothermic reactions

Draw lines to link the statements to form two correct sentences.

| Endothermic reactions | give out heat energy | so temperature increases. |
| Exothermic reactions | take in heat energy | so temperature decreases. |

 Reactions involving energy changes — Grade 4

1. **Table 1** shows some different types of reaction. Complete **Table 1** by placing a tick in each row to show whether the reaction is exothermic or endothermic. **[3 marks]**

Table 1

Type of reaction	Exothermic	Endothermic
Combustion		
Electrolysis		✓
Neutralisation		
Oxidation		
Thermal decomposition		

2. Sherbet is a type of fizzy powdered sweet. It contains citric acid and sodium hydrogen-carbonate. These react together when the sherbet gets wet, making the mouth feel cold. State and explain the type of energy change in this reaction. **[1 mark]**

> Remember if temperature increases the reaction is exothermic. If temperature decreases, then the reaction is endothermic.

....

 Temperature change and data analysis — Grade 5

3. A student adds identical masses of four different powdered metals (**A**, **B**, **C** and **D**) to the same volume of dilute acid. **Table 2** shows the results.

Table 2

Metal	A	B	C	D
Starting temperature (°C)	21	21	22	22
Maximum temperature (°C)	38	26	59	34
Temperature change (°C)		5	37	

> Temperature change = start temperature – max temperature

(a) Complete **Table 2** to show the temperature change for metals **A** and **D**. **[2 marks]**

(b) Determine the order of reactivity of the metals, starting with the most reactive. **[1 mark]**

....

(c) Give a reason for your answer. **[1 mark]**

....

 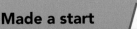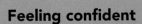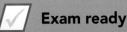

Temperature changes

(5) Quick quiz

Are these reactions exothermic or endothermic changes? Circle the correct answer.

Neutralisation	**Exothermic / Endothermic**
Metal displacement	**Exothermic / Endothermic**
Combustion	**Exothermic / Endothermic**
Photosynthesis	**Exothermic / Endothermic**
Dissolving sodium hydroxide	**Exothermic / Endothermic**

(15) Neutralisation data analysis — Grades 4–5

1. Figure 1 shows the apparatus used by a student to investigate the temperature changes in a neutralisation reaction.

(a) The student has tried to reduce the transfer of energy to the surroundings.

Give **two** ways in which the apparatus reduces heat losses from the reaction mixture. **[2 marks]**

1 There is an air gap between the polystyrene cup and the beaker.

2 ....

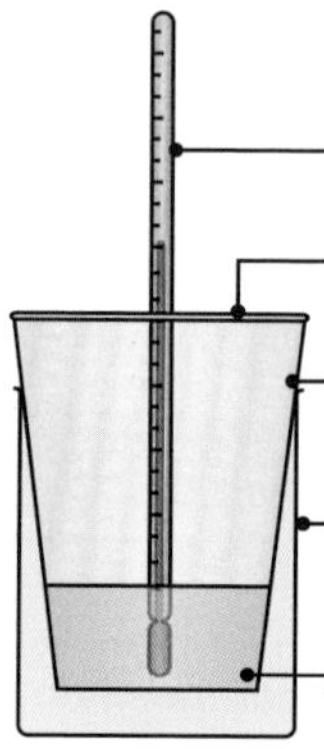

(b) Table 1 shows a student's results from an investigation where 50 cm³ of hydrochloric acid was added to 50 cm³ of sodium hydroxide solution.

Table 1

Concentration of sodium hydroxide (g/dm³)	0.5	1.0	1.5	2.0
Maximum temperature increase (°C)	2.0	3.8	5.4	6.8

thermometer
lid with hole
polystyrene cup
beaker for support
reaction mixture

Figure 1

(i) Identify **two** control variables in this experiment. **[2 marks]**

1 ....

2 ....

(ii) Describe what the results show. **[3 marks]**

....

....

....

> Remember to say in your answer whether the reaction is exothermic or endothermic.

(10) Experimental methods — Grade 4

2. Powdered zinc reacts with dilute hydrochloric acid. Design an experiment to show that this reaction is exothermic. Use the apparatus from the box. **[4 marks]**

beaker	polystyrene cup	thermometer	measuring cylinder

> You only need to describe essential steps in your answer.

....

....

....

....

Made a start | Feeling confident | Exam ready

Crude oil and hydrocarbons

1 Quick quiz

Draw **one** line to match each word to its definition.

alkane	family of molecules with the same general formula
homologous series	the simplest hydrocarbon molecule
methane	a series of molecules with general formula C_nH_{2n+2}

10 Crude oil   Grades 2–3

1. Most of the substances found in crude oil are hydrocarbons. Define the term 'hydrocarbon'. **[2 marks]**

A compound of ....

....

2. Crude oil will run out one day if we keep using it. Name the type of resource that crude oil is. **[1 mark]**

....

3. Most of the hydrocarbons in crude oil are alkanes.

(a) Complete **Table 1** to give the names of the first four alkanes. **[4 marks]**

Table 1

Number of carbon atoms	Name of alkane
1	methane
2	
3	
4	

(b) **Figure 1** shows the structure of one of these substances.

Give the molecular formula of the alkane in **Figure 1**. **[1 mark]**

....

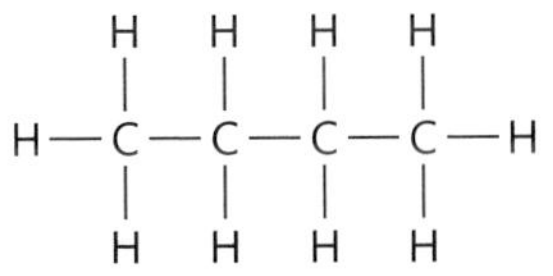

$$H-\overset{\overset{\displaystyle H}{|}}{\underset{\underset{\displaystyle H}{|}}{C}}-\overset{\overset{\displaystyle H}{|}}{\underset{\underset{\displaystyle H}{|}}{C}}-\overset{\overset{\displaystyle H}{|}}{\underset{\underset{\displaystyle H}{|}}{C}}-\overset{\overset{\displaystyle H}{|}}{\underset{\underset{\displaystyle H}{|}}{C}}-H$$

Figure 1

10 General formula of alkanes   Grade 5

4. (a) What is the general formula for the alkane homologous series? Tick **one** box. **[1 mark]**

C_nH_n ☐ C_nH_{n+2} ☐ C_nH_{2n} ☐ C_nH_{2n+2} ☐

(b) Write the molecular formula for:

   (i)   an alkane with two carbon atoms .... **[1 mark]**

   (ii) an alkane with six carbon atoms .... **[1 mark]**

(c) Explain why C_2H_5OH is not a hydrocarbon. **[2 marks]**

....

....

Fractional distillation

True or false?

Fractional distillation separates the components of crude oil by their melting points.	**True / False**
During fractional distillation the hydrocarbon compounds are evaporated.	**True / False**
The hydrocarbon compounds must be solidified before they can be collected from the column.	**True / False**
A hydrocarbon molecule contains carbon, hydrogen and other elements.	**True / False**

---

⑩ **Separating crude oil**   Grade 3

1. **(a) Figure 1** shows a fractionating column used to separate crude oil into useful mixtures called fractions. Label **Figure 1** to show where each of the missing fractions is collected.

   Use the words in the box.   **[2 marks]**

petrol	crude oil	bitumen

   (b) Give **one** use for bitumen.   **[1 mark]**

   ....

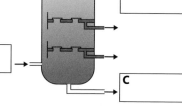

Figure 1

---

⑩ **The fractions**   Grades 3–5

2. Complete **Table 1** to give the names and uses of some of the fractions obtained in fractional distillation of crude oil.

                                                             [4 marks]

Table 1

Fraction	Use
Petrol	
	Fuel for aircraft
	Fuel for large ships
Bitumen	

> If you are asked about uses of crude oil you must say 'fuel for …' if the fraction is used as a fuel because just saying 'for cars' would not be enough for the mark.

3. **Table 2** gives the boiling points of three fractions.

Table 2

Fraction	Number of carbon atoms in molecule	Boiling point (°C)
Petrol	4–12	30–205
Kerosene	11–15	150–300
Diesel oil	14–20	200–350

(a) Describe how the molecules in a fraction are similar to each other.   **[1 mark]**

....

(b) Explain how **Table 2** shows that fractions are mixtures.   **[2 marks]**

....

....

✓ **Made a start**   ✓ **Feeling confident**   ✓ **Exam ready**

Properties of hydrocarbons

 Quick quiz

Circle the formulae of hydrocarbons.

C_3H_8 $C_5H_{11}OH$ $C_{12}H_{24}$ $C_{100}H_{202}$ $CH_3CH_2CH_3$ $CH_3CHCHCH_2Br$ CH_2CHCH_3

Combustion of hydrocarbons

1. **Figure 1** shows the apparatus used to investigate the products of complete combustion of hydrocarbons.

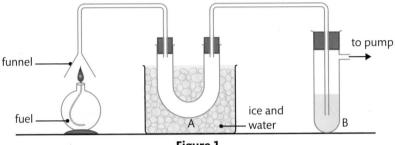

Figure 1

> **Exam focus**
> Learning the products of complete combustion of a hydrocarbon will enable you to write equations for combustion of hydrocarbon fuels.

(a) Name the products of complete combustion of a hydrocarbon. **[2 marks]**

....

(b) Describe changes that would be observed in the U-tube (tube A). **[1 mark]**

....

(c) Name the solution in the side-arm tube (tube B). **[1 mark]**

....

(d) Describe changes that would be observed in the solution. **[2 marks]**

The solution would change from colourless to ....

(e) If oxygen is limited, then incomplete combustion can happen with a hydrocarbon. Explain why combustion of a hydrocarbon in limited oxygen is dangerous. **[2 marks]**

....

....

Properties of hydrocarbons

2. The fractions from crude oil have different properties. These include viscosity and flammability.

(a) State what is meant by the term 'high viscosity'. .... **[1 mark]**

(b) State what is meant by the term 'high flammability'. .... **[1 mark]**

(c) Describe what happens to the viscosity and flammability as the size of the hydrocarbon molecule increases. **[2 marks]**

Viscosity ....

Flammability ....

Atmospheric pollutants

① Quick quiz

Draw **one** line to match each pollutant to its impact.

carbon dioxide		toxic gas
sulfur dioxide		acid rain
carbon monoxide		greenhouse effect

⑩ Producing pollutants
Grades 3–4

1. Complete combustion happens when a fuel burns in a good supply of oxygen.

(a) Complete the word equation for the complete combustion of a hydrocarbon fuel. **[2 marks]**

hydrocarbon + oxygen → .... + water

....

(b) Incomplete combustion happens in a limited supply of air.

(i) Name the gas produced during incomplete combustion that is not produced during complete combustion. **[1 mark]** | It is an oxide of carbon.

....

(ii) Name a solid product formed during incomplete combustion of a hydrocarbon fuel. **[1 mark]** | This is black in colour.

....

2. Fuels such as coal, oil and natural gas may contain some sulfur. The sulfur is present as a natural impurity. Write a word equation for the reaction between sulfur and oxygen. **[2 marks]**

....

3. Air is mainly a mixture of nitrogen and oxygen. These two gases react together in hot engines and furnaces to produce oxides of nitrogen.

(a) Write a word equation for the reaction that produces oxides of nitrogen. **[1 mark]**

....

(b) Oxides of nitrogen can cause respiratory problems. Give **one** other environmental problem caused by oxides of nitrogen. **[1 mark]**

....

⑤ Pollution problems
Grade 3

4. Why is carbon monoxide not easily detected? Tick **one** box. **[1 mark]**

It is colourful and has a smell. ☐

It is colourful and does not have a smell. ☐

It is colourless and has a smell. ☐

It is colourless and does not have a smell. ☐

5. Describe the problem caused by soot in an appliance. **[1 mark]**

....

 Made a start   Feeling confident   ☑ Exam ready

Comparing fuels

(2) Quick quiz

Sort the following resources according to whether they are renewable or non-renewable.

| coal | vegetable oil | diesel oil | natural gas | petrol | wood |

Renewable	Non-renewable

(10) Hydrogen as a fuel — Grade 4

1. Natural gas is mainly methane. Hydrogen is produced by reacting natural gas with steam. Hydrogen can also be obtained by electrolysis of water.

(a) Complete the balanced equation for the reaction of methane with steam to produce carbon monoxide and hydrogen. **[2 marks]**

$CH_4(g) + H_2O(g) \rightarrow CO(g) + \underline{\hspace{2cm}}(g)$

(b) Hydrogen can be produced by the reaction of natural gas with steam. Identify whether hydrogen produced this way is a renewable or non-renewable fuel. **[1 mark]**

(c) State a disadvantage of using hydrogen as a fuel in cars. **[2 marks]**

Hydrogen is flammable and so

(10) Renewable fuels — Grades 3–4

2. Energy resources that can be replaced are: **[1 mark]**

finite ☐

non-renewable ☐

saturated ☐

renewable ☐

3. Ethanol can be produced from sugar beet. Give **one** advantage and **one** disadvantage of using ethanol in car engines. **[2 marks]**

Advantage ....

Disadvantage ....

Cracking and alkenes

② Quick quiz

Name the **two** types of cracking: .... and ....

Name the homologous series that is made from cracking: ....

⑩ Cracking — Grades 3–4

1. Which statement correctly describes what happens during cracking? **[1 mark]**

Small hydrocarbons are joined together to form larger more useful molecules. ☐

Small hydrocarbons are joined together to form larger less useful molecules. ☐

Large hydrocarbons are broken down to form smaller less useful molecules. ☐

Large hydrocarbons are broken down to form smaller more useful molecules. ☐

2. Complete the sentences about why cracking is needed. Use words from the box. **[4 marks]**

| cracking | ending | high | large | low | small | starting |

There is a ....high........... demand for fuels that contain .... molecules. Some of the

products of .... are useful as these fuels. They are also useful as .... materials for making other substances such as polymers.

3. Complete the equations to show the cracking of hydrocarbons.

(a) $C_8H_{18} \rightarrow C_4H_{10} + C_4H$.............. **[1 mark]**　　**(c)** ....$\rightarrow C_3H_8 + C_2H_4$ **[1 mark]**

(b) $C_{10}H_{22} \rightarrow C_8H_{18} +$ .... **[1 mark]**　　**(d)** $C_4H_{10} \rightarrow$ .... $+ C_3H_6$ **[1 mark]**

> Make sure the numbers of C and H atoms are the same on both sides of the arrow.

⑩ Crude oil — Grade 5

4. Table 1 has information about supply and demand of fractions in crude oil.

Table 1

| Fractions | Approximate % | |
	Typical supply from crude oil	Global demand
Gases	2	4
Petrol	16	27
Kerosene	13	8
Diesel	19	23
Fuel oil and bitumen	50	38

(a) Give the name of a fraction where supply is greater than demand. **[1 mark]**

....

(b) State which fraction contains small hydrocarbon molecules. **[1 mark]**

....

(c) State the process that is used to make more of the fractions where demand is greater than supply. **[1 mark]**

....

☐ **Made a start**　　☐ **Feeling confident**　　☐ **Exam ready**

Earth's early atmosphere

② Quick quiz

Complete the table to show whether the percentage of each gas in the Earth's atmosphere has **increased** or **decreased** over time.

Gas	% in early atmosphere	% in atmosphere today	Change
Nitrogen	3.50	80	
Oxygen	0.50	20	
Carbon dioxide	95	0.04	

⑩ Changes in Earth's atmosphere   Grades 3–5

1. Which of the following is the reason why evidence for the early atmosphere is limited? Tick **one** box.   **[1 mark]**

Scientists cannot analyse gases in the atmosphere. ☐

The Earth formed over four billion years ago. ☐

Scientists have no interest in the early atmosphere. ☐

The Earth's atmosphere has changed very little. ☐

2. Where do scientists suggest the Earth's early atmosphere came from? Tick **one** box.   **[1 mark]**

photosynthesis by plants and algae ☐

the oceans when they boiled ☐

the Earth's inner core ☐

volcanic activity ☐

3. Describe how the oceans formed.   **[2 marks]**

As the Earth cooled, ...

....

4. The Earth's early atmosphere contained small proportions of compounds that contained hydrogen atoms. These included CH_4 and NH_3. Name these two gases.   **[2 marks]**

CH_4 .... NH_3 ....

5. Nitrogen gradually built up in the atmosphere over millions of years. Give a reason why it did not form compounds with other elements.   **[1 mark]**

....

⑩ Changes over time   Grade 4

6. **Table 1** shows the composition of the atmosphere of Mars today.

Table 1

Gas	nitrogen	oxygen	carbon dioxide	other gases
% in atmosphere	2.7	0.13	95.3	1.87

Describe **three** differences between the atmospheres of Mars and Earth today.   **[3 marks]**

....

....

....

Oxygen and carbon dioxide levels

1 Quick quiz

True or false?

Carbon dioxide is made during photosynthesis. **True / False**

Oxygen is made during photosynthesis. **True / False**

Carbon dioxide is a greenhouse gas. **True / False**

Oxygen causes climate change. **True / False**

10 Changes in oxygen levels — Grade 5

1. Figure 1 shows how the level of oxygen in the Earth's atmosphere has changed over time.

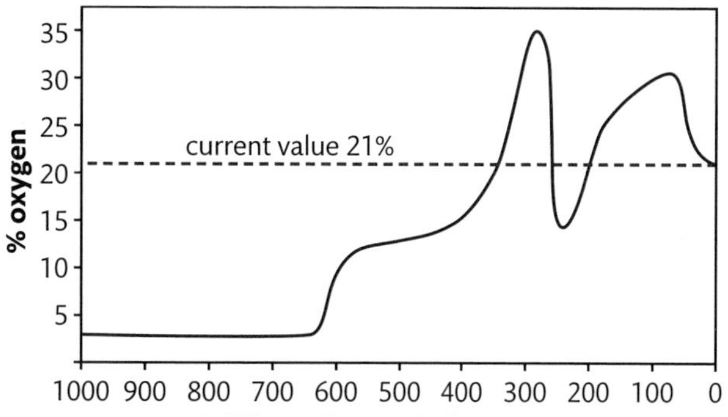

Figure 1

Remember that the *x*-axis is the independent variable – and you choose this. The *y*-axis is what is measured during the investigation and is the dependent variable.

(a) Determine the maximum percentage of oxygen in the Earth's atmosphere over the last billion years. **[1 mark]**

.... %

(b) Explain the overall change in the level of oxygen shown in **Figure 1**. **[2 marks]**

Primitive plants carried out ....

....

2. Write a word equation for photosynthesis. **[1 mark]**

carbon dioxide + ... → glucose + ...

5 Earth's atmosphere today — Grade 3

3. Name the **two** gases that make up most of the Earth's atmosphere today. **[2 marks]**

1 ....

2 ....

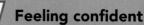

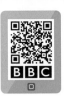

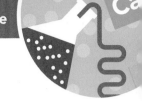

Gases in the atmosphere

2 Quick quiz

(a) Name a relatively unreactive atmospheric gas that is not a noble gas. ....

(b) What gas in the atmosphere is needed for combustion? ....

(c) Which gases in the atmosphere contribute to global warming? .... and ....

5 Percentages of gases — Grade 5

1. Table 1 shows the approximate percentage of gases in today's atmosphere.

Table 1

Gas	oxygen	nitrogen	other gases
% in atmosphere	20	80	<1

Calculate the fraction of the Earth's atmosphere that is nitrogen. Give your answer as the simplest fraction possible. **[1 mark]**

$\frac{80}{100} =$

....

2. Describe the chemical test for oxygen gas. **[2 marks]**

....

15 Gas proportions — Grade 5

3. Nitrogen and oxygen make up most of the dry air in the Earth's atmosphere. There are other very small amounts of gases such as 0.04% carbon dioxide and 0.96% argon.

(a) Calculate the ratio of carbon dioxide to argon in the atmosphere. **[2 marks]**

ratio of carbon dioxide to argon = ...

(b) Give the percentage of argon in dry air to 1 decimal place. **[1 mark]**

....

4. Scientists estimate that there was 95% carbon dioxide in the Earth's early atmosphere. Today there is about 0.04% in the atmosphere.

(a) Calculate the difference between these two values. **[1 mark]**

Difference between early atmosphere and today = ...%

(b) Determine, using your answer in **(a)**, the percentage change from the original carbon dioxide content. **[2 marks]**

percentage change = ...%

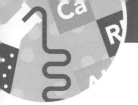

Greenhouse gases

5 Quick quiz

Fill in the gaps using the words in the box.

greenhouse gases	infrared radiation	climate change	warm	carbon dioxide

.... is one of several ....; so called because they trap .... as it is reflected by the Earth's surface. This trapped energy is causing the Earth's surface to .... and leading to ....

12 Greenhouse gases — Grades 3–4

1. Table 1 shows the names and formulae of gases found in the atmosphere.

Table 1

Name of gas	Formula	Number of atoms	Number of elements
carbon dioxide	CO_2	3	2
nitrogen	N_2		
oxygen	O_2		
water vapour	H_2O		

Remember that atoms make up elements. Elements are listed on the periodic table.

(a) Complete **Table 1** to show the number of atoms and elements in a molecule of each substance. **[4 marks]**

(b) A gas can act as a greenhouse gas if its molecules contain two or more different elements.

(i) Name **one** gas in **Table 1** that can act as a greenhouse gas. **[1 mark]**

....

(ii) Name **one** gas in **Table 1** that does **not** act as a greenhouse gas. **[1 mark]**

....

5 The greenhouse effect — Grade 4

2. Complete the sentences about the greenhouse effect. Use words from the box. **[5 marks]**

absorb	atmosphere	emit	infrared	Sun	surface	ultraviolet

Solar energy such as visible light and ....ultraviolet.... light reaches the Earth's surface from the ....

The Earth's .... warms up as it absorbs solar energy. The warm surface emits .... radiation.

Greenhouse gases absorb and re-emit this radiation, warming the Earth's ....

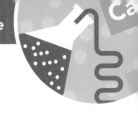

Human contribution to greenhouse gases

2 Quick quiz

Name **two** human activities that increase the amounts of greenhouse gases in the atmosphere.

....

15 Human effect on greenhouse gases — Grade 5

1. (a) Give **two** human activities that are causing an increase in the levels of methane in the atmosphere. **[2 marks]**

1 Livestock farming ....

2 ....

(b) State and explain **one** human activity that contributes to the production of the greenhouse gas carbon dioxide. **[2 marks]**

Combustion of ....

....

You need to give both the human activity and an explanation of how it contributes to the production of carbon dioxide.

5 Predicting climate change — Grade 4

2. The concentration of carbon dioxide in the atmosphere was 302 parts per million in 1918. It was 412 parts per million, one hundred years later, in 2018.

(a) Calculate the increase in the concentration of carbon dioxide between 1918 and 2018. **[1 mark]**

increase in concentration of carbon dioxide = ... parts per million

(b) Calculate the mean change in concentration per year. Use your answer to part **(a)**. **[2 marks]**

mean change in concentration per year = ... parts per million

(c) Which of the following processes takes in carbon dioxide from the atmosphere? Tick **one** box. **[1 mark]**

- respiration ☐
- photosynthesis ☐
- combustion of fossil fuels ☐
- decaying of dead plants ☐

Global climate change

① Quick quiz

True or false?

Climate change is causing sea levels to rise.	**True / False**
Climate change alters the types of crop plants that farmers can grow.	**True / False**
Climate change has no effect on habitats.	**True / False**

⑩ Global climate change issues   Grade 5

1. Global climate change is affecting sea levels. Describe the environmental, social and economic issues caused by changing sea levels. **[6 marks]**

Environmental – as sea levels rise, habitats will be lost, causing

....

Social – rising sea levels will cause erosion of

....

Economic –

....

....

2. Describe a method for reducing the amount of carbon dioxide in the atmosphere. **[1 mark]**

....

⑩ Data processing   Grade 5

3. Figure 1 shows how average global temperature has changed over the 135 years from 1880 to 2015.

(a) Identify the average global temperature in 1960. **[1 mark]**

....

(b) Determine how much the average global temperature rose:

  (i) from 1880 to 1940. **[1 mark]**

....

....

  (ii) from 1960 to 2000. **[1 mark]**

Figure 1 — Global 5-year average temperature (°C) vs Year (1880–2015)

Figure 1

(c) The change in average global temperature is driving global climate change and altering weather patterns. Give **two** ways in which weather patterns are changing around the world. **[2 marks]**

1 ....

2 ....

 Made a start   **Feeling confident**   **Exam ready**

Key concepts in Physics

② Quantities and their units

Draw lines to match each unit to its quantity.

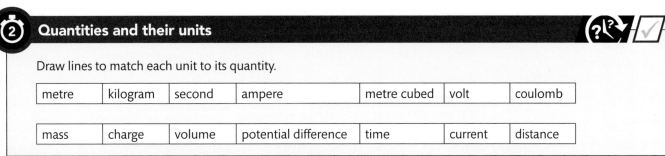

metre	kilogram	second	ampere	metre cubed	volt	coulomb

mass	charge	volume	potential difference	time	current	distance

② Prefixes

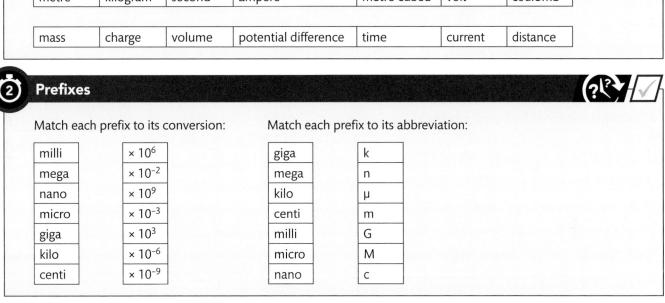

Match each prefix to its conversion:

milli	$\times 10^6$
mega	$\times 10^{-2}$
nano	$\times 10^9$
micro	$\times 10^{-3}$
giga	$\times 10^3$
kilo	$\times 10^{-6}$
centi	$\times 10^{-9}$

Match each prefix to its abbreviation:

giga	k
mega	n
kilo	µ
centi	m
milli	G
micro	M
nano	c

② Conversions and time

1. What is 2.3 nm in m? ....

2. What is 0.0048 kg in g? ....

3. What is 400 MV in V? ....

4. What is 150 000 J in MJ? ....

5. What is 0.0027 A in mA? ....

6. What is 0.00004 s in µs? ....

7. What is 180 cm in m? ....

8. True or false?

30 minutes is 180 seconds	**True / False**
2 hours is 180 minutes	**True / False**
24 hours is 86 400 seconds	**True / False**
32 400 seconds is 9 hours	**True / False**

② Calculations

Show your working for each question.

1. A woman has a mass of 160 pounds. 1 kg = 2.205 pounds. Calculate her mass in kilograms. Give your answer to 2 significant figures.

....

2. The radius of the Earth is 6370 km. Calculate the diameter of the Earth in metres. Give your answer in standard form.

....

3. Light travels through space at 300 000 km/s. Calculate the speed of light in m/s. Give your answer in standard form.

....

4. The circumference of the Sun is 4 379 000 km. Calculate the radius of the Sun in metres. Give your answer to 1 significant figure.

....

Scalar and vector quantities

② Quick quiz

Scalar or vector?

Distance	**Scalar / Vector**	Acceleration	**Scalar / Vector**
Momentum	**Scalar / Vector**	Weight	**Scalar / Vector**
Efficiency	**Scalar / Vector**	Force	**Scalar / Vector**
Speed	**Scalar / Vector**	Temperature	**Scalar / Vector**

⑤ Comparing scalars and vectors　　　Grade 4

1. Some quantities are scalars and some are vectors.

(a) Explain the difference between a scalar and a vector. **[2 marks]**

....

....

(b) Explain whether density is a scalar or a vector. **[2 marks]**

....

....

⑤ Adding vectors　　　Grade 4

2. Figure 1 shows two people pushing a car to move it. One person is exerting a force of 300 N and the other is exerting a force of 150 N. Both people are pushing the car in the same direction.

(a) The arrow in **Figure 1** represents the 150 N force.

Draw an arrow next to it to represent the 300 N force. **[1 mark]**

(b) Calculate the size of the resultant force on the car. **[1 mark]**

resultant force = ... N + ... N = ...

resultant force = ... N

150 N

Figure 1

Both forces are acting in the same direction so the resultant force is the sum of the individual forces.

⑩ Vectors in opposite directions　　　Grade 5

3. Two teams take part in a tug of war (**Figure 2**). One team pulls on the rope to the right. The other team pulls to the left.

(a) Calculate the resultant force. **[2 marks]**

resultant force = ... N, direction: ....

400 N ← Force　　Force → 300 N

Figure 2

(b) Determine the size and direction of the extra force needed to make the two teams balanced. **[2 marks]**

force = ... N, direction: ....

 Made a start　　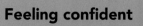 **Feeling confident**　　 **Exam ready**

Distance and speed

② Quick quiz

True or false?

Distance is a scalar quantity.	**True / False**
Displacement has no direction.	**True / False**
Distance has a magnitude and a direction.	**True / False**
Distance measures how far an object has moved in total.	**True / False**

⑩ Final displacement　　　　　　Grade 5

1. Julie's workplace is a 10 kilometre drive away from her home. She drives to work in the morning and home again in the evening.

(a) Calculate the total distance Julie travels each day. **[2 marks]**

total distance = ... km

(b) Give Julie's displacement when she gets home. **[1 mark]**

displacement = ...

2. James runs 2 km to school then realises he has forgotten his homework. He runs home and then back to school.

(a) Calculate the total distance James travelled. **[2 marks]**

total distance = ... km

(b) Give his displacement. **[1 mark]**

displacement = ... km

⑩ Comparing distances　　　　　　Grade 5

3. One person travels 12 km by boat. Another person travels 5 km by car. They start and finish in the same place as each other.

(a) Explain which person travelled the further distance. **[2 marks]**

....

....

(b) Explain whether there is a difference in their displacement. **[2 marks]**

....

....

 Made a start　　 **Feeling confident**　　 **Exam ready**

Speed and velocity

⏱ Quick quiz

Fill in the gaps using the words in the box.

| direction | distance | speed | time |

Velocity is the .... of an object travelling in a particular ....

Speed is a measure of the .... an object has moved in a specific amount of ....

🕙 Speed and velocity   Grade 5

1. A bus travels 100 km in 2 hours.

Calculate its average speed in km/h.   **[2 marks]**

🚏 average speed = $\frac{distance}{time}$ =

....

average speed = ... km/h

2. A cyclist travels 3040 m north (**Figure 1**). It takes him 1600 seconds.

Calculate the cyclist's average velocity in m/s.   **[3 marks]**

🚏 average velocity = $\frac{distance}{time}$ =

....

average velocity = ... m/s ....

Remember, you must give the direction as well as the velocity.

Figure 1

🕙 Average velocity   Grade 5

3. (a) Which of these is a typical speed for a person running? Tick **one** box.   **[1 mark]**

0.5 m/s ☐   3 m/s ☐   12 m/s ☐   25 m/s ☐

(b) Which of these is a typical speed for a car travelling outside town? Tick **one** box.   **[1 mark]**

0.5 m/s ☐   3 m/s ☐   12 m/s ☐   25 m/s ☐

4. A bus is travelling due west and covers 54 km in 1.5 hours.

(a) Calculate the average velocity of the bus in m/s.   **[2 marks]**

velocity = ... m/s ....

(b) Explain why the velocity you calculated in **(a)** is an average velocity.   **[1 mark]**

....

(c) A second bus travels in the same direction, covering twice the distance in the same amount of time.

Calculate the average velocity of the second bus.   **[1 mark]**

average velocity = ... m/s ....

Made a start ☑   Feeling confident ☑   Exam ready ☑

Distance–time graphs

---

2 **Quick quiz**

Draw lines to match the description of the distance–time graph to the motion of the object.

the gradient of the line increases	this means the object is stationary
the gradient of the line decreases	this means the object is accelerating
the gradient of the line is zero	this means the object is decelerating

---

5 **Using distance–time graphs** Grade 5

1. **Figure 1** shows the journey of a cyclist.

Complete the passage below to describe the journey in as much detail as possible.

[3 marks]

A–B: The cyclist travels .... km in .... hours.

The speed of the cyclist is .... km/h.

B–C: The cyclist is .... for .... hours.

C–D: The cyclist travels a further .... km in .... hours.

The speed is .... km/h.

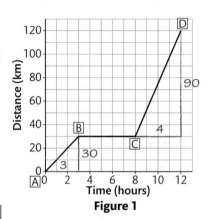

Figure 1

> When asked for the speed, you should consider the distance and refer to the time before calculating speed.

---

15 **Distance–time graphs** Grade 5

2. **Figure 2** shows the distance–time graph for part of a bus journey.

(a) Give the total distance travelled by the bus in the first minute of the journey.

[1 mark]

total distance travelled = ... km

(b) Describe the motion of the bus in the first 20 seconds of the journey.

[1 mark]

....

(c) Give the speed of the bus at 25 seconds. **[1 mark]**

speed = ... m/s

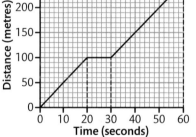

Figure 2

3. A cyclist is stationary at a set of traffic lights. Two seconds after the lights turn green, the cyclist sets off at a constant speed and travels 10 m in the next 5 s.

Sketch a distance–time graph to show the cyclist's motion. **[2 marks]**

Uniform acceleration

2 Quick quiz

Draw lines to match the symbols, quantities and units.

x	time	m/s^2
u	acceleration	m/s
v	initial velocity	m
a	displacement	s
t	final velocity	m/s

10 Using equations of motion — Grade 5

1. A leopard is resting and then accelerates in a straight line to chase a deer. The leopard accelerates to a final velocity of 12 m/s over 6 seconds.

Calculate the acceleration of the leopard. Use the equation: $a = \frac{(v - u)}{t}$. **[2 marks]**

'Resting' or 'at rest' means its velocity is zero.

$a = \frac{(\dots\dots\dots\dots - \dots\dots\dots\dots)}{\dots\dots\dots\dots} = \dots\dots\dots\dots\dots\dots$

acceleration = ... m/s^2

2 Uniform acceleration — Grade 3

2. Which is the correct definition of uniform acceleration? Tick **one** box. **[1 mark]**

- The acceleration changes and is a measure of how quickly an object's velocity changes. ☐
- The acceleration is zero. ☐
- The acceleration is constant and is a measure of how quickly an object's velocity changes. ☐
- The acceleration is constant and is a measure of how quickly an object's distance changes. ☐

5 Acceleration — Grade 5

3. A cyclist accelerates at 3 m/s^2 from a velocity of 2 m/s over a distance of 16 m.
Calculate the cyclist's final velocity.
Use an equation selected from the *Physics equation sheet.* **[3 marks]**

See page 253 for the physics equation sheet.

final velocity = ... m/s

4. A tennis ball falls from rest. It hits the ground 5 s later at a speed of 50 m/s.

(a) Calculate the acceleration of the ball. **[3 marks]**

acceleration = ... m/s^2

(b) State what you have assumed. **[1 mark]**

....

Velocity–time graphs

 Quick quiz

Draw lines to match each feature of a velocity–time graph to the information it gives you.

gradient of the line		constant speed
area under the line		acceleration
a horizontal line		distance travelled

 Velocity–time graphs | Grade 3 |

1. Distance–time graphs and velocity–time graphs give different information about the motion of an object.

Give what can be found from the gradient of a distance–time graph. **[1 mark]**

The gradient = $\frac{\text{distance}}{\text{time}}$ so tells us the

....

 Acceleration | Grade 5 |

2. The velocity–time graph in **Figure 1** shows a car accelerating along a flat road.

Calculate the acceleration of the car. **[3 marks]**

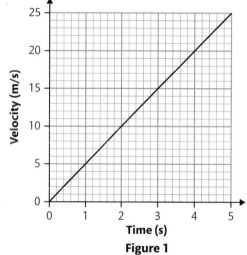

acceleration = ... m/s²

Figure 1

 Distance travelled | Grade 5 |

3. An ice skater's motion is studied for a few seconds and plotted on a graph.

(a) Describe the motion. **[1 mark]**

....

(b) Calculate how far the skater travelled during the study. **[3 marks]**

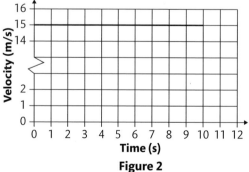

Figure 2

distance travelled = ... m

A 'break' in a graph axis like this shows that the axis has been condensed to save space.

 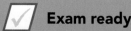

Gravity

2 Quick quiz

Draw lines to match each quantity with its meaning and unit.

mass	the force acting on an object due to gravity	N/kg
weight	the strength of gravity at any one point	kg
gravitational field strength	the amount of matter in an object	N

5 Gravitational field strength — Grade 5

1. A rock has a mass of 2.5 kg on Earth. The gravitational field strength (*g*) on Earth is 10 N/kg.

(a) Calculate the weight of the rock. **[2 marks]**

weight = mass × gravitational field strength

weight = ... × .... = ...

weight = ... N

(b) The rock is taken to the Moon where it weighs 4.1 N.

State its mass on the Moon. **[1 mark]**

Mass is the amount of matter in an object.

mass on Moon = ... kg

15 Mass and weight — Grade 5

2. A moon lander has a mass of 16 000 kg on Earth. (g_{Earth} = 10 N/kg)

(a) Calculate the weight of the moon lander on Earth. **[2 marks]**

weight = ... N

(b) The gravitational field strength on the Moon is 1.6 N/kg.

(i) Give the mass of the moon lander on the Moon. **[1 mark]**

....

(ii) Calculate the weight of the moon lander on the Moon. **[2 marks]**

weight = ... N

(c) Calculate the difference in the weight of the lander on Earth and the weight of the lander on the Moon. **[2 marks]**

difference in weight = ... N

Newton's laws of motion

2 Quick quiz

Draw lines to match each law to the correct statement.

Newton's first law	The acceleration of an object is proportional to the resultant force and inversely proportional to the mass of the object.
Newton's second law	When two objects interact they exert an equal and opposite force on each other.
Newton's third law	An object will continue to move in the same direction at the same speed unless acted upon by a resultant force.

10 Newton's second law — Grade 4

1. (a) Which is the equation for force that comes from Newton's second law? Tick **one** box. **[1 mark]**

force = mass × acceleration ☐

force = $\frac{\text{acceleration}}{\text{mass}}$ ☐

force = $\frac{\text{mass}}{\text{acceleration}}$ ☐

force = $\frac{(\text{acceleration})^2}{\text{mass}}$ ☐

Newton's second law states that resultant force is proportional to acceleration.

(b) Explain why more massive trucks need bigger engines than less massive trucks to produce the same acceleration. **[2 marks]**

When mass is increased, a .... force is needed to produce the .... acceleration.

2. Figure 1 shows a racing bike. The bike and its rider have a combined mass of 70 kg.

Calculate the force needed to accelerate the bike and rider at 4 m/s^2.

Use the equation: $F = ma$ **[2 marks]**

force = ... × .... = ...

force = ... N

Figure 1

When you keep the acceleration the same and increase the mass in Newton's second law equation, what does this do to the force needed?

5 Newton's first law — Grade 4

3. When an object is stationary, the resultant force is zero, according to Newton's first law.

Describe the other situation in Newton's first law where the resultant force on the object is zero. **[2 marks]**

....

3 Unbalanced force — Grade 4

4. Figure 2 shows a ball rolling to the right along flat ground. It slows down and eventually stops.

Explain what caused the ball to slow down. **[3 marks]**

....

....

....

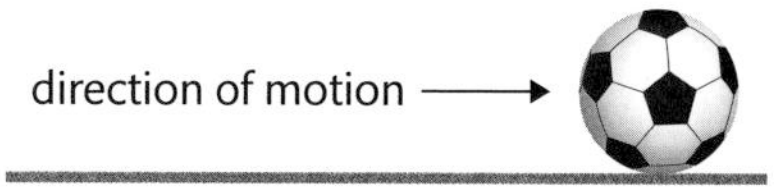

Figure 2

Practical: Investigating acceleration

② Quick quiz

Draw lines to match each quantity to its unit.

speed		m/s^2
mass		N
acceleration		m/s
force		kg

⑮ The effect of force and mass on acceleration　　　　**Grade 5**

1. A student carried out an investigation into the effect of force on the acceleration of an object using the equipment shown in **Figure 1**. The student changed the force by adding more masses to the holder at the end of the bench. The light gate measured the acceleration.

(a) Name the independent variable.　　**[1 mark]**

....

(b) Name the dependent variable.　　**[1 mark]**

....

(c) Predict and explain what the student observes about the acceleration using Newton's second law of motion.　　**[3 marks]**

Newton's second law states that force = ... ×

So if the force is increased and the ....

stays the same, the acceleration must ....

Figure 1

The independent variable is the one that is changed deliberately in the experiment.

The dependent variable is the one that is measured in the experiment.

Remember that the student is changing the force on the object but is not changing the mass of the object. Think about the equation that results from Newton's second law of motion.

⑩ Investigating $F = ma$　　　　**Grade 5**

2. A student investigates the relationship between the mass and the acceleration of an object. The following equipment is available: light gate, trolleys of different masses, mass holder and masses.

(a) Give **one** factor that must be kept constant to ensure the investigation is valid.　　**[1 mark]**

....

(b) Give **one** factor that should be changed.　　**[1 mark]**

....

(c) Give **one** factor that should be measured.　　**[1 mark]**

....

(d) When more mass was added to the trolley, the speed through the light gate decreased.

Explain what this shows about the acceleration.　　**[2 marks]**

....

....

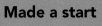 Made a start　 Feeling confident　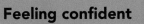 Exam ready

Stopping distance

② Quick quiz

True or false?

Being tired affects your braking distance.	**True / False**
Your stopping distance is the distance travelled while the driver is reacting.	**True / False**
Your thinking distance increases when your reaction time is longer.	**True / False**
Icy roads increase your thinking distance.	**True / False**

⑮ Calculating stopping distance   Grade 4

1. (a) Write the equation linking distance, speed and time.   **[1 mark]**

....

(b) A car travels at a speed of 30 mph (13 m/s). The driver has a reaction time of 1.3 s.

Calculate how far, in **metres**, the car will travel in this time.   **[2 marks]**

distance travelled = ... × .... = ...

distance = ... m

> **Exam focus**
> You need to able to recall and use the equation for distance travelled.

(c) The car's braking distance at 30 mph is 14 m. Calculate the stopping distance.

Use the equation: stopping distance = thinking distance + braking distance   **[2 marks]**   Use your answer to **(b)**.

stopping distance = ... m

⑮ Reaction times   Grade 4

2. Figure 1 shows typical stopping distances for a car travelling at different speeds.

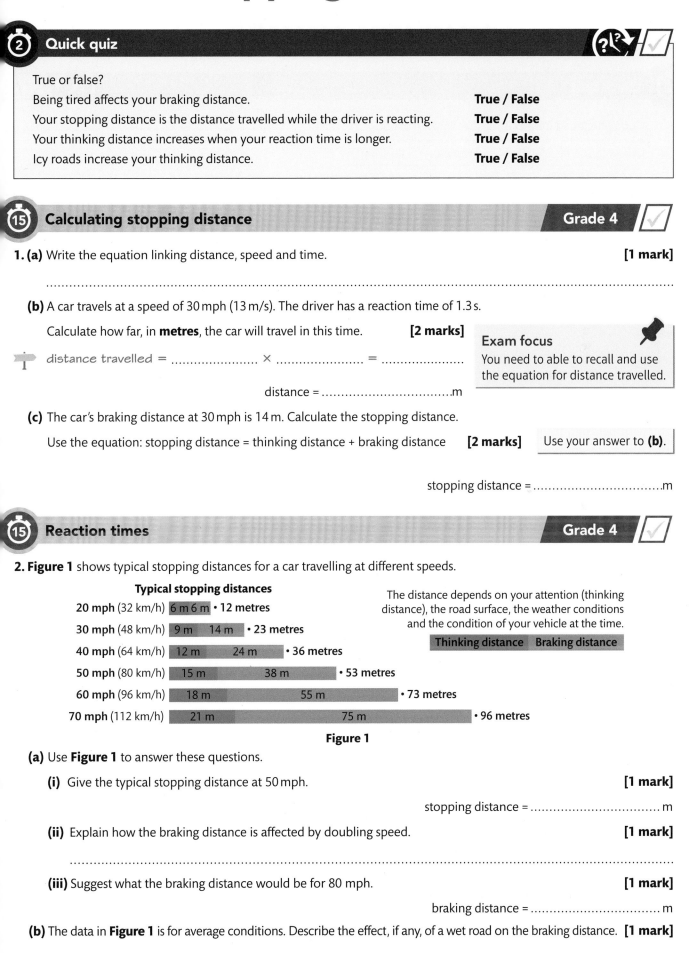

Typical stopping distances

20 mph (32 km/h)	6 m 6 m	• **12 metres**
30 mph (48 km/h)	9 m 14 m	• **23 metres**
40 mph (64 km/h)	12 m 24 m	• **36 metres**
50 mph (80 km/h)	15 m 38 m	• **53 metres**
60 mph (96 km/h)	18 m 55 m	• **73 metres**
70 mph (112 km/h)	21 m 75 m	• **96 metres**

The distance depends on your attention (thinking distance), the road surface, the weather conditions and the condition of your vehicle at the time.

Thinking distance   Braking distance

Figure 1

(a) Use **Figure 1** to answer these questions.

(i) Give the typical stopping distance at 50 mph.   **[1 mark]**

stopping distance = ... m

(ii) Explain how the braking distance is affected by doubling speed.   **[1 mark]**

....

(iii) Suggest what the braking distance would be for 80 mph.   **[1 mark]**

braking distance = ... m

(b) The data in **Figure 1** is for average conditions. Describe the effect, if any, of a wet road on the braking distance. **[1 mark]**

....

Factors affecting braking distance

(2) Quick quiz

Complete the sentences using the words in the box.

| braking | deceleration | stopping | thinking |

Distance travelled under the braking force is the .... distance.

Distance travelled between the driver seeing a hazard and applying the brakes is the .... distance.

The thinking distance plus the braking distance is the .... distance.

If a car crashes there is a large .... and this can cause damage to the brain and the rest of the body.

(5) Braking distance Grade 5

1. Explain how an icy road will affect the braking distance of a vehicle. **[3 marks]**

Friction between the tyres and the road will be
....

so the braking distance will
....

There must be a frictional force between the vehicle's tyres and the road surface for braking to take place.

(2) Braking distance Grade 2

2. Tick the factors that will **increase** braking distance. **[3 marks]**

wet road ☐   damaged brakes ☐   lighter load in the car ☐

tired driver ☐   high speed ☐

(5) Braking and large decelerations Grade 4

3. In a car crash, the car and occupants stop very quickly with a large deceleration.

(a) Explain the danger of a large deceleration. **[2 marks]**

....

....

(b) Explain how the safety features of a car help to protect the occupants in a crash. **[2 marks]**

....

....

(c) Explain why there is a risk that the brakes might overheat when a driver brakes hard. **[2 marks]**

....

....

Think about energy transfers.

 Made a start   **Feeling confident**   **Exam ready**

Gravitational potential energy

② Quick quiz

Complete the equation by selecting words from the box.

force	field	weight	mass	kinetic	potential	position	height

change in gravitational .... energy

= .... × gravitational .... strength × change in vertical ....

⑤ Calculating energy   Grade 5

1. The height of Mount Snowdon is 1090 m above sea level. A 65 kg climber starts at sea level and climbs to the top of Mount Snowdon.

Calculate the change in the climber's gravitational potential energy. Assume g = 10 N/kg. **[2 marks]**

$\Delta GPE = m \times g \times \Delta h$

ΔGPE = ... × .... × .... = ...

change in gravitational potential energy = ... J

⑤ Gravitational potential energy   Grade 5

2. **Figure 1** shows a funicular railway that travels up the side of a steep hill. The mass of a carriage when it is fully loaded with passengers is 2600 kg. Gravitational field strength = 10 N/kg.

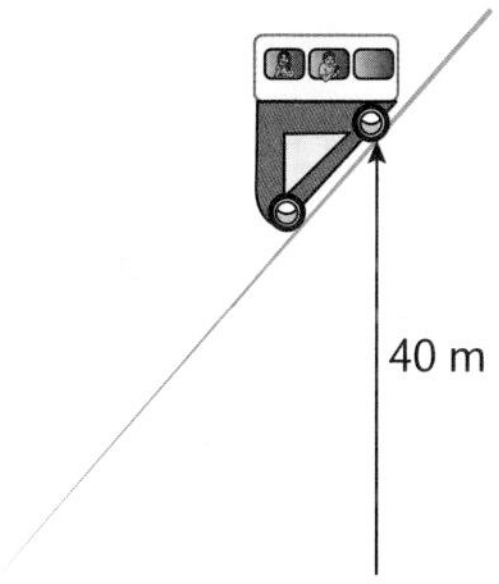

(a) Calculate the change in gravitational potential energy of the carriage when the change in vertical height is 40 m. **[2 marks]**

change in gravitational potential energy = ... J

(b) Suggest how the change in gravitational potential energy would be different if the carriage stopped halfway up the hill. **[1 mark]**

....

40 m

Figure 1

⑤ Energy of a skydiver   Grade 5

3. A skydiver jumps from an aircraft.

Energy is transferred between stores as the skydiver accelerates towards the ground.

Describe the energy transfer. **[2 marks]**

....

....

✓ **Made a start**   ✓ **Feeling confident**   ✓ **Exam ready**

Kinetic energy

 Quick quiz

True or false?

A moving object always has a kinetic energy store.	**True / False**
A stationary object has a kinetic energy store.	**True / False**
When a vehicle is travelling at a constant speed in a straight line, its kinetic energy store does not change.	**True / False**
When a vehicle is accelerating, its kinetic energy store does not change.	**True / False**

 Kinetic energy   Grade 4

1. Which statement about the amount of energy in an object's kinetic energy store is correct? Tick **one** box. **[1 mark]**

The amount of energy is directly proportional to its speed. ☐

The amount of energy is inversely proportional to its speed. ☐

The amount of energy is directly proportional to its (speed)². ☐

The amount of energy is inversely proportional to its (speed)². ☐

> Remember the equation for kinetic energy.

> 'Directly proportional' means that one variable increases as another variable increases. 'Inversely proportional' means that one variable decreases as another increases.

 Kinetic energy   Grade 5

2. A bus with a mass of 10 000 kg is travelling at a speed of 10 m/s.

(a) Calculate the kinetic energy of the bus. **[2 marks]**

> Remember, in the equation for *KE*, *v* is the speed.

$$KE = \frac{1}{2} \times m \times v^2$$

$$KE = \frac{1}{2} \times \text{.....................} \times \text{.....................}^2 = \text{.....................}$$

kinetic energy = ...J

(b) Ten extra passengers get on the bus.

Describe the effect this has on the kinetic energy the bus has when travelling at 10 m/s. **[2 marks]**

An increase in the number of passengers means an increase in mass.

If mass increases, ...

> Use the equation to help you. You could even put numbers into the equation to see the effect.

 Kinetic energy transfers   Grade 5

3. A bullet is shot at a stationary target from a rifle. The bullet's mass is 4.0 g. The bullet travels at 1000 m/s.

> Remember to convert the mass into kg.

(a) Calculate the kinetic energy of the moving bullet. Use the equation

$$\text{kinetic energy} = \frac{1}{2} \times \text{mass} \times (\text{speed})^2$$

[3 marks]

kinetic energy = ...J

(b) Suggest what happens to the kinetic energy of the bullet when it is stopped by the target. **[1 mark]**

....

 Made a start   **Feeling confident**   **Exam ready**

Conservation of energy

② Quick quiz

True or false?

A moving object always has kinetic energy.	**True / False**
Energy is created in electric circuits.	**True / False**
A stretched spring always stores gravitational potential energy.	**True / False**
Friction in the brakes of a car raises the temperature of the brake pads.	**True / False**
A light bulb always wastes energy by heating the surroundings.	**True / False**

⑩ Conservation of energy   Grade 5

1. Figure 1 shows a television. Energy is transferred to it by electricity.

> Remember to list the ways in which energy is wasted as well as the useful energy transfers.

(a) Identify the energy transfers in this device.   **[1 mark]**

🚏 *Energy transferred by heating,*
....

....

(b) State the useful energy transfers for the device.   **[1 mark]**

....

(c) State the wasted energy transfer for the device.   **[1 mark]**

....

Figure 1

⑩ Energy transfers   Grade 5

2. Machinery wastes energy due to friction in the moving parts.

(a) State how the wasted energy is transferred.   **[1 mark]**

....

(b) Give **one** way in which the amount of wasted energy can be reduced.   **[1 mark]**

....

(c) Describe what will eventually happen to the energy wasted in the system.   **[1 mark]**

....

3. Describe the energy transfers when the driver of a moving car applies the brakes and the car stops.   **[2 marks]**

....

....

Efficiency

② Quick quiz

Which statements about efficiency are correct? Tick the correct statements.

Efficiency is measured in joules. ☐

The closer to 1 (or 100%), the more efficient the device. ☐

The lower the number for efficiency, the more efficient the device. ☐

A very efficient device will have an efficiency greater than 100%. ☐

If a device is 40% efficient, 40% of the energy is usefully transferred and 60% is wasted. ☐

⑩ Calculating efficiency **Grade 5**

1. Table 1 shows information about two lamps.

(a) Calculate the efficiency of each lamp as a percentage. Use the

equation: efficiency = $\dfrac{\text{useful energy output}}{\text{total energy input}}$ **[4 marks]**

Table 1

Lamp	Energy input each second (joules)	Useful energy output each second (joules)
A	60	15
B	30	15

Lamp A = $\dfrac{\text{useful energy output}}{\text{total energy input}}$ = ... = ...

Lamp B = ... = ...

> Convert a decimal or fraction into a percentage by multiplying by 100.

efficiency of lamp A = ...%

efficiency of lamp B = ...%

(b) State which lamp is more efficient. **[1 mark]**

....

⑩ Efficiency calculations **Grade 5**

2. A hairdryer transfers 1800 J of useful energy each second. The hairdryer is supplied with 2 kJ of energy each second.

(a) Calculate the energy wasted each second by the hairdryer. **[1 mark]**

energy wasted each second = ...J

(b) Calculate the efficiency of the hairdryer. **[2 marks]**

efficiency = ...

(c) Describe the useful energy transfers in the hairdryer. **[2 marks]**

....

....

   Made a start   **Feeling confident** ✓ **Exam ready**

Renewable energy resources

Quick quiz

Draw lines to match the name of each energy source to a description of its use.

Sun	wind forces turbines to rotate, generating electricity
wind	daily movement of the ocean is used to generate electricity
tides	energy transferred by light is used to generate electricity using solar panels

Wind power
Grade 5

1. **Figure 1** shows some wind turbines.

   Give **two** advantages and **two** disadvantages of using wind power to generate electricity. **[4 marks]**

   Advantages *can be placed in isolated locations*

   ....

   Disadvantages *some people think they spoil the landscape*

   ....

Figure 1

Solar power and hydroelectricity
Grade 3

2. **Figure 2** shows a tidal barrage (left) and a hydroelectric dam (right).

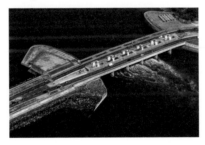 

Figure 2

Give **one** advantage and **one** disadvantage of using each one to generate electricity. **[4 marks]**

Tidal barrage

Advantage ....

Disadvantage ....

Hydroelectric dam

Advantage ....

Disadvantage ....

3. Some towns want to provide electricity to their houses and tower blocks using solar power only. Which statement is a reason why this has not happened? Tick **one** box. **[1 mark]**

Solar panels do not produce constant electricity; other sources of power or very expensive storage batteries are needed. ☐

Solar panels have many moving parts so are unreliable. ☐

Solar panels increase carbon dioxide and pollutant emissions. ☐

Non-renewable energy resources

(2) Quick quiz

Name **three** fossil fuels.

....

(5) Nuclear power
Grade 5

1. **Figure 1** shows a nuclear power station.

   (a) Small amounts of nuclear fuel produce large amounts of energy.

   Give another advantage of nuclear power. **[1 mark]**

   Nuclear power doesn't contribute to
   ....

   (b) It is difficult to dispose of nuclear waste. Give another disadvantage of nuclear power. **[1 mark]**

   Transport of radioactive fuel and waste is
   ....

Figure 1

(5) Renewable and non-renewable energy resources
Grade 4

2. Give **two** disadvantages of using fossil fuel power stations to generate electricity rather than using renewable energy resources. **[2 marks]**

   1 ....

   2 ....

(10) Resources used for transport
Grade 5

3. A hybrid car has a fossil fuel powered engine. It can switch to battery power to reduce pollution. It uses any excess engine power to charge the battery.

   (a) What energy resources does this car use? Tick **one** box. **[1 mark]**

   renewable only ☐   non-renewable only ☐

   renewable and non-renewable ☐   neither renewable nor non-renewable ☐

   (b) **Table 1** gives some typical data about hybrid and electric cars.

Table 1

Data	Hybrid car	Fully electric car
Range in km (maximum distance it can travel before refuelling/recharging)	about 500	about 350
Number of fuel stations or charging stations in the UK	about 8500	about 6000
Number of passengers	4 or 5	4 or 5
Cost to run per 100 km	£7.00	£3.70

Suggest **two** reasons why hybrid cars are currently more popular in the UK than fully electric cars. **[2 marks]**

....

....

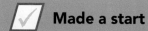 Made a start   Feeling confident   Exam ready

Types of wave

 Quick quiz

Circle the type of wave described.

The vibrations are parallel to the direction the wave is travelling.	**Longitudinal / Transverse**
The vibrations are perpendicular to the direction the wave is travelling.	**Longitudinal / Transverse**
Ripples on water are an example of this type of wave.	**Longitudinal / Transverse**
The wave has compressions and rarefactions.	**Longitudinal / Transverse**
Sound waves are an example.	**Longitudinal / Transverse**

 Types of wave | **Grade 3**

1. Figure 1 shows the pattern of movement of particles in air caused by the vibration of a loudspeaker.

(a) Which type of wave does this diagram show? Tick **one** box. **[1 mark]**

longitudinal sound wave ☐　　longitudinal light wave ☐

transverse sound wave ☐　　transverse light wave ☐

> 'Longitudinal' means 'along the direction of travel'. 'Transverse' means 'across the direction of travel'.

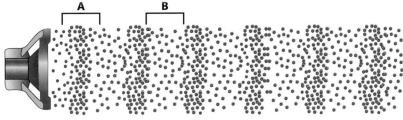

Figure 1

(b) Name the features of the wave labelled **A** and **B**. **[2 marks]**

A ....　B ....

 Speed of sound waves | **Grade 5**

2. Two students measured the speed of sound in air.

This is the method they used.

1. Student 1 stands 50 m away from Student 2.

2. She claps her hands to make a sound.

3. Student 2 starts a stopwatch when she sees the clap and stops it when she hears the clap.

It takes 0.15 seconds for the sound to travel from one student to the other.

Calculate the speed of sound in air from their results. **[2 marks]**

$$\text{speed} = \frac{\text{distance travelled}}{\text{time taken}}$$

speed = ... = ...

....

speed = ... m/s

Properties of waves

② Quick quiz

Draw lines to match each key word with its definition.

amplitude	the number of waves passing a point each second
frequency	the distance from a point on a wave to an identical point on an adjacent wave
wavelength	the time taken to complete one full cycle or wave
time period	the maximum displacement of a point on a wave away from its undisturbed position

⑤ Wave features .... **Grade 3**

1. **Figure 1** shows a diagram of a transverse wave.
   Name the wave features, **B** and **C**, on **Figure 1**. **[2 marks]**

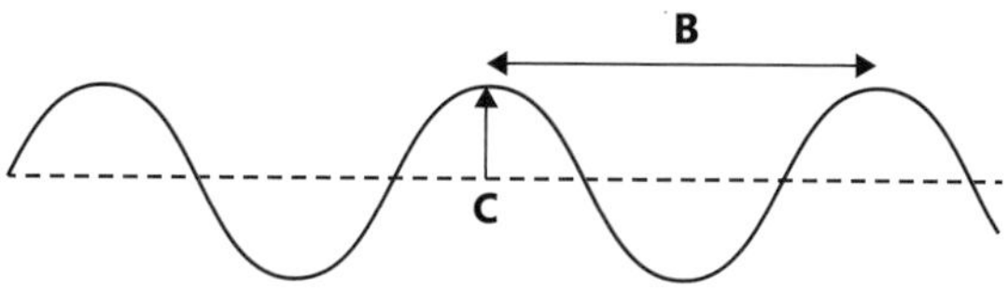

   B ....

   C ....

Figure 1

⑤ Speed of sound in air .... **Grade 4**

2. The frequency of a sound wave is 50 Hz and its wavelength is 6.8 m.
   Calculate the wave speed. **[2 marks]**

   wave speed = frequency × wavelength = ... × .... = ...

   wave speed = ... m/s

⑤ Wave features .... **Grade 5**

3. A stone is thrown into a pond. The stone causes waves in the water. The water waves have a frequency of 5.0 Hz.
   The ripples are 0.10 m apart.

   (a) Write the equation that links frequency, wavelength and wave speed. **[1 mark]**

   ....

   (b) Calculate the speed of the water waves. **[2 marks]**

   wave speed = ... m/s

4. A student measures the frequency of waves on the sea. He counts how many waves go past him in 30 seconds. He then
   divides this number by 30. Explain why he counts the waves over 30 seconds. **[2 marks]**

   ....

   ....

    Made a start   **Feeling confident**   ☑ **Exam ready**

Practical: Investigating waves

2 Quick quiz

Number the steps to show a method for determining the wavelength of waves in a ripple tank. The first one has been done for you.

Measure the distance the wave travelled.	
Calculate the wavelength of the wave.	
Time how long it takes for one wave to travel from the paddle to the edge of the ripple tank.	1
Calculate the wave speed.	
Time 10 rotations of the motor and divide by 10 to get the time period of the wave.	
Calculate the frequency of the wave.	

10 Waves on a string — Grade 5

1. The apparatus in **Figure 1** can be used to investigate the speed of a wave on a string. The frequency of the wave depends on the frequency set on the frequency generator.

(a) Which value does the length L represent?
Tick **one** box. **[1 mark]**

the wavelength ☐

half the wavelength ☐

twice the wavelength ☐

four times the wavelength ☐

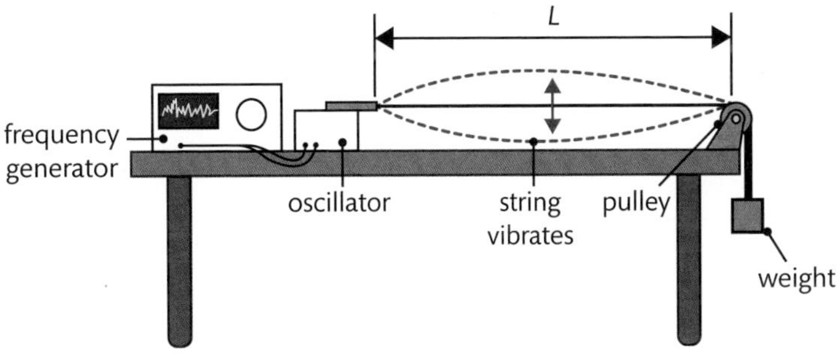

Figure 1

(b) Explain how to determine the speed of the wave on the string. **[3 marks]**

Determine the wavelength by ....

Use the frequency from the frequency generator. Calculate the speed using the equation ....

....

(c) A student investigates the effect of length on the speed of waves on a string using the apparatus in **Figure 1**. The length of the string is changed by moving the oscillator.

Suggest **two** factors the student must keep the same in order to make the experiment a fair test. **[2 marks]**

> Remember that a fair test is one in which only one variable is changed; all others are kept the same.

1 ....

2 ....

5 Investigating speed of waves — Grade 5

2. A student investigates the speed of water waves using a ripple tank.

(a) State what the student should measure, in addition to how far the ripples travel. **[1 mark]**

....

(b) Name the measuring instrument the student should use to measure the distance travelled by the ripples. **[1 mark]**

....

Types of electromagnetic waves

[2] Quick quiz

Are these waves electromagnetic waves (EM) or not (not)? Circle the correct answers.

light	**EM / not**	infrared	**EM / not**	water waves	**EM / not**
sound	**EM / not**	X-rays	**EM / not**	waves on a string	**EM / not**
radio	**EM / not**	microwaves	**EM / not**	ultrasound	**EM / not**

[10] The electromagnetic spectrum — Grade 4

1. Table 1 shows the electromagnetic spectrum.

Complete the electromagnetic spectrum by adding the waves in order of increasing frequency.

Use words from the box. **[3 marks]**

~~gamma rays~~	infrared waves	microwaves	ultraviolet waves	X-rays

Table 1

Lowest frequency → Highest frequency

radio waves			visible light			gamma rays

[5] Light and ultraviolet radiation — Grade 5

2. (a) Give **two** properties of light waves. **[2 marks]**

1 .... **2** ....

(b) Ultraviolet radiation and visible light are both in the electromagnetic spectrum.

Give **one** similarity and **one** difference between ultraviolet radiation and visible light. **[2 marks]**

....

....

Use the wave equation wave speed = frequency × wavelength to help you decide which quantities are different.

[5] Light and ultraviolet radiation — Grade 5

3. A medical handbook says that 'gamma rays are ionising radiation that can cause harm'.

(a) Name the part of an atom that produces gamma rays. .... **[1 mark]**

(b) Explain the term 'ionising radiation'. **[2 marks]**

....

....

(c) Describe how gamma rays can cause harm to a person. **[1 mark]**

....

Practical: Investigating refraction

② Quick quiz

True or false?

The normal is a line drawn parallel to a refracting surface.	**True / False**
The angle of incidence is measured between the incident ray and the refracting surface.	**True / False**
When light travels from air into a glass block, the angle of refraction is always less than the angle of incidence.	**True / False**

③ Defining refraction   Grade 3

1. Explain what is meant by 'refraction'.   **[3 marks]**

Refraction is the change in .... of a ray of light due to a change in .... as it

passes from ....

....

⑩ Investigating refraction   Grade 4

2. A student investigates the refraction of light as it enters a glass block (**Figure 1**). The student uses a ray box with a slit to produce a narrow light ray. The student measures the angle of incidence and the angle of refraction of the light ray at the point where it enters the glass block.

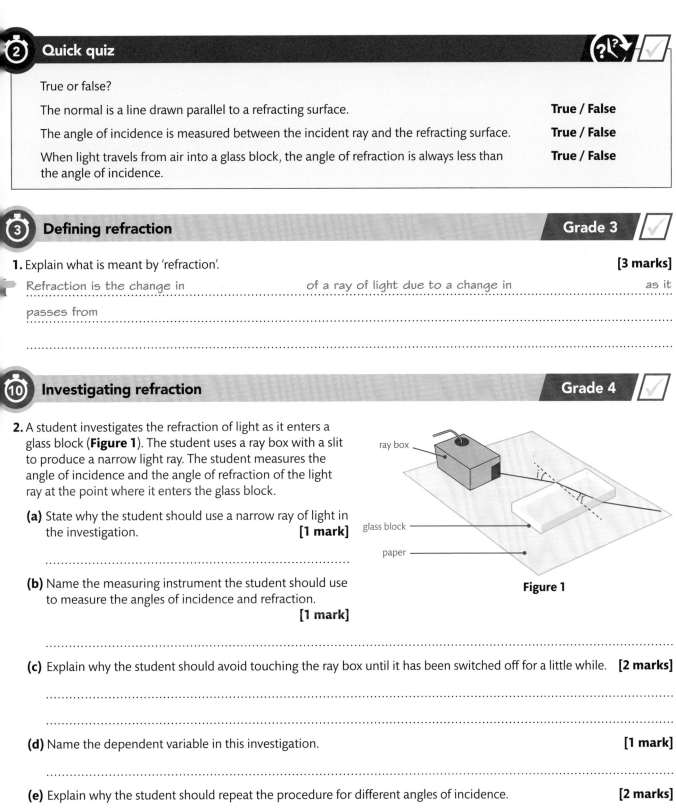

(a) State why the student should use a narrow ray of light in the investigation.   **[1 mark]**

....

(b) Name the measuring instrument the student should use to measure the angles of incidence and refraction.

[1 mark]

Figure 1

....

(c) Explain why the student should avoid touching the ray box until it has been switched off for a little while.   **[2 marks]**

....

....

(d) Name the dependent variable in this investigation.   **[1 mark]**

....

(e) Explain why the student should repeat the procedure for different angles of incidence.   **[2 marks]**

....

....

Applications of EM waves

2 Quick quiz

Draw lines to match each type of wave to one of its applications.

radio waves	medical imaging
infrared	tanning
visible	thermal imaging
ultraviolet	TV and communications
X-rays	lasers

5 Uses of microwaves — Grade 5

1. **Figure 1** shows potatoes being cooked with microwaves.
   Explain how microwaves cook food. **[2 marks]**

   The microwaves are absorbed by ....

   in the food and transfer .... to the food.

Figure 1

5 Communications — Grade 5

2. Radio waves are used for communication.

   (a) Explain why radio waves are used for communication. **[1 mark]**

   ....

   (b) Give **two** types of communications that use radio waves. **[2 marks]**

   1 ....

   2 ....

5 Ultraviolet — Grade 3

3. Ultraviolet light can damage our skin. It is also useful.

   (a) Describe how ultraviolet light damages our skin. **[1 mark]**

   ....

   (b) Give **two** uses of ultraviolet light. **[2 marks]**

   1 ....

   2 ....

   (c) Gamma rays have a higher frequency than ultraviolet light.

   State whether gamma rays are more or less dangerous than ultraviolet light. **[1 mark]**

   ....

The structure of an atom

---

② **Quick quiz**

A carbon-12 atom contains 6 protons, 6 neutrons and 6 electrons. Draw and label the structure of a carbon-12 atom.

---

⑤ **Protons, neutrons and electrons** | **Grade 5** ☑

1. Atoms contain protons, neutrons and electrons.

Give the location of each subatomic particle in the atom and the relative charge of each type of particle. **[3 marks]**

Electrons .... the nucleus. An electron is .... charged.

Protons are found .... A proton is .... charged.

Neutrons are found .... A neutron is ....

---

⑤ **Protons, neutrons and electrons** | **Grade 5** ☑

2. The approximate size of an atom is 1×10^{-10} m. The nucleus of an atom is about 10 000 times smaller than the atom.

> 10 000 times smaller = 1×10^{-4} times

What is the approximate size of the nucleus? Tick **one** box. **[1 mark]**

1×10^{-6} m ☐ 1×10^{-10} m ☐ 1×10^{-14} m ☐ 1×10^{-18} m ☐

3. Protons and neutrons are both types of subatomic particles.

Describe the similarities and differences between protons and neutrons. **[3 marks]**

....

....

....

---

⑤ **Electrons and energy** | **Grade 4** ☑

4. Electrons fill energy levels around the nucleus of an atom.

(a) What happens to an electron in an atom when it absorbs electromagnetic radiation? Tick **one** box. **[1 mark]**

The electron stays in the same energy level. ☐   The electron moves to a lower energy level. ☐

The electron moves to a higher energy level. ☐   The electron is absorbed by the nucleus. ☐

(b) Electrons in an atom absorb electromagnetic radiation. This affects their energy levels.

Give **two** properties of the electrons that stay the same when they absorb electromagnetic radiation. **[2 marks]**

1 ....

2 ....

Mass number, atomic number and isotopes

2 Quick quiz

True or false?

In an atom, the number of protons = the number of electrons.	**True / False**
The mass number of an atom is the total number of protons and electrons.	**True / False**
The atomic number tells you how many electrons an atom has.	**True / False**
mass number – atomic number = number of neutrons	**True / False**
The number of neutrons is always the same as the number of electrons.	**True / False**

5 Isotopes — Grade 5

1. Carbon-12 and carbon-14 are different forms of the element carbon. They are isotopes.

(a) Explain what is meant by 'isotopes' of an element. **[2 marks]**

Isotopes are atoms with the same .... but a different ....

....

(b) Give **one** difference between the isotopes carbon-12 and carbon-14. **[1 mark]**

Carbon-14 has .... extra ....

15 Atomic structure — Grade 5

2. (a) Uranium-238 can be represented by the symbol $^{238}_{92}U$.

Deduce the number of each of these subatomic particles in the uranium atom. **[3 marks]**

protons: .... electrons: .... neutrons: ....

(b) Uranium-238 and uranium-235 are different isotopes of the element uranium.

Describe how the two isotopes are different. **[1 mark]**

....

3. When atoms gain or lose electrons, they become charged.

(a) State what a charged atom is called. **[1 mark]**

....

(b) The atomic number of magnesium is 12. A magnesium atom loses two electrons to become charged.

Give the charge of a charged magnesium atom. **[1 mark]**

....

(c) State the number of electrons remaining on the charged magnesium atom. **[1 mark]**

....

Development of the atomic model

2 Quick quiz

In the plum pudding model, the mass of an atom is distributed throughout the atom.

Where is most of the mass of the atom in the nuclear model?

....

5 Developing the atomic model — Grade 4

1. The following statements describe developments in the accepted model of the atom.

Number the statements from 1 to 5 to place them in the correct historical order. **[3 marks]**

Each development became possible because, over time, scientists were able to see further into atoms at smaller and smaller scales.

Scientists discovered that neutrons existed inside the nucleus of an atom	
The plum pudding model was suggested by scientists who thought that the atom was a positively charged 'pudding' with negatively charged electrons ('plums') stuck inside it	
Niels Bohr suggested that electrons travel in orbits around the nucleus	4
Rutherford's scattering experiment suggested that atoms were mostly empty space with a tiny, massive nucleus in the centre	
The Ancient Greeks thought that atoms were tiny spheres that could not be divided	

5 Plum pudding and nuclear models — Grade 5

2. (a) Describe where the positive and negative charges were thought to be inside the plum pudding model of an atom. **[2 marks]**

Remember that electrons are negatively charged.

The plum pudding model suggested that the atom is a ball of ....

.... with .... embedded in it.

(b) Describe where positive and negative charges are found in the nuclear model of the atom. **[2 marks]**

The positive charge is found ....

The negative charge is found ....

5 The gold foil experiment — Grade 5

3. The scattering experiment with gold foil showed that the plum pudding model was not correct.

(a) What type of particles were fired in a beam at gold foil during the scattering experiment? Tick **one** box. **[1 mark]**

alpha particles ☐ beta particles ☐ gamma particles ☐ electrons ☐

(b) Describe what happened to most of the particles fired at the gold foil. **[1 mark]**

....

(c) Explain what this showed about the inside of an atom. **[1 mark]**

....

Ionising radiation

② Quick quiz

True or false?

All ionising radiation comes from the outer part of the atom.	**True / False**
Some ionising radiation is charged.	**True / False**
All ionising radiation consists of particles.	**True / False**
Some ionising radiation is a type of electromagnetic wave.	**True / False**

⑤ Radioactive decay   Grade 5

1. Radioactive decay is a random process.

Which statements describe what is meant by a 'random process'?   **[3 marks]**

There is no way to tell which nucleus will decay next.

There is a pattern in the order the nuclei decay.

There is no way to predict when a particular nucleus will decay.

We can predict exactly how many nuclei will decay in the next second.

External factors, such as temperature, do not affect the process.

> There are three marks for this question. That means there must be three correct answers.

⑩ Properties of ionising radiations   Grade 5

2. Each type of ionising radiation has different properties.

(a) Name the four charged ionising radiations.   **[4 marks]**

1 ....   3 ....

2 ....   4 ....

(b) Name the ionising radiation made of fast electrons. .... **[1 mark]**

(c) Describe the constituents of an alpha particle.   **[2 marks]**

➤ An alpha particle contains .... and ....

(d) Describe what happens when a radioisotope decays by emitting a positron.   **[3 marks]**

....

....

....

(e) One type of radiation is stopped by a few centimetres of air.

State which type of radiation this is.   **[1 mark]**

....

(f) Explain which type of radiation is the most ionising.   **[2 marks]**

....

....

 Made a start   **Feeling confident**   **Exam ready**

Background radiation

2 Quick quiz

True or false?

Most background radiation comes from nuclear accidents. **True / False**

Some background radiation comes from our food. **True / False**

Cosmic rays are radioactive sources in rocks. **True / False**

Nuclear power stations may be a source of background radiation. **True / False**

5 Detecting and measuring radiation — Grade 4

1. Describe what the activity of a radioactive source means. **[1 mark]**

The activity from a radioactive source is the number of .... that decay every ....

....

15 Detecting and measuring radiation — Grade 5

2. People who work with radiation need to keep track of their exposure.

Name a piece of equipment that they can wear or carry to monitor their long-term exposure to ionising radiation. **[1 mark]**

....

3. Scientists need to measure background radiation.

(a) Name a piece of equipment that can give a count rate immediately. **[1 mark]**

....

(b) Give the units used to measure count rate. **[1 mark]**

....

(c) Describe how you would measure the activity of a source placed in the lab. **[3 marks]**

....

....

....

4. Give **three** sources of background radiation. **[3 marks]**

1 ....

2 ....

3 ....

Beta decay

---

(2) Quick quiz

Does each description match a β– particle, a β+ particle or both?

An electron from the nucleus **β– particle / β+ particle / Both**

A positron from the nucleus **β– particle / β+ particle / Both**

Charge of +1 **β– particle / β+ particle / Both**

Charge of –1 **β– particle / β+ particle / Both**

Negligible mass **β– particle / β+ particle / Both**

---

(5) Beta decay   **Grade 5**

1. Explain why the emission of a β– particle results in the formation of a new element.   **[2 marks]**

When an unstable nucleus decays by β– emission, a neutron changes to a proton and an .... , which is

immediately emitted from the nucleus. The proton remains in the nucleus, so the .... number

increases by .... , forming a new element.

---

(5) Comparing beta emissions   **Grade 4**

2. Tick the boxes to show whether each statement applies to β+, β– or both.   **[5 marks]**

Statement	β+	β–
Positively charged		
Negatively charged		
Negligible mass		
Atomic number of source nucleus increases		
Atomic number of source nucleus decreases		

---

(5) Comparing beta emissions   **Grade 5**

3. (a) Explain why the mass number of a nucleus does not change when a beta particle is emitted.   **[2 marks]**

....

....

....

(b) Describe what happens in a nucleus when it emits a β– particle.   **[2 marks]**

....

....

....

 Made a start   **Feeling confident**   **Exam ready**

BBC

Nuclear decay

2 Quick quiz

Complete the table.

Type of decay	Change to mass number	Change to atomic number
Alpha		
Beta minus		
Beta plus		
Gamma		
Neutron		

5 Decay equations

Grade 5

1. Nuclear equations use symbols such as $^{14}_{6}C$.

(a) State what the numbers 14 and 6 each represent. **[2 marks]**

The number 14 represents the .... number of carbon-14.

The number 6 represents the .... number of carbon-14.

(b) The equation shows the radioactive decay of carbon-14.

Complete the equation so that it is balanced. **[2 marks]**

$^{14}_{6}C \rightarrow {}^{14}_{7}N + {}^{\square}_{\square}e$

Fill in the two missing numbers so that the top and bottom numbers on both sides of the equation add up to the same totals.

(c) State the type of radioactive decay that this equation shows. **[1 mark]**

....

What type of subatomic particle does the 'e' represent?

10 Radioactive decay

Grade 5

2. (a) Which row in **Table 1** shows what happens to the atomic number and the mass number of a nucleus when it undergoes alpha decay? Tick **one** box. **[1 mark]**

Table 1

	Atomic number	Mass number
☐	increases by 2	decreases by 4
☐	decreases by 2	decreases by 4
☐	decreases by 2	increases by 4
☐	increases by 2	increases by 4

(b) The equation shows the alpha decay of an isotope of radon. Complete the equation so that it is balanced. **[3 marks]**

$^{198}_{86}Ra \rightarrow {}^{\square}_{\square}Po + {}^{\square}_{\square}He$

3. Explain why the emission of an α-particle results in the formation of a new element. **[2 marks]**

Which number tells you what an element is?

....

....

Made a start | Feeling confident | Exam ready

Half-lives

② Quick quiz

Use words from the box to fill in the gaps. Some words may be used more than once.

| nuclei | time | half | rate | half-life |

The .... of a radioactive source is the .... it takes for the count ....

to fall to .... its initial value. It is also the .... taken for half of the unstable ....

in a sample to decay.

⑩ Using half-life   Grade 5

1. A sample of caesium-137 has a half-life of 30 years and an initial activity of 1600 Bq. **Table 1** shows how the activity changes after 30 years.

(a) Complete **Table 1** to show the activity after 60, 90 and 120 years.   **[3 marks]**

Table 1

Time (years)	0	30		90	
Activity (Bq)	1600	800			100

(b) The activity of another sample of caesium-137 is found to be 280 Bq.

Estimate the age of the sample. Tick **one** box.   **[1 mark]**

25 years ☐   50 years ☐   75 years ☐   100 years ☐

⑤ Determining half-life   Grade 5

2. Explain why the exact time at which atoms in a radioactive sample will decay cannot be predicted.   **[2 marks]**

....

....

⑩ Using graphs to determine half-life   Grade 5

3. Which two graphs in **Figure 1** show radioactive decay? .... and ....   **[2 marks]**

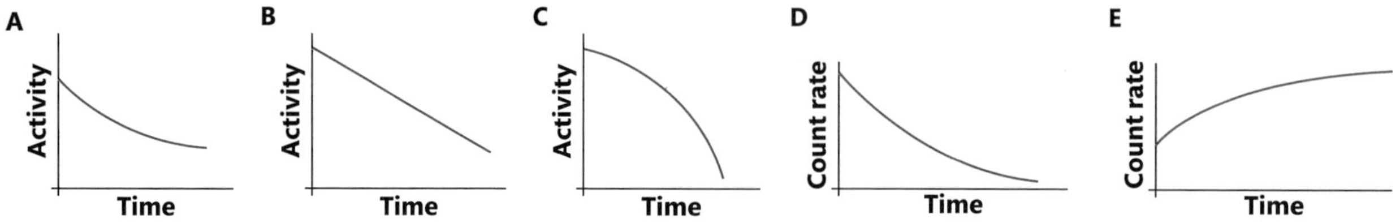

A Activity / Time

B Activity / Time

C Activity / Time

D Count rate / Time

E Count rate / Time

Figure 1

 Made a start   **Feeling confident**   **Exam ready**

Dangers of radioactivity

2 Quick quiz

True or false?

The risk of harm is the same from all radioactive sources. **True / False**

Alpha radiation is always more dangerous than beta radiation. **True / False**

Being exposed to gamma radiation always causes cancer. **True / False**

Alpha emitters are not used as medical tracers. **True / False**

5 Dangers of ionising radiation Grade 5

1. (a) Describe how ionising radiation causes direct damage to humans. **[1 mark]**

Ionising radiation may cause direct damage to body tissue if the radiation collides with .... in the tissue.

(b) Describe how ionising radiation causes indirect damage to humans. **[2 marks]**

Indirect damage can occur if the radiation causes .... to form in tissue.

....

2 Working with radioactive samples Grade 3

2. A student uses a long pair of tongs to handle a sealed alpha source.

Which of these best describes why the student uses tongs rather than holding the source in their fingers? **[1 mark]**

The source will be hot and could burn them. ☐

Alpha particles only travel a few centimetres through air. ☐

The student is less likely to drop the source. ☐

10 Radioactive hazards Grade 5

3. Some people working in hospitals are exposed to radiation during their working day.

(a) Give **three** ways to reduce the radiation dose they receive. **[3 marks]**

1 ....

2 ....

3 ....

(b) If radiation damages the DNA in a human cell, three things can happen. One is that the damage is repaired.

Describe the other **two** things that can happen. **[2 marks]**

1 ....

2 ....

Radioactive contamination and irradiation

2 Quick quiz

Fill in the gaps.

radioactive	damaging	precautions	dose	X-rays

Although they are less powerful and less penetrating than gamma rays, ... can also have a .... effect on the body. When handling .... materials, ... can be taken to minimise the radioactive .... the body receives.

5 Irradiation — Grade 5

1. (a) State what is meant by the term 'irradiation'. **[1 mark]**

Irradiation is the process of exposing an object to ....

(b) State what is meant by the term 'contamination'. **[1 mark]**

Contamination is when radioactive substances stick to or are .... an object.

5 Irradiation — Grade 5

2. (a) Some types of cancer can be irradiated with gamma radiation.

Explain why the doctor stands in another room behind concrete walls when the patient is treated. **[2 marks]**

....

....

Think about the penetrating power of radiation and the safety of the people involved.

(b) Suggest why the patient is only irradiated for a few minutes at a time. **[2 marks]**

....

....

Think about what affects the size of a dose of radiation.

5 Peer review — Grade 5

3. (a) Scientists publish research on the effects of radiation on humans and the environment. Their findings are peer reviewed before publication.

State what is meant by 'peer review'. **[1 mark]**

....

(b) Explain why peer review is important in science. **[1 mark]**

....

Revising energy transfers

② Quick quiz

True or false?

All energy transfers are useful.	**True / False**
Efficient appliances waste a large fraction of their input energy.	**True / False**
Moving objects always have kinetic energy.	**True / False**
Wasted energy is transferred to the surroundings by heating.	**True / False**
When an object is raised through a height it gains elastic potential energy.	**True / False**

⑤ Energy transfer   Grade 5

1. When a hairdryer is switched on, 50% of the input energy is transferred to thermal energy by the heater and 40% is transferred to kinetic energy to drive the fan.

(a) Calculate the percentage of the energy transferred by sound. **[1 mark]**

energy transferred by sound + 50% + 40% = 100%

....

energy transferred by sound = ...

(b) Draw a Sankey diagram for the hairdryer. **[2 marks]**

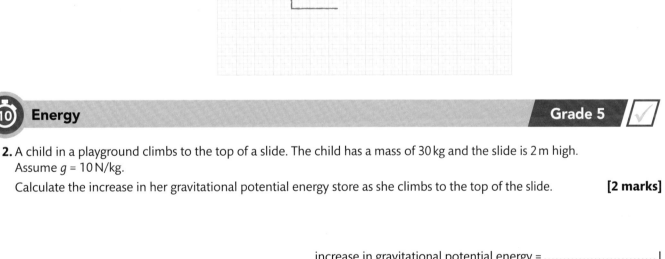

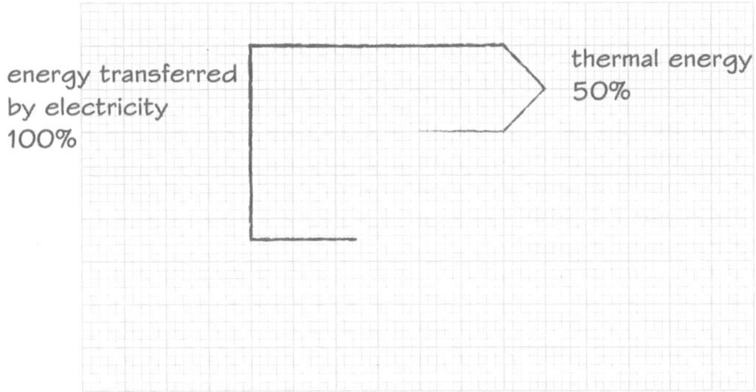

energy transferred by electricity 100%

thermal energy 50%

⑩ Energy   Grade 5

2. A child in a playground climbs to the top of a slide. The child has a mass of 30 kg and the slide is 2 m high. Assume g = 10 N/kg.

Calculate the increase in her gravitational potential energy store as she climbs to the top of the slide. **[2 marks]**

increase in gravitational potential energy = ...J

3. A car is travelling at 12 m/s and has a mass of 1500 kg.

Calculate the kinetic energy store of the car. **[2 marks]**

kinetic energy = ...J

Made a start	Feeling confident	Exam ready	183

Work done and energy transfer

Quick quiz

True or false?

Work done is measured in newtons.	**True / False**
Work is only done if the force is acting in the same direction as the displacement.	**True / False**
Force is measured in joules.	**True / False**
work done = $\dfrac{\text{force}}{\text{distance}}$	**True / False**
force = $\dfrac{\text{work done}}{\text{distance}}$	**True / False**

Energy transfers   Grade 4

1. A crane lifts a container up above the ground. Which energy store has been increased? Tick **one** box. **[1 mark]**

   elastic potential energy store ☐   kinetic energy store ☐

   gravitational potential energy store ☐   thermal energy store ☐

Calculating work done   Grade 5

2. The braking force of a car is 2500 N.

   (a) At a speed of 30 km/h the brakes stop the car in a distance of 12 m.

   Calculate the work done by the brakes to stop the car. Use the equation: work done = force × distance   **[2 marks]**

   work done = ... N × .... m

   work done = ... J

   (b) When the same car stops from a speed of 50 km/h, the work done by the brakes is 60 000 J.

   Calculate the braking distance.   **[3 marks]**

   60 000 J = 2500 N × braking distance

   braking distance = $\dfrac{\text{....................}}{\text{....................}}$

   braking distance = ... m

Energy transfers   Grade 5

3. A lorry has 750 kJ of kinetic energy. The driver applies the brakes. The lorry travels a distance of 75 m as it comes to a stop. Calculate the average braking force of the lorry.   **[4 marks]**

braking force = ... N

Power

② Quick quiz

Which equation is **not** correct? Tick **one** box.

energy transferred = power × time ☐

energy transferred = $\dfrac{power}{time}$ ☐

power = $\dfrac{work\ done}{time}$ ☐

work done = power × time ☐

⑤ Calculating energy from power
Grade 5

1. A kettle has a power of 2.5 kW.

Calculate the energy transferred to the water if it takes 120 seconds to boil 1 kg of water in the kettle.

Use the equation: $P = \dfrac{E}{t}$ **[3 marks]**

2.5 kW = ... W

$P = \dfrac{E}{t}$ so $E = P \times t$

E = ... W × .... s = ...

energy transferred = ...J

Convert to standard units before using the equation. You need to convert from kW to W.

⑮ Calculating power
Grade 5

2. Figure 1 shows a man climbing a set of steps.

The man has a weight of 800 N. The height of the steps is 7.5 m.

(a) Calculate the amount of work done against gravity when the man climbs the steps. Use the equation: $W = F \times d$ **[2 marks]**

work done = ...J

Figure 1

(b) It takes 15 seconds for the man to climb the steps.

Calculate the man's power. Assume all the energy output by the man is transferred to useful energy. **[2 marks]**

power = ...W

Forces

2 Quick quiz

Sort the forces into contact and non-contact forces.

weight tension magnetic friction electrostatic gravitational force

Contact forces	Non-contact forces

5 Types of force — Grade 5

1. (a) Describe what a contact force is. **[1 mark]**

Contact forces act when two objects are ....

(b) Describe what a non-contact force is. **[1 mark]**

Non-contact forces act on objects that are at a ....

2. Force is a vector quantity. Explain what is meant by 'vector quantity'. **[2 marks]**

....

....

5 Labelling forces — Grade 3

3. Figure 1 shows a box being pushed along a flat table. Two forces are labelled for you.

(a) Draw two more labelled arrows on the diagram to show the other forces acting on the box. **[2 marks]**

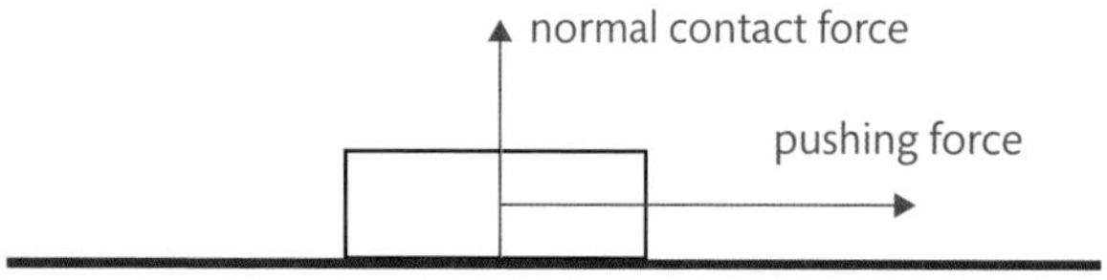

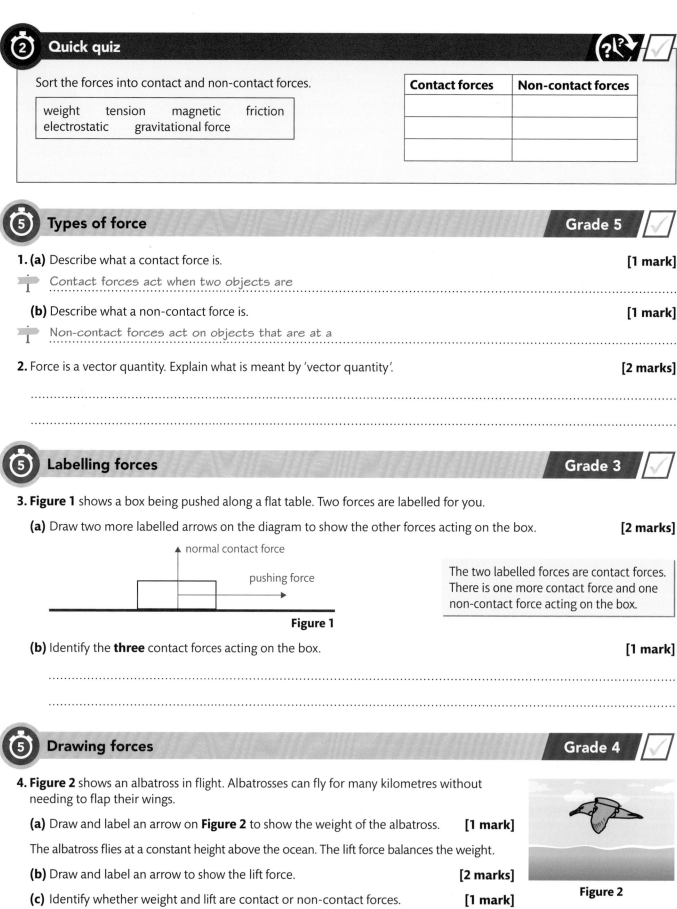

Figure 1

The two labelled forces are contact forces. There is one more contact force and one non-contact force acting on the box.

(b) Identify the **three** contact forces acting on the box. **[1 mark]**

....

....

5 Drawing forces — Grade 4

4. Figure 2 shows an albatross in flight. Albatrosses can fly for many kilometres without needing to flap their wings.

(a) Draw and label an arrow on **Figure 2** to show the weight of the albatross. **[1 mark]**

The albatross flies at a constant height above the ocean. The lift force balances the weight.

(b) Draw and label an arrow to show the lift force. **[2 marks]**

(c) Identify whether weight and lift are contact or non-contact forces. **[1 mark]**

Figure 2

....

Circuit diagrams

5 Quick quiz

Draw the circuit symbol for each component.

thermistor	lamp	ammeter

10 Series and parallel circuits — Grade 5

1. (a) Draw a circuit diagram to show three lamps connected **in series** with a battery. **[2 marks]**

Remember: when components are connected in series they form one single route for charge to flow.

(b) Draw a circuit diagram to show the same three lamps connected **in parallel** with the same battery. **[2 marks]**

In a parallel circuit, each parallel loop is connected to the power supply.

(c) State in which circuit, series or parallel, the lamps would be brighter. **[1 mark]**

The lamps in the .... circuit would be brighter.

5 Test circuits — Grade 5

2. A student wanted to measure the current through a lamp and the potential difference across it.

Draw the circuit the student should use to do this. **[3 marks]**

The circuit is the same for measuring the current and potential difference of any component.

10 Circuits and LEDs — Grade 4

3. A light-emitting diode (LED) is a device that allows current to pass through in one direction and then emits light.

(a) Draw a circuit diagram of a cell in series with a switch, a resistor and an LED. The LED should light up when the switch is closed. **[2 marks]**

(b) Suggest a device that uses an LED. **[1 mark]**

....

Current, resistance and potential difference

Quick quiz

Draw lines to match each key word with its definition.

current	opposition to the flow of charge, measured in ohms (Ω)
potential difference	the flow of charge, measured in amps (A)
resistance	the energy given to each unit of charge, measured in volts (V)

Linking current, pd and resistance

Grade 5

1. Each resistor in the circuit in **Figure 1** has a resistance of 10 Ω. The battery has a potential difference of 6 V.

(a) Explain why the reading on the voltmeter will be 2 V. **[2 marks]**

 The potential difference is shared equally
....
because the three resistors
....

(b) The total resistance of the resistors is 30 Ω.

Calculate the current in the circuit. **[2 marks]**

Use the equation: current = $\dfrac{\text{potential difference}}{\text{resistance}}$

current = $\dfrac{\text{potential difference}}{\text{resistance}}$ = ...

current = ...A

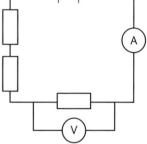

Figure 1

(c) The potential difference is halved.

Explain what effect this will have on the current in the circuit. **[2 marks]**

....

....

> Remember that pd is proportional to current.

$V = I \times R$

Grade 5

2. Figure 2 shows a car headlight. The potential difference from the supply is 12 V and the current is 5 A.

Calculate the resistance of the lamp in the car headlight.

Use the equation: resistance = $\dfrac{\text{potential difference}}{\text{current}}$ **[2 marks]**

Figure 2

resistance = ...Ω

 Made a start **Feeling confident** **Exam ready**

Charge, current and energy

② Quick quiz

True or false?

Charge is the rate of flow of current.	**True / False**
Potential difference is the energy transferred per unit charge.	**True / False**
The unit of potential difference is the joule.	**True / False**
The unit of charge is the volt.	**True / False**
The unit of current is the amp.	**True / False**

⑤ Charge calculations   Grade 4

1. A current of 10 A flows in an appliance. It is switched on for 30 minutes.

(a) Calculate the charge flow in the appliance.

Use the equation: charge = current × time   **[3 marks]**

> **Maths skills**
> Convert quantities into standard units before substituting into the equation.

30 minutes = 30 × 60 = 1800 seconds

charge = current × time = ... × .... s = ...

charge = ...C

(b) The appliance is connected to the mains supply with a potential difference of 230 V.

Calculate the energy transferred in 30 minutes. Use the equation:

energy transferred = charge moved × potential difference   **[2 marks]**

> Use your answer to part **(a)** for charge.

energy transferred = ... × .... = ...

energy transferred = ...J

⑮ Electrical charge   Grade 5

2. A resistor, a lamp, a switch and a battery are connected in series as shown in **Figure 1**. An ammeter is placed in position A. When the switch is closed the reading on the ammeter is 0.75 A.

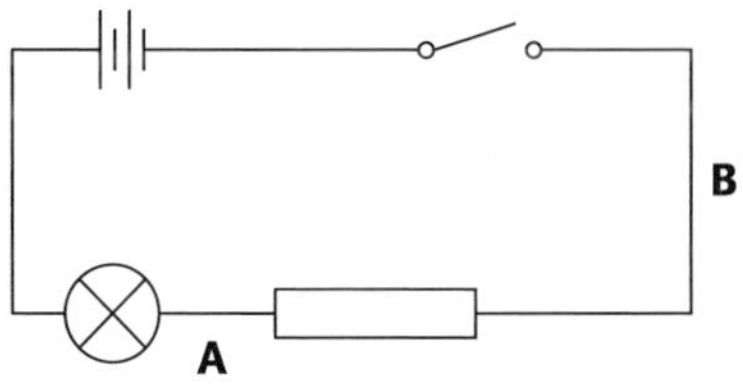

(a) The ammeter is moved so it is placed in position **B**.

Give the reading on the ammeter in position **B**.   **[1 mark]**

....

Figure 1

(b) Calculate the charge transferred when the switch is closed for 120 seconds. Use the equation: $Q = I \times t$ **[2 marks]**

charge = ...C

3. A lamp in a series circuit transfers 50 C of charge. The current in the lamp is 0.5 A.

Calculate how long the lamp was on for. Use the equation: $t = \dfrac{Q}{I}$ **[2 marks]**

time = ...s

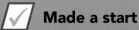 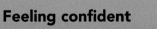

Series and parallel circuits

(2) Quick quiz

Does each statement apply to a **series** or **parallel** circuit? (In the parallel circuits, assume each loop has only one component.)

The current is the same through all components. **Series / Parallel**

The current is the sum of the currents through each component. **Series / Parallel**

The potential difference is the same across each component. **Series / Parallel**

The potential difference is split across the components. **Series / Parallel**

The total resistance is the sum of all the resistances. **Series / Parallel**

(5) Resistance **Grade 3**

1. Two resistors have resistances of 10Ω and 10Ω.

(a) Calculate the total resistance when the resistors are connected in series. **[1 mark]**

 total resistance = ... + ... = ...

> The total resistance in a series circuit is the sum of the individual resistances.

total resistance = ... Ω

(b) The resistors are connected in parallel.

Describe how the resistance changes compared to when they were connected in series. **[1 mark]**

....

(10) Series and parallel circuits **Grade 3**

2. Figure 1 shows two different ways to set up a simple circuit using two lamps and a switch.

(a) The switch is closed in each circuit.

State in which circuit (**A** or **B**) the lamps will shine more brightly. **[1 mark]**

(b) Describe what will happen in circuit **B** when the switch is open and closed. **[2 marks]**

switch open: ....

switch closed: ....

(c) Suggest how to change circuit **B** so that each lamp can be switched on or off separately. **[2 marks]**

....

....

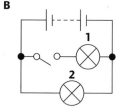

Figure 1

> Look carefully at which circuit loops are closed in each case.

> You need to add a circuit component.

☑ **Made a start** ☑ **Feeling confident** ☑ **Exam ready**

Practical: Resistance

2 Quick quiz

Which is the best definition of resistance? Tick **one** box.

The flow of electrical charge in a wire. ☐

The opposition to the flow of electrical charge in a circuit. ☐

The energy given to the charge as it flows. ☐

A measure of the number of electrons flowing in a circuit. ☐

5 Reducing errors

Grade 5

1. A student investigated the effect of the length of a wire on its resistance. The circuit is shown in **Figure 1**.

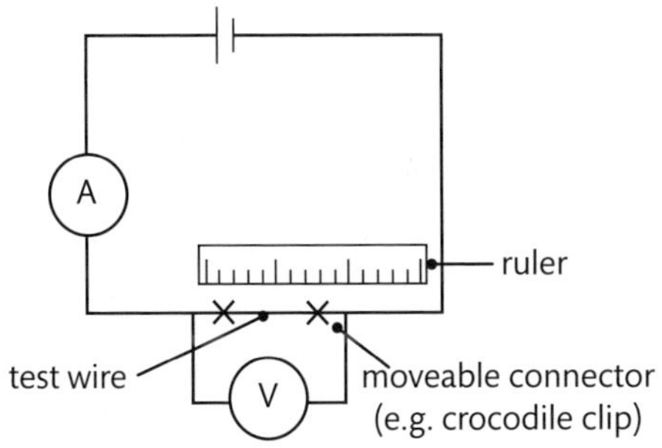
A
ruler
test wire
V
moveable connector
(e.g. crocodile clip)

Figure 1

Think about wire length and current.

(a) The student cleaned the ends of the wire with wire wool before carrying out the experiment.

Explain why the student did this. **[2 marks]**

The wire needed to be cleaned to ....

....

....

....

(b) Give **two** ways to prevent the wire getting too hot in the experiment. **[2 marks]**

1 ....

2 ....

15 Thermistor investigation

Grade 5

2. Describe how to carry out an investigation into the effect of temperature on the resistance of a thermistor. **[6 marks]**

....

....

....

....

....

....

....

....

Exam focus

Remember to write your answers to extended response questions in a structured and logical way.

Resistors

2 Quick quiz

Draw lines to match the shape of each I–V graph to its component.

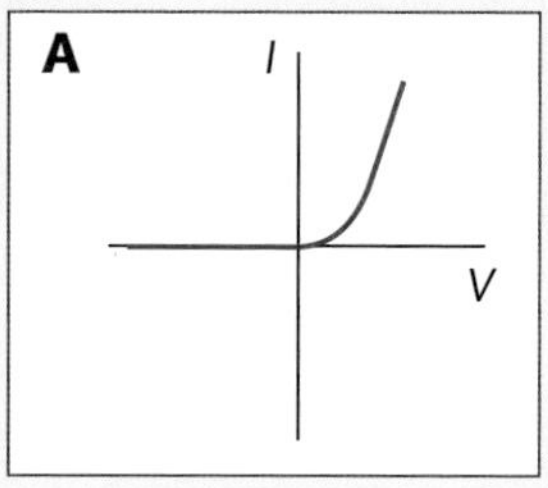

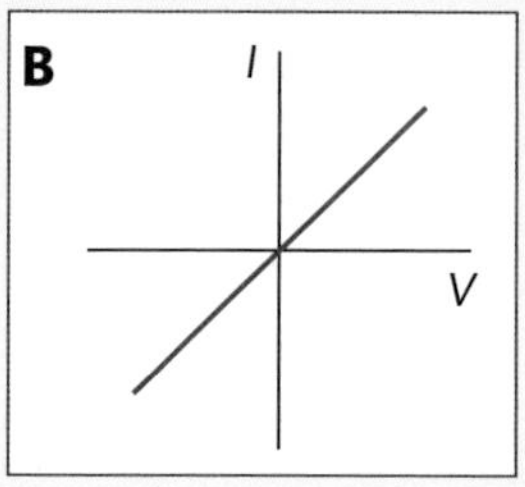

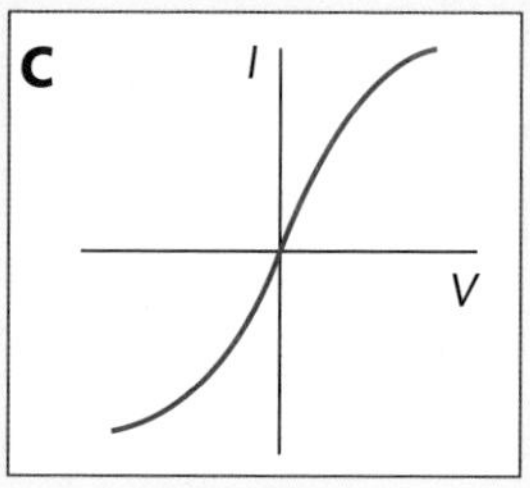

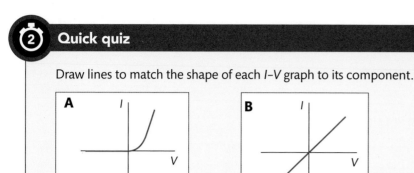

fixed resistor | filament lamp | diode

10 *I*–*V* graphs — Grade 5

1. (a) Explain what the gradient of an I–V graph for a fixed resistor tells you. **[2 marks]**

For a resistor, the gradient of an I–V graph is equal to ....

The steeper the line, the ....

(b) The current through a piece of metal wire at a constant temperature is directly proportional to the potential difference across it. Describe the I–V graph for a metal wire at a constant temperature. **[2 marks]**

....

(c) The filament in a filament bulb is made from a piece of metal wire. Explain why the gradient of an I–V graph for a filament bulb is not constant. **[4 marks]**

A current flowing through the filament causes .... The increased current at higher ....

....

....

5 Thermistors and LDRs — Grade 5

2. A thermistor's resistance changes depending on temperature.

(a) State what happens to the resistance of a thermistor as the temperature increases. **[1 mark]**

....

(b) Suggest a use for a circuit including a thermistor. **[1 mark]**

....

3. An LDR is used in a circuit.

(a) Write down what LDR stands for. **[1 mark]**

....

(b) The light falling on an LDR gets brighter.

Explain what happens to the current through it. **[2 marks]**

....

....

Practical: *I–V* characteristics

② Quick quiz

Number the instructions to show the correct order of how to create an *I–V* graph for a given component. The first one has been done for you.

Plot a graph of current against potential difference.	
Measure the current passing through the component for each potential difference.	
Change the potential difference across the component using a variable resistor.	
Set up a circuit with an ammeter to measure the current through the component and a voltmeter to measure the potential difference across it.	1
Switch the direction of the current and potential difference by swapping the connections on the power supply.	

⑩ Diodes   Grade 5

1. A student investigates how the current in a diode changes with potential difference.

(a) Draw a circuit that could be used to investigate how the current in a diode changes with potential difference.   **[3 marks]**

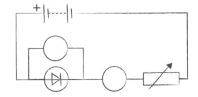

> This will be a simple test circuit with a diode. Something is needed to measure current and something to measure potential difference.

(b) Sketch the current–potential difference (*I–V*) graph the student should expect to obtain using the axes on **Figure 1**.   **[2 marks]**

> The resistance of a diode depends on the direction of the current.

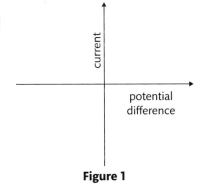

Figure 1

⑩ Resistance from an *I–V* graph   Grade 5

2. A student investigated the relationship between the current and potential difference of a piece of wire with the temperature kept constant.

(a) What shape of the current–potential difference (*I–V*) graph should the student expect to obtain? Tick **one** box.   **[1 mark]**

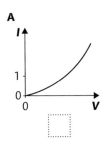
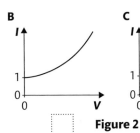
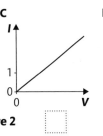
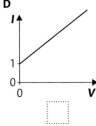

Figure 2

(b) Explain how the *I–V* graph shows that the wire behaves like a fixed resistor.   **[2 marks]**

....

....

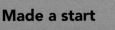 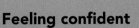

Energy transfer in circuits

② Quick quiz

Complete the sentences using words from the box.

| charge | cools | current | electrons | heats | ions | melts | neutrons | protons | resistance |

When there is an electric .... in a resistor, there is an energy transfer which

.... the resistor. This energy transfer is the result of collisions between ....

and .... in the lattice.

⑩ Electrical power equations **Grade 5**

1. A torch is switched on for 2 minutes. During this time 810 J of energy is transferred to the filament in the torch bulb. The current in the filament is 750 mA.

(a) Calculate the potential difference across the torch bulb.

Use an equation from the formula sheet. **[4 marks]**

🚩 2 minutes = 2 × .... = ...s   750 mA = ...A

energy transferred = current × potential difference × time

$$\text{potential difference} = \frac{\text{energy transferred}}{\text{current} \times \text{time}} = \frac{..............................}{.............. \times ....} = ...$$

potential difference = ... V

(b) Explain why the filament gets hot when the torch is switched on. **[3 marks]**

🚩 The moving .... collide with the .... in the metal lattice of the filament.

This transfers .... to the ions of the filament. ....

⑩ Heating effect of a current **Grade 4**

2. The heating effect of an electrical current can be useful and a disadvantage.

(a) Give **two** examples when the heating effect of an electric current is useful. **[2 marks]**

1 ....

2 ....

(b) Give **two** examples when the heating effect of an electric current is a disadvantage. **[2 marks]**

1 ....

2 ....

⑩ Heating effect of a current **Grade 5**

3. When an electrical appliance is switched on, thermal energy is dissipated to the surroundings. Explain why. **[3 marks]**

🚩 When the appliance is switched on, an electric current ....

....

....

 Made a start 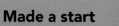 **Feeling confident** 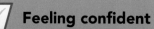 **Exam ready**

Electrical power

---

② Quick quiz

Draw lines to match each quantity to its unit.

power	energy	time	current	potential difference	resistance

seconds (s)	volts (V)	joules (J)	amps (A)	ohms (Ω)	watts (W)

---

⑤ Power   Grade 5

1. An electric kettle transfers 200 000 J of energy when it heats water for 180 seconds.

Calculate the power of the kettle.

Use the equation: $P = \dfrac{E}{t}$ **[2 marks]**

 $P = \dfrac{E}{t} = \dfrac{\text{.....................................}}{\text{.....................................}} = \text{.....................................}$

power = ... W

---

⑮ Electrical power equations   Grade 5

2. An electric oven uses a current of 5 A when connected to the mains supply at 230 V.

Calculate the power of the oven.

Use the equation: $P = I \times V$ **[2 marks]**

power = ... W

3. A hairdryer has a power rating of 2000 W. The hairdryer is connected to a mains supply of 230 V.

Calculate the current in the hairdryer.

Use the equation: $I = \dfrac{P}{V}$ **[2 marks]**

current = ... A

4. A microwave has a power rating of 800 W. It is connected to the mains supply with a potential difference of 230 V.

(a) Calculate the current in the microwave. Give your answer to 2 significant figures.   **[2 marks]**

Use the equation: $I = \dfrac{P}{V}$

current = ... A

(b) The microwave is used for 5 minutes.

Calculate the energy transferred when it is used.

Use the equation: $E = P \times t$ **[3 marks]**

> **Maths skills**
> Always check that the quantities in the question are in the standard units needed for the equation.

energy transferred = ... J

 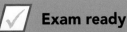

Mains electricity

② Quick quiz

True or false?

Mains electricity is direct current.	**True / False**
There are two or three colour-coded wires in appliance plugs.	**True / False**
The neutral wire in a three-core cable has a blue cover.	**True / False**
The live wire is always at 0 V.	**True / False**

⑤ Earthing　　　　　　　　　　　　　　　　　　　　　　　Grade 3

1. (a) Explain why touching the live wire of an appliance is dangerous.　　**[2 marks]**

Touching the live wire is dangerous because you complete a

.... between the live wire and the ....

You would then receive ....

> **Exam focus**
> Check how many marks each question is worth: for 2 marks you must make two distinct points.

(b) All metal-cased appliances should be earthed.

State what it means when an appliance is 'earthed'.　　**[1 mark]**

....

....

⑩ Mains supply　　　　　　　　　　　　　　　　　　　　Grade 3

2. An appliance plug contains a three-core cable and a fuse.
What is the fuse connected to? Tick **one** box.　　**[1 mark]**

earth wire ☐　　　live wire ☐　　　neutral wire ☐　　　case of the appliance ☐

3. (a) A kettle uses mains electricity, while a torch uses a battery.

Explain the difference between these two supplies of electricity.　　**[2 marks]**

....

....

(b) Give the frequency of the domestic mains electricity supply in the UK. ....**[1 mark]**

② Mains supply　　　　　　　　　　　　　　　　　　　　Grade 5

4. Which graph in **Figure 1** shows the potential difference (V) against time for the domestic mains electricity supply in the UK? Tick **one** box.　　**[1 mark]**

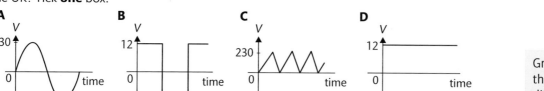

A ... 230 ... V ... time
B ... 12 ... V ... time
C ... 230 ... V ... time
D ... 12 ... V ... time

Figure 1

☐　　　☐　　　☐　　　☐

> Graph D shows the potential difference against time for a battery.

✓ **Made a start**　　　 ✓ **Feeling confident**　　　 ✓ **Exam ready**

Energy transfers in appliances

Quick quiz

Are the energy transfers described below wasted or useful? Circle the correct answer.

A torch transfers energy from its chemical store to its thermal store as light. **Wasted / Useful**

A drill transfers energy to the thermal store in the environment when it is used. **Wasted / Useful**

The heating elements in a toaster transfer energy from its thermal store as light when it is turned on. **Wasted / Useful**

A laptop computer transfers energy from its chemical store to the thermal store in the environment when it is on. **Wasted / Useful**

 Useful and wasted energy transfers **Grade 4**

1. Complete **Table 1** for each of these devices. **[3 marks]**

Table 1

Device	Energy source or store	Useful energy transfers	Wasted energy transfers
Hair dryer	transfer by electricity	kinetic,	
Electric drill	transfer by electricity		
Mobile phone	chemical energy		

Mains appliances transfer energy from the mains to other energy stores. Battery-powered appliances transfer energy from their chemical stores as electricity to other energy stores. Wasted energy is most commonly transferred to thermal stores in the environment, or kinetic stores of particles (as sound).

 **Energy transfers** **Grade 5**

2. Figure 1 shows a television.

(a) Give the energy transfers that take place when the television is turned on. **[1 mark]**

transfer by sound,
....

(b) Identify which of the energy transfers you gave in part **(a)** are wasted and which are useful. **[2 marks]**

....

....

Figure 1

(c) Electricity from the mains carries 2000 J of energy to the television. 1500 J of this energy is usefully transferred to other stores. Calculate how much energy is wasted. **[1 mark]**

wasted energy = ...J

(d) Describe what happens to the wasted energy. **[1 mark]**

....

 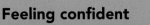

Magnetic fields

② Quick quiz

Draw the magnetic field lines around the bar magnet.

N　　　S

⑤ Types of magnets　　　　Grade 5

1. Figure 1 shows some paper clips hanging from a bar magnet. The paper clips are induced magnets.

Describe what is meant by the term 'induced magnet'. **[2 marks]**

An induced magnet is:

* an object that becomes magnetic when placed in a ....

* always .... to a permanent magnet. ....

Exam focus
You can use bullet points in your answer to make sure you have made two different points.

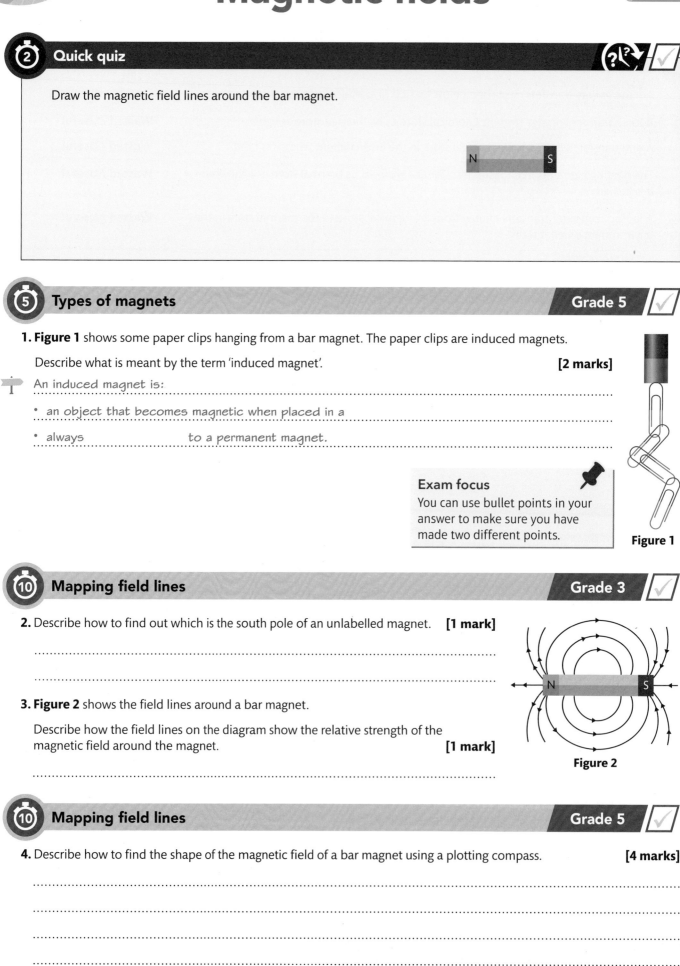

Figure 1

⑩ Mapping field lines　　　　Grade 3

2. Describe how to find out which is the south pole of an unlabelled magnet. **[1 mark]**

....

....

3. Figure 2 shows the field lines around a bar magnet.

Describe how the field lines on the diagram show the relative strength of the magnetic field around the magnet. **[1 mark]**

....

Figure 2

⑩ Mapping field lines　　　　Grade 5

4. Describe how to find the shape of the magnetic field of a bar magnet using a plotting compass. **[4 marks]**

....

....

....

....

✓ **Made a start** ✓ **Feeling confident** ✓ **Exam ready**

Electromagnetism

2 Quick quiz

Is each statement an advantage (**A**) or disadvantage (**D**) of an electromagnet? Circle the correct answer.

Electromagnets use electricity and so cost money to run. **A / D**

The strength of electromagnets can be altered by controlling the current. **A / D**

Electromagnets can be switched on and off. **A / D**

Electromagnets can get hot. **A / D**

5 Solenoids — Grade 3

1. Define the term 'solenoid'. **[2 marks]**

A coil of wire

5 Electromagnets — Grade 4

2. (a) Figure 1 shows a wire carrying a current. Draw the magnetic field around the wire on the diagram. **[2 marks]**

(b) Give **two** things that affect the magnetic field strength of the wire at a particular point. **[2 marks]**

1 ....

2 ....

What can you change about the current or the location of the point?

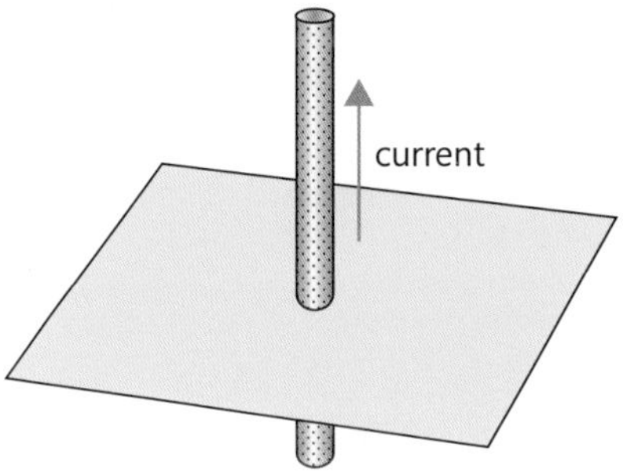

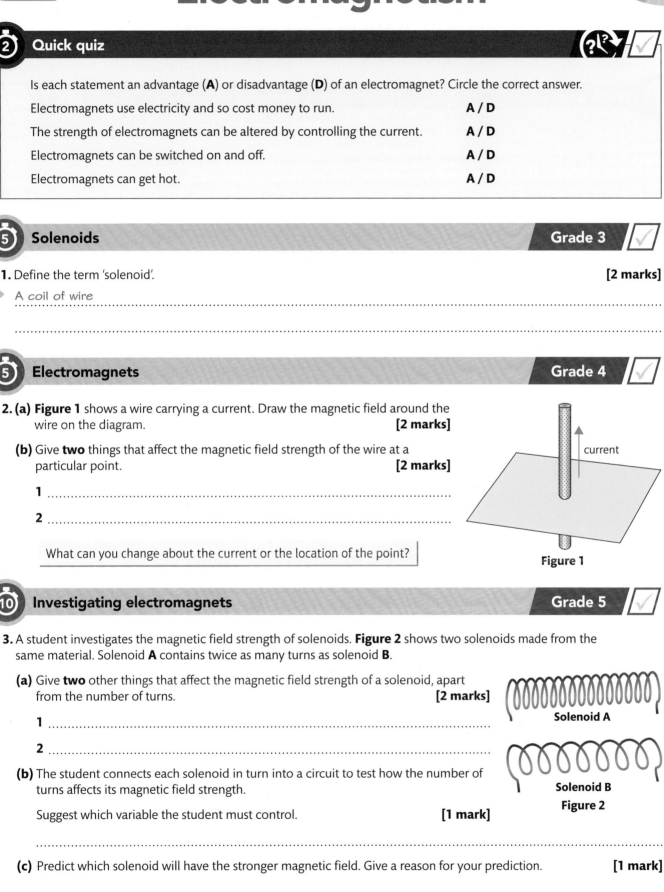

Figure 1

10 Investigating electromagnets — Grade 5

3. A student investigates the magnetic field strength of solenoids. **Figure 2** shows two solenoids made from the same material. Solenoid **A** contains twice as many turns as solenoid **B**.

(a) Give **two** other things that affect the magnetic field strength of a solenoid, apart from the number of turns. **[2 marks]**

1 ....

2 ....

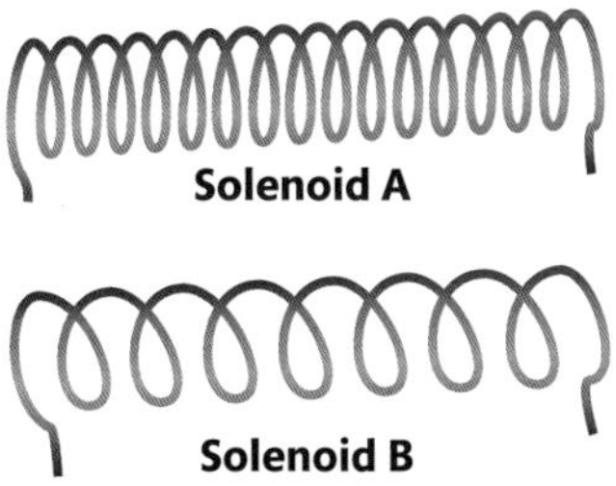

Figure 2

(b) The student connects each solenoid in turn into a circuit to test how the number of turns affects its magnetic field strength.

Suggest which variable the student must control. **[1 mark]**

....

(c) Predict which solenoid will have the stronger magnetic field. Give a reason for your prediction. **[1 mark]**

....

The National Grid and transformers

② Quick quiz

True or false?

Transformers are used to increase the efficiency of the National Grid.	**True / False**
Step-up transformers increase potential difference.	**True / False**
Step-down transformers increase potential difference.	**True / False**
power = $\dfrac{\text{potential difference}}{\text{current}}$	**True / False**

⑩ Transformers   Grade 4 ☑

1. In a transformer, the input potential difference is 230 V and the output potential difference is 10 V.
Explain whether this is a step-up or a step-down transformer.   **[2 marks]**

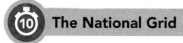 The input is .... V and the output is .... V, so the potential
difference goes .... This means it is a .... transformer.

> Input greater than output = step-down; output greater than input = step-up

⑩ The National Grid   Grade 5 ☑

2. Figure 1 shows the National Grid.

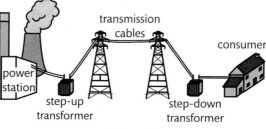

Figure 1

(a) A power station outputs electrical power at a potential difference of approximately 25 kV.

What is the main function of the step-up transformer between the power station and the transmission cables?
Tick **one** box.   **[1 mark]**

increases the power transmitted by the cables ☐

increases the electrical current transmitted in the cables ☐

increases the potential difference at which the electrical power is transmitted ☐

increases the resistance of the cables that transmit the electrical power ☐

(b) What is the main benefit of using a step-up transformer in this way? Tick **one** box.   **[1 mark]**

makes the transmission of electrical power safer ☐

increases the efficiency of appliances in the home ☐

means that the cables can transmit direct current rather than alternating current ☐

reduces the energy wasted in the transmission cables ☐

 Made a start   Feeling confident   ☑ Exam ready

Density

Quick quiz

Draw lines to match each quantity to its correct unit.

mass	m^3
volume	kg/m^3
density	m
length	kg

Calculating density

1. An aluminium block has the dimensions: height 0.5 m; width 0.8 m; depth 0.6 m. It is a cuboid. The block has a mass of 648 kg.

(a) Calculate the volume of the block in m^3. **[2 marks]**

volume = height × width × depth = ... × .... × .... = ...

volume = ... m^3

(b) Calculate the density of aluminium. Use the equation: $\text{density} = \dfrac{\text{mass}}{\text{volume}}$ **[2 marks]**

density = $\dfrac{............}{............}$ = ...

density = ... kg/m^3

(c) A different aluminium block has a mass of 13.5 kg.

Calculate the volume of this block. **[3 marks]**

$\text{density} = \dfrac{\text{mass}}{\text{volume}}$

So, volume = $\dfrac{\text{mass}}{............}$ = $\dfrac{............}{............}$ = ...

volume = ... m^3

Density

2. The mass of 500 cm^3 of cooking oil is 455 g.

(a) Calculate the density of the oil in g/cm^3. **[2 marks]**

density = ... g/cm^3

(b) 10 cm^3 of the cooking oil is added to a pan.

Calculate the mass of cooking oil that was added to the pan. **[3 marks]**

mass = ... g

 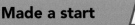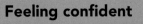

Practical: Density of materials

2 Quick quiz

True or false?

A unit of density is g/mm^3. **True / False**

Density can be measured with a top-pan balance. **True / False**

The mass of a sample of a substance can be calculated using mass = $\frac{\text{volume}}{\text{density}}$ **True / False**

A unit of density is m^3/kg. **True / False**

Volume can be measured using a measuring cylinder. **True / False**

5 Finding volume — Grade 5

1. (a) Describe a method for measuring the volume of a large cuboid. **[3 marks]**

Use a .... to measure the length, ... and height of the cuboid. Use the formula length .... to calculate the volume.

(b) A student suggests the following method for measuring the volume of an irregular rock.

1. Partly fill a displacement can with water.

2. Submerge the rock in the water.

3. Collect the displaced volume of water in a measuring cylinder.

Describe the error in this method and how to correct it. **[2 marks]**

In step 1, the student says to ' .... ' a displacement can.

This will cause an error in the measurement of .... The student should ....

....

10 Finding density — Grade 5

2. Figure 1 shows a bottle of shampoo. A student wants to find the density of the bottle of shampoo.

Figure 1

(a) Name **two** pieces of equipment needed to measure the volume of the bottle of shampoo. **[2 marks]**

1 .... **2** ....

(b) Name **one** other quantity that must be measured to calculate the density of the bottle of shampoo. **[1 mark]**

....

(c) Suggest **one** measuring device that can be used to measure the quantity you identified in part **(b)**. **[1 mark]**

....

(d) Write the equation used to calculate the density of the bottle of shampoo. **[1 mark]**

....

(e) The bottle has a mass of 525 g. The volume of the bottle of shampoo is 500 cm^3.

Calculate the density of the bottle of shampoo in g/cm^3. **[2 marks]**

density = ... g/cm^3

Changes of state

 Quick quiz

True or false?

The temperature a substance freezes at is called the melting point.	**True / False**
The temperature a substance condenses at is called the boiling point.	**True / False**
Changes of state are reversible.	**True / False**
Density is conserved in a change of state.	**True / False**

 State changes `Grade 5`

1. A sample of liquid ethanol at room temperature is heated steadily.
The temperature of the ethanol is measured at regular intervals.
Figure 1 shows a graph of temperature against time (a heating graph) for this experiment.

(a) Describe how the particles of ethanol in section **A** of **Figure 1** are arranged and how they are moving. **[2 marks]**

Ethanol is a liquid so the particles are touching. They move
....
as more energy is taken in.
....

Figure 1

(b) Determine the boiling point of ethanol from **Figure 1**. Tick **one** box. **[1 mark]**

25 °C ☐   78 °C ☐   92 °C ☐   100 °C ☐

(c) What is the best description of the particles of ethanol in section **B** of **Figure 1**? Tick **one** box. **[1 mark]**

> A change of state occurs where a heating graph forms a horizontal line.

The particles of ethanol are touching. ☐

The particles of ethanol bond to each other and the ethanol forms a solid. ☐

The particles of ethanol break apart to form molecules of water and carbon dioxide. ☐

The particles of ethanol separate from each other to move more freely. ☐

> Think about how the particles are moving and the effect of increasing the energy as the ethanol is heated.

 Cooling curve `Grade 4`

2. Stearic acid is a solid at room temperature. The melting point of stearic acid is about 70 °C. Some liquid stearic acid at 180 °C cools to 20 °C in 15 minutes. The temperature is recorded as the liquid cools. The temperature of the stearic acid stays the same between 10 and 12 minutes.

Sketch the shape of the cooling graph on the graph axes **(Figure 2)**. **[3 marks]**

Figure 2

 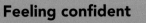

Specific heat capacity

② Quick quiz

The symbol equation for specific heat capacity is $\Delta Q = mc\Delta\theta$. Name each quantity.

ΔQ: change in .... m: ....

c: specific .... $\Delta\theta$: .... in temperature

⑩ Calculating energy transfer   Grade 5

1. An electric kettle heats 1.5 kg of water from 20 °C to 100 °C. The specific heat capacity of water is 4200 J/kg °C.

  (a) Calculate the change in temperature.   **[1 mark]**

    $\Delta\theta$ = ... − .... = ... °C

> Subtract the starting value from the final value.

  (b) Calculate the energy transferred from the kettle to the water.
    Use the equation: $\Delta Q = mc\Delta\theta$ **[2 marks]**

    ΔQ = ... × 4200 × .... = ...

                       energy transferred = ...J

② Specific heat capacity   Grade 3

2. State what is meant by the term 'specific heat capacity'.   **[2 marks]**

....

....

⑩ Measuring energy transfers   Grade 5

3. **Figure 1** shows the equipment used to determine the specific heat capacity of an aluminium block.

  (a) Describe what the insulation is for.   **[1 mark]**

    ....

    ....

  The mass of the aluminium block is 1.0 kg.

  The specific heat capacity of aluminium is 900 J/kg °C.

  The temperature of the block at the start of the experiment was 20 °C. It increased to 32 °C.

  (b) Calculate the energy transferred by the heater to the block.   **[2 marks]**

thermometer

immersion heater

solid aluminium block

insulation

heat resistant mat

Figure 1

> **Exam focus**
> Remember that $\Delta\theta$ means change in temperature.

                       energy transferred = ...J

 Made a start   **Feeling confident**   **Exam ready**

Specific latent heat

2 Quick quiz

True or false?

The specific latent heat of fusion is the energy required to change 1 kg of a liquid into 1 kg of a gas at constant temperature.	**True / False**
The units of specific latent heat of fusion are J/kg.	**True / False**
The specific latent heat of vaporisation is the energy released when 1 kg of a gas is changed to 1 kg of a liquid at constant temperature.	**True / False**
The units of specific latent heat of vaporisation are J/kg °C.	**True / False**

5 Specific latent heat of fusion — Grade 5

1. A block of ice is heated to its melting point. The temperature of the ice is measured throughout the experiment. The amount of energy transferred to the ice is also measured.

(a) The temperature of the ice increases at first, then it stops changing.

Using the particle model, explain what happens to the ice after the temperature stops changing. **[2 marks]**

The particles in the solid ice are starting to ....

so that the ice .... to form a ....

(b) The block of ice has a mass of 5.2 kg. The specific latent heat of fusion of ice is 336 000 J/kg.

Calculate the energy required to melt the ice completely. **[2 marks]**

$Q = mL =$ .... × ....

energy needed = ... J

10 Specific latent heat — Grade 5

2. Figure 1 shows some ice cubes in a glass of lemonade.

The specific latent heat of fusion of water is 336 000 J/kg.

Figure 1

(a) State what is meant by the term 'specific latent heat of fusion'. **[2 marks]**

....

....

(b) 30 g of ice was added to the lemonade. Calculate how much energy from the lemonade was used in melting the ice. **[3 marks]**

Remember to check the units used for mass and convert to kg.

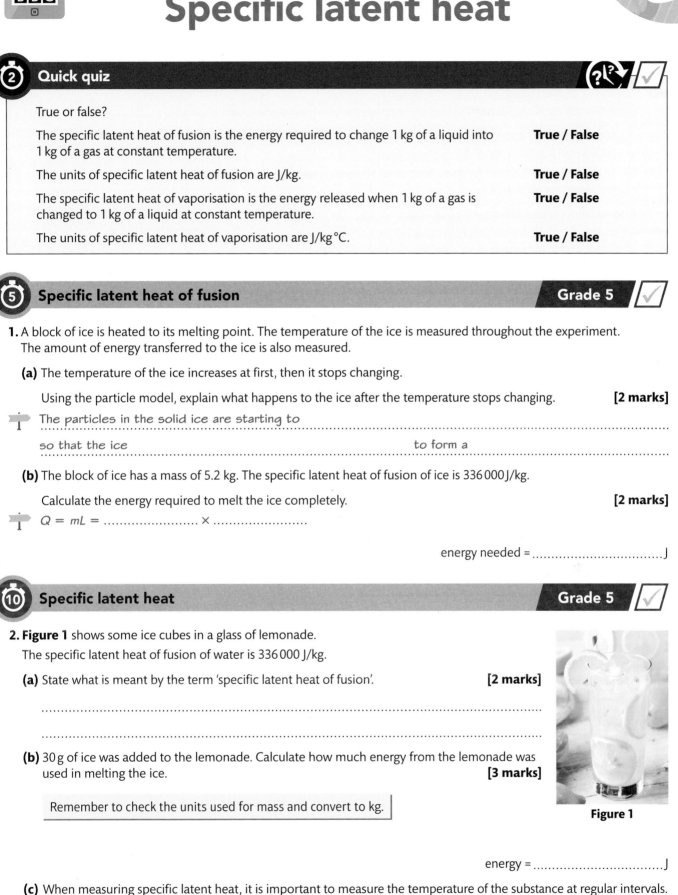

energy = ... J

(c) When measuring specific latent heat, it is important to measure the temperature of the substance at regular intervals. Suggest a reason why this is important. Tick **one** box. **[1 mark]**

To check the temperature is increasing slowly	☐	To check the temperature is falling slowly	☐
To check the temperature stays constant	☐	It is not important to check the temperature	☐

Practical: Properties of water

 Quick quiz

Circle the correct words in **bold** to give correct statements about specific heat capacity.

The **higher / lower** the specific heat capacity of a substance, the more energy it takes to increase the temperature of a given mass of the substance.

The **higher / lower** the specific latent heat of a substance, the more energy it takes to change the state of a given mass of the substance.

A liquid with a **high / low** specific heat capacity would be the most suitable for use in a central heating system.

 Specific heat capacity by electrical heating   **Grade 5**

1. A student has the following equipment to determine the specific heat capacity of water: electric heater, thermometer, stopwatch and calorimeter.

Describe a method the student could use to determine the specific heat capacity of water.   **[6 marks]**

> **Exam focus**
> When asked a question about a required practical, say what you measured and what you measured it with.

Fill the calorimeter with 1 kg of water. Measure the start temperature of the water using the thermometer.

Switch on the electric heater

Measure the highest temperature reached after

Calculate the energy input using

Calculate the specific heat capacity using the equation

change in thermal energy = mass × specific heat capacity × temperature change

rearranged to give specific heat capacity = ...
                                                .... × ....

 Melting ice   **Grade 5**

2. Two students measured the temperature of melting ice every 20 seconds. They melted crushed ice in a beaker and heated it using a Bunsen burner. Their results are shown in **Figure 1**.

(a) The students measured the mass of the ice before starting the experiment.

Their measurements were 0.145 kg, 0.143 kg and 0.147 kg.

Calculate the mean mass.   **[2 marks]**

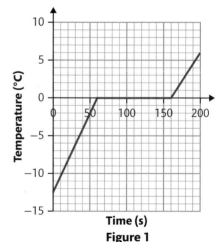

Figure 1

mean mass = ... kg

(b) Predict what will happen to the mass of ice when the ice has melted completely.   **[1 mark]**

....

(c) Determine when the ice was melting from **Figure 1**.   **[1 mark]**

....

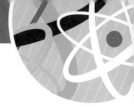

Particle motion in gases

2 Quick quiz

True or false?

Metres squared is a unit of volume.	**True / False**
Kelvin is a unit of temperature.	**True / False**
Pascal is a unit of volume.	**True / False**
N/m^2 is a unit of pressure.	**True / False**
C is a unit of temperature.	**True / False**

5 Absolute zero

Grade 5

1. (a) State what is meant by 'absolute zero'. **[2 marks]**

It is the lowest ....

All the particles in a substance stop ....

(b) Describe the pressure and average kinetic energy of gas particles at absolute zero. **[2 marks]**

At absolute zero, the pressure of a gas is ....

....

15 Gas pressure

Grade 5

2. Figure 1 shows a container of propane gas. Propane gas is used for camping stoves.

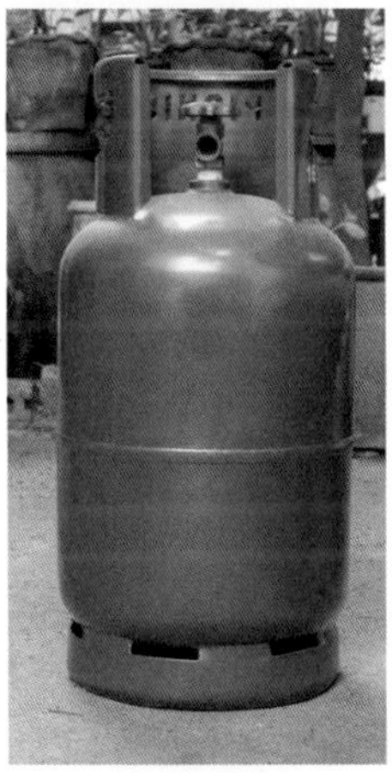

Figure 1

(a) The temperature of the gas is 0 °C.

Calculate the temperature of the gas in kelvin. **[2 marks]**

temperature = ... K

(b) The temperature of the gas in the bottle increases to 298 K.

Calculate the temperature of the gas in degrees Celsius. **[2 marks]**

temperature = ... °C

(c) Describe, using the particle model, what happens when the gas is heated. **[4 marks]**

....

....

....

....

Forces and elasticity

② Quick quiz

True or false?

Elastic distortion means that an object returns to its original shape when an applied force is removed.	**True / False**
Compression usually involves a single force.	**True / False**
Hooke's law states that the extension of an elastic object is inversely proportional to the force applied to it.	**True / False**
The units for the spring constant are N/m.	**True / False**
force = spring constant × extension	**True / False**

⑩ Elastic deformation

Grade 3

1. A mass is added to the end of a rubber band and it extends by 4 cm.

Describe how you could test to confirm that the rubber band had deformed elastically.

> Remember the definition for elastic deformation.

[1 mark]

If the mass is .... from the end of the rubber band, the band should .... its original shape.

⑩ Stretching a spring

Grade 8

2. A spring has a spring constant of 100 N/m. It is stretched by 20 cm.

(a) Calculate the elastic potential energy stored in the spring. Use the equation: $E = \frac{1}{2} \times k \times x^2$ **[3 marks]**

> 20 cm = 0.2 m

elastic potential energy = ... × .... × 0.2^2 = ...

elastic potential energy = ... J

(b) Calculate the force that produced the extension in the spring. Use the equation: $F = k \times x$ **[2 marks]**

force = ... N

⑩ Finding the spring constant
Grade 5

3. A mass of 0.2 kg is added to a spring and it extends by 10 cm.

(a) Calculate the weight added to the spring. Assume g = 10 N/kg.   **[2 marks]**

> **Maths skills**
> Remember that to convert from cm into m you need to divide by 100.

weight = ... N

(b) Calculate the spring constant of the spring.   **[3 marks]**

spring constant = ... N/m

 Made a start   **Feeling confident**   **Exam ready**

Practical: Force and extension

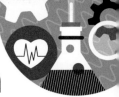

2 Quick quiz

True or false?

The extension of a spring is the final length subtracted from the initial length. **True / False**

The greater the spring constant of a spring, the stiffer the spring. **True / False**

A graph of force applied against extension for a spring will be a straight line through the origin. **True / False**

5 Force and extension — Grade 4

1. A student predicted that the extension of a spring would be directly proportional to the force applied to it. Explain how a graph could be used to show this. **[2 marks]**

Plot a graph of force against .... This should produce a ....

through the origin. Force should .... in proportion to extension.

15 Determining the spring constant — Grade 5

2. A student carried out an experiment to determine the spring constant of a spring. The student added 100 g masses to the end of a spring and measured the extension of the spring. **Table 1** shows the results.

Table 1

Force added (N)	0	1	2	3	4	5	6
Extension (cm)	0	4	8	10	16	20	24

Figure 1 shows a graph of the results.

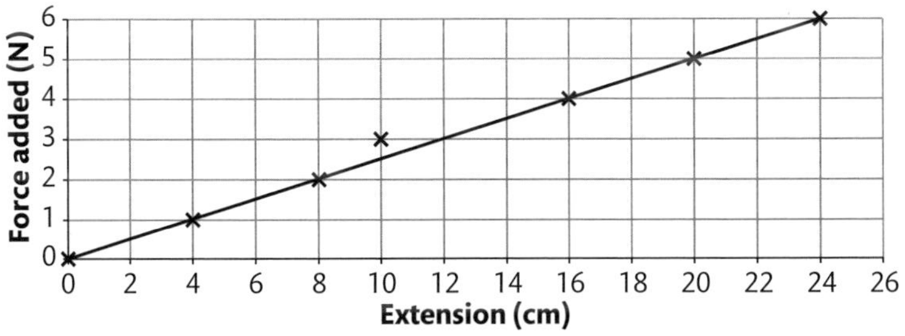

Figure 1

(a) Identify the anomalous reading (outlier) on **Figure 1**. **[1 mark]**

....

(b) Suggest a correct value of extension for the anomalous reading. **[1 mark]**

.... cm

(c) The spring constant can be found by calculating the gradient of the graph.

What is the spring constant of the spring? Tick **one** box. **[1 mark]**

0.25 N/m ☐ 0.4 N/m ☐ 4.0 N/m ☐ 25 N/m ☐

(d) Describe **two** ways that the student could improve the reliability of the method. **[2 marks]**

....

....

Made a start | Feeling confident | Exam ready

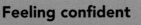

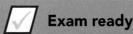

Practice paper: Biology

Time: 1 hour 10 minutes
You must have: ruler, calculator.
The total number of marks for this paper is 60.
Answer **all** questions.

1. **Figure 1** shows three stomata and their guard cells in the lower epidermis of a lily leaf. The photograph was taken using a light microscope.

    (a) Describe the function of stomata and their guard cells in plant leaves.
    [2 marks]

    (b) (i) The magnification of the photograph is ×200.
    Measure the diameter of one stoma on the photograph in cm.
    Use this to calculate the real diameter of the stoma in cm.
    Use the equation:

    $$\text{magnification} = \frac{\text{image size}}{\text{real size}}$$
    [2 marks]

    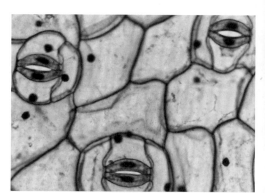

    Figure 1

    (ii) Give your answer from **(i)** in micrometres (μm).
    [1 mark]

    (c) What is the function of the green sub-cellular structures in the guard cells in **Figure 1**?
    [1 mark]

    control what enters and leaves the guard cell ☐

    site of respiration in the guard cell ☐

    site of photosynthesis in the guard cell ☐

    where most cellular reactions take place ☐

    (d) Explain why you need an electron microscope to study the detail inside one of the green sub-cellular structures. **[2 marks]**

    (e) Name **one** other sub-cellular structure found in a plant cell that is also found in animal cells. **[1 mark]**

    (f) Name **one** sub-cellular structure you would find in a plant cell that is **not** found in prokaryotic cells such as bacteria.
    [1 mark]

    (Total for Question 1 = 10 marks)

2. **(a)** Students carried out an investigation into the effect of sugar solution concentration on the mass of potato chips.

    This is the method they used:

    1. Chips were cut from a potato.

    2. The mass of each chip was measured and recorded.

    3. Two beakers of solution were set up, with different sugar concentrations.

    4. One chip was placed in each beaker.

    5. After 10 minutes each chip was reweighed and the new mass recorded.

    Suggest how this method could be improved to produce valid results.
    [4 marks]

(b) **Table 1** shows results from the investigation.

Table 1

Sugar concentration	Mass of chip at start in g	Mass of chip at end in g	Percentage change in mass
0% (pure water)	5.21	5.35	2.69%
30%	5.04	4.28	

Use the measurements in the table to calculate the percentage change in mass in the chip in the 30% solution.
Give your answer to 2 decimal places. **[2 marks]**

(c) Suggest a conclusion that explains the results in the table. **[2 marks]**

(Total for Question 2 = 8 marks)

3. Scientists have genetically engineered mosquitoes using a gene that affects a cell process and causes young mosquitoes to die before they develop into flying adults.

(a) Explain why the new gene was inserted into a cell of an early embryo, rather than a young mosquito. **[2 marks]**

Scientists plan to release adult genetically modified (GM) mosquitoes into the environment to mate with wild mosquitoes, to help control the spread of diseases such as malaria.

(b) Genetic engineering of mosquitoes in this way would reduce mosquito populations. Explain why this could reduce the number of people suffering from malaria. **[3 marks]**

(c) Describe another way that the spread of malaria is being reduced that does not use GM mosquitoes. **[1 mark]**

(d) Some people think that genetically engineered mosquitoes should not be released into the wild. Suggest **one** environmental problem that might result from releasing these mosquitoes into the wild. **[1 mark]**

(Total for Question 3 = 7 marks)

4. Students used the apparatus in **Figure 2** to measure the rate of water loss from a plant in still air and in moving air.
Water loss is measured as the distance the bubble moves over a given time. **Table 2** shows the results of the experiment.

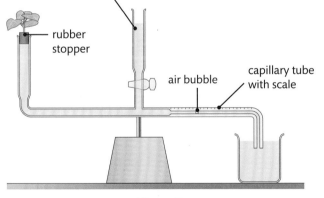

reservoir for pushing air bubble back to right-hand end of capillary tube

rubber stopper

air bubble

capillary tube with scale

Figure 2

Table 2

	Distance moved by bubble in 5 mins (mm)	Rate of water loss (mm/min)
still air	8	1.6
moving air	27	

(a) Describe how water moves through a plant. **[2 marks]**

(b) Complete **Table 2** by calculating the rate of water loss for moving air. **[1 mark]**

(c) Name **two** environmental factors that should be controlled in this experiment. **[2 marks]**

(d) Explain why the bubble moved a greater distance in 5 minutes for the plant in moving air. **[2 marks]**

(Total for Question 4 = 7 marks)

5. In a transect survey from the top to the bottom of a slope in a meadow, students recorded the number of plants of two buttercup species. They also took measurements of soil moisture using a moisture probe. The moisture probe gave a reading of 1 for very dry soil and 10 for very wet soil. **Table 3** shows their results.

Table 3

Sample number	1 (top of slope)	2	3	4	5	6 (bottom of slope)
Number of bulbous buttercups in 1 m²	4	4	1	0	0	0
Number of creeping buttercups in 1 m²	0	0	1	2	2	5
Soil moisture value	1.0	1.5	3.0	5.5	8.5	9.5

(a) Describe a method for carrying out this survey. **[2 marks]**

(b) Describe the relationship between the distribution of plants and the measured abiotic factor shown in **Table 3**. **[2 marks]**

(c) Name **one** biotic factor that could influence the distribution of the two buttercup species. **[1 mark]**

(Total for Question 5 = 5 marks)

6. Cystic fibrosis is an inherited disorder that causes mucus in the lungs and the digestive system to be thick and sticky rather than runny.

(a) Describe how defence systems in the trachea and bronchi of the lungs normally protect against infection. **[2 marks]**

Figure 3 shows a family tree for a family in which one person has cystic fibrosis.

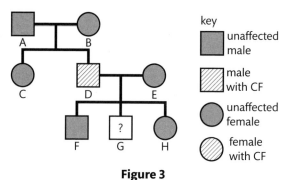

Figure 3

(b) Cystic fibrosis (CF) is caused by a recessive allele. If F represents the unaffected allele, and f represents the allele that causes CF, what is the genotype of person B in this family? **[1 mark]**

FF ☐   Ff ☐

ff ☐   not possible to tell ☐

(c) The genotype of a person who suffers from cystic fibrosis is **[1 mark]**

FF ☐   Ff ☐

ff ☐   not possible to tell ☐

(d) State the meaning of the term 'recessive allele'. **[2 marks]**

(e) Complete the Punnett square to calculate the probability that person G has CF. **[2 marks]**

		father's (D) alleles	
		f	f
mother's (E) alleles	F		
	f		

Cystic fibrosis is a serious condition that affects the daily lives of patients and can decrease lifespan. Genetic engineering is being used to develop potential gene therapy treatments for cystic fibrosis. In one clinical trial for a gene therapy treatment, lung function in the treated group decreased by 0.4% after 12 months, while in the placebo group lung function decreased by 4.0%. Gene therapy treatment can be delivered using a simple inhaler. Some potential gene therapy treatments give only short-term benefits and longer-term approaches carry a greater risk of side effects including cancer.

(f) Comment on the potential benefits and risks of treating cystic fibrosis using gene therapy.   **[4 marks]**

(Total for Question 6 = 12 marks)

7. **Figure 4** shows the relationship between weight and type 2 diabetes. The data were collected from adults aged 16–54 in the UK in 2009–10.

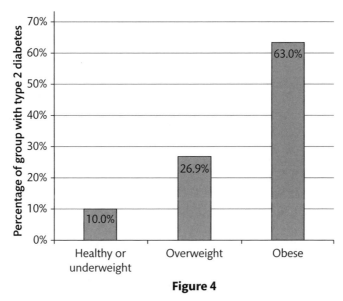

Figure 4

(a) Use **Figure 4** to explain why obesity is described as a risk factor for type 2 diabetes.   **[1 mark]**

Estimates suggest that 79% of the money spent by the NHS on treating diabetes could be saved by helping people to avoid developing diabetes.

(b) Describe **two** ways that a person could change their lifestyle to reduce their risk of developing diabetes.   **[2 marks]**

(c) The body cells of people with type 2 diabetes do not respond effectively to the hormone insulin. Explain how insulin acts to control blood glucose concentration.   **[2 marks]**

(d) Glucose is required by living cells for respiration. The rate of respiration can be measured for small organisms using the equipment shown in **Figure 5**.

Plan an investigation to compare the respiration rates of germinating peas and dried peas.

Include details of how to control important variables.   **[6 marks]**

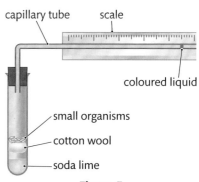

Figure 5

(Total for Question 7 = 11 marks)

TOTAL FOR PAPER = 60 MARKS

Practice paper: Chemistry

Time: 1 hour 10 minutes

You must have: ruler, calculator.

The total number of marks for this paper is 60.

Answer **all** questions.

1. (a) **Figure 1** shows the physical properties of an unknown substance.

Physical properties
conducts electricity when molten
high melting and boiling point
soluble in water
cannot conduct when solid
crystalline solid

Figure 1

What type of bonding is present in the unknown substance? **[1 mark]**

covalent bonding ☐ intermolecular force ☐

ionic bonding ☐ metallic bonding ☐

(b) Complete **Table 1** to give some information about three different ions.

Table 1

Ion	Atomic number	Mass number	Number of protons	Number of electrons	Number of neutrons
Mg^{2+}	12	24			
O^{2-}	8				8
	19	39		18	

[3 marks]

(c) Metals are good conductors of electricity.

Explain why. **[2 marks]**

(Total for Question 1 = 6 marks)

2. (a) What is the structure of carbon dioxide? **[1 mark]**

ionic ☐ simple molecular (covalent) ☐

giant covalent ☐ metallic ☐

(b) State what is meant by the term 'covalent bond'. **[1 mark]**

(c) Graphene is formed from carbon atoms held together by covalent bonds.

Describe the bonding and structure of graphene. **[2 marks]**

(d) Explain why metals have a high melting point. **[2 marks]**

(Total for Question 2 = 6 marks)

3. Alkanes are a homologous series of hydrocarbons.

(a) Which one of the organic molecules in **Figure 2** belongs to the **alkane** homologous series? [1 mark]

A

$$H-\overset{\overset{\displaystyle H}{|}}{C}-\overset{\overset{\displaystyle H}{|}}{C}=\overset{\overset{\displaystyle H}{|}}{C}-\overset{\overset{\displaystyle H}{|}}{C}-H$$

B

C

D

Figure 2

(b) Explain how crude oil is separated into useful mixtures. [3 marks]

(c) Give a use for the diesel oil fraction of crude oil. [1 mark]

(d) Bitumen is a crude oil fraction. Its hydrocarbon molecules have long chains of carbon atoms. The gases fraction contains molecules with short chains of carbon atoms.

Give **three** ways in which the properties of hydrocarbons change as the chain length increases. [3 marks]

(Total for Question 3 = 8 marks)

4. Calcium carbonate reacts with hydrochloric acid. Carbon dioxide is given off in the reaction.

A student adds calcium carbonate to excess dilute hydrochloric acid and measures the volume of gas produced every 10 seconds. **Table 2** shows the results.

Table 2

Time (s)	0	10	20	30	40	50	60
Total volume of gas in syringe (cm³)	0	20	35	45	49	50	50

(a) Describe the test for carbon dioxide gas. [2 marks]

(b) Draw a graph of volume of carbon dioxide gas against time. [3 marks]

(c) Calculate the mean rate of the reaction in cm³/s during the first 20 seconds of the reaction using the graph. [2 marks]

(d) The student repeated the experiment but heated the acid to a higher temperature before adding the calcium carbonate to the flask. All other conditions were the same.

Draw a second line on your graph to show the results you would expect.

Label your line **A**. [2 marks]

(e) The hydrochloric acid solution used contained 7.3 g of hydrochloric acid in 50 cm³ of solution.
Calculate the concentration of the hydrochloric acid in g dm⁻³. [2 marks]

(Total for Question 4 = 11 marks)

215

5. Ethene reacts with steam in a reversible reaction to make ethanol. The equation for this reaction is shown below.

ethene + steam ⇌ ethanol

$C_2H_4(g) + H_2O(g) \rightleftharpoons C_2H_5OH(g)$

This reaction can reach a dynamic equilibrium in a sealed container.

(a) Describe the rates of the forward reaction and reverse reaction at equilibrium. **[1 mark]**

Table 3 shows how the percentage yield of ethanol at equilibrium changes with temperature and pressure.

Table 3

Temperature (°C)	Yield of ethanol (%)	
	30 atmospheres	50 atmospheres
200	35	47
300	19	29

(b) (i) Describe how an increase in the temperature affects the percentage yield of ethanol produced. **[1 mark]**

(ii) Describe how changes in the pressure affect the percentage yield of ethanol produced. **[1 mark]**

(Total for Question 5 = 3 marks)

6. In the periodic table, elements are arranged in order of increasing atomic number and placed in groups and periods.

(a) Give **two** reasons why lithium, sodium and potassium are placed in Group 1. **[2 marks]**

(b) Complete the equation for the reaction of potassium with water.

.... K + ... H_2O → ..... KOH + H_2 **[1 mark]**

(c) Compare the trend in reactivity down Group 1 and Group 7 of the periodic table. **[2 marks]**

(d) Explain the trends in reactivity of Group 1 and Group 7 in terms of electronic configuration.
In your answer, describe each trend and give reasons for it. **[6 marks]**

(Total for Question 6 = 11 marks)

7. The compound CF_3Cl is a refrigerant used in air conditioning systems.

Calculate the relative formula mass of CF_3Cl.

(relative atomic masses C = 12.0, F = 19.0, Cl = 35.5) **[2 marks]**

(Total for Question 7 = 2 marks)

8. The Earth's atmosphere is a mixture of gases.

These gases include carbon dioxide, nitrogen, oxygen and water vapour.

The percentages of these gases remain almost constant.

(a) Complete **Table 4** to show the percentage of different gases in clean air.   **[2 marks]**

Table 4

Gas	% composition
carbon dioxide and other trace gases	<1
	80
oxygen	

(b) The atmosphere today is very different from the atmosphere billions of years ago. Describe the processes that scientists believe led to these changes in the amounts of oxygen, carbon dioxide and water.   **[3 marks]**

(Total for Question 8 = 5 marks)

9. Lead oxide is insoluble. It reacts with an acid to produce lead nitrate and one other product.

(a) Name the acid needed to produce lead nitrate.   **[1 mark]**

(b) Name the other product of this reaction.   **[1 mark]**

(c) Describe how you could prepare a pure, dry sample of lead nitrate.

You should name any essential apparatus in your answer.   **[6 marks]**

(Total for Question 9 = 8 marks)

TOTAL FOR PAPER = 60 MARKS

Practice paper: Physics

> Time: 1 hour 10 minutes
> You must have: ruler, calculator.
> The total number of marks for this paper is 60.
> Answer **all** questions.

1. A rubber ball is dropped from the side of a building. Energy is transferred as the ball falls.

   (a) Which of these describes the correct energy transfer as the ball falls? **[1 mark]**

   Kinetic energy decreases, gravitational potential energy decreases ☐

   Kinetic energy decreases, gravitational potential energy increases ☐

   Kinetic energy increases, gravitational potential energy decreases ☐

   Kinetic energy increases, gravitational potential energy increases ☐

   (b) The mass of the ball is 30 g. What is the mass of the ball in kilograms? **[1 mark]**

   0.3 kg ☐   3 kg ☐   0.03 kg ☐   30 000 kg ☐

   (c) The ball is dropped from a height of 15 m.

   Calculate the change in gravitational potential energy from when the ball is dropped to just before the ball hits the ground. State the unit.

   Use the equation: change in GPE = mass × gravitational field strength × change in height

   The gravitational field strength on Earth is 10 N/kg. **[3 marks]**

   (Total for Question 1 = 5 marks)

2. **Figure 1** shows a representation of a wave.

   ![Figure 1 wave diagram with Displacement on vertical axis, Distance on horizontal axis, label B pointing to amplitude and label A indicating wavelength]

   Displacement   B   Distance   A

   Figure 1

   (a) Complete the labels **A** and **B** on the diagram using words from the box. **[2 marks]**

   | period   amplitude   wavelength   frequency |

   (b) Complete the sentence. **[1 mark]**

   Waves transfer ………………………… and ………………………..

(c) What is the equation that links wave speed v, frequency f and wavelength λ?   **[1 mark]**

$v = \dfrac{f}{\lambda}$ ☐

$\lambda = \dfrac{f}{v}$ ☐

$\lambda = f \times v$ ☐

$v = f \times \lambda$ ☐

(d) A sound wave has a frequency of 40 Hz and a wavelength of 8.5 m. Calculate the speed of this wave in m/s. **[2 marks]**

(e) Electromagnetic waves are useful to us in a number of ways.

    (i) Name the type of electromagnetic waves that are used in airport scanners and medical devices to observe the internal structure of objects.   **[1 mark]**

    (ii) Give **two** uses of microwaves.   **[2 marks]**

(Total for Question 2 = 9 marks)

3. The specific heat capacity is a property of a material.

    (a) Give the meaning of the term 'specific heat capacity'.   **[1 mark]**

    (b) A kettle is used to heat 0.5 kg of water from 20 °C to 80 °C. The specific heat capacity of water is 4200 J/kg °C.
Calculate the energy transferred to the water in J.
Select an equation from the Physics equation sheet.   **[2 marks]**

    (c) A student measures the temperature of a flask of water as it is heated steadily. The measurements are shown in **Table 1**.

Table 1

Time (seconds)	0	30	60	90	120	150	180	210	240	270
Temperature (°C)	20	30	42	58	63	74	86	97	100	100

    (i) Explain whether any of the readings are anomalous.   **[2 marks]**

    (ii) Give **one** way that the student could improve the quality of their data other than by ignoring anomalous results. **[1 mark]**

    (iii) Explain what is happening to the water towards the end of the investigation.   **[1 mark]**

(Total for Question 3 = 7 marks)

4. Potential difference is measured using a voltmeter.

    (a) Give the meaning of the term 'potential difference'.   **[1 mark]**

    (b) An electric kettle is connected to the mains supply with a potential difference of 230 V.
When the kettle is switched on, a current of 8.4 A is measured.
Calculate the power of the kettle. State the unit.
Use the equation:

    power = potential difference × current   **[3 marks]**

219

(c) **Figure 2** shows a circuit diagram containing two different resistors connected in series.

    (i) What is the other component in the circuit?   **[1 mark]**

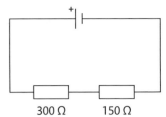

Figure 2

    a mains supply ☐   a battery ☐

    a cell ☐   a switch ☐

    (ii) Calculate the combined resistance of the resistors in **Figure 2** in ohms (Ω).

        [2 marks]

(d) **Figure 3** shows the same circuit as **Figure 2**, with components **X** and **Y** added to make measurements.

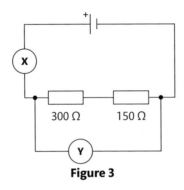

Figure 3

    (i) Which statement about X and Y describes the correct way to connect measuring components?   **[1 mark]**

        Component X is a voltmeter and component Y is an ammeter. ☐

        Component X is an ammeter and component Y is a voltmeter. ☐

        Components X and Y are both voltmeters. ☐

        Components X and Y are both ammeters. ☐

    (ii) The potential difference measured across both resistors is 1.35 V.
Calculate the current in the circuit in amps (A).
Use the equation:
potential difference = current × resistance   **[3 marks]**

(e) The same components are now connected in a different way. **Figure 4** shows the new circuit.

Which statement about the total resistance of the two resistors in **Figure 4** is true?   **[1 mark]**

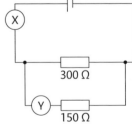

Figure 4

The total resistance is greater than 300 Ω. ☐

The total resistance is 300 Ω. ☐

The total resistance is 150 Ω. ☐

The total resistance is less than 150 Ω. ☐

(Total for Question 4 = 12 marks)

5. The particle model can be used to explain the physical properties of materials.

(a) Which statement about the particles in a gas is true? **[1 mark]**

The particles are close together. ☐

The forces between the particles are very small. ☐

The particles move very slowly. ☐

The forces between the particles keep them in contact. ☐

(b) Solid aluminium has a density of $2700\,\text{kg/m}^3$. Liquid aluminium has a density of $2400\,\text{kg/m}^3$.

Explain the difference in density between solid and liquid aluminium. **[3 marks]**

(c) A student wants to determine the density of an irregular shaped piece of rock.

Describe a method they could use to determine the density of the rock. **[4 marks]**

(Total for Question 5 = 8 marks)

6. $^{12}_{6}\text{C}$ and $^{13}_{6}\text{C}$ are two stable isotopes of the element carbon.

(a) Describe the difference between these two isotopes of carbon. **[1 mark]**

(b) Name **one** quantity that is the same for both isotopes of carbon. **[1 mark]**

(c) $^{14}_{6}\text{C}$ is another isotope of carbon. It is radioactive, and an atom of $^{14}_{6}\text{C}$ decays to form an atom of nitrogen, as shown in the nuclear equation.

$$^{14}_{6}\text{C} \rightarrow {^{14}_{7}\text{N}} + \text{.............................}$$

(i) Complete the nuclear equation. **[3 marks]**

(ii) What type of particle is emitted in this nuclear reaction? **[1 mark]**

proton ☐   electron ☐   neutron ☐   positron ☐

(iii) Name the type of decay that $^{14}_{6}\text{C}$ undergoes in this process. **[1 mark]**

(d) $^{14}_{6}\text{C}$ has a half-life of 5730 years. State the meaning of the term 'half-life'. **[1 mark]**

(e) The amount of $^{14}_{6}\text{C}$ measured in rock samples can be used to estimate the age of the rock. **Figure 5** shows the activity of a sample of $^{14}_{6}\text{C}$ atoms over time.

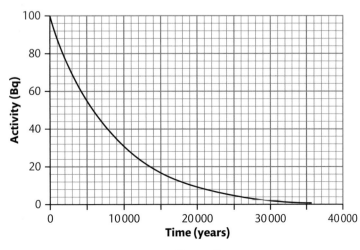

Figure 5

GCSE Science / Practice Papers / Physics

(i) Estimate the activity of the sample after 10 000 years using **Figure 5**. **[1 mark]**

(ii) State how many more years it will take for the activity you estimated in part **(i)** to reduce to half that value. **[1 mark]**

(Total for Question 6 = 10 marks)

7. The UK government is committed to reducing carbon dioxide emissions by 80% by 2050. One way of doing this is to increase the use of renewable energy resources.

   (a) Which one of the following is a renewable energy resource? **[1 mark]**

   oil ☐   gas ☐   biofuel ☐   coal ☐

   (b) **Figure 6** shows the percentage of electricity for the UK generated by using different energy resources in 2018.

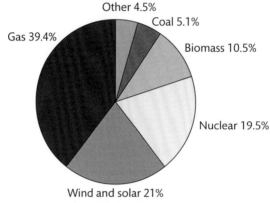

Other 4.5%
Coal 5.1%
Gas 39.4%
Biomass 10.5%
Nuclear 19.5%
Wind and solar 21%

Figure 6

   (i) State the energy resource that produced the third largest amount of electricity for the UK in 2018. **[1 mark]**

   (ii) State whether this energy resource is renewable or non-renewable. **[1 mark]**

   (iii) Justify your choice in part **(ii)**. **[1 mark]**

   (iv) Name **one** type of renewable energy resource that must be included in the section of the chart marked 'Other'. **[1 mark]**

   (v) In 1990, the percentage of electricity for the UK generated by burning coal was 65%.
   Calculate the difference in percentage between 1990 and 2018. **[2 marks]**

   (vi) Suggest **two** reasons why this difference has occurred. **[2 marks]**

(Total for Question 7 = 9 marks)

TOTAL FOR PAPER = 60 MARKS

Answers

Page 1 Levels of organisation
Quick quiz

tissue → a group of similar cells working together

organ system → a group of organs working together

cell → the smallest structural and functional unit of an organism

1. red blood cell → blood → heart → circulatory system

   [1 for each correct box, max = 3]

2. **(a)** An organ is a group of different tissues that work together to perform a role. **[1]**

   (b) the digestive system **[1]**

   (c) It is made up of a group of similar cells **[1]** that work together to carry out particular functions. **[1]**

3. **(a)** Drawing should be made with clean single lines, no shading, label lines drawn with ruler and not crossing each other. **[1]**

   Labels should identify nucleus, cytoplasm, cell membrane. **[1]**

   (b) Estimated diameter in the range 7–12 **[1]** µm **[1]**

Page 2 Eukaryotic and prokaryotic cells
Quick quiz

False; False; True; True; True

1. **(a)** plasmid **[1]**

   (b) flagellum **[1]**

2. Any one each from similarity and difference for 1 mark each:

   Similarity: cytoplasm; ribosomes

   Difference: a cell wall; plasmids; a single loop of DNA; flagella

3. plasmid **[1]**

4. **(a)** micrometre **[1]**

   (b) (i) 0.016 mm **[1]**

   (ii) 16 000 nm **[1]**

Page 3 Animal and plant cells
Quick quiz

A cell wall; **B** chloroplast; **C** permanent vacuole; **D** ribosome; **E** mitochondrion

1. Nucleus → contains genetic material (DNA) that controls what happens in the cell. **[1]**

   Cell membrane → controls which substances enter and leave the cell. **[1]**

   Cytoplasm → gel-like fluid where most cellular reactions take place. **[1]**

   Ribosomes → where proteins are made in the cell. **[1]**

   Mitochondria → where aerobic respiration takes place, producing energy. **[1]**

2.

Cell structure	Description of the structure
Cell wall **[1]**	Made of cellulose which is strong and provides support for the cell.
Permanent vacuole **[1]**	Contains dissolved minerals and sugars (cell sap). Gives the cell support.
Chloroplast **[1]**	Carries out photosynthesis. Contains chlorophyll to trap light energy.

3. Roots are found under the soil where there is no light. **[1]** Photosynthesis could not happen here so chloroplasts are not needed. **[1]**

Page 4 Specialised animal cells
Quick quiz

(a) egg

(b) sperm

(c) ciliated epithelial

1. **(a)** carries the father's genetic material / set of chromosomes **[1]**

   (b) digests part of the cell membrane to make a hole for sperm nucleus to enter the egg / so father's chromosomes can enter **[1]**

   (c) release energy from respiration so that the tail can make swimming movements to reach the egg cell **[1]**

2. **(a) (i)** Provide nutrients for dividing zygote / fertilised egg before placenta forms **[1]**

   (ii) Thickens and hardens so that other sperm nuclei cannot get into the egg cell **[1]**

   (b) fertilisation **[1]**

3. They have tiny hair-like structures called cilia on their surface. **[1]**

   The cilia move from side to side. **[1]**

   The movement carries the mucus along with the dirt and bacteria out of the lungs. **[1]**

Page 5 Microscopy
Quick quiz

From top to bottom: light; sub-cellular structures; lower; more

1. The mitochondria are too small to be seen with a light microscope. **[1]**

2. **(a)** ×160 **[1]**

   (b) ×40 **[1]**

   (c) ×16 **[1]**

3. **(a)** magnification = number of times larger the image appears compared to the actual size of object **[1]**

   (b) Electrons have a much shorter wavelength than light, **[1]** which means that very small structures can be seen with greater clarity / in much greater detail. **[1]**

4. **(a)** real size = $\frac{30}{10\,000}$ **[1]** = 0.003 mm **[1]**

   (b) convert to µm: 0.009 × 1000 = 9.0 µm **[1]**

Page 6 Practical: Using microscopes
Quick quiz

A objective lens; **B** eyepiece lens; **C** coarse focus knob; **D** fine focus knob; **E** lamp; **F** stage clips

1. image size = 3 cm = 3 × 10 000 µm = 30 000 µm **[1]**

   magnification = $\frac{30\,000}{30}$ = ×1000 **[1]**

2. **(a)** comment on drawing line – sharp pencil, not sketchy **[1]**

   comment on labels – add labels / label lines / label nucleus, cytoplasm, membrane **[1]**

   comment on magnification – give magnification / draw magnification bar **[1]**

   (b) to avoid trapping any air bubbles / damaging the specimen **[1]**

Page 7 Enzyme action
Quick quiz

A substrate; **B** active site; **C** enzyme; **D** products

1. **(a)** 40 °C (±2 °C) **[1]**

   (b) As the temperature increases from 0 °C to 30 °C the rate of reaction increases / rises. **[1]**

   (c) The rate of reaction decreases because the enzyme is denatured. **[1]** This means that the shape of the active site changes, **[1]** making it more difficult for the starch substrate to fit into the active site and so be broken down. **[1]**

2. **(a)** C **[1]**

   (b) Because the shape of the substrate **[1]** fits into / is complementary to the active site of the enzyme. **[1]**

Page 8 Practical: Enzymes
Quick quiz

False; True; False; True

1. **(a)** 30 seconds × 4 spots **[1]** [not 5 spots, because the first spot was done at time 0] = 120 seconds **[1]**

   (b) $\frac{1}{90}$; **[1]** answer to 2 significant figures = 0.011 s^{-1} **[1]**

   (c) To keep temperature constant **[1]** because temperature also affects the rate of enzyme-controlled reactions **[1]** / the enzyme will work quite well at 30 °C **[1]**

2. **(a)** the pH at which the rate of reaction of the enzyme is fastest / highest **[1]**

   (b) Iodine solution changes from yellow/ orange to blue/black if starch is present **[1]** but stays orange if there is no starch / the starch has been broken down to sugar. **[1]**

Page 9 Digestion and enzymes
Quick quiz

lipase → fat → fatty acids and glycerol

carbohydrase (e.g. amylase) → carbohydrates (e.g. starch) → glucose

protease → protein → amino acids

1. (a) Food molecules are too large to be absorbed into the blood from the small intestine. **[1]**

Digestive enzymes break down the large food molecules into smaller ones that can be absorbed. **[1]**

(b) amino acids **[1]**

(c) Enzymes are biological because they are made inside living organisms. **[1]**

Enzymes are catalysts because they speed up the rate of reactions. **[1]**

2. (a) lipase **[1]**

(b) fatty acids and glycerol **[1]**

(c) 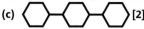 **[2]**

Page 10 Diffusion
Quick quiz

cell membrane
high concentration | low concentration

net movement

1. Diffusion is the net movement of particles from high to low concentration. **[1]**

2. Membrane surface area → The larger the area over which diffusion can occur, the faster the rate. **[1]**

Temperature → Particles with more energy move faster. **[1]**

Concentration gradient → The greater the difference in concentration of particles between two areas, the faster the net movement of particles. **[1]**

3. (a) carbon dioxide **[1]**

(b) Gas A is at higher concentration in the blood than in the air / alveolus **[1]** so it moves down the concentration gradient / from high to low concentration **[1]** by diffusion. **[1]**

(c) Thin walls mean that the distance / path for diffusion is smaller / shorter **[1]** so the rate of diffusion will be higher. **[1]**

Page 11 Osmosis
Quick quiz

	Concentration of salt molecules is	Concentration of water molecules is
Salt solution	high	low
Pure water	low	high

1. (a) Water moves into the cell by the process of osmosis **[1]** causing the cell to increase in size. This is because the solute concentration inside the cell is higher than in the distilled water. **[1]**

(b) The cell shrinks / gets smaller **[1]** as water moves out of the cell by osmosis. **[1]**

2. (a) A membrane that only allows certain molecules to pass through. **[1]**

(b) low; high; water; sugar

low and high correct **[1]**; water and sugar correct **[1]**

(c) The mass increased **[1]** because there was more water inside the tubing after 1 hour. **[1]**

Page 12 Practical: Osmosis
Quick quiz
arrow pointing from left to right across the membrane

1. (a) Because water on the outside of the cylinders would cause the mass to increase / appear higher **[1]** making the results less accurate / have errors. **[1]**

(b) Water enters or leaves the cylinder across its outer surface. **[1]** A bigger surface area could result in a bigger / faster change in mass. **[1]**

(c) Any one for 1 mark from: time left in solution, temperature of solution, type of potato, age of potato

2. (a) (i) change in mass = 1.25 – 1.13 = 0.12 grams **[1]**

(ii) percentage change in mass = $\frac{0.12}{1.13}$ × 100 = 10.6% / 11% **[1]**

(b) by osmosis **[1]**

(c) The mass would fall **[1]** because water would move (by osmosis) out of the potato cells / into the surrounding solution which has a higher solute concentration. **[1]**

Page 13 Active transport
Quick quiz

Statement	Diffusion	Osmosis	Active transport
Movement of substances against a concentration gradient			✓
Movement of water across a partially permeable membrane		✓	
Requires energy to take place			✓
Can describe the movement of gases	✓		
Net movement of dissolved solute molecules down their concentration gradient	✓		

1. (a) They increase the surface area of the root (for absorption). **[1]**

(b) The concentration of mineral ions is higher in the root hair cells than in the surrounding soil solution. **[1]** Therefore, the mineral ions need to be moved against their concentration gradient. **[1]**

2. (a) Because glucose concentration is lower inside the gut than inside the cell. **[1]** Only active transport can move the glucose against the concentration gradient. **[1]**

(b) Mitochondria carry out (aerobic) respiration. **[1]** Respiration releases energy for active transport. **[1]**

Page 14 Mitosis and the cell cycle
Quick quiz

Metaphase	2
Cytokinesis	5
Anaphase	3
Prophase	1
Telophase	4

1. Cell division takes place. **[1]**

2. (a) anaphase **[1]**

(b) interphase **[1]**

3. (a) two **[1]**

(b) Both daughter cells would be genetically identical / have identical sets of chromosomes to the parent cell. **[1]** Daughter cells would be diploid / have four chromosomes. **[1]**

Page 15 Importance of mitosis
Quick quiz
True; False; True; False

1. (a) asexual **[1]**

(b) mitosis **[1]**

(c) The flowers of the daughter bulbs would be white, **[1]** because offspring produced by asexual reproduction are genetically identical to the parent. **[1]**

2. (a) mitosis **[1]**

(b) the division of cells is uncontrolled **[1]**

Page 16 Cell differentiation and growth
Quick quiz
False; True

1. Differentiation is when an unspecialised cell develops to become a specialised cell. **[1]**

2. The first stage is cell division which produces many new unspecialised cells. **[1]** The second stage is cell differentiation which produces cells specialised for a particular function. **[1]**

3. (a) Cell division takes place / meristem cells divide. **[1]**

(b) The small, unspecialised cells produced by the meristem get bigger by the process of <u>elongation</u>. **[1]** Cells must also undergo <u>differentiation</u> **[1]** to form specialised cells.

4. (a) The growth of a baby with the median size of the population / half (50%) of all babies in the population will show growth above this curve and half (50%) will be equal to or below the curve. **[1]**

(b) They show if the baby is growing properly / if there may be any health problems affecting growth. **[1]**

Page 17 Stem cells

Quick quiz

embryonic stem cell → unspecialised cell that can give rise to all of the different types of cell in a human body

adult stem cell → unspecialised cell in tissue that can produce some types of differentiated cell

meristem → plant cells that divide and differentiate into any type of plant cell

1. New blood cells are produced by division **[1]** of adult stem cells **[1]** which are found in bone marrow tissue.

2. **(a)** Embryonic stem cells can divide to produce many kinds of differentiated cell. **[1]** Adult stem cells can produce few types of cells / it may be difficult to find adult stem cells that produce the right kind of specialised cell. **[1]**

    (b) Stem cells could be used to replace faulty cells in the pancreas with healthy ones. **[1]** The healthy cells would then produce insulin. **[1]**

    (c) The cells will be genetically identical to the patient's cells **[1]** and so will not be rejected / destroyed by the immune system. **[1]**

3. **(a)** meristem **[1]**

    (b) Any one for 1 mark from: new plants have identical good characteristics to parent / can select disease free cells / produce large numbers of identical plants quickly. **[1]**

    (c) Meristem cells can divide **[1]** and differentiate into all the cell types needed (for a new plant). **[1]**

Page 18 The human nervous system

Quick quiz

Sensory receptor cells	1
Relay neurone in spinal cord	3
Effector cells	5
Motor neurone	4
Sensory neurone	2

1. **(a)** A synapse is where two neurones meet. **[1]**

    (b) Step 2: The impulse causes the axon terminal to release neurotransmitter into the gap between the neurones. **[1]**

    Step 3: The neurotransmitter diffuses across the gap to the next neurone / diffuses across the gap and binds to receptors on the next neurone. **[1]**

    Step 4: This causes a new electrical impulse to start in the next neurone. **[1]**

2. **(a)** Reflex actions are fast. **[1]** This helps protect the eye from harm caused by something hitting the eye. **[1]**

    (b) to detect stimuli / changes in the environment **[1]**

3. Any two for 2 marks from: they have many dendrites and terminals to connect with sensory receptor cells / neurones in the central nervous system **[1]**; they have a

long dendron / axon to carry electrical impulses through the body **[1]**; they have a myelin sheath to speed up transmission of impulses. **[1]**

Page 19 Meiosis

Quick quiz

True; False; True

1. **(a)** 19 **[1]**

    (b) Meiosis produces gametes that have half the normal number of chromosomes. **[1]** When two gametes fuse during fertilisation their chromosomes are combined in the fertilised cell. **[1]** This restores the full chromosome number in the fertilised cell. **[1]**

2. **(a)** chromosomes / genetic material must be copied / doubled / duplicated **[1]**

    (b) four **[1]**

3. **(a)** sexual (reproduction) **[1]**

    (b) Genetic differences between cells / gametes produce genetic variation in offspring. **[1]** This variation enables offspring to survive in different environments. **[1]**

    (c) Mitosis produces cells with one set of chromosomes while meiosis produces cells with two sets. **[1]**

Page 20 The structure of DNA

Quick quiz

Stage	Stage order
Pour ice-cold ethanol down the inside of the tube very carefully.	4
Remove the banana skin and mash it up very thoroughly.	1
Filter the mixture.	3
Mix the banana mash with a mixture of salt, detergent and water and warm in a water bath for 20 minutes.	2

1. **(a)** double helix **[1]**

    (b) two **[1]**

    (c) A particular base will only pair with one other particular base. **[1]**

    (d) four **[1]**

2. **(a)** nucleotide **[1]**

    (b) It is a long molecule made of repeating units (nucleotides). **[1]**

Page 21 DNA and the genome

Quick quiz

DNA; polymer; two; helix; chromosomes

1. **(a)** It means the whole genetic material of a human. **[1]**

    (b) A gene is a short section of DNA **[1]** that codes for a particular protein. **[1]**

    (c) within the nucleus **[1]**

2. **(a)** chromosome; protein **[2]**

    (b) Any one for 1 mark from: they can be treated before the disease develops **[1]**; change lifestyle to reduce risk. **[1]**

Page 22 Genetic inheritance

Quick quiz

A homozygous recessive allele pair

B different genes

C alleles of gene A

D homozygous dominant allele pair

E heterozygous allele pair

1. multiple interacting genes **[1]**

2. **(a)** A recessive allele is only expressed if an individual has two copies of the recessive allele / if both alleles in a pair are recessive. **[1]**

    (b)

	F	f
F	FF	Ff
f	Ff	ff

    [1 mark for correct offspring genotypes]

    (c) probability expressed in one of the following ways: 0.25, $\frac{1}{4}$, 25%, 1 in 4 **[1]**

3. **(a)**

	T	t
t	Tt	tt
t	Tt	tt

    Correct parent alleles T and t, **[1]** written in correct columns **[1]**

    (b) 2 out of 4 = 50% **[1]**

Page 23 Genetic diagrams

Quick quiz

inherited disorder → a disorder caused by a faulty allele

recessive allele → affects the phenotype only when there are two copies in the genotype

dominant allele → affects the phenotype even if only one copy of the allele is present in the genotype

1. **(a)** four **[1]**

    (b) The genotype must be Dd **[1]** because they have offspring that have the disorder and ones that are healthy, so they must be able to pass on either allele. **[1]**

    (c) Person 6 must have the genotype dd. **[1]** They cannot be a carrier because this disorder is caused by a dominant allele, **[1]** so if they were a carrier with one faulty allele they would suffer from the disorder. **[1]**

2. **(a)** tall **[1]**

    (b) possible offspring genotypes, from left: TT, Tt, Tt, tt **[1 for all correct]**

    possible offspring phenotypes, from left: tall, tall, tall, dwarf **[1 for all correct]**

    (c) 25% **[1]**

Page 24 Sex determination

Quick quiz

fertilisation; zygote; genes; XX; XY

1. **(a)** meiosis **[1]**

    (b) half / 50% **[1]**

    (c) The egg cell from the mother can contain only an X chromosome. **[1]**

Sperm cells may contain either an X chromosome or a Y chromosome. **[1]**

So, the sex chromosome that is present in the sperm that fertilises the egg determines the sex of the baby / if it will be XX or XY. **[1]**

2. (a)

		Sperm cells from father	
		X	Y
Egg cells from mother	X	XX	XY
	X	XX	XY

[1 mark for mother's chromosomes, 1 mark for correct genotypes of offspring]

(b) 50% **[1]**

(c) 50% **[1]**

(d) The baby will be a girl. **[1]**

Page 25 Variation and mutation
Quick quiz
genetic; environmental; environmental; genetic

1. (a) Variation is the differences in characteristics that are seen between individuals. **[1]**

(b) A mutation is a change in the DNA. **[1]**

(c) They are likely to have no effect on the baby **[1]** because most genetic mutations have no effect on phenotype. **[1]** Very rarely a mutation may have a significant / noticeable effect. **[1]**

2. (a) sexual reproduction and mutations in DNA **[1]**

(b) Height is controlled by multiple genes. **[1]** Each child may inherit different alleles of each gene from the parents. **[1]**

(c) Any one from: nutrition **[1]** / food quality **[1]** / food quantity **[1]** / disease (not genetic) **[1]**

(d) as a result of mutation **[1]**

Page 26 Evolution by natural selection
Quick quiz
evolution; natural; characteristics; adapted; offspring; alleles

1. Level 3: A detailed and coherent explanation is provided which includes use of antibiotics and existing variation in resistance to show how a population of resistant bacteria evolves via natural selection. **[5–6]**

Level 2: An attempt to relate natural selection to the evolution of resistant bacteria. The ordering of ideas may be weak but builds towards a coherent argument. **[3–4]**

Level 1: Discrete relevant points made. The ordering of the explanation may be unclear, and the link between natural selection and evolution of antibiotic resistance may be weak or with some errors. **[1–2]**

No relevant content. **[0]**

Indicative content:
The population of bacteria has existing genetic variation.

Some bacteria are more resistant to antibiotics than others.

This is caused by mutations.

People misuse antibiotics by using them too frequently or not finishing courses.

Those bacteria that are not resistant die. The resistant bacteria survive and reproduce, passing on their favourable characteristics.

This is an example of natural selection.

The population of bacteria changes due to natural selection. This is evidence of evolution.

2. (a) Evolution is the change in a population over time **[1]** of inherited characteristics **[1]**

(b) Any one for 2 marks from: thicker fur **[1]** for insulation; **[1]** wider feet **[1]** to stop sinking in snow or slipping on ice; **[1]** white fur **[1]** for camouflage **[1]**

Page 27 Evidence for human evolution
Quick quiz
True; False; True

1. (a) Lucy's leg bone is nearer in length to a modern chimp **[1]** than a modern human. This suggests she was a similar height to a modern chimp. **[1]**

(b) This shows that her knees would have been close together **[1]** and suggests that she would have walked upright like a modern human. **[1]**

2. The more recent hand axe shows more careful working / older axe is more roughly worked. **[1]** The newer axe has a more obvious point / is more specialised / less simple than the older axe. **[1]** This is evidence of evolution of greater human skill / higher human intelligence over the time period. **[1]**

Page 28 Classification
Quick quiz
prokaryotes → single cells with genetic material free in cytoplasm

protists → usually single cells with nucleus and other sub-cellular structures

fungi → usually multi-celled organisms that digest food outside their bodies

plants → usually multi-celled organisms that are able to photosynthesise

animals → multi-celled organisms that digest food inside their bodies

1. (a) phylum; **[1]** species **[1]**

(b) Knowledge about genetic material and how to analyse it was not available **[1]** at the time.

2. (a) Any two for 2 marks from: protists, fungi, animals, plants

(b) (i) Using genetic analysis / by looking at their genes **[1]**

(ii) The genetic material of archaea has similarities with both bacteria and eukaryota / archaea are more similar to eukaryotes than they are to bacteria. **[1]** Bacteria and eukaryota have fewer similarities with each other. **[1]**

Page 29 Selective breeding
Quick quiz
Any suitable responses, such as: dog – markings, size, gentle nature; cow – high milk yield, high meat yield; flower – unusual or large flowers, brightly-coloured flowers, attractive scent, disease resistance

1. (a) Selective breeding is the process by which humans choose and breed plants and animals for particular genetic characteristics. **[1]**

(b) First select male and female cattle that produce the most meat. **[1]** Breed these cattle together. **[1]** Then breed the biggest offspring together. **[1]**

2. (a) Closely related individuals with similar alleles tend to be bred together. **[1]**

(b) Limited genetic variation can make them more likely to suffer from inherited diseases. **[1]** Genetic similarity means the whole population will be vulnerable to the same disease(s). **[1]**

(c) People may think that it is wrong if selective breeding of cows for the benefit of humans **[1]** causes the cows to suffer. **[1]**

Page 30 Genetic engineering
Quick quiz
A gene is added to rice cells so that a plant can produce vitamin A.

Disease-resistant cotton plants that have had a gene from a bacterium inserted into them.

Bacteria that have had their genome modified so they will produce an antibiotic.

Plum trees that are made disease resistant by modifying their chromosomes.

1. (a) The gene for human insulin is obtained from a human chromosome. **[1]**

The gene is then inserted into a bacterium. **[1]**

The modified bacterium will then produce human insulin. **[1]**

(b) Any one for 1 mark from: Genetically engineered insulin is the same as that produced by human genes. **[1]**; Human insulin may be better than pig insulin. **[1]**; No pigs need to be killed to produce it. **[1]**; It is more readily available (as bacteria can be cultured easily). **[1]**

2. (a) This type of GM maize kills caterpillars that try to eat it **[1]** so there is less damage to the plant and it can grow better / produce more food. **[1]**

(b) Any two for 2 marks that give a suitable explanation that shows how the inserted gene could lead to harm in the environment, such as: The poison gene could transfer to wild plants nearby by pollination. **[1]** Wild plants growing from the seed will also kill caterpillars, leaving less food for insect-eating birds. **[1]**

Page 31 Health issues

Quick quiz

lung cancer; cardiovascular disease

1. Physical well-being (or example such as being pain or injury free) **[1]** and mental / social well-being (or example such as lack of mental disorder / adequate nutrition / not being lonely) **[1]**

2. Communicable diseases are caused by a pathogen and can be passed from an infected person to others. **[1]**

   Non-communicable diseases have other causes, such as genes or faults in the way cells work, and cannot be passed to another person by infection. **[1]**

3. $\frac{441}{5507}$ **[1]** × 100 = 8% **[1]**

4. The main peaks in asthma cases and in flu cases match. **[1]** There is a positive correlation between flu and asthma. / An outbreak in flu infections increases the likelihood of asthma attacks. / People who have asthma may be more likely to have an attack if they also have flu. **[1]**

Page 32 Communicable diseases

Quick quiz

chalara ash dieback → fungus

chlamydia → bacterium

HIV → virus

malaria → protist

1. a microorganism that causes disease **[1]**

2.

	Water	Airborne	Animal vector
Tuberculosis		✓	
Chalara ash dieback		✓	
Malaria			✓

[1 mark for each correct row]

3. sterilising drinking water **[1]**

   careful treatment and disposal of sewage **[1]**

4. **(a)** 3.2 (%) **[1]**

   (b) Smoking fewer than 10 cigarettes a day does not increase the chance of developing tuberculosis again. **[1]**

   Smoking more than 10 cigarettes a day increases the chance of developing tuberculosis again **[1]** by more than double. **[1]**

Page 33 Viral diseases

Quick quiz

True; False; True; False

1. **(a)** HIV is spread through exchange of body fluids, for example, during sexual activity / by sharing injection needles. **[1]**

   (b) The risk of spreading HIV during sexual activity can be reduced by using a condom. **[1]**

   (c) White blood cell **[1]**

   (d) White blood cells are part of the immune system. **[1]** With fewer white blood cells, the body is not able to destroy pathogens that enter

the body. **[1]** So AIDS develops, in which a person suffers from / may die due to infection with other diseases. **[1]**

2. **(a)** As the proportion of people with HIV increases, the proportion of people with TB also increases. / There is a positive correlation between proportion of people with HIV and proportion with TB. **[1]**

   (b) HIV damages the immune system so people with HIV are more likely to be infected with TB. **[1]**

Page 34 Bacterial diseases

Quick quiz

chlamydia; cholera; tuberculosis

1. The age groups most likely to be infected are tested. **[1]** More effective targeting of resources / money is saved by only testing those most likely to have the disease. **[1]**

2. **(a)** Any one for 1 mark from: watery diarrhoea **[1]**; vomiting **[1]**; fast heart rate **[1]**; low blood pressure **[1]**

   (b) Human waste may contain cholera bacteria **[1]** which cause cholera if a person drinks water with human waste in it / drinks contaminated with water that isn't boiled. **[1]**

   (c) Any suitable method that prevents ingestion of pathogen, such as: only drink bottled water; boil water to kill pathogens before drinking; do not eat uncooked food. **[2]**

3. **(a)** lung damage **[1]**

   (b) Any two for 2 marks from: cover mouth and nose when coughing; wear a mask; improve ventilation; vaccination of population; treatment of infected persons with antibiotics so they do not pass TB on.

Page 35 Fungal diseases

Quick quiz

eukaryota

1. **(a)** Chalara ash dieback causes damaged areas of bark called lesions **[1]** and loss / death of leaves. **[1]**

   (b) Stopping water and nutrients reaching the leaf and stem cells **[1]** will prevent them carrying out the processes needed for life. **[1]**

   (c) Small spores are released from fruiting bodies on infected twigs. **[1]** These can be carried long distances through the air by the wind. **[1]**

2. **(a)** Clearing dead wood and leaves will remove the fruiting bodies that release spores. **[1]**

   (b) Biodiversity is reduced **[1]** as there will be fewer habitats and food sources **[1]** and so fewer types of animal. **[1]**

Page 36 Protist diseases

Quick quiz

True; False; False; True

1. **(a)** Any two for 2 marks from: recurrent bouts of fever; blood damage / destruction of red blood cells; liver damage

   (b) Any two for 4 marks from: Spray water with insecticide to kill young / larval mosquitoes **[1]** so they will not develop into adults that bite humans. **[1]**

   Spray resting areas with insecticide / chemicals that kill mosquitoes **[1]** to reduce numbers that could spread malaria. **[1]**

   Sleep inside mosquito net **[1]** to prevent bites from night-flying females. **[1]**

   Isolate infected people **[1]** so they cannot be bitten by and infect mosquitoes (which can then infect other people). **[1]**

2. **A** → Mosquito bites a person with malaria, taking in the protist in blood that it feeds on. **[1]**

   B → The mosquito bites another person, passing on malaria when the pathogens enter the human bloodstream. **[1]**

Page 37 Human defence systems

Quick quiz

False; True; True

1. **(a) (i)** Thick skin makes it difficult for pathogens to get into the body. **[1]**

   (ii) Sticky mucus in the nose traps pathogens before they can attack cells lining the nose / enter the lungs. **[1]**

   (iii) Cells lining the trachea and bronchi have cilia (tiny hairs) on their surface that move pathogens out of the lungs (to the throat where they can be swallowed). **[1]**

   (b) Any one for 2 marks from: stomach acid **[1]** destroys pathogens that enter the body in food and drink; **[1]** lysozymes **[1]** break down / digest pathogens that enter the eyes. **[1]**

2. **(a)** It recognises / acts on particular **[1]** pathogens that have entered the body and destroys them. **[1]**

   (b) (Phagocytes) ingest / engulf pathogens by phagocytosis. **[1]** (Lymphocytes) produce antibodies that attack and destroy specific pathogens. **[1]** Produce memory lymphocytes that respond rapidly after a second infection by the same pathogen. **[1]**

3. antigens, lymphocytes, antibodies, pathogens

   antigens / antibodies correct; **[1]** lymphocytes / pathogens correct **[1]**

Page 38 Immunisation

Quick quiz

antigens; communicable; specific; illness

1. **(a)** The weakened form of the virus contains the antigens that trigger an immune response **[1]** but it is not able to cause the polio disease. **[1]**

   (b) The memory lymphocytes specific to polio will remain in the body. **[1]**

   This means that if the child is infected later with the polio virus, antibodies will be produced very rapidly by these lymphocytes. **[1]**

This will destroy the virus before symptoms can occur and prevent the child developing (symptoms of) polio disease. [1]

2. (a) Any two for 2 marks from: to prevent lots of people dying from smallpox; [1] to reduce the spread of smallpox to people who hadn't had the vaccine or disease; [1] some people don't like being immunised [1]

(b) Memory lymphocytes for the smallpox antigen remained in the body [1] so antibodies against the antigen of the smallpox disease were produced very quickly when the person was exposed to the pathogen later on. [1]

(c) There is no longer any risk of them being infected by the smallpox pathogen because the disease has been eradicated. [1]

Page 39 Antibiotics
Quick quiz
antibiotic → medicine used to cure bacterial disease

antibody → produced by immune system in response to infection

painkiller → medicine used to reduce symptoms of disease

antigen → stimulates the immune system to attack a pathogen

1. Antibiotics only kill bacteria, [1] so they will have no effect on a disease caused by viruses. [1]

2. Antibiotics only inhibit cell processes in bacteria such as the pneumonia pathogen. [1]
   They do not affect cell processes in human cells so do not cause harm. [1]

3. (a) Improved cleanliness reduced the number of deaths before 1940. [1] Deaths fell further after the introduction of antibiotics around 1940 [1] but then levelled off / remained at a low level. [1]

(b) Antibiotic-resistant strains cannot be killed by using antibiotics, [1] so the number of deaths from infections is likely to increase. [1]

Page 40 Development of drugs
Quick quiz
placebo → appears exactly like the drug but without any active ingredients

side effect → unintended harm caused by a drug

dose → how much drug to use at a time

1. (a) discovery, [1] development [1]

(b) Computers will be able to compare molecules more quickly / more cheaply. [1]

2. (a) The drug is tested on human cells and tissues. [1] The drug is tested on animals. [1]

(b) To make sure it is safe to use in living cells and systems / make sure it won't poison human cells. [1]

(c) Test on healthy volunteers: to make sure it is safe [1] Test on patients: to find the most effective dose and check for side effects. [1]

(d) Because the potential benefits may outweigh the possible risks / or example, e.g. drug may show potential to save lives of people who might die before the tests are completed. [1]

Page 41 Non-communicable diseases
Quick quiz
False; False; True; True

1. (a) air pollution [1]

(b) Any two for 2 marks from: smoking; genes; high blood pressure; lack of exercise; high blood cholesterol; diabetes; alcohol

2. (a) The person has enough energy intake but may not be getting enough protein / vitamins / minerals. [1]

(b) iron [1]

3. (a) The number of cases of cervical cancer should decrease. [1]

(b) Fewer women should be infected with the virus that triggers the cancer. [1]

Page 42 Effects of lifestyle
Quick quiz
smoking tobacco → lung cancer

obesity → type 2 diabetes

drinking large amounts of alcohol → liver disease

high dose of UV radiation from sunshine → skin cancer

1. (a) People who smoke 1–14 g/day have a risk of heart attack that is 1.6 times that of someone who has never smoked. [1]

(b) As the mass of tobacco smoked per day increases the risk of having a heart attack also increases. [1]

2. (a) Alcohol consumption increased from about 7 dm^3 per person per year in 1970 to about 10 dm^3 per person per year in 2009. [1]

(b) High alcohol consumption can damage the liver / cause cirrhosis [1] so increasing alcohol consumption could be the cause of the increased deaths. [1]

Page 43 Cardiovascular disease
Quick quiz
blood vessels; arteries; blood flow; oxygen

1. (a) Heart valves prevent blood from moving backwards through the heart / in the wrong direction. [1]
   So, with faulty valves the amount of blood flowing through / pumped by the heart is reduced. [1]

(b) The risk of death over 15 years after surgery is the same / similar for both types of valve. [1] The probability of needing a replacement valve is much higher / rises more quickly for biological valves. [1] In the long term, a mechanical valve is a better replacement for a faulty valve. [1]

2. (a) It will help to strengthen the heart muscle and improve circulation. [1] Exercise reduces other risk factors such as obesity / high blood cholesterol / high blood pressure. [1]

(b) Any one for 1 mark from: increase the proportion of foods that help protect against cardiovascular disease (e.g. fruit and vegetables); reduce the intake of foods that cause high cholesterol (e.g. saturated fats or salt); reduce overall energy intake per day to reduce body weight

Page 44 Photosynthesis
Quick quiz
water + carbon dioxide → glucose + oxygen

1. (a) Plants are producers that use photosynthesis to make glucose / food / biomass. [1]
   This is the source of food / energy / biomass in the food chain. [1]

(b) More energy is transferred from the environment to the reaction [1] than is transferred from the reaction to the environment. [1]

(c) Light provides the energy for the reaction. [1] Energy is needed to allow carbon dioxide and water to react together / to be converted into oxygen and glucose. [1]

2. (a) chloroplasts [1]

(b) chlorophyll [1]

(c) Palisade cells contain the most chloroplasts [1] and they are close to the upper surface of the leaf where there will be the most light. [1]

(d) carbon dioxide [1]

(e) Any one for 1 mark from: used for the plant to grow and increase in biomass [1] / used to make other useful substances (or named substance, e.g. starch, protein, lipid, cellulose) [1] / used for respiration which releases the energy from glucose [1]

Page 45 Rate of photosynthesis
Quick quiz
light intensity; carbon dioxide concentration; temperature

1. (a) Because on this part of the graph, as carbon dioxide concentration increases rate of photosynthesis also increases. [1]

(b) Carbon dioxide is needed as one of the reactants in photosynthesis. [1]

(c) At point Y some other factor [1] has become the limiting factor. [1]

2. (a) Between 5 °C and 25 °C the rate of photosynthesis increases. [1] The rate of photosynthesis falls as temperatures rise above 25 °C. [1]

(b) The rate falls above 25 °C because the enzymes for photosynthesis are denatured / shape of active site is changed. [1]

3. (a) Line starting at zero and showing increasing rate of photosynthesis initially, [1] followed by a levelling off to a constant rate of photosynthesis. [1]

(b) the volume of oxygen produced per hour [1]

Page 46 Practical: Photosynthesis
Quick quiz
increase; light intensity; limiting factor; carbon dioxide

1. **(a)** Light intensity (distance from lamp) **[1]**

   (b) Any two for 2 marks from: temperature **[1]**; length of time to record change; mass / number of algal balls; volume of indicator solution in each bottle **[1]**; initial CO_2 concentration **[1]**

   (c) red **[1]**

2. graph similar to below, axes correctly labelled, **[1]** points correctly drawn and joined by straight lines or line of best fit **[1]**

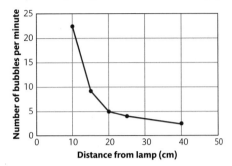

Page 47 Specialised plant cells
Quick quiz
xylem → transports water and minerals → dead and lignified

phloem → transports sucrose (sugar) → holes in end wall, lots of mitochondria

root hair → absorbs water and minerals from soil → large surface area

1. **(a)** Root hair cells have a large surface area **[1]** which increases the rate at which substances can be absorbed into the plant. **[1]**

   (b) Active transport requires energy. **[1]** Mitochondria are the site of respiration and provide the energy needed. **[1]**

2. **(a)** transports water and dissolved mineral ions through plant **[1]**

   (b) Dead cells have no cytoplasm / contents so water can flow more easily. **[1]**

   (c) Dissolved sucrose is transported around the plant **[1]** from the leaves / where it is made to where it is needed. **[1]**

   (d) Energy is needed for translocation **[1]** and only living cells can respire to release energy. **[1]**

Page 48 Transpiration
Quick quiz
water and dissolved mineral ions; xylem; sucrose; phloem

1. **(a)** roots, **[1]** osmosis, **[1]** transpiration **[1]**

   (b) Water evaporates from the surface of cells inside the leaf **[1]** and then diffuses out through the stomata. **[1]**

2. **(a)** root hair cells **[1]**

   (b) Diffusion can only move substances down a concentration gradient. **[1]** Active transport is needed because mineral ions must be moved against the concentration gradient. **[1]**

3. **(a)** to allow gases to diffuse into and out of the leaf **[1]**

   (b) The guard cells change shape / take in water and swell up **[1]** so changing the size of the opening (stomata) between them. **[1]**

   (c) Opening during the day allows carbon dioxide **[1]** to diffuse into the leaf for use by cells in photosynthesis. **[1]**

   (d) Closing at night when photosynthesis doesn't happen reduces water loss from the leaf. **[1]**

Page 49 Water uptake in plants
Quick quiz
False; True; True

1. **(a)** Stomata are opened more as light intensity increases **[1]** so more water molecules can evaporate from the leaf when it is sunnier. **[1]**

   (b) On a warm day more water is lost by evaporation from leaves. **[1]**

   So, on a warm day more water is taken up into the plant through the roots. **[1]**

2. **(a)** Water is taken up by the plant to replace **[1]** water that is lost from the leaves by evaporation. **[1]**

   (b) $\frac{28.5 + 26.4 + 29.1}{3}$
   = 28.0 (mm in 5 min) **[1]**

   (c) $\frac{38.9}{5}$ = 7.78 mm per min **[1]**

   (d) Greater surface area would mean a greater number of stomata. **[1]** More stomata would allow a faster rate of evaporation of water from the leaf. **[1]**

Page 50 Human endocrine system
Quick quiz
A thyroid gland

B adrenal glands

C pituitary gland

D pancreas

1. **(a)** endocrine **[1]**

   (b) adrenal → adrenalin

   thyroid → thyroxine

   pancreas → insulin

   [2 marks for all correct; 1 mark for 1 correct]

2. Any one for 1 mark from: stimulates sperm production; promotes secondary sexual characteristics.

3. **(a)** Insulin is carried in the bloodstream. **[1]**

   (b) Because the insulin only has an effect on certain cells / organs / liver cells. **[1]**

4. The endocrine / hormone system is slower to respond than the nervous system. **[1]** The effects of hormones usually last much longer than the effects of nervous responses. **[1]**

Page 51 Hormones in reproduction
Quick quiz
puberty → time when the body starts developing in ways that will allow reproduction

oestrogen → female hormone that causes development of breasts and start of menstrual cycle

secondary sexual characteristics → features that develop in response to increasing sex hormone concentrations

1. **(a)** Oestrogen: It causes the lining of the uterus to start to build up / repair **[1]**

and causes the release of another hormone that triggers the release of an egg cell / ovulation. **[1]**

   (b) Progesterone: It maintains the uterus lining during the later part of the cycle. **[1]**

2. **(a)** when an egg is released from an ovary **[1]**

   (b) ovary **[1]**

3. **(a)** Oestrogen levels increase / peak first followed by progesterone. **[1]**

   Oestrogen reaches its peak at day 13 / just before ovulation. **[1]**

   (b) The lining of the womb is lost along with some blood. **[1]**

   (c) A fall in progesterone and oestrogen concentration **[1]** means that the uterus lining is no longer maintained. **[1]**

Page 52 Contraception
Quick quiz
prevent pregnancy

1. **(a)** Progesterone stops any eggs from maturing in the ovaries. **[1]**

   So there are no eggs available that can be released from the ovary and fertilised. **[1]**

   (b) 100 − 82 = 18 **[1]**

   (c) hormone implant or patch **[1]**

   (d) The male condom does not cause any side effects that are possible with hormones. **[1]** Condoms also protect against becoming infected with sexually transmitted diseases. **[1]**

2. condom → provides a physical barrier so sperm don't reach the egg

   IUD → prevents fertilised egg from implanting in the uterus

   spermicide → kills sperm

   contraceptive pill → stops ovulation
   [3 marks for all correct, 2 marks for 3 correct, 1 mark for 2 correct, 0 marks for none or 1 correct.]

Page 53 Control of blood glucose
Quick quiz
internal; external; blood glucose; constant; cells

1. **(a)** After each meal the blood glucose concentration rises. **[1]**

   (b) An increase in blood glucose concentration is followed by an increase in blood insulin concentration. **[1]**

   (c) Insulin causes blood glucose levels to fall and return to a normal level / set point. **[1]**

2. **(a)** blood; **[1]** glycogen **[1]**

   (b) pancreas **[1]**

Page 54 Diabetes
Quick quiz
True; True; False

1. **(a)** Between 1990 and 2000, mean body mass changed from about 72.5 kg to about 77.2 kg. **[1]**

   Over the same time, the percentage of people with type 2 diabetes increased from about 4.9% to about 7.3%. **[1]**

This means that mean body mass and percentage with type 2 diabetes show a positive correlation. **[1]**

(b) Because tall people would be heavier even if they weren't obese. **[1]**

2. (a) Type 1: caused when the pancreas does not produce enough insulin **[1]**

Type 2: caused when body cells do not respond to insulin **[1]**

(b) Insulin is injected just before eating. **[1]** It helps to reduce blood glucose concentration to a safe / normal level. **[1]**

(c) Type 2 is controlled by:
- eating a low-sugar / low-carbohydrate diet **[1]** to reduce the amount of glucose entering the bloodstream **[1]**
- regular exercise **[1]** to reduce blood glucose concentration by faster removal of glucose from the blood (due to increased respiration). **[1]**

Page 55 Transport in animals
Quick quiz
urea; oxygen; out of; lungs

1. (a) volume = 4^3 = 64 **[1]**

surface area : volume ratio = 96 : 64 = 3 : 2 OR 1.5 : 1 **[1]**

(b) As length increases, surface area : volume ratio decreases. **[1]**

(c) Increasing surface area : volume ratio would increase the rate of diffusion. **[1]**

2. (a) absorbs dissolved food molecules into the blood **[1]**

(b) They greatly increase the surface area of the small intestine **[1]** so that more dissolved food molecules can be absorbed at the same time / rate of absorption of dissolved food molecules is greater. **[1]**

(c) Food is carried to cells in the blood. **[1]**

Page 56 Alveoli
Quick quiz
lungs; alveoli; oxygen; carbon dioxide; air

1. (a) diffusion **[1]**

(b) Carbon dioxide concentration is higher in the blood because the blood is coming from cells where respiration has taken place. **[2]**

(c) They increase the surface area for diffusion. **[1]**

2. membranes of the alveolus and capillary are very thin → reduces distance for diffusion **[1]**

alveoli are ventilated by breathing → refreshes the air and so maintains a high concentration gradient for diffusion **[1]**

alveoli are surrounded by many capillaries → good blood flow increases the concentration gradient between air and blood **[1]**

Page 57 The blood
Quick quiz
red blood cell → carries oxygen

white blood cell → destroys pathogens

plasma → carries dissolved substances

platelet → causes blood to clot where blood vessels are damaged

1. (a) Erythrocytes carry oxygen from the lungs to body cells. **[1]**

(b) The red colour is caused by a pigment called haemoglobin. **[1]** This binds to oxygen and so carries it round the body in the blood. **[1]**

(c) The shape gives the cell a large surface area. **[1]**

This means that exchange of gases by diffusion is faster. **[1]**

2. (a) The clot blocks the wound and prevents loss of blood. **[1]** It also stops harmful bacteria / pathogens from entering the body. **[1]**

(b) Phagocytes engulf **[1]** and destroy any pathogens that have entered the wound. **[1]**

(c) Any two for 2 marks from: Pathogens cause infection; **[1]** lymphocytes produce antibodies which can destroy the pathogen, so numbers increase when infection is present. **[1]** / Lymphocytes produce antitoxins **[1]** that neutralise toxins produced by pathogens. **[1]**

Page 58 Blood vessels
Quick quiz
A heart; **B** vein; **C** capillary; **D** artery

1. Veins have a wide lumen / internal diameter. **[1]** This allows blood to flow easily with little friction / resistance. **[1]**

Veins have valves. **[1]** These close to stop the blood from flowing backwards. **[1]**

2. (a) The pressure is higher in the artery / aorta **[1]** because it is close to the heart, so most affected by heart contraction. **[1]** The artery also has more elastic tissue to maintain the high pressure. **[1]**

(b) carry blood from the capillaries to the heart **[1]**

(c) Thin walls decrease the distance for diffusion and so increase the rate of diffusion / exchange. **[1]**

Page 59 The heart
Quick quiz
A vena cava; **B** valve; **C** atrium; **D** ventricle

1. vena cava; **[1]** right atrium; **[1]** right ventricle; **[1]** pulmonary arteries; **[1]** pulmonary veins; **[1]** aorta **[1]**

2. (a) circulatory system **[1]**

(b) The heart is made of muscle **[1]** which contracts to pump the blood. **[1]**

(c) Valves close when the chamber walls contract **[1]** to prevent blood flowing backwards through the heart. **[1]**

(d) The atria pump blood only as far as the ventricle. **[1]** The ventricles need to generate a larger force to push blood out of the heart (to the lungs and body). **[1]**

(e) The left ventricle needs to generate a much larger force to push blood all through the body, **[1]** while the right ventricle only pumps blood through the lungs. **[1]**

Page 60 Aerobic and anaerobic respiration
Quick quiz
aerobic → glucose, oxygen → carbon dioxide, water

anaerobic (in muscle cells) → glucose → lactic acid

1. (a) mitochondria **[1]**

(b) glucose + oxygen **[1]** → carbon dioxide + water **[1]**

(c) Heat energy is released from the reaction. / More energy is released from forming bonds (in products) than is needed to break bonds (in reactants) in the reaction. **[1]**

2. (a) glucose → lactic acid **[1]**

(b) because lactic acid build-up is damaging to cells / causes fatigue or pain **[1]**

(c) ethanol; **[1]** carbon dioxide **[1]**

3. (a) Anaerobic respiration occurs when oxygen supply is not sufficient **[1]** to meet energy demands using aerobic respiration. **[1]**

(b) Aerobic respiration releases more energy from each glucose molecule than anaerobic respiration. **[1]**

(c) lactic acid **[1]**

Page 61 Practical: Rate of respiration
Quick quiz
True; False; True

1. (a) It moves because the organisms are using up oxygen **[1]** in the process of aerobic respiration. **[1]**

(b) Soda lime absorbs carbon dioxide produced during respiration. **[1]**

(c) Same apparatus / same glass tubing, bung and soda lime **[1]** but without any live organisms / with same mass of inert object e.g. glass beads **[1]**

2. (a) The measurement at 20 °C **[1]** (too low to fit the pattern of the other results)

(b) Repeat the investigation several times at each temperature **[1]** and discard any results that are anomalous / calculate a mean at each temperature. **[1]**

(c) As temperature increases, **[1]** the rate of respiration increases. **[1]**

Page 62 Response to exercise
Quick quiz
First row: Rest; Second row: Exercise

1. (a) via the blood / circulatory system **[1]**

(b) (i) Breathing rate increases so more oxygen is taken into the body for aerobic respiration **[1]** and more carbon dioxide from respiration is removed. **[1]**

(ii) Heart rate increases **[1]** so that blood transports oxygen and glucose to cells more quickly and removes carbon dioxide from cells more rapidly. **[1]**

(c) Count the number of pulses **[1]** felt in 1 minute (or in suitable timescale multiplied e.g. 15 seconds multiplied by 4). **[1]**

2. (a) cardiac output = 0.081 × 55 **[1]**
= 4.46 (l/min) **[1]**

(b) stroke volume = $\frac{4.46}{69}$ **[1]** = 0.065 (l) **[1]**

3. The volume of blood pumped by the left ventricle with each beat. **[1]**

Page 63 Communities
Quick quiz
the same; the same area

different; the same area

1. ecosystem **[1]**

2. (a) Blackbirds depend on blackberry plants for food / shelter / nest sites. **[1]**

Blackberry plants depend on blackbirds for seed dispersal. **[1]**

(b) If the number of blackberry plants in the area decreased, the number of blackbirds might also decrease **[1]** because they would have less food / fewer places to nest. **[1]**

3. (a) rabbit and field mouse **[1]**

(b) food / grass **[1]**

(c) Rabbit numbers might decrease **[1]** because more deer would eat more grass / would mean less grass for rabbits. **[1]**

Page 64 Abiotic factors
Quick quiz
light intensity; temperature; water availability; soil nutrient concentration; carbon dioxide concentration in air; pollutants

1. (a) The trend is a continuing rise in temperature. **[1]**

(b) As the temperature increases this could cause more male insects to have reduced fertility / be unable to reproduce **[1]** which could cause the size of insect populations to fall. **[1]**

2. (a) Pollution is something added to the environment that causes harm to living organisms. **[1]**

(b) If corals are killed by plastic pollution, this will reduce the amount of shelter and food the reef provides for other animals **[1]** so biodiversity will decrease. **[1]**

3. An explanation that makes reference to the following points:
- The loss of leaves from trees increases light intensity nearer the ground. **[1]**
- Mineral ions will be released from decaying leaves. **[1]**
- More mineral ions increase growth / increased photosynthesis increases growth. **[1]**

Page 65 Biotic factors
Quick quiz
parasitism; mutualism

1. (a) Most white-clawed crayfish are larger when the signal crayfish are absent. **[1]** The most frequent size class with signal crayfish is 20–29 mm but most individuals are in the 30–39 mm size class when signal crayfish are absent. **[1]**

(b) Signal crayfish compete more successfully than white-clawed for same food. **[1]** Predation by signal crayfish on white-clawed crayfish. **[1]**

2. (a) If they eat the same food there will be competition. **[1]** Less food for red squirrels will mean they are likely to starve and have fewer offspring. **[1]**

(b) Grey squirrels could spread the virus to new areas. **[1]** Red squirrels are not resistant to the virus and are killed by it, so their numbers fall rapidly. **[1]**

(c) Grey squirrels may be more likely to suffer from predation from / be eaten by pine martens. **[1]** Red squirrel survival would then increase due to reduced competition. **[1]**

Page 66 Practical: Population studies
Quick quiz
belt transect; distribution; abundance; quadrat

1. (a) The buttercups may not be spread evenly through the area. **[1]**

(b) Random sampling may help to avoid bias in the results from choosing positions for the quadrat where there are many / few buttercup plants. **[1]**

(c) $\frac{3 + 2 + 0 + 0 + 2 + 1}{6}$ = 1.3 **[1]**

(d) total area of field = 25 × 34 = 850 m^2 **[1]**

total area of quadrat = 100 cm^2

$= \frac{100}{100 \times 100}$ = 0.01 m^2 **[1]**

population size = $\frac{850}{0.01}$ × 1.3 = 110 500 plants **[1]**

2. (a) Any abiotic factor that is affected by the presence of the tree, such as: light intensity; mineral ions; soil moisture. **[1]**

(b) Because this allows the students to see how the tree affects daisies compared with the open field / allows the students to see effects along a gradient from the tree. **[1]**

Page 67 Biodiversity
Quick quiz
species; ecosystem; food; less

1. (a) Eutrophication is a problem caused when high levels of plant nutrients / organic matter enter a watercourse **[1]** stimulating excessive plant growth / bacterial decay. **[1]**

(b) As oxygen concentration decreases, the number of species also decreases. **[1]**

When oxygen concentration increases, the number of species increases. **[1]**

2. (a) Growing fish in ponds or cages to supply food for people. **[1]**

(b) Eating farmed fish could reduce the amount of fish taken from the wild for human food. **[1]**

Page 68 Maintaining biodiversity
Quick quiz
False; False; True; True

1. (a) The national trend for skylarks is a decreasing population. **[1]**

The trend on the farm for skylarks is an increasing population. **[1]**

(b) More yield means the farmer has more to sell / can earn more money. **[1]**

(c) Planting field edges with a greater diversity of plants **[1]** means that skylarks can find food in the area all year round. **[1]**

2. Level 3: The suggestions throughout are supported by linkage and application of knowledge and understanding of scientific enquiry, techniques and procedures. Logical connections are made between elements in the context of the question. (AO2)
- Lines of reasoning are supported by sustained application of relevant evidence. (AO2) **[5–6]**

Level 2: The suggestions are mostly supported through linkage and application of knowledge and understanding of scientific enquiry, techniques and procedures. Some logical connections are made between elements in the context of the question. (AO2)
- Lines of reasoning are mostly supported through the application of relevant evidence. (AO2) **[3–4]**

Level 1: The explanation attempts to link and apply knowledge and understanding of scientific enquiry, techniques and procedures. Flawed or simplistic connections are made between elements in the context of the question. (AO2)
- Lines of reasoning are unsupported or unclear. (AO2) **[1–2]**

No awardable content **[0]**

Indicative content:
- Plant a large variety of tree species to increase biodiversity of trees.
- More tree species will provide a greater range of habitats.
- More habitats will result in a greater variety of available shelter and food.
- This will increase biodiversity of animals.
- Create different habitats, such as open areas within the forest, wetter / drier areas, to increase plant and animal biodiversity.
- Consideration should be given to species that are in need of conservation in the UK and the conditions they require.
- Consideration should be given to existing plants and animals that may be displaced by the forest, especially if they need conservation.

Page 69 Carbon cycle
Quick quiz
respiration: increase; photosynthesis: decrease; decay by microorganisms: increase

1. (a) combustion / burning **[1]**

(b) photosynthesis **[1]**

(c) respiration **[1]**

(d) They are broken down by microorganisms / bacteria **[1]** that release carbon dioxide in the process of respiration. **[1]**

2. (a) microorganisms such as bacteria and fungi **[1]**

(b) Because carbon dioxide is released by respiration during decomposition / by microorganisms. **[1]**

(c) Decomposition releases mineral ions to the soil for new plant growth. **[1]**

Page 70 Water cycle

Quick quiz

cytoplasm; reactions; vacuole; plasma; xylem; phloem

1. (a) The water cycle provides fresh water that organisms living on land need to absorb into their cells for many cell processes. **[1]**

   The water also dissolves mineral ions from the soil that plants absorb to make proteins and other substances. **[1]**

   (b) **A:** Evaporation is when liquid water in the sea changes to water vapour in the air. **[1]**

   B: Condensation is when water vapour cools and forms liquid water droplets in clouds. **[1]**

   C: Precipitation is when liquid or solid water (ice, snow) falls from clouds onto land or sea. **[1]**

2. (a) Water that is suitable for drinking. **[1]**

   (b) Water evaporates from the sea water due to energy from sunlight. **[1]**
   The water vapour condenses on the cooler cover and is collected in a separate container. **[1]**

   (c) Only the water evaporates from the sea water, leaving the dissolved salts behind and so separating the water and salt. **[1]**

Page 71 Nitrogen cycle

Quick quiz

True; False; False; True

1. (a) As the mass of nitrogen is increased, the yield increases. **[1]**

   (b) nitrate **[1]**

   (c) Nitrogen is needed so the plant can make protein (and DNA) **[1]** which is an important substance for growth. **[1]**

2. (a) (i) Soil bacteria / decomposers will break down dead plant material **[1]** releasing nitrogen compounds / ammonia from the material into the soil (eventually leading to increased nitrate levels). **[1]**

   (ii) Artificial fertiliser contains nitrates which can be absorbed directly by plants. **[1]**

   (b) reduce the amount of soil nitrogen available to plants **[1]**

Page 72 Atoms, elements and compounds

Quick quiz

atom → the smallest part of an element that can exist

element → made of only one type of atom

compound → consists of two or more different elements chemically joined

1. calcium + oxygen → calcium oxide **[1]**

2. copper carbonate → copper oxide + carbon dioxide **[1]**

3.

Element name	Element symbol
Sodium **[1]**	Na
Bromine	Br **[1]**
Lead **[1]**	Pb
Iron	Fe **[1]**

4. 3 **[1]**

5. barium chloride **[1]**

6. (a) 5 **[1]**

   (b) 2 **[1]**

7. zinc carbonate → carbon dioxide + zinc oxide **[1]**

Page 73 The model of the atom

Quick quiz

The order from top to bottom: 4, 1, 3, 2

1.

Feature	Plum pudding model	Nuclear model
Protons in a nucleus		✓
Contains electrons	✓	✓
Contains positive charges	✓	✓
Electrons at fixed distances		✓

[1 mark for each correct row]

2. Most alpha particles passed straight through. → Most of the atom is empty space. **[1]**

   Some alpha particles were deflected. → The nucleus is positively charged. **[1]**

   A very small number of alpha particles were deflected backwards. → The nucleus has most of the atom's mass. **[1]**

Page 74 Subatomic particles

Quick quiz

(a) A = electron; B = neutron; C = proton

(b) nucleus

1.

Name of subatomic particle	Position in the atom
proton	nucleus
neutron	nucleus
electron	shell

[1 mark for each correct row]

2. proton **[1]**

3. Atoms contain equal numbers of protons and electrons. **[1]**

4. 6 **[1]**

5. 11 **[1]**

6. 0.000 000 000 1 m **[1]**

Page 75 Size and mass of atoms

Quick quiz

Name of subatomic particle	Relative charge
proton	1
neutron	0
electron	−1

1. Mass number is the total number of protons and neutrons in an atom. **[1]**

2. (a) 79 **[1]**

   (b) 197 **[1]**

3. 27 − 13 = 14 **[1]**

4. atomic number = number of protons
   For iron, protons = electrons = 26 **[1]**
   For Fe^{3+}, 3 fewer electrons = 23 **[1]**

5. Protons = 4 **[1]** Neutrons = 5 **[1]**

6. nucleus **[1]**

Page 76 Isotopes and relative atomic mass

Quick quiz

False; True; False; True

1. (a) protons 8; **[1]** neutrons 8; **[1]** electrons 8 **[1]**

   (b) Isotopes are atoms of an element that have the same number of protons **[1]** but different numbers of neutrons. **[1]**

2. (a) protons 2; **[1]** neutrons 1; **[1]** electrons 2 **[1]**

   (b) There are other isotopes of helium (which are heavier). **[1]**

3. 10, 10, 10 and 10, 10, 12 (both correct for 1 mark)

Page 77 Developing the periodic table

Quick quiz

Mendeleev arranged elements in order of their increasing relative atomic mass. He put elements with similar properties into groups. He changed the order of some elements to fit the trend better.

1. Elements were arranged in atomic weight order in groups of eight **[1]**

2. (a) He grouped elements with similar properties together **[1]** and left gaps where elements did not fit the pattern. **[1]**

   (b) Some elements were not in the correct group / elements with similar properties were not under each other, e.g. Te and Ir **[1]**

3. (a) For elements that were yet to be discovered / for elements that Mendeleev predicted would be discovered. **[1]**

   (b) Group 0 had not been discovered / today no elements share a box in the periodic table / elements that he predicted have been found / new elements have been found. **[1]**

   (c) Ga **[1]**

Page 78 The periodic table

Quick quiz

1. potassium → Group 1
   nitrogen → Group 5
   argon → Group 0

2. True; True; True; False

1. (a) Group 7 **[1]**

   (b) F **[1]**

2. (a) 4 **[1]**

   (b) 2 **[1]**

   (c) 6 **[1]**

   (d) 4 **[1]**

3. (a) chlorine [1]

  (b) 7 [1]

4. It will form an alkaline solution [1] because elements in the same group have similar chemistry. [1]

Page 79 Electronic configuration
Quick quiz
(a)

Shell	Maximum number of electrons
1	2
2	8
3	8

(b) group 6

(c) period 3

1. (a)

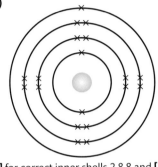

  [1] for correct inner shells 2.8.8 and [1] for 1 electron in outer shell

  (b) 19 [1]

2. 2.8.2 [1]

3. (a) (i) 2.6 [1]

    (ii) 1 [1]

  (b) The number of electrons in the outer shell is the same as the group number. [1]

4. [1] for correct electrons in inner shells; [1] mark for correct electrons in outer shells

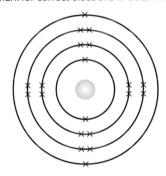

Page 80 Metals and non-metals
Quick quiz

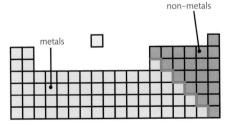

metals   non–metals

1.

Property	Metals	Non-metals
Poor conductor of electricity		✓
Good conductor of heat	✓	
Brittle		✓
Dull		✓
Malleable	✓	

[1 mark for each correct column]

2. Metals lose electrons to form positively charged ions. [1]
Non-metals gain electrons to form negatively charged ions. [1]

3. (a) Metal, because it has three electrons in its outer shell. [1]

  (b) Helium is a non-metal [1] but it has fewer than four electrons in its outer shell. [1]

4. Li → 2.1

  Ca → 2.8.8.2

  Na → 2.8.1

  F → 2.7 [3]

Page 81 Chemical bonds
Quick quiz
True; False; False; False; True

1. (a) A bond that is formed when two atoms share a pair of electrons. [1]

  (b) Both hydrogen and chlorine are non-metals and so can only form covalent bonds with each other. [1]

2. Covalent: water; carbon dioxide; methane [1] Ionic: sodium chloride; iron sulfide; magnesium oxide [1]

3. Metallic bonding is an electrostatic [1] force of attraction [1] between ions and delocalised electrons. [1]

4. Metallic bonding [1] with positive metal ions [1] in a 'sea' of delocalised electrons. [1]

Page 82 Ionic bonding
Quick quiz
magnesium Mg^{2+}; oxygen O^{2-}; sodium Na^+; aluminium Al^{3+}; fluorine F^-; calcium Ca^{2+}

1. Non-metals gain electrons to form negative ions. [1]

2. Atoms of Group 2 elements will lose two electrons, [1] because all atoms of elements in Group 2 have two electrons in the outer shell. [1] To be stable, they need a full outer shell. [1]

3.

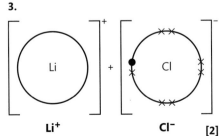

[2]

4. (a) magnesium + chlorine → magnesium chloride [1]

  (b) Mg [1]$^{2+}$ [1]

(c) Ionic bonding [1] with electrostatic forces of attraction [1] between oppositely charged ions. [1]

Page 83 Ionic compounds
Quick quiz
two-dimensional; three-dimensional; ball and stick; dot and cross

1. (a) giant [1]

  (b) ions [1]

  (c) It is strong electrostatic forces of attraction [1] between oppositely charged ions. [1]

  (d) Ratio of ions is 6:6 which simplifies to 1:1 [1] so the empirical formula is CaS. [1]

2. (a) There is a regular arrangement of ions [1] held by strong electrostatic forces between oppositely charged ions. [1]

  (b) MgO [2]

Page 84 Properties of ionic compounds
Quick quiz
sodium chloride; magnesium oxide; copper sulfate

1. (a) conduct electricity when dissolved [1]

  (b) there are strong forces of attraction between ions [1]

2. Ionic bonding is the electrostatic [1] force of attraction in all directions between oppositely [1] charged ions [1].

3. The ions in a solid are in fixed positions. [1] In order to conduct electricity, ions need to be free to move. [1]

4. The ions are free to move [1] and carry the charge. [1]

Page 85 Covalent bonding
Quick quiz
(a) electrons; (b) small molecules, giant covalent structures

1. (a) B [1]

  (b) NH_3 [1]

  (c) water [1]

2. (a) Any one for 1 mark from: models are not to scale; does not show position of electrons.

  (b) Any one for 1 mark from: only a two-dimensional representation; does not show relative shape and size of molecule.

3. double bond / two shared pairs of electrons; [1] rest of molecule correct / four unbonded electrons / two lone pairs [1]

4. two double bonds [1]; rest of molecule correct / four unbonded electrons / two lone pairs [1]

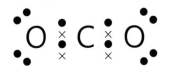

Page 86 Properties of simple molecular substances

Quick quiz

Substances that consist of simple molecules are usually **liquids** or gases at room temperature. Simple molecular substances consist of simple molecules that contain **covalent** bonds and have intermolecular forces between molecules.

They:

- have relatively **low** melting and boiling points.
- are **poor** conductors of electricity.
- are usually **insoluble** in water.

1. Carbon dioxide is a gas at room temperature because the forces of attraction between the molecules are weak / easily overcome. **[1]** Therefore little energy is needed to separate the molecules and the boiling point of carbon dioxide is low. **[1]**

2. **(a)** ethene **[1]**
   (b) As the size of the molecule increases, the boiling point increases. **[1]**

3. Carbon dioxide gas has a simple molecular structure and does not have an overall electric charge / mobile charged particles / electrons **[1]** so there are no charge carriers / no particles to carry the charge. **[1]**

Page 87 Giant covalent structures

Quick quiz

simple molecular; simple molecular; simple molecular; giant covalent

1. **(a)** In a giant structure with a regular pattern **[1]**
   (b) To conduct electricity, a substance needs charged particles that can move about **[1]** but silicon dioxide does not have particles like these. **[1]**

2. **(a)** Covalent bonds **[1]** joining atoms together in a giant structure **[1]** with a regular pattern. **[1]**
   (b) Any two for 2 marks from: high melting / boiling point; solid at room temperature; insoluble in water

Page 88 Diamond

Quick quiz

Each atom in diamond is bonded to four other atoms. All the atoms are joined by covalent bonds. Diamond has a high melting point. Diamond is suitable for cutting tools because it is hard.

1. **(a)** 4 **[1]**
   (b) covalent **[1]**
   (c) The atoms in diamond have a giant **[1]** structure with a regular **[1]** arrangement.

2. It has no free electrons / ions. **[1]**

3. High; Strong **[1]**

Page 89 Graphite

Quick quiz

Any two from: pencils, lubricants, electrodes

1. **(a)** covalent **[1]**
   (b) three / 3 **[1]**

2. Graphite forms layers of carbon atoms. **[1]** These are arranged in hexagons. **[1]** Between the layers there are weak forces of attraction. **[1]**

3. **(a)** covalent **[1]**
   (b) In graphite each carbon atom has 3 bonds, but in diamond each carbon atom has 4. **[1]**
   (c) Because layers of atoms **[1]** can easily slide over each other. **[1]**
   (d) Graphite **[1]** because free moving delocalised electrons **[1]** can easily move and carry the charge. **[1]**

Page 90 Graphene and fullerenes

Quick quiz

True; False; True; False

1. **(a)** three / 3 **[1]**
   (b) Both have high melting and boiling points so are solid at room temperature. **[1]** Both conduct electricity. **[1]**

2. Graphene is a giant covalent structure. **[1]** It has covalent bonds between the atoms. **[1]** These bonds are very strong / need a lot of energy to break. **[1]**

3. high tensile strength, very high length to diameter ratios **[1]**

4. **(a)** covalent bonds **[1]** simple molecular structure **[1]**
   (b) No **[1]** as there are no free moving **[1]** charged particles / ions / electrons. **[1]**

Page 91 Polymers

Quick quiz

Poly(ethene) molecules are **large**. The atoms are held together by **covalent** bonds. The intermolecular forces between poly(ethene) molecules are **stronger** than the intermolecular forces between ethene molecules. Properties of poly(ethene) include:

- relatively **high** melting point
- **does not** conduct electricity.

1. **(a)** A polymer is a large molecule made from smaller molecules / monomers joined together. **[1]**
   (b) covalent **[1]**

2. **(a)** carbon **[1]**
   (b) H **[1]**
   (c) Large molecules **[1]** containing chains of carbon atoms **[1]**

3. There are no free electrons or ions in the structure. **[1]**

Page 92 Metals

Quick quiz

(a) one large grey circle labelled 'metal particle'; one small green circle labelled 'delocalised electron'

(b) True; False; False

1. **(a)** electrostatic **[1]**
   (b) 1 **[1]** + **[1]**

2. can be hammered into shape without breaking **[1]**

3. They have strong (metallic) bonds. **[1]**

4. Metals have delocalised electrons **[1]** which can move freely (and carry charge). **[1]**

Page 93 Relative formula mass

Quick quiz

False; False; False

1. **(a)** 12 **[1]**; 23 **[1]**; 201 **[1]**
   (b) 32 **[1]**; 38 **[1]**; 71 **[1]**

2. **(a)** 159.5 **[1]**
   (b) 106 **[1]**
   (c) 58.5 **[1]**
   (d) 35 **[1]**
   (e) 74 **[1]**

3. **(a)** 152 **[1]**
   (b) 158 **[1]**
   (c) 187.5 **[1]**

Page 94 Empirical formulae

Quick quiz

molecular formula → shows the number and type of atom → C_6H_6

empirical formula → smallest whole number ratio of atoms in a compound → CH

displayed formula → shows every atom and every bond → H–O–O–H

1. **(a)** C_2H_6 **[1]**
   (b) 30 **[1]**
   (c) CH_3 **[1]**

2. Relative formula mass of C_2H_5 = (2 × 12) + (5 × 1) = 29
   Then divide 58 by this value $\frac{58}{29}$ = 2
   This shows that you need 2 empirical formulae to make the molecular formula. So, the molecular formula must be C_4H_{10} **[3]**

3. An explanation including some of the following points for 6 marks:
   - Find mass of crucible / suitable container (+ lid)
   - Find mass of container (+ lid) + magnesium
   - Heat container (+lid) + magnesium
   - Lift lid occasionally to allow oxygen in
   - Minimise loss of magnesium oxide
   - Heat until no further change
   - Allow to cool
   - Find mass of container (+ lid) + magnesium oxide
   - Repeat heating
   - Until constant mass

Page 95 Balancing equations

Quick quiz

Balanced equations:

$2Ca + O_2 \rightarrow 2CaO$; $CH_4 + 2O_2 \rightarrow CO_2 + 2H_2O$

1. **(a)** $BaO + 2HCl \rightarrow BaCl_2 + H_2O$ **[1]**
   (b) $2Na + Br_2 \rightarrow 2NaBr$ **[1]**
   (c) $Mg + CuSO_4 \rightarrow MgSO_4 + Cu$ **[1]**
   (d) $2Li + 2H_2O \rightarrow 2LiOH + H_2$ **[1]**
   (e) $2Al_2O_3 \rightarrow 4Al + 3O_2$ **[1]**

2. **(a)** potassium + oxygen → potassium oxide **[1]**
   (b) $2K + 2H_2O \rightarrow 2KOH + H_2$
   correct formulae for reactants and products **[1]**; correct balancing **[1]**
   (c) $2K + Cl_2 \rightarrow 2KCl$
   correct reactants **[1]**; correct products **[1]**; correct balancing **[1]**

3. (a) carbon + oxygen → carbon monoxide + carbon dioxide **[1]**

(b) $2CuO + C \rightarrow 2Cu + CO_2$
correct formulae for reactants and products **[1]**; correct balancing **[1]**

(c) $C + O_2 \rightarrow CO_2$
correct formulae for reactants and products **[1]**; correct balancing **[1]**

Page 96 Conservation of mass
Quick quiz
Heating copper carbonate; Reacting hydrochloric acid and magnesium

1. (a) $2Ag_2O \rightarrow 4Ag + O_2$
correct formulae for reactants and products **[1]**; correct balancing **[1]**

(b) 6.22 – 5.79 = 0.43 g **[1]**

(c) Any one for 1 mark from: Some of the reactant was left; **[1]** Not all of the product was collected and weighed. **[1]**

2. mass of magnesium = 0.24 g; mass of magnesium oxide = 0.40 g **[1]**; mass of oxygen = 0.16 g **[1]**

3. (a) copper + iodine → copper iodide **[1]**

(b) (The mass would increase) because copper combines with iodine in the reaction **[1]** so the mass is due to copper and iodine, not just copper. **[1]**

Page 97 Calculating masses in reactions
Quick quiz
128 g

1. (a) Student 1: The reaction produces a gas. **[1]** Unless the gas is collected, the mass of the products will appear less than that of the reactants as the gas will have escaped. **[1]**

Student 2: If a closed system is used, all of the products will be collected. **[1]**

(b) $CaCO_3(s) + 2HCl(aq) \rightarrow CaCl_2(aq) + H_2O(l) + CO_2(g)$
correct formulae **[1]**; correct balancing **[1]**; correct state symbols **[1]**

(c) Top pan balance **[1]** 'Scales' is not an acceptable answer.

2. The total mass after a reaction is the same as the total mass before the reaction. **[1]**

3. A closed system means the reactants and products cannot escape to the surroundings. **[1]**

4. (a) 50 – 28 = 22 g **[1]**

(b) $\frac{22}{50} \times 100\%$ **[1]** = 44% **[1]**

Page 98 Concentrations of solutions
Quick quiz
concentration → g/dm³; mass → g; volume → dm³

1. 0.25 dm³ **[1]**

2. (a) $\frac{100}{1000}$ = 0.1 dm³ **[1]**

(b) concentration = $\frac{\text{mass in g}}{\text{volume in dm}^3}$ **[1]**

$= \frac{3.7}{0.1}$ **[1]** = 37 g/dm³ **[1]**

3. 50 cm³ = 0.05 dm³ **[1]**

concentration = $\frac{2}{0.05}$ **[1]** = 40 g/dm³ **[1]**

4. 125 cm³ = 0.125 dm³ **[1]**

4 × 0.125 **[1]** = 0.5 g **[1]**

Page 99 States of matter
Quick quiz

State	Particle arrangement	Particle movement	Forces of attraction
solid	close together regular lattice arrangement	vibrate in one place	strong
liquid	close together random arrangement	move around each other	weak
gas	far apart random arrangement	move around freely in all directions	very weak / none

1. (a) The energy of the particles increases. **[1]**

(b) The particles move further apart **[1]** because the strength of the forces between the particles decreases. **[1]**

(c) The particles move faster. **[1]**

2. (a) Particles can only vibrate in fixed positions in a solid **[1]**. In a gas, particles move quickly **[1]** in all **[1]** directions.

(b) As the strength of the forces increases, **[1]** the boiling point increases. **[1]**

(c) The particles move more slowly **[1]** and move closer together / move to a more regular arrangement. **[1]**

Page 100 Pure substances
Quick quiz
A; B; D

1. Sample B is the pure benzoic acid **[1]** as its melting point is closest / identical to the melting point of benzoic acid. **[1]**

2. A pure substance contains only a single element or compound. Oxygen is made of atoms / molecules of oxygen only, **[1]** but air contains different gases / atoms / molecules and so is not pure. **[1]**

3. salty water **[1]**

4. C **[1]** because it has a <u>sharp</u> melting point matching that given for paracetamol **[1]**

5. Orange juice straight from the orange contains several different substances (water, sugars, flavour compounds, vitamins and so on) **[1]** and so is not made up of a single element or compound. **[1]**

Page 101 Mixtures
Quick quiz
coal from slurry → filtration and drying

ethanol from a mixture of alcohols → fractional distillation

water from coal slurry → filtration

salts from sea water → crystallisation

pure water from sea water → simple distillation

coloured substances from leaves, dissolved in ethanol → paper chromatography

1. (a) A mixture consists of two or more elements / compounds / substances not chemically bonded. **[1]**

(b) To remove unreacted copper oxide the student should filter the solution through filter paper **[1]** in a filter funnel. **[1]**

To get the copper sulfate solute from the solution the student should pour the solution into an evaporating basin **[1]** and use the Bunsen burner to evaporate approximately half of the water. **[1]** Then leave the solution to allow all of the water to evaporate. **[1]**

The blue copper sulfate crystals can be removed and dried by leaving them in the air. **[1]**

2. (a) Sand is insoluble in water **[1]** so its particles are too large to pass through the filter paper. **[1]** The particles in sea water are small enough to pass through the filter paper. **[1]**

(b) simple distillation **[1]**

Page 102 Chromatography
Quick quiz
True; False; False

1. vertical line of three dots above the black ink cross and at the same heights as those for the blue, yellow and red inks (**[2]** for all correct, **[1]** if two correct, as long as green dot not included)

2. $R_f = \frac{3.7}{7.3}$ **[1]** = 0.506849 **[1]** = 0.51 (2 s. f.) **[1]**

3. Answers could include the following points in a logical order for 4 marks:
- The paper contains the stationary phase.
- The mobile phase / solvent moves through the paper.
- The substances in the sample are attracted to the two phases.
- Substances travel further if they are more strongly attracted to the mobile phase than to the stationary phase.

Page 103 Practical: Investigating inks
Quick quiz
stationary phase → the chromatography paper

R_f value → the distance a substance travels relative to the solvent

mobile phase → the liquid solvent

solvent front → the level reached by the solvent

1. Step 1: Draw the base line using a ruler and pencil on chromatography paper. **[1]**

Step 2: Put small spots of ink onto the base line (with spaces between). **[1]**

Step 3: Pour water (the mobile phase) into a beaker. **[1]**

Step 4: Fix the chromatography paper (the stationary phase) in the beaker so that the bottom edge of the paper dips into the water with the water level below the pencil line. **[1]**

2. (a) The original green ink contains three spots / coloured substances. **[1]**

(b) The original green ink and the ink from the suspected forgery have a different number of spots / coloured substances. **[1]** One of the spots is the same in both inks but the other spots are different. **[1]** So, the suspected forgery is not drawn with the same ink as the original green ink. **[1]**

3. (a) Pencil would be used **[1]** because it is insoluble in the solvent. **[1]**

(b) **1** The distance moved from the base line by each spot **[1]**; **2** The distance from base line to solvent front **[1]**

Page 104 Potable water
Quick quiz
(a) rivers and reservoirs; ground water

(b) sea water

1. (a) Potable water is water that is drinkable. **[1]**

(b) Potable water contains dissolved substances, but pure water does not. **[1]**

(c) **1** The sea water is heated to evaporate the water (leaving the salt behind). **[1]** **2** The water vapour is then condensed to give pure water. **[1]**

2. filtration; **[1]** sedimentation; **[1]** chlorination **[1]**

3. The water must not contain dissolved salts. **[1]**

Page 105 The pH scale and neutralisation
Quick quiz
left-hand end 0–6 labelled 'acidic'; 7 labelled 'neutral'; right-hand end 8–14 labelled 'alkaline'

1. It is a measure of the acidity or alkalinity of a solution. **[1]**

2. (a) battery acid, **[1]** vinegar, **[1]** tomato juice **[1]**

(b) shampoo **[1]**, baking soda **[1]**

3. (a)

	Acidic solutions	Alkaline solutions
Name of ion	Hydrogen **[1]**	Hydroxide **[1]**
Formula of ion	H^+ **[1]**	OH^- **[1]**

(b) $H^+ + OH^- \rightarrow H_2O$ **[1]**

4. Add a small spot of the solution to the indicator paper / dip the indicator paper in the solution. **[1]** (Leave for 30 seconds) and record the colour. **[1]** Match the colour to the nearest colour on a pH colour chart. **[1]**

Page 106 Practical: pH change
Quick quiz
True; False; True

1. (a) calcium chloride + water **[1]**

(b) calcium chloride + water **[1]**

2. (a) hydrogen ion **[1]**

(b) hydroxide ion **[1]**

3. universal indicator solution **[1]**

4. (a) pipette / burette **[1]**

(b) balance **[1]**

(c) hydrochloric acid + calcium hydroxide → calcium chloride + water **[1]** for each product

(d) pH would start less than 7 (accept any number from 0 to 3) **[1]** and would increase **[1]** on the addition of calcium hydroxide. The pH would finish at a value of more than 7 (accept any value from 10 to 14). **[1]**

Page 107 Salt production
Quick quiz
hydrochloric → chloride; sulfuric → sulfate; nitric → nitrate

1. (a) magnesium oxide + sulfuric acid → magnesium sulfate + water **[1]**

(b) magnesium hydroxide + sulfuric acid → magnesium sulfate + water **[1]**

(c) copper carbonate + nitric acid → copper nitrate + water + carbon dioxide **[1]**

(d) iron oxide + hydrochloric acid → iron chloride + water **[1]**

(e) zinc carbonate + hydrochloric acid → zinc chloride + water + carbon dioxide **[1]**

2. Bubble through limewater / calcium hydroxide **[1]**; turns cloudy. **[1]**

3. (a) sodium chloride **[1]**

(b) copper sulfate **[1]**

(c) zinc nitrate **[1]**

4. (a) Mg^{2+} and Cl^- **[1]**

(b) Ag^+ and NO_3^- **[1]**

5. (a) $CaCl_2$, calcium chloride **[1]**

(b) $PbBr_2$, lead bromide **[1]**

Page 108 Reactions of acids with metals
Quick quiz
hydrogen

1. (a) A salt is a compound made from the neutralisation of an acid and a base. **[1]**

(b) magnesium + hydrochloric acid → magnesium chloride **[1]** + hydrogen **[1]**

(c) sulfuric acid **[1]**

(d) H_2 **[1]**

2. (a) magnesium chloride **[1]**

(b) Observation: Bubbles / fizzing / effervescence **[1]**; Reason: A gas / hydrogen is made **[1]**

OR Observation: Magnesium metal would get smaller **[1]** Reason: As the metal reacts and forms a soluble salt **[1]**

3. (a) magnesium nitrate **[1]**

(b) hydrogen **[1]**

4. (a) $Zn + H_2SO_4$ **[1]** $\rightarrow ZnSO_4 + H_2$ **[1]**

(b) A lit splint **[1]** will cause the hydrogen to ignite with a squeaky pop. **[1]**

Page 109 Soluble salts
Quick quiz
True; True; False; True

1. (a) It is too reactive / it would be unsafe to use. **[1]**

(b) Silver does not react with dilute acids. **[1]**

2. (a) The magnesium ribbon would become smaller or disappear, **[1]** and the student would see bubbling / fizzing. **[1]**

(b) Filter the mixture **[1]**

3. (a) zinc **[1]**; zinc oxide **[1]**; zinc carbonate **[1]**

(b) Any one for 1 mark from:

zinc + hydrochloric acid → zinc chloride + hydrogen

zinc oxide + hydrochloric acid → zinc chloride + water

zinc carbonate + hydrochloric acid → zinc chloride + water + carbon dioxide

Page 110 Practical: Making salts
Quick quiz
From left to right: evaporating dish; filter funnel; beaker; tripod; Bunsen burner

1. Correct order (top to bottom): 3, 4, 6, 1, 2, 7, 5 **[5 or 6 correct for 5 marks; 4 correct for 4 marks; 3 correct for 3 marks; 2 correct for 2 marks; 1 correct for 1 mark]**

2. Warm some nitric acid gently in a beaker with a Bunsen burner. **[1]** Add zinc oxide, one spatula at a time, until no more reacts, stirring gently. **[1]** Filter to remove unreacted zinc oxide. **[1]** Heat the zinc nitrate solution gently and leave to crystallise in an evaporating basin. **[1]** Pat the crystals dry with filter paper. **[1]**

Page 111 Titration
Quick quiz
red to yellow

1. (a) A pipette filler **[1]** B pipette **[1]** C conical flask

(b) Makes the colour change at the end point easier to see **[1]**

(c) burette **[1]**

(d) From pink **[1]** to colourless **[1]**

2. A method including the following points in a logical order for 6 marks:

- pipette
- burette
- wash with appropriate solution
- acid or alkali in flask
- indicator
- swirling
- use white tile

End point

- correct starting colour of indicator
- controlled addition until indicator changes colour
- add dropwise near endpoint
- correct end colour of indicator
- repeat titration until concordant results

Obtaining crystals

- mix volumes without indicator
- evaporate to half volume / until crystallisation starts
- leave to crystallise
- dry between filter paper

Page 112 Solubility rules
Quick quiz

Rule	Soluble (observation: dissolves in water)	Insoluble (observation: makes a precipitate)
All common sodium, potassium and ammonium salts	✓	
Nitrates	✓	
Common chlorides (except for silver chloride)	✓	
Common sulfates (except for lead sulfate, barium sulfate and calcium sulfate)	✓	
Common hydroxides (except for sodium, potassium and ammonium salts)		✓
Common carbonates (except for sodium, potassium and ammonium salts)		✓

1. **(a)** ammonium sulfate + barium chloride → ammonium chloride + barium sulfate **[1]**
   (b) barium sulfate **[1]**
2. **(a)** potassium iodide + lead nitrate → potassium nitrate + lead iodide correct reactants **[1]**; correct products **[1]**
   (b) sodium chloride + silver nitrate → sodium nitrate + silver chloride; correct reactants **[1]**; correct products **[1]**
3. lead chloride **[1]**
4. Filter the mixture. **[1]** Wash / rinse the residue / solid with water. **[1]** Dry between filter paper / dry in a warm oven. **[1]**

Page 113 Electrolysis
Quick quiz
(a) electrode → a solid electrical conductor

electrolysis → using electricity to decompose a compound

electrolyte → a liquid or solution that can conduct electricity

(b) ions

1. **(a)** cathode **[1]**
   (b) anode **[1]**
2. They become free to move about. **[1]**
3. **(a)** carbon / graphite **[1]**
   (b) Dissolve it in water. **[1]** Melt it. **[1]**
4. During electrolysis, positive **[1]** ions move to the negative electrode. Negative ions move to the positive **[1]** electrode. Ions **[1]** are discharged at the electrodes, producing elements. **[1]**
5. Place two copper electrodes **[1]** in a solution of copper sulfate. **[1]** Connect to a dc power supply or battery. **[1]** If copper ions are positively charged, the negative electrode will gain copper / get heavier. **[1]**

Diagram could be included:

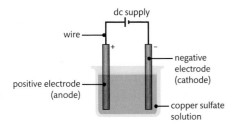

Page 114 Electrolysis of molten ionic compounds
Quick quiz
solid; an electrolyte; cathode; anode

1. **(a)** Magnesium ions have a positive charge **[1]** so they are attracted to the negative charge of the cathode / the opposite charge **[1]** where they gain electrons to form magnesium metal. **[1]**
   (b) chlorine **[1]**
2. **(a)** cathode / negative electrode **[1]**
   (b) bromine / Br_2 **[1]**
   (c) lead bromide → lead **[1]** + bromine **[1]**
   (d) Any appropriate answer for 1 mark such as: Use a fume cupboard / complete in a well-ventilated room; Wear eye protection; Tie long hair back / secure loose clothing; Do not touch the hot equipment, use tongs instead.

Page 115 Electrolysis of aqueous solutions
Quick quiz
(a) anode, **(b)** cathode, **(c)** the solution used in electrolysis

1. **(a)** hydrogen **[1]**
   (b) copper **[1]**
   (c) hydrogen **[1]**
   (d) silver **[1]**
2. **(a)** chlorine **[1]**
   (b) oxygen **[1]**
   (c) bromine **[1]**
   (d) oxygen **[1]**
3. **(a)** hydroxide ions, OH^-, **[1]** and hydrogen ions, H^+ **[1]**
   (b) hydroxide ions / OH^- ions **[1]**
4. **(a)** cathode: hydrogen; anode: oxygen **[1]**
   (b) cathode: hydrogen; anode: iodine **[1]**

Page 116 Practical: Electrolysis of copper sulfate
Quick quiz
A cell; **B** cathode; **C** anode; **D** electrolyte

1. **(a)** oxygen **[1]**
   (b) Cu **[1]**
   (c) Inert electrodes **[1]** are placed in the electrolyte, which is copper sulfate solution. **[1]** The electrodes are connected to a dc power supply **[1]** and left to run for a few minutes. **[1]**
   (d) an unreactive electrode **[1]**
2. **(a)** Inert electrodes do not become involved in the chemistry of the electrolysis but copper electrodes do. **[1]**
   (b) cathode – copper **[1]** anode – oxygen **[1]**

Page 117 The reactivity series
Quick quiz
sodium; magnesium; iron

1. **(a)** Metal Z **[1]** because it reacted the most vigorously. **[1]**
   (b) Z, X, Y **[1]**
   (c) Metal Z **[1]**
2. **(a)** (Most reactive to least reactive) B, C, A **[1]**
   (b) Because metal B reacted with two metals (A and C) **[1]**; metal C reacted with A but not with B **[1]**; metal A did not react with B or C **[1]**

Page 118 Extraction of metals and reduction
Quick quiz
1, 3, 2, 4 (aluminium, iron, copper, gold)

1. **(a)** A naturally occurring rock **[1]** that contains a sufficient amount of metal or metal compounds to be extracted for profit. **[1]**
   (b) gold **[1]**
2. **(a)** zinc / copper **[1]**
   (b) K / Mg **[1]**
3. **(a)** iron oxide + carbon → iron + carbon dioxide **[1]**
   (b) Iron is less reactive than carbon. **[1]**
   (c) Oxidised: carbon because it gains oxygen. **[1]** Reduced: iron oxide because it loses oxygen. **[1]**

Page 119 Electrolysis to extract metals
Quick quiz
3, 4, 1, 2 (potassium, zinc, iron, copper)

1. sodium / magnesium **[1]**
2. When the compound is dissolved in water **[1]** and when it is molten. **[1]**
3. **(a)** Aluminium oxide is insoluble / it does not dissolve in water. **[1]**
   (b) Cryolite melts at a lower temperature than aluminium oxide, **[1]** so this reduces the energy needed to produce an electrolyte. **[1]**
4. **(a)** A large amount of electricity is needed. **[1]**
   (b) oxygen **[1]**
   (c) Hot carbon reacts with oxygen to produce carbon dioxide **[1]** which uses up the anodes. **[1]**

Page 120 Metal oxides
Quick quiz
True; True; False

1. **(a)** calcium oxide **[1]**
   (b) iron oxide **[1]**
   (c) magnesium oxide **[1]**

2. (a) lead oxide **[1]**

(b) zinc oxide **[1]**

(c) sodium oxide **[1]**

(d) aluminium oxide **[1]**

3. (a) aluminium + oxygen → aluminium oxide **[1]**

(b) In the reaction, aluminium gains oxygen. **[1]**

4. Copper oxide is reduced because it loses oxygen. **[1]** Hydrogen is oxidised because it gains oxygen. **[1]**

5. Iron oxide is reduced **[1]** as it loses oxygen. **[1]** Carbon is oxidised **[1]** as it gains oxygen. **[1]**

Page 121 Recycling and life-cycle assessment
Quick quiz
Any three from: extracting the raw materials; manufacture and packaging of the product; use of the product; disposal of the product.

1. A life-cycle assessment assesses the impact of a product at every stage **[1]** to see how it affects the environment. **[1]**

2. Any three for 3 marks from: energy used to extract the raw materials; **[1]** amount of waste produced / toxicity of water produced during manufacture; **[1]** amount of carbon dioxide / greenhouse gases produced; **[1]** cost of any added resources; **[1]** renewability of raw materials. **[1]**

3. (a) Using the plastic bag more times will reduce the amount of plastic bags needed to be made **[1]** and reduce the amount of landfill. **[1]**

(b) Energy is needed to collect and process the bags for recycling. **[1]** Also new bags will be needed to replace those that have been recycled. **[1]** Re-using a bag requires less energy use and less production of new bags. **[1]**

(c) Any from: Capture the energy from burning **[1]** to make electricity. **[1]** / Treat any waste gases **[1]** to stop air pollution. **[1]**

4. Answers could include the following points in a logical order for 6 marks; any five comments and a justified response:

Paper cups – made from a renewable resource; **[1]** are biodegradable; **[1]** the carbon dioxide created by paper cups is offset by photosynthesis in growing wood. **[1]**

However, paper cups – cannot be recycled; **[1]** create more CO_2; **[1]** produce more waste; **[1]** require more energy to manufacture; **[1]** require more fresh water. **[1]**

Plastic cups – are made from a non-renewable / finite resource. **[1]**

Page 122 Reversible reactions
Quick quiz
reversible → a reaction that can proceed in either direction

reactants → substances found to the left of the arrow in an equation

equilibrium → rate of forward reaction is equal to rate of backward reaction

products → substances found to the right of the arrow in an equation

1. (a) The damp pink **[1]** paper will turn blue after it has been dried in the oven. **[1]**

(b) blue cobalt salt + water **[1]** ⇌ **[1]** pink cobalt salt **[1]**

(c) The forward and backward reactions are happening at the same rate. **[1]** The concentrations of the reactants and products do not change. **[1]**

2. reversible reaction **[1]**

3 (a) $2SO_2(g) + O_2(g) \rightleftharpoons 2SO_3(g)$ **[1]**

(b) Temperature, **[1]** pressure **[1]**

4. (a) anhydrous copper sulfate + water **[1]** ⇌ hydrated copper sulfate **[1]**

(b) Colour change from white **[1]** to blue **[1]**

Page 123 Dynamic equilibrium and the Haber process
Quick quiz
False; True; True; False

1. (a) Dynamic equilibrium occurs in a closed system when the rate of the forward and reverse reactions are equal **[1]**. The concentrations of the reactants and products remain constant. **[1]**

(b) Temperature of 450 °C **[1]**; pressure of 200 atmospheres **[1]**; iron catalyst **[1]**

(c) ammonia **[1]**

2. (a) nitrogen from air **[1]**; hydrogen from natural gas **[1]**

(b) Reaction mixture is cooled. **[1]** The ammonia liquefies but unreacted gases do not **[1]** so the ammonia is run / tapped off. **[1]**

Page 124 Group 1
Quick quiz
True; False; True; False; False

1. (a) They all fizz in the water. **[1]**

The water turns universal indicator purple after all the reactions. **[1]**

(b) potassium + water → potassium hydroxide + hydrogen **[1]**

2. (a) lithium + oxygen → lithium oxide **[1]**

(b) red **[1]**

3. (a) soft **[1]** and have relatively low melting points **[1]**

(b) Any two for 2 marks from: effervescence / bubbles / hydrogen gas; sodium disappears; orange flame; sodium moves on surface; pop / smoke at end

(c) $2K(s) + 2H_2O(l) \rightarrow 2KOH(aq) + H_2(g)$ **[1]**

Page 125 Group 7
Quick quiz
low; non-metals; poor; molecules

1. Iodine, Grey, Solid **[1]**

2. (a) 7 **[1]**

(b) Damp blue litmus paper **[1]** goes red **[1]** then bleaches. **[1]**

(c) The boiling point increases as you go down the group **[1]** because the molecules get bigger / relative atomic mass increases **[1]** so there are larger intermolecular forces of attraction. **[1]**

3. (a) bromine **[1]**

(b) I_2 or At_2 **[1]**

(c) chlorine, accept Cl_2 **[1]**

(d) solid **[1]**

Page 126 Group 7 reactivity
Quick quiz
reactivity; electron configuration; seven; one; easier; fluorine

1. (a) A more reactive element **[1]** takes the place of a less reactive element from its compound. **[1]**

(b) chlorine **[1]**

(c) The same halogen / halide was used **[1]** so there would not be a reaction. **[1]**

(d) potassium iodide + bromine → potassium bromide **[1]** + iodine **[1]**

2. (a) chlorine **[1]**

(b) Br^- **[1]**

Page 127 Group 0
Quick quiz
True; False; True; True; True

1. melting point −189 °C; **[1; note that answers can vary slightly but should be between the values missing above and below in the table]** boiling point −186 °C **[1]**

2. (a) They both have eight electrons in their outer shells, **[1]** so they both have full outer shells / stable arrangements. **[1]**

(b) It only has two electrons in its outer shell (rather than eight). **[1]**

(c) They all have full outer shells / stable arrangements. **[1]**

3. (a) melting point in range −190 to −271 °C (−248 °C); **[1]** boiling point only slightly higher than melting point and in range −187 to −268 °C (−246 °C) **[1]**

(b) increases down the group **[1]**

(c) It has a low density **[1]** and is non-flammable / inert. **[1]**

Page 128 Calculating rate of reaction
Quick quiz
A and **D** are correct; **B**: mol/s; **C**: cm³/s

1. $\frac{0.12}{50} = 0.0024$ (2.4×10^{-3}) **[1]** g/s **[1]**

2. (a) The volume of gas stops increasing. **[1]**

(b) Tangent drawn at 10 s **[1]** (red line on graph)

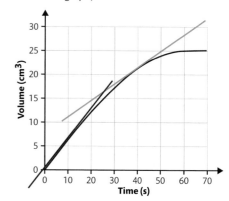

(c) The slope decreases, for example, from 10 s to the end of the reaction. **[1]** This means that the rate decreases as the reaction goes on. **[1]**

3. (a) $\frac{25}{60}$ = 0.42 **[1]** cm³/s **[1]**

   (b) Tangent drawn at 40 s **[1]** (green line on graph)

Page 129 Factors affecting rate of reaction

Quick quiz
increase; decrease; increase; decrease

1. Particles collide more often **[1]** and with more energy. **[1]**

2. It reduces the activation energy. **[1]**

3. (a) The larger the chips, the smaller the mass lost **[1]** so the lower the rate of reaction. **[1]**

   (b) surface area of the chips **[1]**

   (c) change the temperature; **[1]** change the concentration of the acid **[1]**

Page 130 Practical: Monitoring rate of reaction – colour change

Quick quiz
measure the volume of gas produced; measure the change in mass; measure the time taken for a colour change

1. (a) Draw a cross on the paper **[1]** and time how long it takes until the cross can no longer be seen through the liquid. **[1]**

   (b) $Na_2S_2O_3 + 2HCl \rightarrow 2NaCl + H_2O + SO_2 + S$ **[1]**

   (c) Any suitable answer for 2 marks such as: Wear eye protection **[1]** as the acid is an irritant and could damage eyes. **[1]** / Complete in a well ventilated room / under a fume hood **[1]** as sulfur dioxide is an irritant. **[1]**

2. (a) A = thermometer; **[1]** B = conical flask; **[1]** C = white tile **[1]**

   (b) temperature **[1]**

   (c) stopwatch **[1]**

   (d) Any one for 1 mark: keep the volume the same; keep the concentrations the same; use the same flask and cross each time; use the same person to judge when the cross can no longer be seen **[1]**

Page 131 Practical: Monitoring rate of reaction – gas production

Quick quiz
magnesium + hydrochloric acid

calcium carbonate + hydrochloric acid

zinc + sulfuric acid

1. (a) D **[1]**

   (b) B **[1]**

   (c) gas syringe **[1]**

   (d) some carbon dioxide may escape / not be collected **[1]**

2. (a) hydrogen **[1]**

   (b) Any one for 1 mark: bubbles / fizzing **[1]**; metal seems to disappear **[1]**

(c) Any one for 1 mark: mass of magnesium ribbon **[1]** / size of magnesium ribbon **[1]** / volume of acid **[1]** / temperature **[1]**

(d) magnesium ribbon disappears or fizzing stops / volume on syringe doesn't increase any further **[1]**

Page 132 Collision theory and activation energy

Quick quiz
temperature → Particles have more energy and move faster, colliding more frequently.

concentration → There are more particles present in the same volume and so a higher chance of collisions.

pressure → The volume in which the particles are located is reduced, therefore the particles are more likely to collide.

1. (a) **[3]**

Change in reaction condition	Reaction rate increased	Reaction rate decreased
Concentration decreased		✓
Surface area to volume ratio increased	✓	
Temperature increased	✓	

   (b)

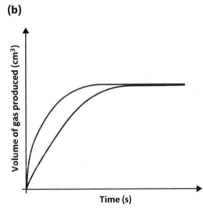

curve is steeper at start; **[1]** curve flattens at same volume of gas as original curve **[1]**

   (c) The rate of reaction will decrease **[1]** as the lower temperature means that the particles have less energy **[1]** and they are less likely to collide. **[1]** This means there are fewer successful collisions in a given time and there will be fewer reactions. **[1]**

2. (a) As the reaction continues the rate of reaction reduces. **[1]** The reaction stops when the line becomes flat. **[1]**

   (b) As the reaction continues, the concentration of the reactants reduces **[1]** as they are being used up to make the products. **[1]** This means that there are fewer successful collisions in a given time as the reaction continues and so the rate decreases. **[1]**

Page 133 Reaction profiles

Quick quiz

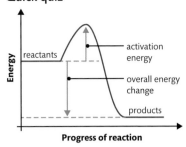

1. (a) The products have less energy than the reactants. **[1]**

   (b) X is the overall energy change of the reaction / the overall difference between the energy of the reactants and the energy of the products. **[1]**

   (c) The minimum energy required to start a reaction **[1]**

2.

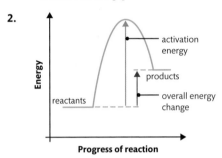

- reactant(s) and product(s) labelled in their correct positions **[1]**
- energy of reactants lower than energy of products **[1]**
- activation energy **[1]**

Page 134 Catalysts

Quick quiz
False; False; True; False

1. (a) Catalysts provide a different pathway for the reaction **[1]** which has a lower activation energy. **[1]** This means there are more successful collisions between particles **[1]** per second / minute. **[1]**

   (b) iron **[1]**

2. (a) A substance that changes the rate of a chemical reaction **[1]** but is not used up during the reaction. **[1]**

   (b) Manganese dioxide does not appear in the word equation. **[1]**

3. (a)

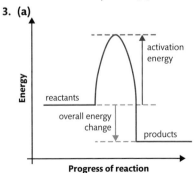

reactants and products labelled in their correct positions; **[1]** energy of reactants higher than energy of products; **[1]** activation energy correctly identified **[1]**

(b) The height of the activation energy would be lower. [1]

(c) The catalyst provides an alternative pathway for the reaction with a lower activation energy [1] so there are more successful collisions. [1]

Page 135 Exothermic and endothermic reactions
Quick quiz
Endothermic reactions → take in heat energy → so temperature decreases.

Exothermic reactions → give out heat energy → so temperature increases.

1.

Type of reaction	Exothermic	Endothermic
Combustion	✓	
Electrolysis		✓
Neutralisation	✓	
Oxidation	✓	
Thermal decomposition		✓

[3 marks if all correct; 2 marks if 3 or 4 correct; 1 mark if 1 or 2 correct]

2. Endothermic because the temperature of the surroundings goes down [1]

3. (a) A: 17 [1]; D: 12 [1]

(b) C, A, D, B [1]

(c) The greater the temperature increase, the more reactive the metal is. [1]

Page 136 Temperature changes
Quick quiz
exothermic; exothermic; exothermic; endothermic; exothermic

1. (a) Any two for 2 marks from: There is an air gap between the polystyrene cup and the beaker. [1] There is a lid on the cup. [1] The cup is standing inside a beaker. [1]

(b) (i) Any two for 2 marks from: same volume of sodium hydroxide [1]; same volume of hydrochloric acid [1]; same concentration of hydrochloric acid [1]; same size of beaker [1]; same type of acid / alkali used. [1]

(ii) The reaction is exothermic. [1] The greater the concentration, [1] the greater the temperature increase. [1]

2. Any four for 4 marks from: Measure some acid into a polystyrene cup using a measuring cylinder. [1] Put the cup in a beaker to stop it falling over / to insulate it more. [1] Record the starting temperature using a thermometer. [1] Add some zinc and record the maximum / end temperature. [1] The temperature should increase. [1]

Page 137 Crude oil and hydrocarbons
Quick quiz
alkane → a series of molecules with general formula C_nH_{2n+2}

homologous series → family of molecules with the same general formula

methane → the simplest hydrocarbon molecule

1. A compound [1] of hydrogen and carbon only [1]

2. non-renewable [1]

3. (a)

Number of carbon atoms	Name of alkane
1	methane [1]
2	ethane [1]
3	propane [1]
4	butane [1]

(b) C_4H_{10} [1]

4. (a) C_nH_{2n+2} [1]

(b) (i) C_2H_6 [1]

(ii) C_6H_{14} [1]

(c) It contains oxygen, so not just hydrogen and carbon. [1] It does not have the formula C_nH_{2n+2}. [1]

Page 138 Fractional distillation
Quick quiz
False; True; False; False

1. (a) A petrol; B crude oil; C bitumen [2]

(b) used to surface roads / roofs [1]

2. petrol = fuel for cars [1], kerosene [1] = fuel for aircraft, fuel oil [1] = fuel for large ships, bitumen = surface roads / roofs [1]

3. (a) They have similar numbers of carbon atoms. [1]

(b) They have a boiling point range [1] but pure substances have an exact boiling point. [1] / There is a range of numbers of carbon atoms in the molecules [1] but in a pure substance all molecules would have the same number of carbon atoms. [1]

Page 139 Properties of hydrocarbons
Quick quiz
C_3H_8, $C_{12}H_{24}$, $C_{100}H_{202}$, $CH_3CH_2CH_3$, CH_2CHCH_3

1. (a) carbon dioxide [1]; water [1]

(b) Droplets of water / colourless liquid would appear. [1]

(c) limewater [1]

(d) The solution would change from colourless [1] to cloudy white / milky. [1]

(e) It produces carbon monoxide / carbon [1] which is toxic / causes breathing problems. [1]

2. (a) liquid is thick and not runny [1]

(b) material will catch fire easily [1]

(c) Viscosity: increases with the size of the hydrocarbon [1]

Flammability: decreases with the size of the hydrocarbon [1]

Page 140 Atmospheric pollutants
Quick quiz
carbon dioxide → greenhouse effect; sulfur dioxide → acid rain; carbon monoxide → toxic gas

1. (a) hydrocarbon + oxygen → carbon dioxide [1] + water [1]

(b) (i) carbon monoxide [1]

(ii) soot / carbon [1]

2. sulfur + oxygen → sulfur dioxide

[1 mark for correct reactants; 1 mark for correct product]

3. (a) nitrogen + oxygen → oxides of nitrogen [1]

(b) acid rain [1]

4. It is colourless and does not have a smell. [1]

5. blocks appliances [1] / may cause fires [1]

Page 141 Comparing fuels
Quick quiz
Non-renewable: coal; diesel oil; natural gas; petrol

Renewable: vegetable oil; wood

1. (a) $CH_4(g) + H_2O(g)$ [1] → $CO(g) + 3H_2(g)$ [1]

(b) renewable [1]

(c) Hydrogen is flammable [1] and so difficult to store safely in a car. [1]

2. renewable [1]

3. Advantage: ethanol is renewable [1] / saves resources of crude oil [1] Disadvantage: produces less energy per litre so more must be burnt [1]

Page 142 Cracking and alkenes
Quick quiz
catalytic cracking and steam cracking; alkanes

1. Large hydrocarbons are broken down to form smaller more useful molecules. [1]

2. There is a high [1] demand for fuels that contain small [1] molecules. Some of the products of cracking [1] are useful as these fuels. They are also useful as starting [1] materials for making other substances such as polymers.

3. (a) $C_8H_{18} → C_4H_{10} + C_4H_8$ [1]

(b) $C_{10}H_{22} → C_8H_{18} + C_2H_4$ [1]

(c) $C_5H_{12} → C_3H_8 + C_2H_4$ [1]

(d) $C_4H_{10} → CH_4 + C_3H_6$ [1]

4. (a) kerosene / fuel oil and bitumen [1]

(b) gases [1]

(c) cracking [1]

Page 143 Earth's early atmosphere
Quick quiz
nitrogen increased; oxygen increased; carbon dioxide decreased

1. The Earth formed over four billion years ago. [1]

2. volcanic activity [1]

3. As the Earth cooled, [1] water vapour condensed. [1]

4. CH_4 – methane [1]; NH_3 – ammonia [1]

5. Nitrogen is (relatively) unreactive. [1]

6. Any three for 3 marks from: The percentage of nitrogen is less. [1] The percentage of oxygen is less. [1] The percentage of carbon dioxide is greater. [1] / The percentage of other gases is greater. [1]

Page 144 Oxygen and carbon dioxide levels

Quick quiz

False; True; True; False

1. **(a)** 35% **[1]**
   (b) Primitive plants carried out photosynthesis, **[1]** which released oxygen into the atmosphere. **[1]**
2. carbon dioxide + water → glucose + oxygen **[1]**
3. oxygen **[1]** and nitrogen **[1]**

Page 145 Gases in the atmosphere

Quick quiz

(a) nitrogen; **(b)** oxygen; **(c)** carbon dioxide and water vapour

1. $\frac{80}{100} = \frac{4}{5}$ **[1]**
2. relights **[1]** a glowing splint **[1]**
3. **(a)** carbon dioxide : argon = 0.04 : 0.96 **[1]** = 1 : 24 **[1]**
   (b) 1.0% **[1]**
4. **(a)** Difference: 95% − 0.04% = 94.96% **[1]**
   (b) Percentage change: $\frac{94.96}{95} \times 100\%$ **[1]** = 99.96% decrease in CO_2 **[1]**

Page 146 Greenhouse gases

Quick quiz

carbon dioxide; greenhouse gases; infrared radiation; warm; climate change

1. **(a)**

Name of gas	Formula	Number of atoms	Number of elements
carbon dioxide	CO_2	3	2
nitrogen	N_2	2	1
oxygen	O_2	2	1
water vapour	H_2O	3	2

[1 mark for each correct row]

   (b) (i) carbon dioxide / water vapour **[1]**
   (ii) nitrogen / oxygen **[1]**
2. Solar energy such as visible light and ultraviolet **[1]** light reaches the Earth's surface from the Sun. **[1]** The Earth's surface **[1]** warms up as it absorbs solar energy. The warm surface emits infrared **[1]** radiation. Greenhouse gases absorb and re-emit this radiation, warming the Earth's atmosphere. **[1]**

Page 147 Human contribution to greenhouse gases

Quick quiz

Any two from: farming; use of fossil fuels; industry

1. **(a)** Any two for 2 marks from: livestock farming, **[1]** landfill sites, **[1]** rice paddy fields **[1]**
   (b) Combustion of fossil fuels **[1]** releases carbon dioxide as a waste product. **[1]**
2. **(a)** 412 − 302 = 110 (parts per million) **[1]**
   (b) $\frac{110}{100}$ **[1]** = 1.1 (parts per million) **[1]**
   (c) photosynthesis **[1]**

Page 148 Global climate change

Quick quiz

True; True; False

1. Environmental – as sea levels rise, habitats will be lost, **[1]** causing species of plants and animals to die out / decreasing food sources. **[1]**

   Social – rising sea levels will cause erosion of coastlines, **[1]** damaging habitats / damaging natural beauty of the areas / putting homes at risk. **[1]**

   Economic – coastal areas will no longer be attractive to the tourist industry **[1]** thus reducing the revenue of businesses in the area **[1]** / land and business premises will be put at risk. **[1]**
2. carbon capture and storage **[1]** / encourage more plants to be grown **[1]**
3. **(a)** Answer in the range of 13.85–13.88 °C (accept ±0.02) **[1]**
   (b) (i) 13.87 − 13.65 = 0.22 °C (accept ±0.02) **[1]**
   (ii) 14.65 − 13.95 = 0.70 °C **[1]** (accept ±0.02)
   (c) Any two for 2 marks from: more intense storms; more storms / hurricanes; higher summer temperatures; lower / higher precipitation; warmer winters; unpredictable weather patterns; flooding

Page 149 Key concepts in physics

Quantities and their units

metre → distance; kilogram → mass; second → time; ampere → current; metre cubed → volume; volt → potential difference; coulomb → charge

Prefixes

Conversion: milli → $\times 10^{-3}$; mega → $\times 10^{6}$; nano → $\times 10^{-9}$; micro → $\times 10^{-6}$; giga → $\times 10^{9}$; kilo → $\times 10^{3}$; centi → $\times 10^{-2}$

Abbreviation: giga → G; mega → M; kilo → k; centi → c; milli → m; micro → μ; nano → n

Conversions and time

1. 0.000 000 0023 m
2. 4.8 g
3. 400 000 000 V
4. 0.15 MJ
5. 2.7 mA
6. 40 μs
7. 1.8 m
8. False; False; True; True

Calculations

1. mass in kg = $\frac{160}{2.205}$ = 72.56 = 73 kg to 2 s.f.
2. diameter = 2 × 6370 = 12 740 km; 12 740 km = 12 740 000 m = 1.274×10^{7} m
3. speed of light = 300 000 km/s = 300 000 000 m/s = 3.0×10^{8} m/s
4. circumference = 4 379 000 km = 4.379×10^{9} m; radius = $\frac{4.379 \times 10^{9}}{2\pi}$ = 6.9694×10^{8} = 7×10^{8} m to 1 s.f.

Page 150 Scalar and vector quantities

Quick quiz

distance → scalar; momentum → vector; efficiency → scalar; speed → scalar; acceleration → vector; weight → vector; force → vector; temperature → scalar

1. **(a)** A scalar has magnitude but does not have direction, **[1]** but a vector has both magnitude and direction. **[1]**
   (b) A scalar **[1]** because it has magnitude but does not have a direction. **[1]**
2. **(a)** arrow pointing in the same direction that is twice as long as the one given **[1]**
   (b) 300 N + 150 N = 450 N **[1]**
3. **(a)** Resultant force = 400 − 300 **[1]** = 100 N (to the left) **[1]**
   (b) force = 100 N **[1]** to the right **[1]**

Page 151 Distance and speed

Quick quiz

True; False; False; True

1. **(a)** 10 + 10 **[1]** = 20 km **[1]**
   (b) zero (as she ends at the place she began) **[1]**
2. **(a)** 2 + 2 + 2 **[1]** = 6 km **[1]**
   (b) 2 km (school is 2 km from home) **[1]**
3. **(a)** The person in the boat travelled further (12 km). **[1]** The person in the car only travelled 5 km. **[1]**
   (b) There is no difference in their displacement **[1]** because they start and finish in the same place. **[1]**

Page 152 Speed and velocity

Quick quiz

speed; direction; distance; time

1. average speed = $\frac{\text{distance}}{\text{time}} = \frac{100}{2}$ **[1]** = 50 km/h **[1]**
2. average velocity = $\frac{\text{distance}}{\text{time}} = \frac{3040}{1600}$ **[1]** = 1.9 m/s north **[1]**
3. **(a)** 3 m/s **[1]**
   (b) 25 m/s **[1]**
4. **(a)** velocity = $\frac{\text{distance}}{\text{time}} = \frac{54\,000}{5400}$ **[1]** = 10 m/s west **[1]**
   (b) The speed will not have been constant throughout the journey. Moving objects have varying speeds (as do sound and wind). **[1]**
   (c) distance of second bus = 108 km; average velocity = $\frac{108\,000}{5400}$ = 20 m/s west **[1]** (twice the velocity of the first bus) accept 2 × 10 = 20 m/s

Page 153 Distance–time graphs

Quick quiz

the gradient of the line increases → this means the object is accelerating

the gradient of the line decreases → this means the object is decelerating

the gradient of the line is zero → this means the object is stationary

1. A–B: The cyclist travels 30 km in 3 hours. The speed of the cyclist is 10 km/h. **[1]**

   B–C: The cyclist is stationary for 5 hours. **[1]**

   C–D: The cyclist travels a further 90 km in 4 hours. The speed is 22.5 km/h. **[1]**

2. (a) 250 m **[1]**

(b) constant speed (of 5 m/s) **[1]**

(c) 0 m/s **[1]**

3. Distance on the y-axis and time on the x-axis **[1]**; a straight line drawn from (0, 0) to (2, 0) then from (2, 0) to (7, 10) **[1]**

Page 154 Uniform acceleration

Quick quiz

$x \rightarrow$ displacement $\rightarrow$ m; $u \rightarrow$ initial velocity $\rightarrow$ m/s; $v \rightarrow$ final velocity $\rightarrow$ m/s; $a \rightarrow$ acceleration $\rightarrow$ m/s^2; $t \rightarrow$ time $\rightarrow$ s

1. $a = \dfrac{12-0}{6}$ **[1]** = 2 m/s^2 **[1]**

2. The acceleration is constant and is a measure of how quickly an object's velocity changes. **[1]**

3. $v^2 = u^2 + 2ax = 2^2 + 2 \times 3 \times 16$ **[1]** = 100; **[1]** so $v = \sqrt{100} = 10$ m/s **[1]**

4. (a) $a = \dfrac{v-u}{t} = \dfrac{50-0}{5} = 10$ m/s^2 **[3]**

(b) Assumed that acceleration is constant or uniform. **[1]**

Page 155 Velocity-time graphs

Quick quiz

gradient of the line $\rightarrow$ acceleration; area under the line $\rightarrow$ distance travelled; a horizontal line $\rightarrow$ constant speed

1. speed **[1]**

2. $a = \dfrac{25-0 \, \textbf{[1]}}{5-0 \, \textbf{[1]}} = 5$ m/s^2 **[1]**

3. (a) travelling at a constant speed of 15 m/s **[1]**

(b) distance = area under the graph **[1]** 15 × 10 **[1]** = 150 m **[1]**

Page 156 Gravity

Quick quiz

mass $\rightarrow$ the amount of matter in an object $\rightarrow$ kg; weight $\rightarrow$ the force acting on an object due to gravity $\rightarrow$ N; gravitational field strength $\rightarrow$ the strength of gravity at any one point $\rightarrow$ N/kg

1. (a) $W = mg = 2.5 \times 10$ **[1]** = 25 N **[1]**

(b) 2.5 kg **[1]**

2. (a) $W = mg = 16\,000 \times 10$ **[1]** = 160 000 N **[1]**

(b) (i) mass = 16 000 kg **[1]** (same as mass on Earth)

(ii) $W = mg = 16\,000$ kg × 1.6 N/kg **[1]** = 25 600 N **[1]**

(c) difference = 160 000 – 25 600 **[1]** = 134 400 N **[1]**

Page 157 Newton's laws of motion

Quick quiz

Newton's first law $\rightarrow$ An object will continue to move in the same direction at the same speed unless acted upon by a resultant force.

Newton's second law $\rightarrow$ The acceleration of an object is proportional to the resultant force and inversely proportional to the mass of the object.

Newton's third law $\rightarrow$ When two objects interact they exert an equal and opposite force on each other.

1. (a) force = mass × acceleration **[1]**

(b) When mass is increased, a larger force is needed **[1]** to produce the same acceleration. **[1]**

---

2. $F = m \times a = 70 \times 4$ **[1]** = 280 N **[1]**

3. moving in a straight line **[1]** at a constant speed **[1]**

4. Forces of friction and air resistance act on the moving ball, **[1]** so the resultant force on the ball is in the opposite direction to its motion **[1]** causing it to slow down. **[1]**

Page 158 Practical: Investigating acceleration

Quick quiz

speed $\rightarrow$ m/s; mass $\rightarrow$ kg; acceleration $\rightarrow$ m/s^2; force $\rightarrow$ N

1. (a) force **[1]**

(b) acceleration **[1]**

(c) Newton's second law states that force = mass × acceleration. **[1]** So if the force is increased and the mass stays the same, **[1]** the acceleration must increase. **[1]**

2. (a) force applied (i.e. the number of masses on the mass holder pulling the trolley through the light gate) **[1]** OR distance between trolley and light gate **[1]**

(b) the (mass of the) trolley **[1]**

(c) acceleration of the trolley through the light gate **[1]**

(d) It shows that acceleration is inversely proportional to mass **[1]** when the force is kept constant. **[1]**

Page 159 Stopping distance

Quick quiz

False; False; True; False

1. (a) distance = speed × time **[1]**

(b) distance travelled = 13 × 1.3 **[1]** = 16.9 m **[1]**

(c) stopping distance = 16.9 + 14 **[1]** = 30.9 m **[1]**

2. (a) (i) 53 m **[1]**

(ii) approximately quadruples / × 4 **[1]**

(iii) answers in the range 90–100 m **[1]**

(b) increases **[1]**

Page 160 Factors affecting braking distance

Quick quiz

braking; thinking; stopping; deceleration

1. Friction between the tyres and the road **[1]** will be reduced **[1]** so the braking distance will be increased. **[1]**

2. wet road, **[1]** damaged brakes, **[1]** high speed **[1]**

3. (a) A large deceleration requires a large force **[1]** which means that the occupants can be injured. **[1]**

(b) They reduce the forces on the occupants **[1]** by increasing the time taken for the occupants to come to a stop. **[1]**

(c) Friction transfers energy to the brakes and causes them to heat up. **[1]** When a driver brakes hard, a lot of energy is transferred in a short time. **[1]**

Page 161 Gravitational potential energy

Quick quiz

potential; mass; field; height

1. $\Delta GPE = 65 \times 10 \times 1090$ **[1]** = 708 500 J **[1]**

2. (a) 2600 × 10 × 40 **[1]** = 1 040 000 J **[1]**

(b) It would be half / halved / 520 000 J. **[1]**

3. Gravitational potential energy **[1]** is transferred to kinetic energy. **[1]**

Page 162 Kinetic energy

Quick quiz

True; False; True; False

1. The amount of energy is directly proportional to its (speed)^2. **[1]**

2. (a) $KE = \dfrac{1}{2} \times m \times v^2 = \dfrac{1}{2} \times 10\,000 \times 10^2$ **[1]** = 500 000 J **[1]**

(b) An increase in the number of passengers means an increase in mass. **[1]** If mass increases, so does the kinetic energy. **[1]**

3. (a) 4.0 g = 0.004 kg; **[1]** kinetic energy = 0.5 × 0.004 × (1000)^2 **[1]** = 2000 J **[1]**

(b) Any one for 1 mark from: energy dissipated as heat; energy transferred as sound (eventually dissipated as heat); energy transferred as kinetic energy of part of target that flies off

Page 163 Conservation of energy

Quick quiz

True; False; False; True; True

1. (a) Energy transferred by heating, light and sound **[1]**

(b) transfers by light and sound **[1]**

(c) transfer by heating **[1]**

2. (a) heating **[1]**

(b) lubrication **[1]**

(c) It will be dissipated to the surroundings. **[1]**

3. The kinetic energy store of the car **[1]** is transferred by friction to thermal energy in the brakes and the surroundings. **[1]**

Page 164 Efficiency

Quick quiz

The closer to 1 (or 100%), the more efficient the device; If a device is 40% efficient, 40% of the energy is usefully transferred and 60% is wasted.

1. (a) Lamp A: $\dfrac{15}{60}$ **[1]** = 0.25 = 25% **[1]**

Lamp B: $\dfrac{15}{30}$ **[1]** = 0.5 = 50% **[1]**

(b) Lamp B (is more efficient) because its efficiency is higher. **[1]**

2. (a) 2000 – 1800 = 200 J **[1]**

(b) $\dfrac{1800}{2000}$ **[1]** = 0.9 or 90% **[1]**

(c) Energy is usefully transferred to kinetic energy in the motor **[1]** and thermal energy in the heating element. **[1]**

Page 165 Renewable energy resources

Quick quiz

Sun $\rightarrow$ energy transferred by light is used to generate electricity using solar panels

wind $\rightarrow$ wind forces turbines to rotate, generating electricity tides → daily movement of the ocean is used to generate electricity

1. Advantages (any two for 2 marks from): can be placed in isolated locations; **[1]** no fuel costs **[1]**

   Disadvantages (any two for 2 marks from): some people think they spoil the landscape; **[1]** some maintenance costs; **[1]** danger to birds; **[1]** noisy; **[1]** only work when windy; **[1]** cannot be used in storms **[1]**

2. Tidal barrage: Advantage (any one for 1 mark from): free energy; **[1]** low maintenance costs once built; **[1]** predictable energy output; **[1]** tides store a large amount of energy; **[1]** Disadvantage (any one from): change movement of water in estuaries so can disrupt wildlife; **[1]** costly to build; **[1]** limited location options; **[1]** low power output; **[1]** Hydroelectric dam: Advantage (any one from): reliable; **[1]** high power output; **[1]** small water wheels work in isolated locations; **[1]** free energy; **[1]** Disadvantage (any one from): some maintenance costs; **[1]** dams flood valleys, destroying habitats **[1]**

3. Solar panels do not produce constant electricity; other sources of power or very expensive storage batteries are needed. **[1]**

Page 166 Non-renewable energy resources
Quick quiz
coal, oil, natural gas

1. (a) Nuclear power doesn't contribute to global warming. **[1]**

   (b) Transport of radioactive fuel and waste is dangerous and expensive. **[1]**

2. Any two for 2 marks from: Carbon dioxide is produced. **[1]** Smoke and sulfur dioxide can cause breathing problems. **[1]** Fossil fuels will eventually run out. **[1]**

3. (a) renewable and non-renewable **[1]**

   (b) Hybrid cars can travel further than electric cars without having to stop for fuel or to recharge **[1]**. There are more fuel stations for hybrid cars than there are charging stations for fully electric cars. **[1]**

Page 167 Types of wave
Quick quiz
longitudinal waves: statements 1, 4, 5; transverse waves: statements 2 and 3

1. (a) longitudinal sound wave **[1]**

   (b) **A:** compression; **[1] B:** rarefaction **[1]**

2. speed = $\frac{50}{0.15}$ **[1]** = 333 m/s **[1]**

Page 168 Properties of waves
Quick quiz
amplitude → the maximum displacement of a point on a wave away from its undisturbed position

frequency → the number of waves passing a point each second

wavelength → the distance from a point on a wave to an identical point on an adjacent wave

time period → the time taken to complete one full cycle or wave

1. **B:** wavelength, **[1] C:** amplitude **[1]**

2. wave speed = frequency × wavelength = 50 × 6.8 **[1]** = 340 m/s **[1]**

3. (a) wave speed = frequency × wavelength **[1]**

   (b) 5.0 × 0.10 **[1]** = 0.5 m/s **[1]**

4. To reduce timing error **[1]** because any error he makes in timing will be spread out over the total number of waves. **[1]** / Because there may be less than one wave every second **[1]** so he needs to time over a longer period. **[1]**

Page 169 Practical: Investigating waves
Quick quiz
From top: 2, 6, 1, 3, 4, 5

1. (a) half the wavelength **[1]**

   (b) Determine the wavelength by measuring length L and doubling it. **[1]** Use the frequency from the frequency generator. **[1]** Calculate the speed using the equation speed = frequency × wavelength. **[1]**

   (c) Same frequency of oscillation; **[1]** Same tension / weight on the string. **[1]**

2. (a) The number of waves that pass a point in a fixed period of time. **[1]**

   (b) a metre rule **[1]**

Page 170 Types of electromagnetic waves
Quick quiz
EM: light; infrared; X-rays; radio; microwaves

Not: water waves; sound; waves on a string; ultrasound

1. Missing labels, from left to right: microwaves; infrared waves; ultraviolet waves; X-rays; gamma rays. **[3 marks: all 5 correct; 2 marks: 3 or 4 correct; 1 mark: 1 or 2 correct.]**

2. (a) Any two for 2 marks from: transverse; electromagnetic; travel in straight lines; all travel at the same speed (in a vacuum)

   (b) Similarity: The wave speed is the same for light and ultraviolet radiation. **[1]**

      Difference: Any one for 1 mark from: The frequency is different. The wavelength is different.

3. (a) nucleus **[1]**

   (b) Ionising radiation is radiation / electromagnetic waves **[1]** that can change the electric charge on an atom. **[1]**

   (c) Any one for 1 mark from: gene damage; mutation; cancer

Page 171 Practical: Investigating refraction
Quick quiz
False; False; True

1. Refraction is the change in direction **[1]** of a ray of light due to a change in speed **[1]** as it passes from one material into another. **[1]**

2. (a) So the angles can be measured more accurately. **[1]**

   (b) protractor **[1]**

   (c) The ray box could be hot **[1]** and the student could burn their hand. **[1]**

   (d) angle of refraction **[1]**

   (e) So that a set of values of angle of incidence and corresponding angle of refraction can be recorded **[1]** and any patterns identified. **[1]**

Page 172 Applications of EM waves
Quick quiz
radio waves → TV and communications; infrared → thermal imaging; visible → lasers; ultraviolet → tanning; X-rays → medical imaging

1. The microwaves are absorbed by the water in the food **[1]** and transfer energy to the food. **[1]**

2. (a) Radio waves can be used for communication because they can transfer information / not blocked by the atmosphere / easily converted into electrical signals. **[1]**

   (b) Any two for 2 marks from: (broadcast) radio / music / sound; television; walkie talkies

3. (a) Can cause premature ageing and skin cancer **[1]**

   (b) Any two for 2 marks from: security marking, **[1]** tanning, **[1]** fluorescent lamps, **[1]** detecting forged bank notes, **[1]** disinfecting water **[1]**

   (c) more dangerous (because they are higher frequency and can kill cells easily) **[1]**

Page 173 The structure of an atom
Quick quiz

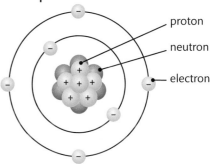

carbon atom

1. Electrons orbit the nucleus. An electron is negatively charged. **[1]** Protons are found in the nucleus. A proton is positively charged. **[1]** Neutrons are found in the nucleus. A neutron is neutral. **[1]**

2. 1×10^{-14} m **[1]**

3. They both have a relative mass of 1. **[1]** Protons have a relative charge of +1 whereas neutrons have a relative charge of 0. **[1]** They are both found in the nucleus. **[1]**

4. (a) The electron moves to a higher energy level. **[1]**

   (b) Any two for 2 marks from: mass of electron; **[1]** charge of electron; **[1]** number of electrons. **[1]**

Page 174 Mass number, atomic number and isotopes
Quick quiz
True; False; True; True; False

1. (a) Isotopes are atoms with the same atomic number **[1]** but a different mass number / number of neutrons. **[1]**

   (b) Carbon-14 has 2 extra neutrons. **[1]**

2. **(a)** 92 protons; **[1]** 92 electrons; **[1]** 146 neutrons **[1]**

   (b) Uranium 238 has 3 more neutrons than uranium-235. **[1]**

3. **(a)** ion **[1]**

   (b) 2+ **[1]**

   (c) 10 **[1]**

Page 175 Development of the atomic model

Quick quiz
In the nucleus of the atom.

1. from top: 5, 2, 4, 3, 1 **[3 marks for all in the correct order; 2 marks for 3 or 4 in the correct order; 1 mark for 1 or 2 in the correct order]**

2. **(a)** The plum pudding model suggested that the atom is a ball of positive charge **[1]** with negative charge / electrons embedded in it. **[1]**

   (b) The positive charge is found in a small nucleus at the centre. **[1]** The negative charge is found spread out on orbiting electrons. **[1]**

3. **(a)** alpha particles **[1]**

   (b) They passed (straight) through. **[1]**

   (c) Most of an atom is empty space. **[1]**

Page 176 Ionising radiation

Quick quiz
False; True; False; True

1. There is no way to tell which nucleus will decay next. **[1]** There is no way to predict when a particular nucleus will decay. **[1]** External factors, such as temperature, do not affect the process. **[1]**

2. **(a)** alpha particle, **[1]** beta-plus particle, **[1]** beta-minus particle, **[1]** gamma ray **[1]**

   (b) beta-minus particle **[1]**

   (c) An alpha particle contains two protons **[1]** and two neutrons. **[1]**

   (d) A proton decays **[1]** into a neutron and a positron. **[1]** The positron is emitted from the nucleus **[1]**

   (e) alpha particles **[1]**

   (f) Alpha particles **[1]** because they are the largest / have the most mass. **[1]**

Page 177 Background radiation

Quick quiz
False; True; False; True

1. The activity from a radioactive source is the number of nuclei that decay every second. **[1]**

2. film badge or dosimeter **[1]**

3. **(a)** G-M tube and rate meter **[1]**

   (b) Becquerel (Bq) **[1]**

   (c) Measure the background radiation, **[1]** then measure the activity of the source **[1]** and subtract the background count from the measured activity of the source. **[1]**

4. Any three for 3 marks from: radon; ground and buildings; medical procedures; food and drink; cosmic rays; nuclear power

Page 178 Beta decay

Quick quiz
β– particle, β+ particle, β+ particle, β– particle, both

1. When an unstable nucleus decays by β– emission, a neutron changes to a proton and an electron, **[1]** which is immediately emitted from the nucleus. The proton remains in the nucleus, so the atomic number increases by one, **[1]** forming a new element.

2. β+ particles: positively charged; negligible mass; atomic number of source nucleus decreases.

   β– particles: negatively charged; negligible mass; atomic number of source nucleus increases.

   [1 mark for each correct row in the table]

3. **(a)** A proton decays into a neutron and a positron and the neutron stays in the nucleus. **[1]** The positron is emitted from the nucleus but it has negligible mass. **[1]**

   (b) A neutron decays into a proton and a β–particle. **[1]** The β–particle is emitted from the nucleus. **[1]**

Page 179 Nuclear decay

Quick quiz

Type of decay	Change to mass number	Change to atomic number
Alpha	–4	–2
Beta minus	0	+1
Beta plus	0	–1
Gamma	0	0
Neutron	–1	0

1. **(a)** The number 14 represents the mass number of carbon-14. **[1]** The number 6 represents the atomic number of carbon-14. **[1]**

   (b) $_{-1}^{0}e$ **[1 mark for each correct value for the electron]**

   (c) beta (decay) **[1]**

2. **(a)** decreases by 2, decreases by 4 **[1]**

   (b) $_{86}^{198}Ra \rightarrow _{84}^{194}Po + _{2}^{4}He$

   [1 mark for 194, 1 mark for 84, 1 mark for both 4 and 2 correct]

3. The atomic number / number of protons decreases by 2. **[1]** When the atomic number changes, there is a different element. **[1]**

Page 180 Half-lives

Quick quiz
half-life; time; rate; half; time; nuclei

1. **(a)**

Time (years)	0	30	60	90	120
Activity (Bq)	1600	800	400	200	100

   [1 mark for each correct column]

   (b) 75 years **[1]**

2. Radioactive decay is a random process **[1]** which means that you cannot predict when a nucleus will decay. **[1]**

3. **A [1]** and **D [1]**

Page 181 Dangers of radioactivity

Quick quiz
False; False; False; True

1. **(a)** Ionising radiation may cause direct damage to body tissue if the radiation collides with cells in the tissue. **[1]**

   (b) Indirect damage can occur if the radiation causes ions to form in tissue. **[1]** These ions can destroy cells in our body, or they can mutate the genes within the cells. **[1]**

2. Alpha particles only travel a few centimetres through air. **[1]**

3. **(a)** reduce the exposure time; **[1]** wear protective clothing and / or stay behind a screen; **[1]** keep your distance from sources, for example, using long tweezers, tongs or robotic arms **[1]**

   (b) The cell may be destroyed. **[1]** Genes within the cell may mutate. **[1]**

Page 182 Radioactive contamination and irradiation

Quick quiz
X-rays; damaging; radioactive; precautions; dose

1. **(a)** Irradiation is the process of exposing an object to ionising radiation. **[1]**

   (b) Contamination is when radioactive substances stick to or are taken inside an object. **[1]**

2. **(a)** Gamma radiation can penetrate skin and cause damage / harm / cancer. **[1]** Standing in another room means that the doctor is protected from / receives less gamma radiation. **[1]**

   (b) The amount of radiation a patient receives depends on the time they are exposed to the source. **[1]** A longer time means a larger dose. **[1]**

3. **(a)** Peer review is when scientific research is checked and evaluated by other scientists. **[1]**

   (b) It makes scientists more confident about each other's findings. **[1]**

Page 183 Revising energy transfers

Quick quiz
False; False; True; True; False

1. **(a)** energy transferred by sound = 10% **[1]**

   (b)

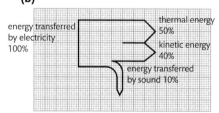

   Arrow for kinetic energy correct **[1]**

   Arrow for sound correct **[1]**

2. $\Delta GPE = m \times g \times \Delta h = 30 \times 10 \times 2$ **[1]** $= 600J$ **[1]**

3. $KE = \frac{1}{2} \times m \times v^2 = \frac{1}{2} \times 1500 \times 12^2$ **[1]** $= 108\,000J$ **[1]** (or 108 kJ)

Page 184 Work done and energy transfer
Quick quiz
False; True; False; False; True

1. gravitational potential energy store **[1]**
2. **(a)** work done = 2500 × 12 **[1]** = 30 000 J **[1]**
   (b) 60 000 J = 2500 × braking distance **[1]**
   braking distance = $\frac{60\,000}{2500}$ **[1]** = 24 m **[1]**
3. 750 kJ = 750 000 J; **[1]** 750 000 = F × 75; **[1]**
   $F = \frac{750\,000}{75}$ **[1]** = 10 000 N **[1]**

Page 185 Power
Quick quiz
energy transferred = $\frac{\text{power}}{\text{time}}$

1. 2.5 kW = 2500 W; $P = \frac{E}{t}$ so E = P × t **[1]**
   E = 2500 W × 120 s **[1]** = 300 000 J **[1]**
2. **(a)** W = 800 × 7.5 **[1]** = 6000 J **[1]**
   (b) $P = \frac{6000}{15}$ **[1]** = 400 W **[1]**

Page 186 Forces
Quick quiz
Contact forces: tension; friction; gravitational force

Non-contact forces: weight; magnetic; electrostatic

1. **(a)** Contact forces act when two objects are touching. **[1]**
   (b) Non-contact forces act on objects that are at a distance from each other. **[1]**
2. A quantity that has both magnitude **[1]** and direction **[1]**
3. **(a)** One arrow labelled 'weight' starting from centre of box pointing vertically downwards, **[1]** one arrow labelled 'friction' pointing horizontally backwards **[1]**
   (b) normal contact force; pushing force; friction **[1]**
4. **(a)** arrow labelled 'weight' pointing vertically downwards from approximate centre of albatross **[1]**
   (b) arrow labelled 'lift' pointing vertically upwards from the approximate centre of the albatross **[1]** and the same length as the weight arrow **[1]**
   (c) weight: non-contact; lift: contact **[1]**

Page 187 Circuit diagrams
Quick quiz

Component	Circuit symbol
thermistor	
lamp	
ammeter	

1. **(a)** correct symbols, **[1]** correct circuit **[1]**

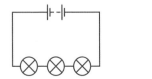

(b) correct symbols, **[1]** correct circuit **[1]**

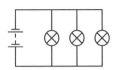

(c) The lamps in the parallel circuit would be brighter. **[1]**

2.

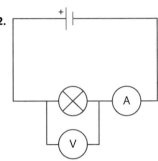

All symbols drawn correctly; **[1]** ammeter shown connected in series with the lamp; **[1]** voltmeter connected in parallel with the lamp. **[1]**

3. **(a)**

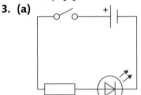

All symbols drawn correctly; **[1]** LED in correct orientation. **[1]**

(b) Any suitable device, such as lighting or cameras. **[1]**

Page 188 Current, resistance and potential difference
Quick quiz
current → the flow of charge, measured in amps (A)

potential difference → the energy given to each unit of charge, measured in volts (V)

resistance → opposition to the flow of charge, measured in ohms (Ω)

1. **(a)** The potential difference is shared equally between the resistors **[1]** because the three resistors have the same resistance. **[1]**
   (b) $I = \frac{V}{R} = \frac{6}{30}$ **[1]** = 0.2 A **[1]**
   (c) It will halve **[1]** as current is proportional to potential difference. **[1]**
2. $R = \frac{12}{5}$ **[1]** = 2.4 Ω **[1]**

Page 189 Charge, current and energy
Quick quiz
False; True; False; False; True

1. **(a)** 30 minutes = 30 × 60 = 1800 s; **[1]**
   charge = current × time = 10 × 1800 **[1]** = 18 000 C **[1]**
   (b) energy transferred = charge moved × potential difference = 18 000 × 230 **[1]** = 4 140 000 J **[1]**
2. **(a)** 0.75 A **[1]**
   (b) Q = I × t = 0.75 × 120 **[1]** = 90 C **[1]**
3. $t = \frac{50}{0.5}$ **[1]** = 100 s **[1]**

Page 190 Series and parallel circuits
Quick quiz
series; parallel; parallel; series; series

1. **(a)** 10 + 10 = 20 Ω **[1]**
   (b) Total resistance will be less than when they were connected in series. **[1]**
2. **(a)** B **[1]**
   (b) Switch open: lamp 1 off, lamp 2 on **[1]**
   Switch closed: both lamps on **[1]**
   (c) Add a switch **[1]** to the loop for lamp 2. **[1]**

Page 191 Practical: Resistance
Quick quiz
The opposition to the flow of electrical charge in a circuit.

1. **(a)** The wire needed to be cleaned to remove dirt / oxide **[1]** in order to provide a better contact. **[1]**
   (b) Any two for 2 marks from: Use longer lengths of wire. **[1]** Keep the current low. **[1]** Switch off the current between readings **[1]**
2. Answers could include the following points in a logical order for 6 marks:
   - Connect the thermistor in a series circuit with a power supply and ammeter.
   - Place a voltmeter in parallel with the thermistor.
   - Put the thermistor in a beaker of hot water.
   - Avoid contact of the other electrical equipment with water.
   - Measure the temperature of the water with a thermometer.
   - Measure the potential difference across the thermistor with the voltmeter.
   - Measure the current through the thermistor with the ammeter.
   - Calculate the resistance of the thermistor using $R = \frac{V}{I}$
   - Repeat for different temperatures as the water cools.
   - Plot a graph of resistance against temperature.
   - As temperature decreases, the resistance of the thermistor increases.

Page 192 Resistors
Quick quiz
A → diode; B → fixed resistor; C → filament lamp

1. **(a)** For a resistor, the gradient of an I–V graph is equal to $\frac{1}{\text{resistance}}$. **[1]** The steeper the line, the lower the resistance. **[1]**
   (b) A straight line **[1]** through the origin **[1]**
   (c) A current flowing through the filament causes heating. **[1]** The increased current at higher potential differences increases the temperature of the filament, and so increases its resistance. **[1]** As the resistance is not constant, **[1]** the gradient of the I–V graph (which is $\frac{1}{\text{resistance}}$) will not be constant. **[1]**

2. (a) It decreases. **[1]**

(b) a thermostat **[1]**

3. (a) light dependent resistor **[1]**

(b) As the light intensity increases, the resistance decreases. **[1]** If the potential difference across the LDR remains the same, the current will increase. **[1]**

Page 193 Practical: *I–V* characteristics

Quick quiz
From top: 5, 3, 2, 1, 4

1. (a)

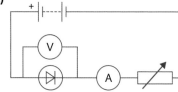

ammeter in series with diode; **[1]** voltmeter in parallel with diode; **[1]** variable resistor and power supply in series with diode **[1]**

(b)

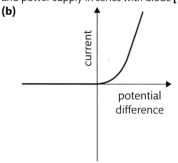

shape of the curve for positive pd; **[1]** shape of the curve for negative pd **[1]**

2. (a) C **[1]**

(b) A straight line through the origin (0,0) **[1]** shows that current is proportional to potential difference. **[1]**

Page 194 Energy transfer in circuits

Quick quiz
current; heats; electrons / ions; ions / electrons

1. (a) 2 minutes = 2 × 60 = 120 s; 750 mA = 0.75 A **[1]**

energy transferred = current × potential difference × time
so potential difference =
$\frac{\text{energy transferred}}{\text{current} \times \text{time}}$ **[1]** $= \frac{810}{(0.75 \times 120)}$ **[1]**
= 9 V **[1]**

(b) The moving electrons collide **[1]** with the ions in the metal lattice of the filament. **[1]** This transfers energy to the ions of the filament. **[1]**

2. (a) Any two for 2 marks from: heating water in an electric kettle; heating in a toaster / coffee machine or other heating device; heating the filament in a light bulb till it glows; melting the fuse in a circuit when the current is too high.

(b) Any two for 2 marks from: energy is wasted heating power transmission cables; electric motors become warm when used for a long time; devices such as laptops require cooling fans to prevent overheating.

3. When the appliance is switched on, an electric current does work **[1]** against electrical resistance. **[1]** Energy is transferred as thermal energy, heating the appliance, and this energy is then dissipated to the surroundings. **[1]**

Page 195 Electrical power

Quick quiz
power → watts (W); energy → joules (J); time → seconds (s); current → amps (A); potential difference → volts (V); resistance → ohms (Ω)

1. $P = \frac{E}{t} = \frac{200\,000}{180}$ **[1]** $= 1111\,W$ (1.1 kW) **[1]**

2. $P = I \times V = 230 \times 5$ **[1]** $= 1150\,W$ **[1]**

3. $I = \frac{2000}{230}$ **[1]** $= 8.7\,A$ **[1]**

4. (a) $I = \frac{800}{230}$ **[1]** $= 3.5\,A$ **[1]**

(b) $t = 5 \times 60 = 300\,s$ **[1]** $E = P \times t = 800 \times 300$ **[1]** $= 240\,000\,J$ (240 kJ) **[1]**

Page 196 Mains electricity

Quick quiz
False; True; True; False

1. (a) Touching the live wire is dangerous because you complete a new circuit between the live wire and the ground. **[1]** You would then receive an electric shock. **[1]**

(b) An earth wire (from the three-core cable) is connected to the metal casing (of the appliance) to stop the case becoming live. **[1]**

2. live wire **[1]**

3. (a) Supply from a battery is direct current and supply from the mains is alternating current. **[1]** Direct current travels in one direction and alternating current continually changes direction. **[1]**

(b) 50 Hz or hertz **[1]**

4. A **[1]**

Page 197 Energy transfers in appliances

Quick quiz
From top to bottom: useful; wasted; wasted; wasted

1.

Device	Energy source or store	Useful energy transfers	Wasted energy transfers
Hair dryer	transfer by electricity	kinetic, thermal	transfer by sound
Electric drill	transfer by electricity	kinetic	thermal, transfer by sound
Mobile phone	chemical energy	transfers by sound and light	thermal

[1 mark for each correct row.]

2. (a) transfer by sound, light and heating **[1]**

(b) useful: transfer by sound and light; **[1]** wasted: transfer by heating (to thermal store of the environment) **[1]**

(c) 2000 − 1500 = 500 J **[1]**

(d) transferred to the surrounding environment as thermal energy **[1]**

Page 198 Magnetic fields

Quick quiz

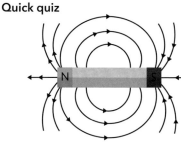

1. An induced magnet is: an object that becomes magnetic when placed in a magnetic field; **[1]** always attracted to a permanent magnet. **[1]**

2. Use a plotting compass: the compass will point toward south (and away from north). **[1]** OR It will repel a known south pole / attract a known north pole. **[1]**

3. The closer the field lines, the stronger the field. **[1]**

4. Any four for 4 marks from:

- Place a plotting compass at the north pole of a bar magnet and draw a dot where it points. Move the compass so that the back of the needle is on the dot.

- Draw a second dot where the compass points.

- Repeat until the compass reaches the other side of the magnet.

- Join the dots together and add arrows on the line showing the direction of the field, north to south.

- Repeat this for other starting points near the north pole of the magnet.

Page 199 Electromagnetism

Quick quiz
D; A; A; D

1. A coil of wire **[1]** carrying a current that generates a magnetic field. **[1]**

2. (a)

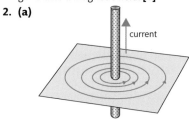

circles around wire, **[1]** correct direction **[1]**

(b) distance of the point from the wire, **[1]** current in the wire **[1]**

3. (a) Any two for 2 marks from: current in the solenoid; whether an iron core is placed inside the solenoid; distance from the solenoid.

(b) current in the circuit **[1]**

(c) Solenoid **A** because it has more turns. **[1]**

Page 200 The National Grid and transformers

Quick quiz
True; True; False; False

1. The input is 230 V and the output is 10 V, so the potential difference goes down. **[1]** This means it is a step-down transformer. **[1]**

2. **(a)** increases the potential difference at which the electrical power is transmitted **[1]**

(b) reduces the energy wasted in the transmission cables **[1]**

Page 201 Density
Quick quiz
mass → kg; volume → m³; density → kg/m³; length → m

1. **(a)** volume = 0.5 × 0.8 × 0.6 **[1]**
= 0.24 m³ **[1]**

(b) density = $\frac{mass}{volume}$ = $\frac{648}{0.24}$ **[1]**
= 2700 kg/m³ **[1]**

(c) density = $\frac{mass}{volume}$ so volume
= $\frac{mass}{density}$ **[1]** = $\frac{13.5}{2700}$ **[1]** = 0.005 m³ **[1]**

2. **(a)** density = $\frac{mass}{volume}$ = $\frac{455}{500}$ **[1]**
= 0.91 g/cm³ **[1]**

(b) mass = density × volume **[1]**
= 0.91 × 10 **[1]** = 9.1 g **[1]**

Page 202 Practical: Density of materials
Quick quiz
True; False; False; False; True

1. **(a)** Use a ruler / metre rule / tape to measure **[1]** the length, width and height of the cuboid. **[1]** Use the formula length × width × height to calculate the volume. **[1]**

(b) In step 1, the student says to 'partly fill' a displacement can. This will cause an error in the measurement of volume. **[1]** The student should fill the can right up to the level of the spout. **[1]**

2. **(a)** measuring cylinder; **[1]** displacement can **[1]**

(b) mass **[1]**

(c) mass balance / digital balance **[1]**

(d) density = $\frac{mass}{volume}$ **[1]**

(e) density = $\frac{525}{500}$ **[1]** = 1.05 g/cm³ **[1]**

Page 203 Changes of state
Quick quiz
True; True; True; False

1. **(a)** Ethanol is a liquid so the particles are touching. **[1]** They move more quickly as more energy is taken in. **[1]**

(b) 78 °C **[1]**

(c) The particles of ethanol separate from each other to move more freely. **[1]**

2. Straight line from (0 min, 180 °C) to (10 min, 70 °C) **[1]**

Horizontal line from (10 min, 70 °C) to (12 min, 70 °C) **[1]**

Straight line from (12 min, 70 °C) to (15 min, 20 °C) **[1]**

Page 204 Specific heat capacity
Quick quiz
ΔQ: change in energy, m: mass, c: specific heat capacity, Δθ: change in temperature

1. **(a)** Δθ = 100 − 20 = 80 °C **[1]**

(b) ΔQ = 1.5 × 4200 × 80 **[1]** = 504 000 J **[1]**

2. The amount of energy needed **[1]** to raise the temperature of 1 kg of a material by 1 °C. **[1]**

3. **(a)** to reduce heat / energy loss to the surroundings **[1]**

(b) ΔQ = 1 × 900 × (32 − 20) **[1]** = 10 800 J (10.8 kJ) **[1]**

Page 205 Specific latent heat
Quick quiz
False; True; True; False

1. **(a)** The particles in the solid ice are starting to move apart **[1]** so that the ice melts to form a liquid. **[1]**

(b) Q = mL = 5.2 × 336 000 **[1]**
= 1 747 200 J **[1]**

2. **(a)** The energy required to change 1 kg of a solid into 1 kg of a liquid **[1]** without changing the temperature. **[1]**

(b) 30 g = 0.03 kg **[1]** Q = 0.03 × 336 000 **[1]**
= 10 080 J **[1]**

(c) To check the temperature stays constant **[1]**

Page 206 Practical: Properties of water
Quick quiz
higher; higher; low

1. Answer could include the following points in a logical order for 6 marks.
- Fill the calorimeter with 1 kg of water. Measure the start temperature of the water using the thermometer.
- Switch on the electric heater
- and record its power output rating.
- Measure the highest temperature reached after a measured amount of time.
- Calculate the energy input using the equation: energy input = power rating of heater × time
- Calculate the specific heat capacity using the equation: ΔQ = mcΔθ
- rearranged to give $c = \frac{\Delta Q}{m \times \Delta \theta}$

2. **(a)** $\frac{0.145 + 0.143 + 0.147}{3}$ **[1]** = 0.145 kg **[1]**

(b) It will remain the same. **[1]**

(c) Between 60 and 160 seconds **[1]**

Page 207 Particle motion in gases
Quick quiz
False; True; False; True; False

1. **(a)** It is the lowest temperature theoretically possible. **[1]** All the particles in a substance stop vibrating. **[1]**

(b) At absolute zero, the pressure of a gas is zero **[1]** and the average kinetic energy of the gas particles is zero. **[1]**

2. **(a)** 0 + 273 **[1]** = 273 K **[1]**

(b) 298 − 273 **[1]** = 25 °C **[1]**

(c) The kinetic energy of the particles increases. **[1]** This causes the particles to move faster and spread out. **[1]** As the gas bottle is sealed it has a fixed volume **[1]** so the pressure inside the container will increase as the particles collide with the walls of the container more often and with more energy. **[1]**

Page 208 Forces and elasticity
Quick quiz
True; False; False; True; True

1. If the mass is removed from the end of the rubber band, the band should return to its original shape. **[1]**

2. **(a)** 20 cm = 0.2 m; **[1]** elastic potential energy = 0.5 × 100 × 0.2² **[1]** = 2 J **[1]**

(b) force = 100 × 0.2 **[1]** = 20 N **[1]**

3. **(a)** weight = 0.2 × 10 **[1]** = 2 N **[1]**

(b) 2 = k × 0.1; **[1]** $k = \frac{2}{0.1}$ **[1]** = 20 N/m **[1]**

Page 209 Practical: Force and extension
Quick quiz
False; True; True

1. Plot a graph of force against extension **[1]**. This should produce a straight line through the origin. Force should increase in proportion to extension. **[1]**

2. **(a)** the reading of 10 cm against 3 N **[1]**

(b) 12 cm **[1]**

(c) 25 N/m (spring constant = $\frac{6.0}{0.24}$) **[1]**

(d) Any two for 2 marks from: Repeat each reading one or two more times and take an average. / Measure the spring length from the same point on the spring each time. / Make sure the spring is at eye level when measuring it.

Practice paper: Biology Answers
1. **(a)** The guard cells change shape to open the stoma during the day and close it at night. **[1]**

The stomata allow gases / carbon dioxide and oxygen to be exchanged between the leaf and the air. **[1]**

(b) **(i)** image diameter = 1.2 cm (± 0.1 cm) **[1]**

real diameter = $\frac{1.2}{200}$

= 0.006 (cm) **[1]**

(ii) 60 (μm) **[1]**

(c) site of photosynthesis in the guard cell **[1]**

(d) The structures are very small so detail would not be seen with a light microscope. **[1]**

Electron microscopes produce much higher magnification than light microscopes. **[1]**

(e) Any one for 1 mark from: mitochondrion; nucleus; ribosome.

(f) Any one for 1 mark from: nucleus; mitochondrion; chloroplast; vacuole.

2. **(a)** A suggestion that makes reference to at least four of the following points for 4 marks:
- wipe chips dry with paper towel before measuring mass, both before and after immersion
- use accurate balance, e.g. measures to 0.05 g or less
- make sure each chip is fully covered by solution in beaker
- use wider range of concentrations with smaller differences between them

- use several chips / do repeats at each concentration
- calculate means of repeats
- control for temperature, e.g. using a water bath
- one valid aspect relating to the potato e.g. same variety, same age, approximately same size / surface area

(b) $\dfrac{4.28 - 5.04}{5.04} \times 100 = -15.07936$ **[1]**

$= -15.08\ (\%)$ **[1]**

[total of 1 mark only if minus sign is missing]

(c) Water enters the potato cells by osmosis when the concentration inside the cells / cytoplasm is greater than that of the solution (0% solution). **[1]**

Water leaves the potato cells by osmosis when the solution concentration is greater than the concentration inside the cells / cytoplasm (30% solution). **[1]**

3. (a) The cells containing the gene will divide by mitosis **[1]** so all the cells of the developing mosquito contain the gene. **[1]**

(b) Mosquitoes suck blood from infected people which contains the protist that causes malaria. **[1]** The protist enters another person's blood when the mosquito bites them. **[1]**

Killing mosquitoes prevents the protist being spread from person to person. **[1]**

(c) Any one for 1 mark from: spraying water with insecticide to kill young mosquitoes; spraying doorways and windows with insecticide to kill resting mosquito adults; using mosquito nets while sleeping to prevent mosquitoes getting to skin to bite.

(d) Any one for 1 mark from: difficult to predict impact on other organisms; may have harmful effects on food webs / food chains e.g. populations of mosquitoes' predators may decrease.

4. (a) Water is transported through the plant in xylem **[1]** from roots to leaves. **[1]**

(b) $\dfrac{27}{5} = 5.4$ (mm/min) **[1]**

(c) Any two for 2 marks from: temperature; humidity; light intensity.

(d) More water is lost from the stomata / leaf in moving air **[1]** because the rate of evaporation is greater in moving air / moving air removes humid air from around the stomata. **[1]**

5. (a) A method that makes reference to the following points:
- samples of plant number and soil moisture taken using quadrats **[1]**
- quadrats placed at regular distances along a line / tape measure from top to bottom of slope **[1]**

(b) Bulbous buttercups are more common where the ground is drier. **[1]**

Creeping buttercups are more common where the ground is wetter / more moist. **[1]**

(c) Any one for 1 mark from: competition (e.g. between the buttercup species); predation / grazing.

6. (a) Pathogens are trapped in the runny mucus **[1]** and the mucus is moved out of the trachea and bronchi (by ciliated cells) to the back of the mouth where it is swallowed. **[1]**

(b) Ff **[1]**

(c) ff **[1]**

(d) Two copies of the allele are needed **[1]** for the effect of the allele to be seen/expressed. **[1]** / The allele is not expressed **[1]** in the presence of the dominant allele. **[1]**

(e) Punnett square completed **[1]**

		father's (D) alleles	
		f	f
mother's (E) alleles	F	Ff	Ff
	f	ff	ff

probability: 0.5 / 50% / 1 in 2 chance **[1]**

(f) Any four for 4 marks. At least one benefit and one risk:

Benefits:
- results show a far smaller loss of lung function in treated group than placebo group (0.4% compared to 4%)
- treatment is non-invasive / easy to administer
- disease is serious so any reduction in symptoms would be of benefit

Risks:
- treated group still suffered some loss of lung function, so this is not a cure
- no safe long-term treatment yet available / will need repeated treatments
- some methods have potential for serious side effects

7. (a) Answer should indicate the strong relationship between weight and type 2 diabetes for 1 mark, such as:
- there is a strong positive correlation between weight and type 2 diabetes

- a much higher proportion of obese people have type 2 diabetes than people with lower weight
- as weight / mass increases the percentage of people with type 2 diabetes increases.

(b) Exercise more to reduce mass / weight; **[1]** eat a carbohydrate-controlled / healthy diet to reduce mass / weight. **[1]**

(c) Insulin reduces excess blood glucose **[1]** by increasing the uptake of glucose into body / liver cells. **[1]**

(d) Level 3: A detailed and coherent plan including several aspects of using the equipment. A reference to at least two variables and an explanation of how to control at least one variable. Logical connections made between elements of the answer. **[5–6 marks]**

Level 2: Plan includes more than one aspect of equipment or names more than one controlled variable or names and explains reason for control. Some logical connections made between elements of the answer. **[3–4 marks]**

Level 1: Simple plan referring to at least one aspect of the equipment and one controlled variable. Overall understanding of equipment may be flawed and order may not be logical. **[1–2 marks]**

No relevant content **[0 marks]**

Indicative content:
Use of equipment:
- Place peas into the boiling tube / on cotton wool
- Mark the starting position of the drop of liquid
- Close tap / seal tube
- Use a stopwatch
- Mark position of the drop of liquid at end of test
- Calculate the distance moved / volume change
- Same approach for dried and germinating peas
- Repeat measurements (for each type of pea)

Control of variables:
- Same mass of each type of pea
- Control temperature with a water bath
- Same time period / stated time period for each experiment
- Same quantity / mass of soda lime

Practice paper: Chemistry Answers

1. (a) ionic bonding **[1]**

(b) [1 mark for each correct row]

Ion	Atomic number	Mass number	Number of protons	Number of electrons	Number of neutrons
Mg^{2+}	12	24	**12**	**10**	**12**
O^{2-}	8	**16**	**8**	**10**	8
K^+	19	39	**19**	18	**20**

(c) Metals contain delocalised electrons. **[1]** As the electrons move, they carry charge / electricity through the metal. **[1]**

2. (a) simple molecular (covalent) **[1]**

(b) A covalent bond is formed when a pair of electrons is shared between atoms. **[1]**

(c) In graphene, each carbon atom forms three covalent bonds with other carbon atoms **[1]** in a single layer of hexagonal rings. **[1]**

(d) Metallic bonds are strong **[1]** and many metallic bonds need to be broken to melt a metal crystal. **[1]**

3. (a) B **[1]**

(b) Crude oil is heated / boiled / vaporised; **[1]** vapours rise and cool; **[1]** fractions condense at different temperatures / heights. **[1]**

(c) Fuel for cars or trains **[1]**

(d) As the chain length increases:
- boiling points increase **[1]**
- hydrocarbons become more viscous / thicker / less easy to pour **[1]**
- hydrocarbons become less flammable. **[1]**

4. (a) Pass the gas through limewater. **[1]** If carbon dioxide is present, it will turn cloudy / milky. **[1]**

(b)

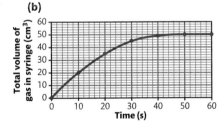

All points plotted correctly ± 0.5 square **[2]**; 6 points correct **[1]**; line of best fit **[1]**

(c) $\frac{35 - 0}{20 - 0} = 1.75\,cm^3/s$

[1 mark for correct calculation; 1 mark for correct answer (with or without working)]

(d) Steeper line, levelling off sooner **[1]** and finishing at same level **[1]**

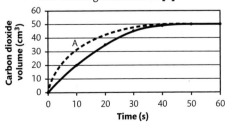

(e) $50\,cm^3 = \frac{50}{1000} = 0.05\,dm^3$ **[1]**

$\frac{7.3}{0.05} = 146\,g/dm^3$ **[1]**

5. (a) The rate of the forward reaction is equal to / the same as the rate of the reverse reaction. **[1]**

(b) (i) As temperature increases, the percentage yield of ethanol decreases. **[1]**

(ii) As pressure increases, the percentage yield of ethanol increases. **[1]**

[Accept reverse statements]

6. (a) They all have one electron in their outermost (electron) shell **[1]** which gives them similar chemical properties. **[1]**

(b) $2K + 2H_2O \rightarrow 2KOH + H_2$ **[1]**

(c) Reactivity increases as you go down group 1, but decreases as you go down group 7. **[2]**

(d) Level 3 **[5–6 marks]** – thorough explanation of why the trends in reactivity change down the groups, linked to the attraction between the nucleus and electrons and the distance between them.

Level 2 **[3–4 marks]** – relevant comment made about the trends in reactivity of both groups, showing understanding that reactivity is linked to the ability to gain or lose electrons.

Level 1 **[1–2 marks]** – general comment made about the trends in reactivity of both groups.

[0 marks] – no relevant comment made.

Indicative content:
- In group 1 reactivity increases down the group. In group 7 reactivity decreases down the group. **[1]**
- Reactivity is linked to an atom's ability to gain or lose electrons to acquire a full outer electron shell. **[1]**
- Atoms of group 1 elements have 1 electron in the outer electron shell, so they need to lose this electron to gain a stable full outer electron shell. **[1]**
- Atoms of group 7 elements have 7 electrons in their outer shell, so they need to gain an electron to gain a stable full outer electron shell. **[1]**
- (In atoms of elements) further down each group, the outer electron(s) is/are further from the nucleus, so the attraction between the nucleus and the outer electrons decreases. **[1]**
- In group 1 elements, this means the outer electron is more easily lost and so reactivity increases. **[1]**
- In group 7 elements, atoms gain an extra electron less easily and so reactivity decreases. **[1]**

7. $M_r = 12.0 + (3 \times 19.0) + 35.5$ **[1]** $= 104.5$ **[1]**

8. (a)

Gas	% composition
carbon dioxide and other trace gases	<1
nitrogen **[1]**	80
oxygen	20 **[1]**

(b)
- Water vapour in the atmosphere condensed, forming the oceans. **[1]**
- Photosynthesis reduced the amount of carbon dioxide and increased oxygen. **[1]**
- Primitive plants / Algae used carbon dioxide and released oxygen by photosynthesis and consequently the amount of oxygen in the atmosphere gradually increased / the amount of carbon dioxide decreased. **[1]**

9. (a) nitric acid **[1]**

(b) water **[1]**

(c) Level 3 **[5–6 marks]** – All techniques described correctly in order with named equipment throughout.

Level 2 **[3–4 marks]** – Some relevant techniques described correctly with equipment in the correct order.

Level 1 **[1–2 marks]** – Some relevant techniques mentioned but may not be described or correctly described.

[0 marks] – No relevant detail or description of techniques.

Indicative content:
- Warm the acid using a Bunsen burner / electric heater / suitable apparatus.
- Add lead oxide to nitric acid until it is in excess / no more will dissolve.
- Use a filter funnel and filter paper to separate the excess lead oxide from the salt solution.
- Gently heat the salt solution with a Bunsen burner / water bath / electric heater / suitable apparatus to remove about $\frac{1}{3}$ of the water.
- Leave the solution to cool – crystals should form.
- Crystals can be filtered and dried to produce a pure dry sample of lead nitrate.

Practice paper: Physics Answers

1. (a) Kinetic energy increases, gravitational potential energy decreases **[1]**

(b) 0.03 kg **[1]**

(c) change in GPE = $0.03 \times 10 \times 15$ **[1]** = 4.5 **[1]** J **[1]**

2. (a) **A** = wavelength **[1]**; **B** = amplitude **[1]**

(b) energy, information **[1]**

(c) $v = f \times \lambda$ **[1]**

(d) wave speed = 40×8.5 **[1]** = 340 (m/s) **[1]**

(e) (i) X-rays [1]

    (ii) Any two for 2 marks from: mobile phone communications; cooking; satellite communications.

3. (a) The amount of energy required to raise the temperature of 1 kg of a material by 1 °C. [1]

   (b) 0.5 × 4200 × (80 − 20) [1] = 126 000 (J) (or 126 kJ) [1]

   (c) (i) Reading at 90 seconds/58 °C is anomalous [1] because it does not fit the regular pattern of increases in temperature with time [1] (Note that the measurements at 240 and 270 seconds are NOT anomalous.)

    (ii) Any one for 1 mark from: take more readings / at shorter intervals; repeat the readings / repeat the investigation.

    (iii) Water is boiling / all the energy is being used to turn the liquid to a gas, so temperature does not change. [1]

4. (a) Energy transferred per unit charge [1]

   (b) power = 230 × 8.4 [1] = 1932 [1] (allow 1900, 1930) W [1] (also allow 1.9 if unit is stated as kW)

   (c) (i) a cell [1]

    (ii) Combined resistance = 300 + 150 [1] = 450 Ω [1]

   (d) (i) Component X is an ammeter and component Y is a voltmeter. [1]

    (ii) 1.35 = I × 450 [1] so I = $\frac{1.35}{450}$ [1] = 0.003 (A) [1]

(e) The total resistance is less than 150 Ω. [1]

5. (a) The forces between the particles are very small. [1]

   (b) In the solid the particles are packed more closely than in the liquid [1] which means there is more mass in the same volume, [1] so the density will be higher in the solid. [1]

   (c) Any four clearly-made points in a logical order. [4]

- Measure the mass of the rock using a balance.
- Determine the volume of the rock by displacement of water from a displacement can into a measuring cylinder.
- Lower the rock into the displacement can carefully to avoid splashing and loss of water.
- density = $\frac{\text{mass}}{\text{volume}}$

6. (a) Each atom of $^{12}_{6}$C contains one fewer neutrons than each atom of $^{13}_{6}$C. [1]

   (b) Any one for 1 mark from: number of protons (per atom); number of electrons (per atom).

   (c) (i) $^{14}_{6}$C → $^{14}_{7}$N + $^{0}_{-1}$e

    1 mark for the correctly placed 0, 1 mark for the correctly placed −1, 1 mark for the 'e'

    (ii) electron [1]

    (iii) beta minus decay [1] [accept beta decay for 1 mark]

(d) The (average) time it takes for the number of unstable nuclei in the radioisotope in a sample to halve. [1] / The (average) time it takes for the count rate from a sample containing the isotope to fall to half of its initial value. [1]

(e) (i) 30 Bq [1] [allow estimates in the range 28 to 32]

    (ii) 6000 years [1] [allow estimates in range of 5000 to 7000 years]

7. (a) biofuel [1]

   (b) (i) nuclear [1]

    (ii) non-renewable [1]

    (iii) Nuclear fuel is a limited resource that cannot easily be replaced in a short time. [1]

    (iv) hydroelectricity [1]

    (v) Change in percentage = 65 − 5.1 [1] = 59.9% reduction [1]

    (vi) Any two sensible reasons for 1 mark each; reasons can include: coal is a polluting / dirty fuel so people / governments want to use less; coal is a fossil fuel / hydrocarbon that produces carbon dioxide, a greenhouse gas, leading to global warming so people / governments want to use less; coal is a non-renewable resource and people / governments want to move to use more renewable resources.

Equations for physics

In the exam, you could be asked about any of the equations on this page. Make sure you know how to rearrange each of the equations and learn the units that match each quantity.

10 Equations to learn

Word equation	Symbol equation
weight = mass × gravitational field strength	$W = m \times g$
work done = force × distance moved in the direction of the force	$E = F \times d$
force exerted on a spring = spring constant × extension	$F = k \times x$
distance travelled = average speed × time	
acceleration = change in velocity ÷ time taken	$a = \dfrac{(v - u)}{t}$
force = mass × acceleration	$F = m \times a$
kinetic energy $= \dfrac{1}{2} \times$ mass × (speed)^2	$KE = \dfrac{1}{2} \times m \times v^2$
change in gravitational potential energy = mass × gravitational field strength × change in vertical height	$\Delta GPE = m \times g \times \Delta h$
power = energy transferred (J) ÷ time taken	$P = \dfrac{E}{t}$
power = work done ÷ time taken	$P = \dfrac{E}{t}$
efficiency $= \dfrac{\text{(useful energy transferred by the device)}}{\text{(total energy supplied to the device)}}$	
wave speed = frequency × wavelength	$v = f \times \lambda$
wave speed = distance ÷ time	$v = \dfrac{x}{t}$
charge = current × time	$Q = I \times t$
potential difference = current × resistance	$V = I \times R$
electrical power = current × potential difference	$P = I \times V$
electrical power = (current)^2 × resistance	$P = I^2 \times R$
energy transferred = charge moved × potential difference	$E = Q \times V$
density = mass ÷ volume	$\rho = \dfrac{m}{v}$

5 Physics equation sheet

You will be given a list of some of the more complicated equations in the exam.

Word equation	Symbol equation
(final velocity)^2 – (initial velocity)^2 = 2 × acceleration × distance	$v^2 - u^2 = 2 \times a \times x$
change in thermal energy = mass × specific heat capacity × change in temperature	$\Delta Q = m \times c \times \Delta\theta$
thermal energy for a change of state = mass × specific latent heat	$Q = m \times L$
energy transferred = current × potential difference × time	$E = I \times V \times t$
For transformers with 100% efficiency, potential difference across primary coil × current in primary coil = potential difference across secondary coil × current in secondary coil	$V_p \times I_p = V_s \times I_s$
energy transferred in stretching = 0.5 × spring constant × (extension)^2	$E = \dfrac{1}{2} \times k \times x^2$

Periodic Table

Key

| relative atomic mass |
| **atomic symbol** |
| name |
| atomic (proton) number |

Example:

| 1 |
| **H** |
| Hydrogen |
| 1 |

Group 1	Group 2											Group 3	Group 4	Group 5	Group 6	Group 7	Group 0
																	4 **He** Helium 2
7 **Li** Lithium 3	9 **Be** Beryllium 4											11 **B** Boron 5	12 **C** Carbon 6	14 **N** Nitrogen 7	16 **O** Oxygen 8	19 **F** Fluorine 9	20 **Ne** Neon 10
23 **Na** Sodium 11	24 **Mg** Magnesium 12											27 **Al** Aluminium 13	28 **Si** Silicon 14	31 **P** Phosphorus 15	32 **S** Sulfur 16	35.5 **Cl** Chlorine 17	40 **Ar** Argon 18
39 **K** Potassium 19	40 **Ca** Calcium 20	45 **Sc** Scandium 21	48 **Ti** Titanium 22	51 **V** Vanadium 23	52 **Cr** Chromium 24	55 **Mn** Manganese 25	56 **Fe** Iron 26	59 **Co** Cobalt 27	59 **Ni** Nickel 28	63.5 **Cu** Copper 29	65 **Zn** Zinc 30	70 **Ga** Gallium 31	73 **Ge** Germanium 32	75 **As** Arsenic 33	79 **Se** Selenium 34	80 **Br** Bromine 35	84 **Kr** Krypton 36
85 **Rb** Rubidium 37	88 **Sr** Strontium 38	89 **Y** Yttrium 39	91 **Zr** Zirconium 40	93 **Nb** Niobium 41	96 **Mo** Molybdenum 42	98 **Tc** Technetium 43	101 **Ru** Ruthenium 44	103 **Rh** Rhodium 45	106 **Pd** Palladium 46	108 **Ag** Silver 47	112 **Cd** Cadmium 48	115 **In** Indium 49	119 **Sn** Tin 50	122 **Sb** Antimony 51	128 **Te** Tellurium 52	127 **I** Iodine 53	131 **Xe** Xenon 54
133 **Cs** Caesium 55	137 **Ba** Barium 56	139 **La** Lanthanum 57	178 **Hf** Hafnium 72	181 **Ta** Tantalum 73	184 **W** Tungsten 74	186 **Re** Rhenium 75	190 **Os** Osmium 76	192 **Ir** Iridium 77	195 **Pt** Platinum 78	197 **Au** Gold 79	201 **Hg** Mercury 80	204 **Tl** Thallium 81	207 **Pb** Lead 82	209 **Bi** Bismuth 83	[201] **Po** Polonium 84	[210] **At** Astatine 85	[222] **Rn** Radon 86
[223] **Fr** Francium 87	[226] **Ra** Radium 88	[227] **Ac** Actinium 89	[261] **Rf** Rutherfordium 104	[262] **Db** Dubnium 105	[266] **Sg** Seaborgium 106	[264] **Bh** Bohrium 107	[277] **Hs** Hassium 108	[268] **Mt** Meitnerium 109	[271] **Ds** Darmstadtium 110	[272] **Rg** Roentgenium 111							

Elements with atomic numbers 112–116 have been reported but not fully authenticated.

* The Lanthanoides (atomic numbers 58–71) and the actinides (atomic numbers 90–103) have been omitted.
Relative atomic masses for copper and chlorine have not been rounded to the nearest whole number.